# Multiple Personality, Allied Disorders, and Hypnosis

# Multiple Personality, Allied Disorders, and Hypnosis

EUGENE L. BLISS, M.D.

New York   Oxford
OXFORD UNIVERSITY PRESS
1986

Oxford University Press

Oxford   New York   Toronto
Delhi   Bombay   Calcutta   Madras   Karachi
Petaling Jaya   Singapore   Hong Kong   Tokyo
Nairobi   Dar es Salaam      Cape Town
Melbourne   Auckland

and associated companies in
Beirut   Berlin   Ibadan   Nicosia

Published by Oxford University Press, Inc.,
200 Madison Avenue, New York, New York 10016

Oxford is a registered trademark of Oxford University Press.

Library of Congress Cataloging-in-Publication Data

Bliss, Eugene L.
  Multiple personality, allied disorders, and hypnosis.

  Bibliography: p.
  Includes index.
  1. Multiple personality.   2. Schizophrenia.
3. Hypnosis.   4. Hypnotism—Therapeutic use.   I. Title.
RC569.5.M8B568   1986      616.85′236      85-13666
ISBN 0-19-503658-1

Printing (last digit): 9 8 7 6 5 4 3 2 1

Printed in the United States of America
on acid free paper

# Preface

A chance telephone call five years ago started me on this adventure. My caller was the chief nurse at a local hospital, who said she had encountered a difficult problem that demanded my expert help. The history at first appeared to be routine. A nurse at the hospital was probably addicted to Demerol. She had been intoxicated while on duty, and it was suspected that she had been injecting herself with narcotics intended for patients. But now came the unexpected twist. When the nurse was summoned into the chief nurse's office, accused of the offense, and the needle marks identified on her arms, she underwent a strange transformation. Her demeanor, facial expression, and tone of voice changed. She denied her name was Sue, claiming it was Sarah. The chief nurse excused herself momentarily, and when she returned to her office Sue was now present in the place of Sarah, but she was bewildered and tearful.

I accepted the referral immediately, suspecting a case of multiple personality. What I didn't say was that I had never seen a case, and certainly didn't know how to treat one. Fortunately, Sue proved to be a simple case of multiple personality with only two alter egos. If there had been more, I would have been overwhelmed.

Astonishingly, another case was identified by a resident in the emergency room a few weeks later, and admitted to the ward. She proved to have a large number of personalities that defied our ministrations. I then began the quest in earnest for more cases. Slowly, as my diagnostic skills improved, I was able to detect subtler cases. It became apparent that the reason I had never seen a case in the past thirty years of psychiatric practice as an academician—a teacher, investigator, and therapist—was simply ignorance. Many such patients must have escaped my detection over the years as they passed through the psychiatric service.

After six months of work with a number of these patients, I was beginning to collect data and to formulate some tentative hypotheses. By then, I was using hypnosis extensively, after discovering that these patients were excellent hypnotic subjects and that hypnosis could reveal reasons for their psychopathology. Gradually I recognized that I was exploring not only multiple personality but also its related syndrome hysteria and the nature of hypnosis. In my quest for understanding, the different personalities in these patients proved to be excellent teachers, but I had to ask them many questions, be humble in the face of their superior knowledge, and yet be critical and careful in their delusional world. Insights came slowly. At first I had tentative ideas—hunches —that I tested on new patients, and gradually my understanding expanded.

At some point in the process, I realized that my endeavor was in some ways a recapitulation of Freud's early clinical experience. He had begun with hysteria and hypnosis, and it was primarily out of this context that his theories had evolved. This led me to a careful re-reading of his early studies of hysteria and a recognition of our fundamental differences. It was chastening to recognize that no one recently, as far as I knew, had repeated Freud's early studies of hysteria to determine whether his insights had been correct, or whether there might be other ways to interpret his observations.

It was only much later, when I had decided to write this monograph, that I examined the nineteenth- and early twentieth-century literature on hypnosis and hysteria in detail and learned that others, notably Braid, Bramwell, Janet, Bernheim, Forel, Prince, and Sidis, had spent years exploring the nature of these phenomena and had arrived at valuable insights.

Patients with multiple personalities also began to upset my conventional notions about a host of clinical entities, until I came to wonder who was deluded—the patients or me. I had believed and taught that hysteria was a syndrome early described by the Egyptians and the Greeks. It had been studied by Hippocrates and had survived as a clinical entity through the ages, but always as an enigma. Earlier physicians had attributed it to everything from a wandering uterus, to demonic possession, to a weakness in the synthetic capabilities of the mind. Cases were to be found almost exclusively in females, but why there should be a sex difference was never well explained. These women had a plethora of symptoms which led them to seek medical care, to abuse drugs, and to undergo surgery. They were impulsive and unreasonable, emotional and suggestible. In fact, they often seemed to act but not to think. They had hysterical tantrums, were infantile, and made silly suicidal gestures.

In recent years, severe hysteria has been precisely defined, renamed Briquet's syndrome, and studied carefully. There seemed to be a curious relationship between Briquet's syndrome in females and sociopathy and alcoholism in males because they coexisted in the same families. This was somehow linked to criminality, but the connections were not understood.

Hysteria appeared to be a potpourri of disturbances. Perhaps it did not deserve to be perpetuated as a syndrome despite its venerable history. Freud had identified conversion symptoms in hysterical patients, and had seen them as body language that enacted unconscious sexual traumas. Unfortunately, I had never encountered these unconscious complexes in my previous practice. If they existed, they had been beyond my reach; they were either to be accepted on faith or discarded. Furthermore, the treatment of hysteria remained symptomatic and unsatisfactory. Respectable scientific studies confirmed the persistence and constancy of the syndrome over a period of many years, but a rational therapy was not apparent. The best one could expect was temporary relief. I hope to show that these preconceptions must now be reexamined, that hysterics are fascinating people whose problems ordinarily are well hidden from usual clinical scrutiny, and that therapy is possible.

Textbook writers and medical historians claimed that the earlier explorations of hysteria and hypnosis laid the groundwork for the emergence of "dynamic" psychiatry. But how hypnosis, induced by a hypnotist, related to psychiatry escaped me. Hypnosis simply seemed to be an exotic phenomenon with a lurid history, and I never used it.

As a psychiatric resident, I had experimented with hypnosis on a few cases of chronic schizophrenia and severe character disorder, but nothing happened. There certainly were no dramatic results. I had read that hypnosis could be helpful in allaying anxiety and in relieving pain. The nineteenth-century literature was full of remarkable cures by hypnosis, but any treatment that is alleged to cure everything from migraine to warts is obviously suspect. In general, my abortive attempts with hypnosis were embarrassing and awkward, and so, like most psychiatrists, I had avoided it. The explanation that its essence was enhanced suggestibility seemed plausible. It appeared to have little relevance to the practice of psychiatry, and certainly no direct relationship to any form of psychopathology.

One must be wary of converts, but I must admit that the last five years have changed my opinion. I now see hypnosis as important to many forms of psychopathology, and wonder how I treated some of my patients without it.

But my experience with multiple personality also recast my thinking about that broad category of disturbances termed schizophrenia. It seemed obvious that if there were severe forms of schizophrenia, there should also be milder cases, since most diseases in medicine are spectral, running from mild to severe. In fact, there is good evidence supporting a borderline variety of schizophrenia.

The cause of schizophrenia remains obscure, but many psychiatrists, as early as Kraepelin, claimed an organic derangement. Recently, dilated ventricles have been identified in some of these patients, and even biochemical defects have been proposed; but overriding all has been the recurring evidence for a genetic cause for schizophrenia. Evidence from family, twin, and adoptee studies is virtually conclusive. A learned form of schizophrenia has its supporters, but the evidence is less precise and certainly less convincing.

Practically, the diagnosis of schizophrenia is made when the patient has auditory hallucinations, delusions, and a thought disorder, if mania or some intoxication is not present. A thought disorder, at least in flagrant form, is often absent or so subtle as to be uncertain, so hallucinations and delusions had usually decided the issue for me and most clinicians whom I observed.

My experience with cases of multiple personality and kindred disorders has shaken this firm view about schizophrenia, or rather *some* cases of schizophrenia. Delusions and hallucinations no longer necessarily connote schizophrenia for me, since the mechanism responsible for multiple personalities can produce both symptoms. I now must reluctantly admit that there is such a thing as "learned schizophrenia," but learned in ways that I had never previously suspected.

In this maze of uncertainties, patients with multiple personalities led me further afield to new considerations of criminality and antisocial behaviors. There might be a subgroup of antisocial individuals whose deviant behaviors could be partially explained by this mechanism, since many multiples exhibit antisocial traits.

Antisocial people have long histories dating back to childhood of perverse relationships with family, friends, teachers, the law, authority, and later with spouses and employers. They are bad actors with defective consciences, who don't seem to learn from disastrous experiences. They repeatedly get into trouble, often committing antisocial acts stupidly as if to court punishment. Some psychiatrists even have believed that many were unconsciously seeking punishment. There is no simple explanation of sociopathy, but even here "multiple personality" has offered insights into the nature of some cases—into the reasons for driven behaviors and the inability to learn from experiences.

Other syndromes are accessible to a comparable scrutiny, and these will be discussed later. This monograph is an attempt to present these observations and experiences in some detail together with the theories I have evolved, so that others can reexamine these findings, define the errors which must exist, and determine where the truth lies.

My procedure at first was simply to grope, as I listened, observed, and tried to penetrate the confusion. A helpful early decision was to abandon my preconceptions and to believe the patients. For example, when they claimed to "not remember," I accepted this as true. Astonishingly, this complaint was not rare in the general psychiatric population. I never realized how many patients have amnestic periods, but who ever asks?

This naiveté led to discoveries, but all did not withstand persistent scrutiny; many lovely hypotheses had to be discarded. Gradually the pieces in the puzzle began to fit together, until the entirety seemed too elegant not to be valid. When I turned to the older literature to learn what the nineteenth-century hypnotists had to say, the result was chastening but reassuring. Many of my "original" discoveries were not original, for they had been made before. At best, my synthesis was somewhat different and perhaps more complete.

When I reviewed the modern literature on hypnosis, it sharpened my perspective. A scientific rigor had been introduced, sometimes to prove the obvious; but often to detect variables, to examine them critically, and to study them precisely. In the process, many old problems were resurrected, sometimes without recognition of the wealth of earlier observations. Even the existence of hypnosis was again disputed. But amid the clutter of science there had been advances. Some extravagant earlier claims for hypnosis were disproved, and this was helpful. A major advance was the creation of reliable procedures to measure hypnotizability. The trait could now be given numbers and studied more objectively. It was now possible to identify this trait with greater assurance; then to relate it to variables such as age, sex, imagination, gullibility, creativity, and psychopathology.

Finally, when I assembled the information about hypnosis, both historical and contemporary, our knowledge about hysteria, and data about multiple personality, the entirety formed a coherent story. The ensemble has led me to conclude, and I shall present data to support this view, that this hypnotic capability of the mind has importance to the theory and practice of psychiatry, which deserves attention and research.

*Salt Lake City, Utah*                                                                                     E.L.B.
*October 1985*

# Acknowledgments

When I scan the books in my collection or wander through the stacks of a great library, I wonder why anyone undertakes the painful chore of writing another volume when it only adds to an already overburdened literature, much destined for rapid oblivion. Nevertheless, I gathered information until it seemed mandatory to consolidate the material into a volume to assist others concerned with these problems.

In the process, many individuals—colleagues, friends, family, editors, and patients—offered valuable assistance. Prominent among them were Fredrick Redlich, Lester Cooper, Robert Anderson, Bernard Grosser, Paul Wender, and David Tomb. E. Alan Jeppsen, Randall Stutman, Jonathan Bliss, Esther Larson, and Stanley Nakashima collaborated with me on various studies. Alice Blanchard, my kind, capable secretary, typed and retyped the manuscript with unfailing patience. When the bulky manuscript was accepted for publication by the Oxford University Press, Jeffrey House gently but firmly suggested deletions and reorganizations which I recognized reluctantly as improvements. Finally, Betty Gatewood edited the book with meticulous care. Her comments and changes improved the prose and drove me to clarify murky passages. Throughout the entire process, my wife supported my efforts, encouraged me when I faltered, and tolerated those long periods of scribbling in my study. To all I offer my thanks and gratitude.

Finally, I would like to acknowledge the editors and publishers of the American Journal of Psychiatry, the Archives of General Psychiatry, the Journal of Nervous and Mental Diseases, the American Journal of Hypnosis, and the Psychiatric Clinics of North America who were kind enough to allow me to reproduce tables and data from articles of mine and my colleagues which appeared in those publications.

# Contents

*Multiple Personality,
Allied Disorders, and Hypnosis*

# 1 / *The History of Hypnosis*

Many physicians view the history of medicine as a dull recital of the ignorance of our ancestors, their quaint therapies and strange theories. The common impulse is to rush toward the present, where contemporary truths and reliable information will be found, uncluttered by past errors. But history can be an adventure, the unraveling of a mystery—in this case, the gradual deciphering of a capability of the mind, now termed hypnosis.

Over several centuries this mental process, with its strange capacities, was examined and delineated. Its history involves the discovery of unsuspected unconscious processes, but also shows how fixed preconceptions can block understanding. There is the tantalizing question why, once perceived, this remarkable faculty of mind did not remain a focus of scientific interest or why the importance of spontaneous self-hypnosis was neglected.

## Early History

Early medicine was an affair of charms and spells, plant lore, and efforts to counteract supernatural forces (103, 249). Our ancestors regarded disease as the emanation of superhuman influences—the gods, an enemy, offended spirits of the dead—to be nullified by spells and sorcery. Whether healing powers were embodied in a king, priest, shaman, prophet, or physician, healers often employed tactics that we would now term hypnotic.

### The Shaman or Witch Doctor

Just as we have appointed specialists to handle our societal needs—doctors, lawyers, carpenters, barbers, and ministers—so our predecessors designated and trained shamans to cope with disease. The shamans frightened away the demons of illness by assuming a terrifying aspect, by covering themselves with animal skins, or by resorting to shouting, raving, slapping their hands, or shaking rattles. They might extract the active principle of a disease by sucking it through a hollow tube, or they might provide the patient with a special fetish or amulet to ward off the malign spirit.

Sigerist (249) wrote at length about these medicine men in primitive cultures. It would appear that diverse tribes have used similar methods to select and train their shamans. Those chosen usually were thought to acquire supernatural power from the spirits, animal gods, or the spirit of lightning, thunder, earth, water, wind, and mountains. Some chosen to be shamans underwent a long period of training to acquire their power. They lived alone, praying, fasting, and often suffering self-inflicted torture. Visions often were imperative, and the novitiate usually also had to learn a repertoire of songs, prayers, and ceremonies. Most powerful shamans had to acquire a close relation with the spirits—the faculty to call them, be possessed by them, and speak through them.

Those seeking to be shamans sought out ecstatic experience. Some candidates ran through the woods, jumped through fire, and submerged themselves in rivers. This intense excitement might be followed by a state of deep and protracted unconsciousness. Sigerist noted this in his description of Koryak shamans: "People about to become shaman have fits of wild paroxysms alternating with a condition of complete exhaustion. They will lie motionless for two or three days without partaking of food or drink. Finally they retire to the wilderness, where they spend their time enduring hunger and cold in order to prepare themselves for their calling."

The anthropologist Jenness (150) described the shamans whom he studied among the Canadian Eskimos from 1913 to 1918. Those shamans whose ceremonies he witnessed appeared to be excellent hypnotic subjects, for they went into trancelike states in which they had visions, heard voices, and experienced remarkable personal transformations. He wrote:

In concluding this sketch of shamanism, I may remark that nothing that I actually saw with my own eyes appeared to suggest the operation of any spiritual or mental forces with which we ourselves are not familiar. Hysteria, self-hypnosis, and delusions caused by suggestion are well known to every psychologist and medical practitioner, and everything that I witnessed could be explained on one or other of these grounds.

The implication that may be drawn from anthropological studies of shamans and medicine men is that these primitive doctors had more than an armamentarium of nostrums, herbs, rituals, incantations, and culturally prescribed ceremonies. Many or perhaps most were excellent hypnotic subjects. Those who were so endowed probably were selected in part for this ability, but others were forced to cultivate this skill by self-deprivation, fasting, and other tactics conducive to the development of trances. In a trance state (123, 205) it is possible to have a wide variety of "supernatural" experiences that would reflect the expectations and mores of the particular culture. Hypnosis allows frenzies, periods of apparent unconsciousness, visions, and even communication with the dead—anything that the imagination can contrive, but with a sense of reality for the subject. Descriptions of the behavior and experiences of shamans during their ministrations strongly suggest that these hysterical transformations often happened. But it also seems likely that their patients who had hypnotic capabilities also went into trances, in which they could have realistic fantasies, which were frequently therapeutic. What historians have called "suggestive" remedies often must have included hypnotic states that facilitated recovery.

## The Cult of Aesculapius

This is but one example of early medical therapy that must have benefited from the unrecognized induction of trance states. The cult of Aesculapius (103, 168, 178, 249) thrived near Corinth, Greece, in 500 B.C. By 400 B.C., there were hundreds of temples throughout Greece, and by 300 B.C., the movement had spread to Rome. The patients were received by physician-priests, who stirred their imaginations by recounting the deeds of Aesculapius, the success of temple treatment, and the remedies employed. The walls of the Aesculapian temples were adorned with bas-reliefs, some of which are still preserved. One represents a recumbent patient with a physician seated at his bedside while nearby stands a tall, erect person, representing the god of health. Oracular prescriptions were inscribed upon marble slabs. They included such statements as, "Lucius, having a pleurisy, and being given over by everyone, received from the god this oracle, that he should come and take the ashes off his altar, and mixing them with wine, apply them to his side. Which done, he was cured, and returned thanks to the god, and the people congratulated him upon his happy recovery."

In the Aesculapian cult, the proper cure would be revealed in the patient's dreams. The interpretation of the dream was the task of the priest, who was the intermediary between Aesculapius and the patient. The priests exerted a powerful influence by reciting wonderful tales of miraculous cures. Hydrotherapy, massage, and fumigation were adjunctive treatments, but the core therapy was sleeping in the sanctuary of the temple to attain relief either through revelations, dreams, or divine visitation. The philosophy of oneiromancy, the art of interpreting omens from dreams, held that during sleep the soul was released from the body to soar into spiritual regions, where it communed with celestial beings. Ideas revealed in dreams or trances were revered as divine revelations.

Aesculapian therapy was enhanced by dim light, since the main treatment took place at night after the candles were extinguished. Assisted by sacristans carrying bandages and poultices, a priest dressed in white moved from patient to patient, listening to the dreams they recounted.

The atmosphere was conducive to the induction of hypnotic states, and many cures may have been the result of unrecognized trances.

The techniques of the cult of Aesculapius have appeared in other cultures. For example, the Yogis of India have for centuries used meditation—going back to at least the second century A.D. This involves the repetitive chanting of a mantra or the focused attention on an object, often a candle flame. Incense, soft music, and a darkened room are often used. Furthermore, witch doctors of Africa and the North American Indians have used comparable tactics, such as the rhythmic beat of a drum or a repetitive chant, to focus attention and to achieve trancelike states.

## The Royal Touch

The healing of illness by the laying on of hands goes back to prehistoric times. In the New Testament there are these injunctions: "Neglect not the gift that is in thee, which was given thee by prophecy with the laying on of hands of the Presbytery" (Timothy). "And he could there do no mighty work, save that he laid his hands upon a few sick folk, and healed them" (Mark).

Druid priests effected cures by stroking the sick with their hands. Likewise, royal personages, exalted by their birth, were often invested with extraordinary healing powers. By the touch of their hand they could transmit some of this supernatural power to cure patients (168). The treatment of scrofulous patients by the reigning sovereign's hand may have originated in France with Clovis I (466–511); Louis I (778–840) is reported to have added to this the sign of the cross. Philip I (1052–1108) utilized "the touch" but lost his power of healing, it was said, because of his immorality. Louis IX (1214–1270) practiced the art, and Francis I while a prisoner at Madrid after the battle of Pavia in 1525 "cured multitudes of people daily of the evil."

The Royal Touch was a privilege of the kings and queens of England from before the Norman Conquest until the beginning of the Hanoverian dynasty, a period of nearly seven hundred years. Queen Elizabeth I (1533–1603) continued this practice, especially upon indigent persons who were unable to pay for private care. The ceremony of the Royal Touch reached its height of popularity during the reign of Charles II (1630–1685). John Evelyn wrote that the king put his hands upon the sick who approached, healed them, then hung a gold angel around the neck of each one. In the Parliamentary Journal (July 2–9, 1660) there is the statement, "His sacred majesty, on Monday last, touched 250 in the banquetting house . . . His majesty hath, for the future, appointed every Friday for the cure, at which 200, and no more are to be presented to him." On March 28, 1684, the congestion of people with their children eager to be cured was so large that six or seven were crushed to death as they pressed at the door for tickets.

Queen Anne (1665–1714) was the last of the English sovereigns to exercise this royal prerogative. Like many others, Samuel Johnson, then a child, was taken to London by his mother upon the advice of her physician, to be touched by the Queen for his scrofula, but the treatment was unsuccessful. The Royal Touch was not a panacea; there were many failures as well as successes. Dr. Wiseman, the favorite surgeon of Charles II, contended that the imagination of the patient was doubtless powerfully affected by the magnificence and splendor of the ceremony. But when therapeutic failures occurred these were ascribed to a lack of faith.

## Valentine Greatraks

The efficacy of "suggestive therapies" was well known in the sixteenth century. There were many practitioners of the art, but probably the most famous was Valentine Greatraks (1628–1666), the Irish stroker (168). He followed a long line of predecessors who advocated the efficacy of sympathetic or magnetic cure of wounds, and the healing of disease by "stroking." Paracelsus originated sympathetic medicine, but it was developed by Goclenius (1608) and Rattray (1658). Fludd (1619), Von Helmont (1621), Kircher (1643), and Maxwell (1679) were all early theorists of magnetism, in this respect predecessors of Mesmer.

Greatraks continued this tradition. He was born in Ireland on Saint Valentine's Day, hence his first name. At the outbreak of the Civil War in 1641, his mother fled with him to England, where he devoted himself to the study of the classics and divinity. Afterward he served for seven years in Cromwell's army as a cavalry lieutenant. He then returned to Ireland, where he was appointed a magistrate. Soon after the restoration, in obedience to a divine impulse, he began practice as a healer of disease by the laying on of hands, stroking, and touching. Greatraks's success was immediate and sensational. People flocked to him in such large numbers that "his barns and outhouses were crammed with innumerable specimens of suffering humanity." In 1665, he returned to England, where he continued to perform marvelous cures. But after an investigation and an adverse report by members of the Royal Society, his practice fell into disrepute; he retired to Ireland, where he died in obscurity.

Greatraks has been described as a man of integrity, one who was highly respected and incapable of fraud. Notoriety was distasteful to him, for he was driven to cure by the conviction that he possessed a healing power inspired by God. He is said to have had an agreeable personality, a pleasant manner, a fine figure, gallant bearing, a handsome face, a musical voice, and great energy.

Greatraks was versatile, and he adapted his manipulations to suit the individual case. Sometimes gently stroking a patient would suffice, but when the evil spirits were malignant, energetic massage would be necessary. Occasionally the demon fled "like a well-bred dog" at command, but more frequently he succeeded only after he became wet with perspiration and red in the face. One patient with rheumatism and gout is said to have been told, "I have seen a good many spirits of this kind. . . . They are watery spirits who bring on cold shivering and excite an overflow of aqueous humor in our poor bodies. . . . Evil spirit, who has quitted thy dwelling in the waters, to come and afflict this miserable body, I command thee to quit thy abode, and to return to thine ancient habitation."

A David Lloyd issued a tract entitled *Wonders no Miracles or Valentine Greatraks' Gift of Healing Examined*, in which he claimed that the "Irish stroker" was an impostor. In reply, Greatraks published a volume (110) entitled *A Brief Account of Mr. Valentine Greatraks and Divers of the Strange Cures By him lately Performed* (1666). It was written as a letter addressed to Robert Boyle, certainly one of England's scientific giants. In the book he indicated his outrage at the unjust vilification, listed his impressive lineage and credentials, and documented his miraculous cures. He even admitted to failures, but those were attributed to divine decision. There were testimonials by patients, verified by Boyle and others. An example was Anne Field. "Afflicted with a violent headache for five years, a blindness in both eyes, insomuch that she was not able to distinguish one person from another, at four yards distance; after three or four times stroking was perfectly freed of her pain in her head, and her eyes so mended, that she can now read a small Print."

More than fifty cures by Greatraks were described, witnessed, and documented by reliable individuals. These included the cure of every variety of intractable pain, the passage of urinary stones, rheumatism, ulcers, epilepsy, wounds, sciatica, the King's Evil, deafness, the ague, intractable coughing, and paralyses. Many illnesses were long-standing and previously had been treated unsuccessfully by various physicians.

In a letter (134) dated 1872, Sam Hocking referred to some manuscripts in the British Museum—the Dr. Birch Collection—that give accounts of the healing powers of Mr. Greatraks. There is a notation in the letter that "All disorders were not obedient to his touch, but he failed in few. Mr. Greatraks was of large stature and surprising strength. He had the largest, heaviest and softest hand of any man of his time." Hocking continued, "I am familiar with the cures, of every kind, named in Mr. Greatraks' book; most of which I have succeeded in curing by my own hand (King's Evil excepted, a disease never met with); and I have found the 'laying on of hands' practiced with various success in all the different countries I have visited; namely Mexico, the United States of America, Spain, France and Germany."

## Mesmer and Animal Magnetism

Franz Anton Mesmer (1734–1815) is often credited with the discovery of hypnosis, designated by him as animal magnetism (61, 71). However, he neither discovered nor did he understand this remarkable mental process. What he did, however, was to bring it to the attention of the Western world. It is an irony that a capability of the mind that had been expressed for centuries should finally receive widespread attention by dint of Mesmer's flamboyant antics, implausible theories, and fanatical dedication. There may simply have been a conjunction of elements—the emergence of an effective protagonist promulgating a principle at a moment in history when people were receptive. But whatever the reason, the result was that Mesmer attained an eminence hardly justified by his scientific acumen.

Mesmer was born in 1734 in Iznang, a small Swiss village near Lake Constance, where his father served as a game warden to the Prince-Bishop. Thanks to his many talents, he was privileged to study theology, philosophy, and law before he finally chose medicine as his vocation. In his graduation thesis (188), he expounded an old theory that the heavenly bodies influence people by way of a "fluidum" that possesses curative powers. His thesis is said to have been influenced (some have believed that it was plagiarized) from the work of the English physician Richard Mead (184), who had published in 1704 *De Imperio Solis et Lunae in Corpora Humana* (A Treatise Concerning the Influence of the Sun and Moon upon Human Bodies and the Diseases thereby produced). Mead, Newton's personal physician, had been influenced by the great discoveries in physics—those of Copernicus, Galileo, Kepler, Torricelli, and Newton, as well as Halley's theory of the tides. He therefore propounded a theory relating mechanics to medicine. Newton had enunciated a universal law of gravitational attraction between all bodies, this being a function of the product of their masses divided by the square of the distance between the bodies. To Mead it seemed sensible to extend this general principle to man. Accordingly, the sun and the moon would cause "various alterations in the human body, according to their different positions with respect to the earth." This was supported by his observation that various diseases were periodic and seemed to synchronize with lunar changes, just as the tides rose and receded according to the moon's gravitational pull upon the oceans. Furthermore, the moon's influence was "necessarily greater on the nervous fluid or animal spirits, than on the blood or any other fluid of the animal body." The chief medical culprits were epileptic diseases, raving fits of mad people, vertigo, hysterical disorders, nephritic paroxysms, asthma, epidemic fevers, and other periodic diseases.

Mesmer reproduced Mead's system and named the property of the animal body that renders it responsive to the action of heavenly bodies "animal magnetism." The theory was gradually elaborated into the concept that this was in accord with "the familiar principles of universal attraction . . . how the planets mutually affect one another in their orbits . . . [but] those spheres also exert a direct action on all the parts that go to make up animate bodies, in particular on the nervous system, by an all-penetrating fluid." There followed a confusion of gravity with cohesion, elasticity, irritability, and electricity. Mesmer was clearly not a keen student of Newton, and the attractive force between all bodies somehow was transformed into an invisible fluid, animal magnetism, and other physical modalities.

Most simply stated, his proposition was that planets influence the human body through a universal fluid, an invisible gas in which all bodies are immersed. Since he thought that this fluid acted upon living beings and had many "attractive" properties resembling those of a magnet, he termed it "animal magnetism." Disease was a disturbance of the harmonious distribution of these fluids. Therefore, the proper treatment was to reestablish harmony by the use of magnets. The theory was not a scientific tour de force—Newton would have been horrified—but it set Mesmer's direction and would lead him unwittingly to the brink of a quite different phenomenon.

In 1766, Mesmer began the practice of medicine in Vienna, married a well-to-do widow, and would have become an affluent doctor long since forgotten, if it were not for his concern with the principle that heavenly spheres irradiated a force that penetrated everywhere, exercising a direct effect upon the nervous system of living organisms. In 1773, he tested his concept by treating a woman named Franzeska Oesterlin, who was a twenty-eight-year-old hysteric with many conversion symptoms. Mesmer cured her through the use of magnets. This was not a novel method: others at the time were employing the same tactics. But Mesmer's cures created a sensation in Vienna, and he traveled to Bavaria and Munich to demonstrate this remarkable phenomenon. However, there was professional skepticism and opposition when he attempted to cure a member of a prominent family who was blind. The furor generated by this case presumably led him to leave Vienna for Paris in 1778, at the age of forty-three.

In Paris, Mesmer again became a controversial figure. Despite the antagonism of the medical profession, he established a clinic on the Place Vendôme, and in 1779 he published his most important volume (189), *Mémoire sur la découverte du Magnétisme animal*. It is a thin, unprepossessing monograph, now rare and expensive, in which he described the evolution of his theory, the success of his treatment, the opposition he had encountered to his work, and the twenty-seven propositions clarifying the nature of animal magnetism. The theory (189, 193) was embellished to indicate that this force—animal magnetism—could act at a distance; was intensified and reflected by mirrors like light; could be stored, concentrated and transported; and was affiliated with magnetism and electricity. Since sickness resulted from an obstacle to the flow of this fluid through the body, therapy was simply the overcoming of this block by inducing crises, often in the form of convulsions, and so restoring health or the harmony of the patient with nature.

Mesmer was a dedicated and persistent zealot, and in Paris he immediately put his magnetic principles into practice. He created a *baquet*, a tub filled with water in which bottles were arranged concentrically. The bottom of the tub was covered with iron filings and pieces of glass, and the tub was closed with a cover from which iron rods projected. Patients would grasp these rods to receive the magnetic fluid.

Subjects sat in a circle about the *baquet* with their hands joined or connected by a cord. The room was dimly lighted and hung with mirrors. Strains of soft music filled the air. Mesmer would appear in ornate dress, pass about the circle of patients, touching one, making passes over another, and fixing a third with a glance. An eyewitness described the scene. "Some patients remained calm—others cough, spit, feel slight pain, a local or general heat, and fall into sweats; others are agitated and tormented by convulsions. . . . It is impossible not to admit, from all these results, that some great force acts upon and masters these patients, and that this force appears to reside in the magnetizer." Not all crises took a violent form. Some subjects fell into a deep sleep, where many were able to communicate with dead or distant spirits.

The fact that many cures occurred awakened enormous public interest. Charles d'Eslon, physician to the king's youngest brother, became a supporter, but this was counterbalanced by the opposition of the medical faculty. Mesmer's friends organized themselves as a Society of Harmony to promote animal magnetism. The house in Place Vendôme became too small, and Mesmer purchased the Hotel Bullion, in which he built four *baquets*. Since even this did not suffice, he magnetized a tree, and thousands of sick people attached themselves to it with cords in the hope of a cure.

Mesmerism prevailed as an epidemic that overcame all of France. The great subject of conversation in Paris was animal magnetism. It was investigated by the police, patronized by the queen, ridiculed on the stage, burlesqued in songs and cartoons, and publicized by an avalanche of pamphlets and books (61). The craze for mesmerism was a reflection of the scientific ambiance of the time. Newton's theory of gravitation had been publshed in 1687; Franklin's electricity was being demonstrated at lyceums and museums in Paris; huge gas balloons were lifting people into the air for the first time in 1783. In view of these apparent miracles,

Mesmer's invisible fluid had plausibility, but it never became respectable in cautious scientific circles.

After Mesmer's early cures became known, the intrepid maestro invited the professors to verify his cures, his request was ignored. He then requested attention from the Royal Society of Medicine, only to quarrel with the commissioners, who refused to traffic with him further. In the midst of the furor, Marie Antoinette intervened. The government offered Mesmer a life pension of 20,000 livres and another 10,000 to set up a clinic if he would accept the surveillance of three government representatives. The tempestuous Mesmer refused to be judged by overseers, had a well-publicized tantrum, and finally demanded a country estate—which was not granted.

Nevertheless, through the organization of the Society of Harmony and its support by his wealthy friends, as well as sumptuous payments by patients, Mesmer lived in grand style, traveling about Paris in an elegant coach. Miraculous cures were reported everywhere, while faith and skepticism were joined in battle. At last the king interceded in 1784, appointing a prestigious commission to determine whether Mesmer was a quack or a healer. The panel included Bailly, the celebrated astronomer; Lavoisier, the preeminent chemist; Benjamin Franklin, statesman and scientist; Guillotin, of decapitation fame; and de Jussieu, a renowned botanist. In all, there were four doctors from the faculty of medicine and five members of the Academy of Sciences.

M. Desson, representing Mesmer, demonstrated "animal magnetism" to the commission. In their report (190, 192) this jury described the magnetic responses of patients. "Some are calm; tranquil and unconscious to any sensations; others cough, spit . . . or [experience] an universal burning and perspiration; a third class are agitated and tormented with convulsions . . . by shrieks, tears, hiccuppings and immoderate laughter." When the commissioners allowed themselves to be subjects, however, none detected any difference in sensations, nor did they experience multiple symptoms or violent crises. The commissioners also noted that the bizarre sensations occurred only if patients were aware of the magnet, not when the magnetism was directed toward them while they were blindfolded.

During the course of his demonstrations, Desson magnetized one tree and then brought a boy who was a susceptible subject to the scene. The boy did not know which tree had been magnetized. He responded to all four trees—and the fourth, which had not been magnetized, produced a crisis with a stiffening of his limbs. Another patient was brought for examination to Lavoisier's house, but she had a crisis in the antechamber before seeing the commissioners or Desson. An electrometer was also applied to one of the buckets containing "magnetized" fluid, but there was no response—the substance was neither electrical nor magnetic.

After many experiments, the scientists concluded, "Imagination, imitation are therefore the true causes of the effects attributed to this new agent, known by the appellation of animal magnetism. . . . This agent, this fluid has no existence." When confronted with their opinion, Desson agreed that imagination might be the explanation. However, he contended that imagination itself had therapeutic powers. The commissioners disagreed, perceiving no virtue in crises that could be hurtful. Their final judgment was, "Imagination without magnetism produces convulsions and magnetism without imagination produces nothing."

Unfortunately, this group, behaving like many committees, condemned the most vulnerable aspect of Mesmer's theory, animal magnetism, which could not survive scientific scrutiny. But the commission ignored the formidable problem of the nature of the psychological states of "magnetized" patients and the cures that emanated from them. Only one member of the committee, de Jussieu, the botanist, wrote a dissenting opinion, suggesting that Mesmer might be on the track of an important truth.

In fact, two government committees were appointed to investigate animal magnetism; a separate committee of the Royal Society of Medicine issued another report (191) five days later. Both reports were condemnatory, and they marked the end of Mesmer's popularity and influence. Now branded a quack, he rapidly sank into obscurity, leaving his followers to continue his practices.

Mesmer brought to international attention a bewildering and mysterious mental process—and a therapeutic tactic that would continue to perplex and antagonize the scientific community for two hundred years. But his bizarre performances also gave rise to attitudes toward animal magnetism or hypnosis that would become rigid and restrict later thinking about the phenomenon.

The first monumental obstacle would be the role of the mesmerist. Henceforth, there would be a focus on the mesmerist or hypnotist and his overwhelming importance to the process. It had been made doctrine that a mesmerist induced the trance state, but Mesmer's spectacle gave reason to discount this dogma. Subjects too poor to pay for the *baquet*, a privilege of the affluent, attached themselves by cords to a "magnetized" tree. Yet many fell into trances, convulsed, or were "cured," without benefit of a therapist.

Furthermore, Mesmer only touched some subjects and made ceremonial passes over others while glancing hither and yon—unremarkable behaviors to produce such dramatic responses. One might conclude that neither the hypnotist nor a specific technique was necessary, for all these effects might be generated by the setting, the patient's expectations, and the emotional state that ensued. This, in fact, was precisely the inference drawn by the commission. But whatever the process, an altered state of consciousness had been demonstrated in which remarkable behaviors occurred and cures were possible.

Another dilemma was the nature of the hypnotic state. To many, as in Mesmer's day, it would become a hoax and a fraud—certainly not respectable science. To others, it would become a miraculous process with universal curative properties. Some, like the members of the commission, would be able to explain any therapeutic outcome or remarkable occurrence as the result of imitation or imagination (later to be dignified as suggestion)—but such an attribution is hardly an explanation. Finally, there would be an alignment of mesmerism with parapsychological experiences, since many subjects in Mesmer's time and thereafter reported communications with the deceased or distant spirits. Such an association would not enhance the scientific respectability of mesmerism.

## Amand-Marie-Jacques de Chastenet, The Marquis de Puysegur

Mesmer's writings had been meager and his tenure brief. His condemnation and disgrace might have terminated the movement—earlier exponents of magnetism, like Fludd, Von Helmont, Kircher, and Maxwell, had disappeared into historical obscurity—if the Marquis de Puysegur (1751–1825), favored by the prestige of his lineage, had not supported and publicized the cause (71, 224). Puysegur was a member of the French nobility and a convert to mesmerism.

Puysegur tested subjects and discovered that they could diagnose their own disease, foresee its course, and prescribe their own treatment. When the number of patients seeking help became unmanageable, Puysegur resorted to the use of an old elm tree in the village square. Ropes were hung from the tree, and patients wrapped the ends around their bodies. Patients held hands, forming a human chain, until they felt the fluid circulating. Puysegur then touched some with an iron rod, whereupon the patients diagnosed their diseases and prescribed their treatments. They were instructed to kiss the tree to awaken. In one month, sixty-two of the three hundred patients were cured of their ailments

The similarity between magnetic sleep—a deep trance—and somnambulism—natural sleepwalking—became apparent to Puysegur since subjects in hypnosis superficially may have the appearance of sleep, although they may walk and talk. Therefore, he called this state, induced by an operator and often attended by amnesia, "artificial somnambulism," and characterized it as a profound trance.

One of his early patients was Victor, a young peasant whose family had served the Puysegurs for several generations. Victor was an excellent subject, but his "magnetism" was not accompanied by convulsions.

Instead he entered a strange sleep in which he was awake and responsive. He could answer questions and seemed to be more intelligent than in his alert state, but when he returned to "consciousness" he had no memory for the mesmeric experience. Furthermore, in a trance state, Victor could talk freely about his problems, which ordinarily he would be reluctant to confide. They could then be discussed and resolved.

In 1818, Puysegur revisited Victor, then severely ill, and again magnetized him. Puysegur was impressed by Victor's ability in this altered state to remember every detail of his former trance states—another feat that would be rediscovered repeatedly.

Victor and other subjects had taught the Marquis certain basic principles of hypnosis. Puysegur recognized, contrary to Mesmer, that convulsions or crises were not necessary or central to the process. He identified the amnesias, the insights possible in trances, the facilitation of a therapeutic discourse, and the latent memories. These observations led him to decide that Mesmer's fluid was not responsible for the phenomenon. Instead he concluded that the active agent was the magnetizer's will. He thus recognized the psychological nature of the process.

Puysegur organized a group to train magnetizers and to create centers for treatment. By 1789, there were two hundred members of this group of the Strasbough society, including many aristocrats. The society published an annual report listing cures with case histories. All the society's activities were terminated by the French revolution, which relegated Puysegur to prison for two years and led to the execution of many of his colleagues. Puysegur's writings were gradually forgotten, and it was not until the late nineteenth century that his original observations were exhumed and appreciated.

## The Early Magnetists

In this early period, there was dispute between the "fluidists" and the "animists," the "fluidists" contending that the mesmeric induction of subjects was due to a fluid emanating from the magnetizer, the "animists" attributing changes to the subject's mental state (71, 148). There was thus competition between a physical and a psychological explanation. Puysegur had been the first to support the psychological interpretation, but Faria, Alexandre Bertrand, and others would soon espouse the same thesis. In this period, the exploration of hypnosis entered the descriptive phase, in which many of its salient features would be identified and its therapeutic capabilities discovered—although these were often exaggerated.

## Abbé Faria

Abbé Faria (1756–1819) was a Portuguese priest who claimed to be an Indian Brahman, but nothing is known about him until he came to Paris in 1813 at the age of fifty-seven. He died six years later in 1819, leaving one book—*On the Cause of Lucid Sleep* (71, 217).

In Paris, he initially enjoyed popularity as a hypnotist. One of his more dramatic feats involved the suggestion to hypnotized subjects that the water they were drinking was really wine. However, in 1815 he was discredited when a subject at one of his demonstrations simulated hypnosis and then burst into laughter, saying "I have fooled you."

But despite this opprobrium, he made important contributions. In his book he referred to hypnosis as "lucid sleep," a concept that Braid (1843) later would elaborate by coining the term *hypnosis* from the Greek *hypnos,* "sleep." Furthermore, Faria referred to magnetism as a form of concentration, and considered highly susceptible subjects to be *epoptes*—those who could experience all of the alterations of hypnosis. He also noted differences between subjects. Predicated on experience with more than five thousand people, he estimated that the ability to be a highly susceptible subject could be found in one out of five or six persons in the general population.

Finally, Faria's induction technique was novel, since he asked his subjects to sit, close their eyes, and focus their attention on sleep. If that failed, he would ask the subject to fixate on his open hand, which he would move slowly toward the subject's face, commanding in a loud voice, "Sleep!" If that failed, he would lightly touch the person on the head, face, and body. To terminate what he termed lucid sleep, he would simply say "Wake up."

Faria was aware of Puysegur's notion that hypnosis was a matter of the will—the motivation of the subject—but he made the pertinent observation that this was often not the case, since subjects entered trances when motivated, unmotivated, or sometimes despite their opposition. Furthermore, some people would enter a trance as they crossed the threshold of his salon, even before he could attempt an induction. This led him to dismiss the view that hypnosis was primarily due to the power of the magnetist over the subject.

The commission that examined Mesmer's work had concluded that hypnosis was simply a matter of imagination, but Faria rejected this verdict as inadequate. He reasoned that what is imagined is ordinarily not forgotten, whereas what happens during hypnosis is forgotten: in fact, posthypnotic amnesia was a common occurrence. A paramount contribution of Faria's was the recognition that 15 to 20 percent of the population have the natural ability to attain deep trances. He attributed this to people's powers of concentration, but he also perceived that the hypnotist must engender trust to allow the development of this natural phenomenon.

## *Joseph-Philippe-Francois Deleuze and Contemporaries*

Deleuze (1753–1835) was an officer in the French army and later a botanist who was one of many attracted to the movement. His first experience with hypnosis was a personal one when, as he later wrote, "I joined the chain and in a few minutes saw the patient asleep. I looked with astonishment, but falling asleep myself in less than fifteen minutes I ceased to observe. During my sleep I talked much and was so much excited as to trouble the chain. Of this I had no recollection when I awoke and found them all laughing around me."

After this initial experience, Deleuze began to study and to practice mesmerism. His *Critical History of Magnetism* (63) (1813) represented years of investigation and reflection, including the analysis of nearly three hundred publications. Deleuze (63, 64, 65) recognized that children older than seven magnetized easily. He noted a resemblance to sleepwalking. He also observed astutely that "the process . . . may be regarded as the effect of a concentration upon one single class of sensations, upon one order of ideas." This anticipated Braid's later explanation of the monoidea as the essence of hypnosis.

Deleuze described the retrogression to childhood caused by mesmerism; he gave detailed instructions about the technique of induction; he defined problems encountered and methods of therapy. He warned about rapport. "When magnetism is accompanied with somnambulism it generally imparts to the somnambulist a very lively affection for her magnetizer." But there was also the admonition, "Avoid being magnetized when it is no longer necessary. If you continue after being cured . . . you will become habituated to it." Hypnosis could become an addiction. Like all those who practiced this technique, Deleuze could enumerate a long list of cures, of everything from suppurative ulcers to asthma; paralyses, hysterical afflictions and hypochondriasis; pains, spasms, early cases of mental alienation, and the pains of childbirth.

A contemporary of Deleuze's was Alexandre Bertrand (12) (1795–1831) who gave lectures on magnetism from 1819 to 1821. Students attended "to the great scandal of the faculty." Bertrand opposed the doctrine of a magnetic fluid, and published a tome in 1826 with descriptions of behaviors and experiences of hypnotized subjects—their movements, hallucinations, negative hallucinations (the obliteration of objects), amnesias, and posthypnotic behaviors.

It was early recognized by several practitioners of hypnosis that a rapport between the subject and the operator was important. It was also noted that subjects would resist any command they considered to be immoral. As practice continued, details of the initiation and termination of treatment were defined, and the dangers of frequent inductions and prolonged therapy were recognized. But many quacks and stage performers tarnished the reputation of the movement. Further contamination came with the impact of spiritualism, first in the United States and then in England and Germany. Mediums appeared who could, in trances, communicate with the dead—objects would apparently rise into the air, musical instruments would play at command, and spirits would be heard. Although scientists and physicians pursued the study of mesmerism throughout Europe and the United States, these other influences counteracted and denigrated this effort. Hypnosis experienced and was to experience an unsavory reputation in respectable scientific circles.

## Jules Dupotet de Sennevoy

Dupotet (1796–1881) was one of the most famous hypnotists of his day. A follower of Mesmer, he gathered about him many students and disciples, and his seances were famous throughout Paris. Dupotet is included here because of his descriptions (68) in 1838 of trance states, but also because of his conviction that supernatural feats could be performed in a hypnotic state—a conviction he shared with many other mesmerists. Concerning the status of a person in a trance, he wrote:

In this peculiar state of sleep, the surface of the body is sometimes acutely sensible—but more frequently the sense of feeling is absolutely annihilated. The jaws are firmly locked, and resist every effort to wrench them open; the joints are often rigid, and the limbs inflexible; and not only is the sense of feeling, but the senses of smell, hearing, and sight, also, are so deadened to all external impressions, that no pungent odour, loud report, or glare of light, can excite them in the slightest degree. The body may be pricked, pinched, lacerated, or burnt; fumes of concentrated liquid ammonia may be passed up the nostrils; the loudest reports suddenly made close upon the ear; dazzling and intense light may be thrown upon the pupil of the eye; yet so profound is the physical state of lethargy, that the sleeper will remain undisturbed, and insensible to tortures, which, in the waking state, would be intolerable.

Dupotet described how hypnotized subjects failed to react when their lips and nostrils were tickled with feathers; when their skin was pinched until bruises were produced; and when smoke was introduced into their nasal passages. Even a woman whose feet were plunged into a strong infusion of mustard-seed at a high temperature apparently felt nothing. Even in the presence of all these stimuli, Dupotet wrote, "not the slightest sign of pain did they evince. The expression of the countenance remained unchanged, nor was the pulse in any degree affected. On being awakened, however, out of the magnetic sleep, they all experienced the pain usually attendant on such applications, and were exceedingly angry at the treatment they had received."

He also referred to a surgical procedure done under hypnosis as further evidence to support his own observations. A woman suffering from an abscess on the front of the thigh was put into a magnetic sleep to produce insensibility to pain. The surgeon repeatedly plunged a probe into the abscess to drain the purulent matter. During the operation the patient remained motionless as a statue. Upon being awakened, she was asked whether she would submit to the operation, to which she replied, "I suppose I must, since it is necessary." She was then informed that it was unnecessary as the operation already had been performed. The patient was astonished, for she had seen nothing and felt nothing. She also remembered nothing, except for the hypnotist's laying the palm of his hand upon her forehead to induce sleep.

As further proof of the powers of hypnosis, Dupotet cited an even more drastic surgical operation. In 1829, a sixty-four-year-old woman consulted M. Cloquet, an eminent surgeon, for an ulcerated cancer in her right breast. During the two days before the operation, the woman was magnetised several times to prepare her to submit without fear to the operation. On the day appointed for the operation, the surgeon found the patient seated in an armchair, in the attitude of a person in a tranquil natural sleep. The first incision, commencing at the axilla, was carried around the upper part of the tumor as far as the inner border of the breast; the second, beginning at the same point, was carried around the lower part of the tumor until it met the first. The enlarged glands were then dissected with precaution, on account of their vicinity to the axillary artery, and the tumor was extirpated. The operation lasted from ten to twelve minutes,and during the whole time, the patient continued conversing tranquilly with the operator, and gave not the slightest indication of sensibility—no motion of the limbs or the features; no change in respiration or voice. These were early reports of surgical procedures using hypnosis as an anesthetic agent; many more would follow in later years.

Dupotet reached the conclusion that the hypnotic state had extraordinary features. Of those hypnotized, he wrote:

They converse clearly and intelligently with all those persons with whom they are en rapport, or in mental relation. Their perceptions in regard to the objects of their attention are more than ordinarily acute; but the organs of the senses are closed against other impressions. They manifest a clearness or lucidity of ideas, and a temporary knowledge and intellectual activity, beyond that which they possess in their ordinary waking state. They forget when they are awakened everything which may have taken place during their somnambulism; but on returning into the same state, they recollect everything which occurred during their former fits.

But Dupotet, like so many of his confreres, made extravagent statements sure to alienate scientists and to give hypnosis a bad name. He contended that

> they [hypnotized subjects] mentally take cognizance of the conditions and rela-
> tions of surrounding objects, through some other channel than the organs
> through which such impressions are usually conveyed. There is in many cases an
> obvious vicarious transference of the senses from their appropriate organs to
> other parts of the nervous system, as to the tips of the fingers, epigastrium, and
> other parts of the body. The lucidity of their vision penetrates through interven-
> ing opaque objects, and even takes cognizance of events passing at a distance.
> They appear endowed with a knowledge beyond that which they ordinarily pos-
> sess, and prescribe for themselves, as well as for those with whom they are en
> rapport, remedies for such complaints as they may be afflicted with; and these
> are generally found successful. Their lucid vision often extends beyond the pres-
> ent existence, and they foretell events with circumstantial minuteness, even the
> day and hour—the very moment—when such predictions will be verified is accu-
> rately specified.

Dupotet made no original discoveries, but his work does reflect the state of the art during this period, the nature of the observations being made, and the excitement of these pioneers. It also illustrates their mis-conceptions. Many early hypnotists were convinced that parapsychologi-cal experiences were authentic. Excellent hypnotic subjects continue to report them even today, but their existence remains unproved.

## The Revival of Hypnosis and the Dispute Between the Salpêtrière and Nancy Schools

During the nineteenth century, interest in hypnosis was erratic. Periods of renewed investigation alternated with decades of scientific ostracism and neglect. For nearly twenty years before Charcot's studies, hypnotism was abandoned to charlatans and infrequent public demonstrations; only a few healers secretly still used it (148).

The resurgence of scientific interest prompted by Charcot's work brought with it renewed controversy about the basic nature of hypnosis reminiscent of the earlier conflict between "fluidists" and "animists." Now the precise behaviors of subjects were opposed to the inexactitude of the mental process of "suggestibility." Charcot at the Salpêtrière, sup-ported by his associates Bourneville, Brissand, Chambard, and Richer, would seek the essence of hypnosis by studying the movements and re-flexes of subjects, whereas Liébeault and Bernheim, the Nancy School, would focus on subjects' suggestibility. It was an acrimonious wrangle, but it resulted in further clarification of an elusive phenomenon.

## *Jean-Martin Charcot—The Salpêtrière School*

During the latter part of the nineteenth century, Charcot (1835–1893) was perhaps the most eminent or at least the most publicized neurologist in the Western World (71, 148). Physician to kings and princes, Charcot through his clinics at the Salpêtrière attracted visitors from distant places.

The turning point in Charcot's medical career occurred in 1862, when he was appointed chief physician to one of the clinics at the Salpêtrière in Paris. This huge metropolitan hospital had historical credentials, but its medical facilities were antiquated. By dint of a forceful personality and unswerving direction, Charcot refurbished the institution, adding laboratories, examining rooms, teaching facilities, consulting staffs, and an illustrious photography service. Later came an anatomical-pathological museum, an outpatient service, and a large auditorium where the great man presented cases and gave carefully prepared, precise lectures before students and international dignitaries. A brilliant teacher and a born actor, he would mimic the gait, voice, and behavior typical of the syndrome he was discussing. He was a man who attracted disciples, but he had critics and enemies as well. Charcot was a controversial figure who fascinated—and alienated—many. His scientific achievements were nonetheless impressive. He made contributions to the understanding of pulmonary and kidney diseases; gave substance to geriatric medicine; and in neurology delineated disseminated sclerosis, amyotrophic lateral sclerosis, locomotor ataxia, luetic arthropathies, cerebral and medullar localization, and aphasias.

Charcot's most controversial studies were of hysteria and hypnosis (148). During a period in which hypnosis was unsavory and in disrepute, he brought to these investigations what he perceived to be a scientific rigor. Charcot defined three states of hysteria: lethargy, catalepsy, and somnambulism. In lethargy, there was the appearance of a deep sleep in which the subject was deaf and unresponsive to stimuli, but had neuromuscular hyperactivity. When the subject's eyes were opened by the physician, the subject progressed into catalepsy, in which limbs retained any position in which they were placed and the posture was one of paralysis. Finally, the subject could be put into a somnambulistic state, in which he or she could hear and speak. Now the subject would respond to suggestion and produce contractures by stimulation of the skin. These were the leading ideas that Charcot presented in a paper before the Academy of Sciences in 1882—the various states found in hysterical patients when hypnosis was induced. It was a singular achievement for anyone to give a paper on hypnosis before the Academy, since this august body had twice condemned all research in animal magnetism. Only Charcot's eminence and his obvious scientific objectivity made this possible.

Charcot's notion that there were three predictable stages of hypnosis we now know to be incorrect. At the time, however, this mattered little, because animal magnetism had been brought back into the scientific forum, where it could again be a legitimate object for investigation. Why Charcot made his error about the nature of hypnosis is an interesting tale. According to Janet (148), this was the result of a conjunction of circumstances. Charcot was an imperious academician in the nineteenth-century tradition. Subordinates deferred and listened while he pontificated and tolerated little opposition. Although many hysterics must have passed through the clinics and hospital, his studies of hysteria were based primarily on perhaps a dozen severe cases, including three women—called only Witt., Bar. and Glaiz, to conceal their identities—who were his favorite subjects.

Charcot never hypnotized anyone. Before his demonstrations, the patients were prepared by assistants, who had drilled them to undergo a change of state at a sign from the professor. Charcot merely gave this sign before his audience. It is unlikely that his assistants were consciously deceiving the professor. A more plausible explanation is that they were unwittingly reinforcing those behaviors that both they and Charcot expected. The patients, few in number, were quick to learn their roles—unconsciously—and they became compliant puppets. It must also be remembered that Charcot was primarily a neurologist. Unlike Janet, who spent countless hours doing hypnosis with thousands of patients, Charcot had little personal familiarity with the peculiarities of hypnosis, for he only demonstrated it with patients at his clinics. There he examined these subjects in the way familiar to him, with a neurological precision quite appropriate to diseases of the central nervous system, but not applicable to these strange mentalistic aberrations.

What Charcot had really uncovered was the contagion or suggestibility peculiar to the hypnotic trance. In this state, ideas or behaviors may be introduced if they are acceptable to the subject—the prime example of this being posthypnotic instructions. Presumably Charcot's stages, repeated so frequently in demonstrations, were of this nature. But it would be a mistake to believe that all ideas can be instilled successfully. Even in hypnosis a subject can be remarkably stubborn, and an idea must be acceptable if the patient is to act on it.

Charcot's thesis of three immutable stages was soon gingerly and then vigorously disputed. The Salpêtrière school of Charcot's disciples defended the professor, but gradually it became apparent that he had erred. His greatest contribution to psychiatry was to make the study of hypnosis respectable, which encouraged others to investigate it. Immediately following Charcot's studies, an avalanche of papers and books appeared. Once again there was interest, ferment, and scientific controversy.

## *Ambroise-Auguste Liébeault—The Nancy School*

In 1860, Liébeault (1823–1904) began to study mesmerism seriously. Sixteen years before he had begun a humble general practice of medicine in France. Since his patients were not accustomed to mesmeric therapy, and as they initially had little faith in such a practice, he promised to treat them for nothing if they would allow him to practice mesmerism upon them. He soon was deluged with patients, and in 1864 he settled in Nancy, where he practiced hypnosis gratis among the poor. For two years he worked on a book, *Du Sommeil et Etats Analogues* (173). It is said that only one copy was sold, but this is an unlikely story since this volume, although rare, occasionally appears in antiquarian catalogues. It does, however, suggest Liébeault's initial obscurity. Although his colleagues considered him a madman, the poor esteemed him as "the good father Liébeault" because many of them were helped by his treatments after other physicians had failed.

Bramwell (32) visited him in 1889. Afterward, he reported:

I was shown a few hypnotic experiments; but cure alone seemed the sole object of his work . . . The patients told to go to sleep apparently fell at once into a quiet slumber, then received their dose of curative suggestions, and when told to awake either walked quietly away or sat for a little while to chat with their friends; the whole process rarely lasting longer than ten minutes. I noticed that in some instances curative suggestions appeared to be perfectly successful, even when the state produced was only that of somnolence. The cases varied widely, but most of them were either cured or relieved.

Liébeault treated thousands of patients with continuing success; he was primarily a skilled practitioner dedicated to therapy. His observations and studies were incidental to his daily ministrations to the poor, and it was only through his association with Bernheim, who publicized his work and ideas, that he became known. Together they represented the School of Suggestive Therapy in opposition to Charcot's rigid explanation of hypnosis.

## *Hippolyte-Marie Bernheim—The Nancy School*

Bernheim (1840–1919) was a professor at the university in Nancy. In 1882, Liébeault cured a patient with sciatica of six years' duration whom Bernheim had failed to treat successfully. The professor visited to observe Liébeault's practice. At first he was critical and skeptical, but it became increasingly difficult for him to deny the cures by hypnotic suggestion that he first witnessed and later discovered in his own practice. Like so many of his predecessors, Bernheim found that his initial disbelief yielded to conviction as he experienced therapeutic triumphs by hypnosis in cases in which all previous treatments had failed.

In 1884, Bernheim published his researches in a book (11), which he revised and expanded in 1886. According to this book, his use of hypnosis was primarily therapeutic, and suggestion was the vehicle. "The Nancy School [he wrote] placed the study of hypnosis upon its true basis, suggestion, and thus created this most useful and most fruitful application." Bernheim indicated that Liébeault extended the observations of Braid and Durand de Gros. Suggestion, he asserted, became effective by inducing first a hypnotic state. "The concentration of the mind on a single idea, the idea of sleep, facilitated by the fixation of the gaze, brings about the repose of the body, the deadening of the senses, then isolation from the external world."

Bernheim also perceived the strange and elusive relationship between sleep and hypnosis, although this was not fully explained: "Ordinary sleep does not differ from hypnotic sleep. The one is, like the other, due to the fixation of the attention and of the nervous force upon the idea of sleep. The individual who wishes to sleep, isolates his senses, meditates, and remains motionless. The nervous force concentrates itself, so to speak, at one point of the brain upon a single idea, and abandons the nerves of sensation, motion and special sense." In contrast, "the hypnotized subject falls asleep, with his thought fixed, in relationship with the hypnotizer; hence the possibility of the suggestion of dreams, ideas and acts, by this foreign will."

Bernheim described in great detail the changes in sensation, sight, taste, smell, hearing, movement, and vision that could be provoked by hypnosis, as well as the amnesias and posthypnotic suggestions that could be induced. But being a therapist, he was preoccupied by the "peculiar aptitude for transforming the idea received [from the operator] into an act," and "the unconscious transformation of the thought into movement, unknown to the will," during hypnosis. A close connection between hypnosis and hysteria was implied, but it is difficult to determine whether he recognized the nature of this connection. Bernheim wrote in passing about autosuggestion, but only briefly, which suggests that this was not a fundamental concept for him.

Most of Bernheim's book is devoted to describing the remarkable therapeutic results he achieved. Well over a hundred cases are discussed in some detail, perhaps the largest number available for scrutiny from any author. These included cases classified as organic diseases of the nervous system, hysteria, neuropathic affections, neuroses, pareses and paralyses, gastrointestinal afflictions, pains, rheumatic disorders, neuralgias, and menstrual troubles. Several cases of "insanity" with hallucinations were reported that responded favorably to hypnotic suggestion. Not all patients were cured, although many were, but the amelioration of disabling symptoms occurred with impressive regularity.

When one reads these accounts and attends to Bernheim's careful observations and his critical reservations, it is difficult to dispatch the reports as the work of another naive zealot. All patients were not cured, many were only helped, and some had great resistances that negated his efforts. Their "autosuggests" were often more powerful than his suggestions. Furthermore, simple suggestion did not always suffice. "It is sometimes necessary to reason, to prove and to convince," he wrote. Hypnosis "increases the cerebral docility; it makes the automatic activity predominate over the will. But the latter persists to a certain degree, the subject thinks, reasons, discusses, accepts more readily than in the waking condition." Furthermore, he noted, "Therapeutic suggestion is not infallible, though it gives good results in a very large number of cases. . . . The cause of the failure is inherent sometimes in the disease, sometimes in the subject. . . . Sometimes the subject resists."

He recognized as early suggestive therapies the invocations of Egyptian priests, the practice of the Aesculapiads, Paracelsus's sympathetic powder, homeopathic medicine, the Royal Touch; the cures at the tomb of Deacon in Paris, Knock in Ireland, and Lourdes in France; the magnetizers; the therapies of Greatraks, Gassner, and others.

Although Bernheim's experience was extensive, his major emphasis was on suggestion—the suggestibility of excellent hypnotic patients and the use of hypnosis as a means to convey suggestions. His theoretical explanations gave little insight into the nature of hypnosis, although its capabilities were described in detail.

## The English Hypnotists

There was an early interest in hypnosis in Germany that later spread throughout Europe, but England remained a bastion of conservative opposition. Its medical establishment denigrated hypnosis, and pioneers like Braid, Elliotson, and Esdaille pursued their studies in virtual isolation. Despite this disrepute, these pioneers stubbornly persisted, and their insights and observations advanced the understanding of the hypnotic process.

### *James Braid*

Braid (1795–1861) was born in Fifeshire, Scotland, and educated in Edinburgh, where he qualified as a surgeon. In 1841, he was present at a mesmeric seance given by the operator Lafontaine. Despite an initial skepticism, this excited his interest, and he began hypnotic experiments (30, 31, 32).

In 1843, he published his most important book, *Neurypnology or The Rationale of Nervous Sleep* (30). It contains his earliest theories, the most important of which was his view of the subjective nature of the hypnotic process. He coined the terms *neurypnology*—the doctrine of nervous sleep, and *neurohypnotism*—nervous sleep (from which came the term hypnotism), but he later recognized that sleep and hypnosis were dissimilar.

Like so many before him, Braid contended that hypnosis was a powerful therapeutic tool. He experimented with magnets, but concluded that magnetism made no contribution to the process. He believed that hypnosis was capable of curing many diseases for which there were no remedies but that it was not a panacea. Different patients showed varying susceptibility, he contended, and therapeutic results might be rapid or delayed. "I lay no claim for it to produce the marvellous or transcendental phenomena; [he wrote] nor do I believe that the phenomena manifested have any relationship to a magnetic temperament, or some peculiar or occult power, possessed in an extraordinary degree by the operator. . . . Like the originators of all new views, however, hypnotism has subjected me to much contention."

In 1844, Braid suffered an attack of rheumatism. The pain became so intense that

it entirely deprived me of sleep for three nights successively, and on the last of the three nights I could not remain in any one posture for five minutes, from the severity of the pain." After attending patients, he returned home still suffering extreme pain. "In this condition I resolved to try the effects of hypnotism. I requested two friends . . . to watch the effects and arouse me when I had passed sufficiently into the condition. . . . I sat down and hypnotised myself. . . . At the expiration of nine minutes they aroused me, and to my agreeable surprise, I was quite free from pain, being able to move in any way with perfect ease. . . . A week thereafter I had a slight return which I removed by hypnotising myself once more; and I have remained quite free from rheumatism ever since, now nearly six years.

In 1855, he published a pamphlet with the title *Electro-Biological Phenomena and the Physiology of Fascination*. He treated under this name the condition of "fascination" seen in human beings and animals produced by great unexpected danger. This fascination, or the absorption of the entire attention by a single object or idea, was the essence of the hypnotic state. This explained for Braid not only the immobility of a bird confronted with a snake, but also the fixation of people, their immobility in situations of great danger.

At first Braid was convinced that a fixity of gaze was mandatory to hypnotic induction, but later, after successful hypnosis of blind subjects, he concluded that it was not essential. A fixation of the eyes was only one aspect of the riveting of the mind on one idea, he asserted, and this concentration on a single idea was the essence of the process.

Earlier critics had expressed grave concern about the powers of the operator to control the subject during the hypnotic state. It was feared that a subject might be induced to perform immoral or even criminal behaviors. Braid's observations led him to the opposite conviction, that volition and judgment were not abolished in hypnosis, for his subjects were keenly aware and would do nothing that was opposed to their moral sense. But the fact that hypnotized subjects could experience amnesias—might temporarily forget yet later recapture amnestic information, and their susceptibility to posthypnotic suggestions led him to recognize a "double consciousness." In Braid's view, this meant that one state was conscious and the other was outside awareness. This notion foreshadows Janet's dissociation, the preconscious, the subconscious, and the unconscious—important concepts that would concern Braid's successors.

Braid also became convinced of the fundamental difference between sleep and hypnosis. Interestingly, he detected a resemblance between the condition produced by hashish and certain hypnotic states. He admonished operators to recognize the acuity of the special senses in hypnosis—the tendency to imitate others; the extraordinary recall of things long forgotten in the waking state; the vivid state of imagination in hypnosis, which invested memories with the attribute of a present reality; and the ability of subjects to detect unintentional suggestions by the operator.

Braid was a skeptical, sensible scientist and a cautious investigator. His understanding of hypnosis laid the groundwork for much that is now known.

*John Elliotson*

Elliotson (1791–1868), the son of a chemist, received his medical degree from Edinburgh. Immediately after the publication of Laennec's classical volume on auscultation (1819), Elliotson adopted the use of the stethoscope in England. He was one of the first to use the method of percussion and auscultation of the chest, demonstrating his capacity to entertain novel ideas, but he was met with condemnation and ridicule for carrying a piece of wood into a sickroom or "using that hocus-pocus" (32).

When Dupotet visited England in 1837, Elliotson was intrigued by the therapeutic possibilities of hypnosis. Now a professor of Medicine at the University College, he began to mesmerize patients regularly, with favorable results. Students attended his demonstrations in large numbers, but his colleagues objected to his iconoclastic views, and the dean advised him to desist. A stubborn man, Elliotson replied that "the institution was established for the discovery and dissemination of truth. . . . The sole question was whether the matter were the truth or not." In 1838, the Council of the University College passed a resolution "That the Hospital Committee be instructed to take such steps as they shall deem most advisable to prevent the practice of mesmerism or animal magnetism in the future within the Hospital." Elliotson was ordered to cease his studies, and he resigned his appointment in protest.

When Elliotson was privileged to give the illustrious Harveean Oration in 1846, he was attacked in the *Lancet* as a pariah who was striking a vital blow at legitimate medicine. Undeterred, he chose as his subject mesmerism, reminding his audience that the greatest discoveries in medicine had almost always been opposed by the profession. These included the descriptions of the lacteal vessels, the thoracic duct, the circulation of the blood, the sounds of the chest, vaccination, and antisepsis. He cited his studies over the previous decade proving that mesmerism could prevent pain during surgery, produce sleep, ease sickness, and cure many diseases unrelieved by current practices.

In 1843, he began the publication of the *Zoist* (297), a journal of mesmeric and allied studies. It continued through thirteen volumes, and is a rich source of information about the mesmeric successes and practices of the time. Cure or improvement was claimed following mesmeric treatment in hysteroepilepsy, epilepsy, insanity, hysteria, stammering, neuralgia, asthma, torticollis, headache, functional disorders of the heart, rheumatism, and other diseases.

Many operations were reported (72) using hypnosis as an anesthetic agent—a Dr. Parker claimed to have done two hundred—but the subjects of various surgical operations were considered by the medical profession to be impostors or insensible to pain. In 1842, a surgeon, Mr. Ward, amputated a leg during a mesmeric trance, and reported that the patient lay perfectly calm during the operation, without a twitch of a muscle. Critics claimed that the patient had been trained not to experience pain and contended he was an impostor, while one irate physician stated, "Pain was a wise provision of nature, and patients ought to suffer pain while their surgeons were operating."

As a result of the influence of the *Zoist,* mesmeric institutions were formed in London, Edinburgh, and Dublin, but medical journals either ignored or vilified the movement. In the *Lancet* in 1847, an editorial appeared: "Of course the parties concerned in the infamous publication (the *Zoist*) are in a state of perpetual mortification at their fallen and degraded position, and therefore they bite and rail; the leper must be taken with his spots."

Elliotson continued to espouse the use of hypnosis for surgical anesthesia, but he also contended that it was particularly effective in the treatment of hysteria and other functional disorders, for which the current practices of blistering, bleeding, and salivation were both brutal and useless. A common bit of medical advice to women suffering from hysteria at the time was to seek marriage—the supposition being that the disease was of a sexual character. Elliotson, however, contended that hysteria was not connected with the uterus, nor was it even limited to females: boys and men also had it.

Although Elliotson was opposed to spiritualism, he did believe in clairvoyance and phrenology, subjects often discussed in the *Zoist*. He objected strongly to bloodletting, and complained about fashions in medicine—for thirty years the liver had been a favorite organ, and now the kidney had replaced it as the source of all ailments.

Elliotson also was unhappy with his contemporaries' medical treatment of children. He found children easy to hypnotize, and was indignant about the cruelties inflicted upon them by parents, doctors, and teachers, contending that convulsions sometimes arose from overwork, while terror was a common cause of nervous afflictions.

Seen in retrospect, Elliotson's contributions were social and moral. He stubbornly supported the application of hypnosis as an important adjunct to medical practice; opposed the virulent antipathy of orthodox medicine to its use; fostered a journal in which others could publish their unacceptable findings; and helped to sustain the study and application of hypnosis in England.

## James Esdaile

Esdaile (1808–1859), the son of a minister, graduated with a medical degree from Edinburgh, and then received an appointment in the East India Company to work in India. His chief contribution was the application of hypnosis to the practice of surgery (32). Hypnosis had previously been reported as an effective anesthetic agent in surgery by Recamier (1821), Cloquet (1829), Oudet (1837), and others, but Esdaile probably had the largest number of cases ever collected. It must be realized that these experiments took place before the discovery of ether or chloroform, at a time when no effective anesthetic agent was available, and surgery was a grim, brutal, and painful experience. In his book *Mesmerism in India* (1846), Esdaile reported his remarkable successes (76). During eight months, there were seventy-three painless surgical operations, including arm, penis, and breast amputations; straightening of contracted knees; the removal of cataracts; and fourteen surgical excisions of scrotal tumors weighing from eight to eighty pounds.

G. Shah, a shopkeeper aged forty, was one of the patients on whom Esdaile successfully operated using hypnotic anesthesia. "He has got a 'monster tumour' which prevents him from moving; its great weight, and his having used it for a writing desk for many years, has pressed it into its present shape. His pulse is weak and his feet oedematous." There was a low morbidity and low mortality from mesmeric surgery. Healing occurred rapidly, infections were minimal, and there were no deaths in the initial series.

At the end of a year and after more than a hundred operations, Esdaile reported his surgical results to the government, received a favorable response, and was assigned to a small hospital in Calcutta in 1846, where he continued his mesmeric efforts, both surgical and medical. Before Esdaile left India, he had performed thousands of painless minor operations and 261 major procedures. The removal of enormous scrotal tumors resulting from elephantiasis was perhaps his most dramatic achievement, since the mortality of the procedure at the time using conventional nonmesmeric methods was 50 percent. Mortality in 200 consecutive cases of Esdaile's was only 5 percent. At least twenty of the tumors weighed 50 to 103 pounds, and many of the patients were over fifty years of age. No patients died immediately after the operation. All deaths took place days or weeks later due to cholera, lockjaw, or dysentery, hardly unexpected and probably not the surgeon's fault since most of his patients lived in poverty and filth.

Esdaile's mesmeric work was constantly attacked in Indian medical journals, it being alleged that coolies enjoyed operations and simulated anesthesia to please him. There was polite condescension, for he was described as an honest fool who was deceived by his patients, a group of unscrupulous impostors. In reply, Esdaile, who was not a docile man, asserted that he had done more operations on scrotal tumors in a month than had been done in all the native hospitals in Calcutta in a year. During the operations, he noted, patients remained quiet and showed no signs of pain, whereas they always did in the waking state.

He left India in 1851, explaining in a letter to his friend Elliotson, "My reasons for leaving India were simply that I hated the climate, the country, and all its ways from the moment I set foot in it. . . . Knowing that all the wealth of India could not bribe me to remain a moment after the expiration of my period of service."

It was alleged by critics that Esdaile's surgical feats, if true, were a product of the hysteria of the Indian natives. After returning to Britain, Esdaile settled in Perth, where he wrote to Elliotson that the inhabitants of the far North in England were as susceptible to mesmerism as those of the farthest East in India. Like so many pioneers in hypnosis, he became bitter at his rejection by the medical profession. He was urged to send an account of his removals of scrotal tumors during trances to a reputable journal. Esdaile's own account was:

My article was not published, and I then sent a more general paper containing a resume of my surgical work. This was rejected for its unpractical character! I have heard that it is given as a reason for not printing my paper that, though no one now denies my facts, these apply to the Natives of India only. But, as far as I know, no medical journal has admitted the reality of painless mesmeric operations even for India, or inserted one of the numerous European cases reported from London, Paris, Cherbough, etc. . . . To pretend that there is a free medical press in Great Britain is a mockery and a delusion.

## John Milne Bramwell

John Bramwell (1852–?) as a boy witnessed hypnotic experiments by his father, a physician, and he read books on the topic early in life, notably Gregory's *Animal Magnetism*, and a translation of Reichenbach's work.

He attended the medical school at Edinburgh, where Professor John Hughes Bennett included a resume of Braid's work as a regular part of his course in physiology, asserting that one day hypnotism would revolutionize the theory and practice of medicine. Bramwell then entered the general practice of medicine, and after several years first began the use of hypnosis when "a case occurred in my practice in which hypnotic treatment was apparently indicated. . . . Although I told my patient how little I knew of the subject, I had no difficulty in hypnotizing him." This first success encouraged him to try hypnosis with friends and later with patients.

Thereafter he used hypnosis extensively, developed a large referral practice, performed clinical experiments, and lectured and wrote extensively on the subject. But his major contribution was a text on hypnosis, *Hypnosis—Its History, Practice and Theory* (32), published in 1903. It is a scholarly, critical, and detailed analysis of hypnosis, which to my knowledge has never been excelled. I shall summarize some of its salient elements, but it must be read to be appreciated. In Table 1 various induction tactics are listed.

*Table 1. Hypnotic Induction Techniques*

| | |
|---|---|
| Mesmer | He passed his hands over subjects and ran his hands down their shoulders, arms, and fingers. |
| Esdaile | He placed subjects in a darkened room, directing them to close their eyes and try to sleep. He made passes over their bodies without touching. |
| Braid | Patients were instructed to gaze at a bright object held a foot from their eyes above the forehead. They were then asked to look at the object and to think of nothing else. Later this was changed to a request to fixate visually and then to close the eyes. It was finally modified to verbal suggestions. |
| Liébeault | He told subjects to gaze steadily at the operator and to think of nothing. If the subject's eyes did not spontaneously close, he or she was told to close them. |
| Beaunis | He used a fixed gaze. |
| Wetterstrand | He made passes with physical contact in a darkened room with verbal suggestions |
| Richet | He squeezed thumbs and made passes over subjects. There was no need for visual fixation. |
| Luys | Subjects were asked to look at a revolving mirror. |
| Voison | Insane patients were placed in straightjackets. Their eyes were held open, and they were compelled to look at a light or finger, accompanied by suggestions. |
| Bramwell | He used visual fixation with verbal suggestion, "Your eyelids are getting heavy; you can't keep them open, etc." |
| Physical modes | These included loud noises, the ticking of a watch, soft music, a weak electric current to the head, pressure upon certain parts of body, and drugs—including cannabis, chloroform, alcohol, chloral, and morphine. |

These are the means of hypnotic induction cited by Bramwell, but many others can be culled from the literature. Abbé Faria sometimes simply intoned "Sleep." Most operators relied on some form of visual concentration, verbal patter, passes, and relaxation. But visual fixation and verbal messages were not mandatory, since blind subjects and the deaf also could be induced. Janet, not cited by Bramwell, also referred to inductions by shock and emotional arousal. Stage hypnotists would suddenly thrust the head back or apply a sharp blow to the back of the neck, while Charcot at times suddenly flashed a light or sounded a gong, causing surprise and alarm. The aggregate of these disparate tactics, all capable of inducing trances, led Braid and Bramwell to believe that the essential element was focused attention, no matter what the cause might be. All evidence suggested a single mentalistic process that was inherent in the subject and mobilized by the operators.

Those Bramwell called somnambulists were subjects who went into deep trances with posthypnotic amnesia. These constituted 10 to 20 percent of the population, whereas 40 to 50 percent of all subjects were good hypnotic candidates. That meant that 50 to 70 percent of all people had significant hypnotic capabilities, and only 5 to 10 percent were refractory.

Bramwell, it should be noted, had two series of cases. The first hundred patients came from his early general practice; he had known many for over a decade and had their confidence. The second hundred were mostly of strangers, often chronically ill people, who were referred by other physicians for hypnotic therapy. In the first group, 48 percent were somnambulists and none failed to enter hypnosis, whereas in the latter group 29 percent were somnambulists and 22 percent were refractory. The discrepancy between the two groups Bramwell attributed to differences in rapport and confidence, although severity of illness may have been an important variable. Bramwell also tabulated the data then available about hypnotic susceptibility with respect to the ages of subjects (Table 2).

Many studies led him to conclude that race, nationality, social position, and sex did not influence hypnotic susceptibility. Children proved to be excellent subjects, whereas the elderly showed decrements in this capability. The youngest child whom Bramwell could hypnotize was three years old; Wetterstand's youngest was two and a half. Most authorities agreed that low intelligence and severe insanity militated against an induction, as did fear of hypnosis or a determination to resist the process, while the power to concentrate facilitated hypnosis. Although Janet and many others reported hysterics to be excellent subjects, Bramwell, Moll, and Forel experienced difficulty inducing them. Whether this was a matter of selection or of definition is difficult to determine.

A perplexing problem was the number of hypnotic attempts a therapist should make before deciding that the subject was refractory.

*Table 2. Susceptibility to Hypnosis[a]*

| | | Number of subjects | Somnam- bulism | Moderate | Mild | None |
|---|---|---|---|---|---|---|
| Schrenk-Notzing | | 8705 | 15% | 49% | 29% | 6% |
| Liébeault | | 755 | 19 | 42 | 32 | 7 |
| Van Eeden and Van Renterghem | | 1089 | 12 | 41 | 41 | 5 |
| Bramwell | | | | | | |
| Own patients | | 100 | 48 | 40 | 12 | 0 |
| Strangers referred | | 100 | 29 | 13 | 36 | 22 |
| | *Ages* | | | | | |
| Beaunis | – 7 | 23 | 27 | 17 | 56 | 0 |
| Beaunis | 7–14 | 65 | 55 | 31 | 14 | 0 |
| Ringier | 7–14 | | 53 | | | |
| Beaunis | 14–21 | 87 | 23 | 51 | 14 | 10 |
| Ringier | 14–21 | | 42 | | | |
| Beaunis | 21–28 | 98 | 13 | 42 | 35 | 9 |
| Beaunis | 28–35 | 84 | 23 | 40 | 30 | 6 |
| Beaunis | 35–42 | 85 | 11 | 47 | 34 | 8 |
| Beaunis | 42–49 | 106 | 22 | 34 | 32 | 12 |
| Beaunis | 49–56 | 68 | 7 | 50 | 38 | 4 |
| Beaunis | 56–63 | 69 | 7 | 46 | 32 | 14 |
| Beaunis | 63 + | 59 | 12 | 48 | 27 | 14 |

[a] The percentages have been consolidated into fewer categories. The number of subjects under "ages" comes from Hilgard (128); and Beaunis used Liébeault's data.

Tuckey would make three or four; Moll and Forel were persistent and often made many more; Bramwell continued stubbornly because he was often successful after repeated failures—many being cases that eventually yielded the best results.

Bramwell gave many examples of several hypnotic capabilities (Table 3), and referred to his own confirmatory observations. He also noted the claims of telepathy and clairvoyance—abilities attributed to many excellent subjects. Elliotson and Esdaile firmly believed in these phenomena, but Bramwell tersely reported that after many years of hypnotic work including experiments, he had seen nothing to confirm their existence.

These results (Table 4) deserve careful consideration, since severe obsessional neurotics, chronic hysterics, and sexual deviants often prove to be refractory to modern nonhypnotic therapies. Furthermore, it should be remembered that many of Bramwell's successes occurred with chronically disabled patients referred to him only after other means had failed.

*Table 3. Hypnotic Capabilities*

| | |
|---|---|
| Motor movements | Catalepsy, paralyses, and flaccidity could all be induced. Bramwell commented that all were due to direct or indirect suggestion and all could be reproduced by trained unhypnotized subjects. |
| Vasomotor | The pulse could be accelerated, but this was due to emotional causes. Bleeding, local redness of skin, blisters, and change in skin temperature were reported, but Bramwell found the evidence inconclusive. |
| Sensations | Vision, audition, smell, taste, touch, pressure, temperature, and pain all could be made more acute, be diminished, or be arrested. Subjects could be made insensible to all. |
| Delusions, hallucinations, and illusions | All could be induced in some subjects. |
| Anesthesia, analgesia, and amnesia | All were reported by many investigators. |

Bramwell, like Janet, was impressed by cases of multiple personality. He cited over a dozen from the literature as confirmatory evidence of a secondary consciousness—events taking place outside of awareness. These were perceived as comparable to hypnotic automatic writing and amnesias, for in all of these there were identifiable mental activities inaccessible to consciousness. Bramwell even speculated in this regard about hysterics: "May not the difficulty of inducing hypnosis in the hysterical— of making one's suggestions find a resting place in them—be due to the fact that the hypnotic substratum of their personality is already occupied by irrational self-suggestions which their waking will cannot control."

The emphasis in therapy during this period was on the use of suggestion during hypnosis. Many other elements must have crept into the procedure, but this was the basic mode. Bramwell discounted Bernheim's theory that heightened suggestibility was the essential feature of hypnosis. His caustic comment was, "Suggestion no more explains the phenomena of hypnosis than the crack of a pistol explains a boat race. . . . The essential condition is not the means used to excite the phenomena but the peculiar state which enables them to be evoked."

Bramwell reviewed the experiments and opinions of many authorities pertaining to the free will and independence of hypnotized subjects. Like many other experienced operators, he came to the conclusion that they were not "unconscious machines incapable of judgment," because they would frequently refuse suggests that were disagreeable or morally repugnant.

Bramwell also noted Esdaile's observation that mesmerism had long been known in India but that its secrets, stemming from remote antiquity, were confined to certain castes and families. He referred to a Dr. Davidson, residing in India, who visited the mesmeric hospital in

*Table 4. Results of Therapy with Hypnosis*

| Entity | Investigator | Results | | | |
|--------|-------------|---------|---|---|---|
| Hysteria | Bramwell and references | There were many successful treatments of paralyses, contractures, spasms, anesthesias, amauroses, mutism, aphonia, hiccough, and other disorders. | | | |
| | | Cases | Cured | Improved | Unimproved |
| Menstrual problems | Brunnberg | Amenorrhea (9) | 6 | 2 | 1 |
| | | Menorrhagia (9) | 4 | 2 | 3 |
| | | Menorrhagia and dysmenorrhea (5) | 3 | 1 | 1 |
| | | Dysmenorrhea (3) | 1 | 1 | 1 |
| | Bramwell and references | Many cures | | | |
| Profound depressions and manias | Bramwell and references | There were cases of severe melancholia that were cured after about 20 sessions | | | |
| Neurasthenia | Bramwell | Many cures | | | |
| | Schrench-Notzing, etc. | 228 cases; 32% recovered, 37% much improved, 32% no improvement | | | |
| Impotence | Schrench-Notzing | 18 cases; 10 cured | | | |
| Sexual psy-chopathies | Schrench-Notzing | Many cures | | | |
| | Krafft-Ebing | Many cures | | | |
| Insanity | Voisin | At first Voisin was successful with 10% after prolonged therapy. Later percentages became better. He treated several hundred cases over 18 years. | | | |
| | References | Many others reported sporadic occasional successes, but most results were unfavorable | | | |
| Dipsomania and chronic alcoholism | Bramwell | 76 cases of severe, chronic alcoholism; 28 recovered (average length of follow-up 3 years); 36 improved; 12 failures | | | |
| | Hirt | 13 cases with 8 recoveries | | | |
| Morphine addiction | Wetterstrand | 41 cases; 28 cured | | | |
| Children's disorders | References | There were successes with incontinence, twitches, nocturnal terrors, spasms, antisocial behaviors, and other problems. | | | |
| Enuresis | Bramwell | In every case in which genuine hypnosis was induced, with one exception, the patient recovered. By 1890, he had 18 cases—all successful. | | | |
| Obsessions | Bramwell | Many successes | | | |
| | References | Many recoveries | | | |
| Epilepsy | Bramwell | 10 cases; 5 improved but no complete recoveries | | | |
| | Woods | 14 cases; 2 recovered, 10 improved | | | |
| | References | Many successful treatments | | | |
| Stammering | Wetterstrand | 48 cases; 15 cured, 19 improved, 14 unimproved | | | |
| | References | Many successes | | | |

Calcutta and suddenly realized what *jar-phoonk* of India was. It was mesmerism. Many of his patients, after he had failed to cure their complaints, were treated by the *jadoowalla* and, to his great surprise, returned cured after they had gone through a process of being stroked and breathed upon. Furthermore, in Bombay, a native was treated by a local mendicant. A Colonel Bagnold reported that the native doctor caused the patient to look at a string of beads and then made passes over her.

Bramwell was a disciple of Braid. He perceived hypnosis as a highly developed trait in many people, most useful for the treatment of many neuropathic conditions. Focusing of attention was its salient feature, but in this focused state remarkable mentalistic changes would occur. Although he recognized the existence of a secondary consciousness, he paid little attention to Janet's concept of dissociation and hidden complexes; nor did he mention the theories or discoveries of either Breuer or Freud. His therapy was basically hypnotic suggestion, and he did not search for concealed traumas. He did, however, collate much of the available information about hypnosis, making it available in an understandable form.

## The Emergence of the Unconscious

The early mesmerists were delving into one aspect of the unconscious when they discovered posthypnotic amnesias, but there had been earlier recognition of unconscious processes, reviewed by Whyte (286) and summarized in Table 5.

Whyte reached the conclusion that the concept of unconscious mental processes was conceived in post-Cartesian Europe around 1700. It was topical around 1800 and fashionable around 1870 to 1880—in fact, it was a European commonplace. References to the unconscious over the centuries related to many aspects of mental functioning but offered little conceptual clarity. Examples of unconscious mentation came from such diverse sources as memory, perception, reasoning, and ideas; imagination and creativity; instincts, insight, habitual activities, and dreams.

The advent of hypnosis introduced a new scientific instrument to explore the mind. As is true in science, a new instrument or a new technique may probe nature to reveal new understandings. A telescope, a microscope, a chemical test, even a thermometer, will enhance knowledge and open new frontiers. The introduction of hypnosis was such a novel instrument. William James wrote:

In the wonderful explorations by Binet, Janet, Breuer, Freud, Mason, Prince, and others of the subliminal consciousness of patients with hysteria, we have revealed to us whole systems of underground life, in the shape of memories of a

*Table 5. The Unconscious*

| | |
|---|---|
| Galen (c. 130–300 A.D.) | We make unconscious inferences from perceptions. |
| Plotinus (c. 204–270) | Feelings can be present without awareness of them. The absence of conscious perception is no proof of the absence of mental activity. |
| St. Augustine (354–430) | "Great is this power of memory, exceedingly great." |
| St. Thomas Aquinas (1224–1274) | "There are thus processes in the soul of which we are not immediately aware." |
| Dante (1265–1321) | Shameful memories are often forgotten. |
| Paracelsus (1493–1541) | There are influences both biological and spiritual guiding man of which he is seldom aware. |
| Boehme (1575–1642) | "Before God I do not know how the thing arises in me without the participation of my will. I do not know that which I must write." |
| Shakespeare (1564–1616) | "In soothe I know not why I am so sad." (Merchant of Venice) |
| Pascal (1623–1662) | "The heart has its reasons, which reason knows not." |
| Spinoza (1632–1677) | Unconscious memories and motives exist. |
| Norris (1632–1704) | "There are infinitely more ideas impressed on our minds than we can possibly attend to or perceive." |
| Leibnitz (1646–1716) | "Our clear concepts are like islands which arise above the ocean of obscure ones." |
| Vico (1668–1744) | "Common sense is judgment without reflection." |
| Lichtenberg (1742–1799) | "These dreams developed all kinds of ideas that were sleeping in my soul." |
| Rousseau (1712–1778) | "The true and primary motives of the greater part of my actions are not so clear to me as I have for a long time imagined." |
| Kant (1724–1804) | "The dark ideas in man are unmeasurable. The clear ones . . . cover infinitely few points which lie open to consciousness. |
| Platner (1744–1818) | "Ideas with consciousness are often the psychological results of ideas without consciousness." |
| Herder (1744–1803) | Unconscious mental processes have demonic power, but also were sources of imagination, poetry, and dreams. |
| Goethe (1749–1832) | Conscious and unconscious processes are interwoven in the workings of the mind. |
| Herbart (1776–1841) | "Arrested [inhibited] ideas are obscured and disappear from consciousness and these unconscious ideas continue to exert their pressures against consciousness." |
| Carus (1789–1869) | "The key to the understanding of the character of the conscious life lies in the region of the unconscious." |
| Wundt (1832–1920) | "Our mind is so fortunately equipped that it brings us the most important bases for our thoughts without our having the least knowledge of this work of elaboration. Only the results of it become conscious." |
| Von Hartmann | *Philosophy of the Unconscious*—book published in 1868. |

painful sort which lead a parasitic existence, buried outside of the primary fields of consciousness, and making eruptions thereto with hallucinations, pains, convulsions, paralyses of feelings and of motion, and the whole procession of symptoms of hysteric disease of body and of mind (145).

## Pierre Janet

Modern psychiatrists, if familiar with the name Pierre Janet (1859–1947), would link him with the concept that hysteria is due to a congenital weakness of the mind. Those more knowledgeable might list him with many prominent French psychiatrists of the latter half of the nineteenth century such as Briquet, Richet, Binet, and Gilles de la Tourette. Janet certainly lacks at present the historical eminence of Braid or Charcot, and few would compare him to Freud. Yet his contributions were of equal importance, for it was he rather than Freud who discovered this novel "unconscious." Sir William Osler once wrote, "In science the credit goes to the man who convinces the world, not to the man to whom the idea first occurred" (66).

Janet never achieved the influence or recognition that he deserved. He neither founded a school nor collected followers; he has simply been overlooked, Born in Paris, he began his professional career as a philosopher, but became interested in the subject of hallucinations, which led him to study a hysteric named Leonie. This initiated his interest in hypnosis and hysteria, subjects that he would study for the rest of his life. His commitment to research in psychopathology led him to acquire a medical degree (71).

In 1889, he published his first volume (146), *Psychological Automatism*, reflecting his studies over the preceding seven years. In fact, he had begun this work at almost the same time that Breuer had started to treat Anna O. It is a curious coincidence, because both men simultaneously and independently were defining the same remarkable phenomenon. Janet's volume is a medical classic comparable in importance to Breuer's and Freud's monograph on hysteria and Freud's book on dreams. In it he propounded the novel thesis that hysterical symptoms are due to subconscious fixed ideas that have been isolated and usually forgotten. Split off from consciousness—"dissociated"—they embody painful experiences, but become autonomous by virtue of their segregation from the main stream of consciousness. The mode of treatment is hypnosis, which allows them to be identified and reintegrated into consciousness. This antedated Breuer's and Freud's identical discovery, published four years later in 1893.

Janet's volume was based upon the study of fourteen hysterical women, five hysterical men, and eight psychotics and epileptics. But most of the research rested on his clinical studies of four women: Lucie,

Leonie, Marie, and Rose. Lucie had fits of terror for no apparent reason. By means of automatic writing during hypnosis, Janet discovered the forgotten, unconscious experience that had generated the symptoms. This nineteen-year-old girl had been terrified by two men hiding behind a curtain when she was seven. A personality, Adrienne, would relive this experience. Leonie also proved to have multiple personalities. These multiple personalities, which Janet termed successive existences, were studied. He described how the various personalities reacted to one another, and how some personalities are childish.

Another hysteric, Marie, resurrected forgotten memories in hypnosis related to the shock of her first menstrual period. As an adult, she became depressed, suffered pains, nervous spasms, and shivered before each menstrual period. This became understandable when a forgotten experience that had occurred at the age of thirteen with her first menses was resurrected by hypnosis. At that time she had been ashamed of her state and plunged herself into a big bucket of cold water. Her menses did stop, but she shivered violently, became sick, and was delirious for several days. As an adult, she reenacted this forgotten episode monthly, but without recognizing its meaning. Therapy involved the reliving of this experience in hypnosis, but in a corrective fashion by making it conscious. Furthermore, a blindness in her left eye, which had appeared at age six, was discovered in hypnosis to be due to another forgotten experience.

Based on clinical studies and hypnotic experiments, Janet came to the conclusion that these psychological automatisms were divisible into two groups: total automatism, such as catalepsy, in which the subject may be completely out of contact with reality; and partial automatism, in which the person is split, so that a subconscious part follows an independent course unknown to consciousness. This subconscious records information not available to consciousness and manifests itself in automatic writing, retrievable amnesias, forgotten traumas, and posthypnotic suggestions. Furthermore, this subconscious contains ideas that can be responsible for many other actions, feelings, and attitudes, including obsessions, compulsions, and hallucinations. Lucie would say in terror, "I am afraid and I don't know why." Janet explained, "It is because the unconscious has its dream; it sees men behind the curtains, and puts the body in the attitude of terror." According to Janet's thinking, the "field of consciousness" has been narrowed in hysterics, as is evidenced by the "forgetting" of certain unacceptable ideas, memories, and feelings. These can be reached via hypnosis, but they have developed an autonomy of their own; out of consciousness they direct behavior.

In 1889, Janet started his medical studies in Paris while continuing his psychological investigations at the Salpêtriére. One of his early patients there was Justine, who had a morbid fear of cholera. The same pattern of unconscious concealment was found in her. By virtue of some ingenious hypnotic ploys contrived by Janet, she finally revealed an early forgotten memory of two corpses with the stench of putrefaction, at a time when she heard bells tolling and shouts of "cholera, cholera."

Based on a variety of comparable cases, Janet came to the conclusion that these illnesses consisted of the patient's inability to bring into consciousness certain memories that instead operated automatically and irresistibly. "We thus have to deal with a psychological system which escaped the control of consciousness and develops independently." Subconscious fixed ideas are therefore a characteristic feature of hysteria, and various acts performed during fugues or hysterical crises are often disguised reenactments of these fixed unconscious ideas and experiences.

Janet's fundamental views are contained in a two volume work, *Psychological Healing* (148). His summary of the history of hypnosis is one of the most detailed accounts available. Furthermore, he was a collector not only of five thousand case histories recorded in his own handwriting, but of a historical library with most of the works of the old magnetizers and hypnotists in the original volumes. He had a command of that information, but he also had been present and had participated in a part of the history of hypnosis.

Despite his unparalleled experience with cases of hysteria and his long-standing practice of hypnosis, he found no simple explanation for these "dissociations" demonstrated by his patients. As a result, he concluded that hysterics had a congenital weakness of psychological synthesis that led to a fragmentation of their minds (147)—an unsupported genetic hypothesis.

In his work *Psychological Healing* (148), he discussed the current theories of hypnosis. At the time, hypnotic therapy mainly relied on suggestion. It was asserted that suggestion could bring about relief of symptoms, and that by its use many patients could be helped. This led to a general preoccupation with suggestion and the conviction by many that the essence of hypnosis was heightened suggestibility. The facile inference was that hysterics were abnormally suggestible—and therefore weak-minded. Janet had many reservations about this general thesis. He emphasized that some suggestions were not accepted by subjects—in fact, many subjects were remarkably stubborn. Janet concluded that suggestibility did not covary closely with hypnosis—and therefore, suggestibility could not be the key to its nature. Janet also rejected the traditional idea that hypnosis was related to the state of sleep. This was impossible, he concluded, because of the many physiological and behavioral differences between the two states—including the obvious recognition that hypnotized subjects can move, react, and speak, which they could not do if they were asleep.

Charcot had recognized that symptoms found in hysterics could be reduplicated artificially by many excellent hypnotic subjects when these symptoms were suggested by a hypnotist. Janet also perceived the many similarities and parallelisms between hypnosis and hysteria, but like Charcot he did not clarify the precise connection between the two. Instead Janet like his predecessors remained preoccupied with the view that hypnosis was dependent on a hypnotist—a failure to recognize that hypnosis was both a native endowment and a spontaneous reaction. He stated, "Hypnosis is not only a subconscious state; it is an artificial condition determined by the hypnotist."

Janet noted that susceptibility to hypnosis was different in various groups of patients. His clinical impression was that hysterics were the best hypnotic subjects, although some were refractory, but idiots, patients with brain damage, obsessional neurotics, severe depressives and schizophrenics were poor candidates.

Janet's therapeutic results with hypnosis were submitted with scientific candor. In a series of 3,500 patients in whom hypnosis was tried, 250, or 7 percent, responded favorably or were cured for at least one year. Hypnosis and suggestion gave "practical results almost exclusively in cases of hysterical neuroses." The best results were obtained in patients who were young (under thirty), with a recent onset of symptoms. Therapy by simple hypnotic suggestion, for one to four sessions, alleviated symptoms in fifty-four patients with a variety of hysterical symptoms, including paraplegia, mutism, blindness, contractures, chorea, spasms, tics, hiccough, vomiting, convulsions, terrors, and sleepwalking.

But the more numerous cases in which a cure by suggestion was complete and persisted for at least a year were not achieved so rapidly. The patients in this group came for treatment two or three times a week for a period of one to three months. Included were fourteen cases of functional paralyses; twenty-one with hysterical contractures; twenty-five with involuntary movements; seventeen with a variety of fixed ideas and impulses, including hallucinations; sixty-four with hysteria accompanied by somnambulism with delirium. A third category included cases in which hypnotic suggestion brought a temporary relief, failed, or periodically had to be repeated when relapses occurred.

Finally, there was a complex form of hypnotic therapy which went well beyond simple suggestion—a therapy of reintegration into consciousness of the traumatic forgotten memories. The memories had to be searched out, but when patients recounted them and their sufferings, these miseries were "liquidated."

During this period, Freud was publishing his observations and theories. Janet was offended by Freud's failure to recognize his contributions and priorities, but he also took exception to many psychoanalytic concepts. Janet stated that Breuer's and Freud's publications of 1893 and 1895 were merely confirmations of his own views, which he had presented in 1889. Their "traumatic memories," found in hysterics, were his "fixed ideas." Both he and they, he said, described an identical unconscious, termed by Janet the subconscious. Freud's concept of repression was also his, what he had described as a weakness of mental synthesis. The term "conversion" was used by Freud to denote precisely what Janet had described as the many symptoms emanating from the traumatic fixed ideas in his patients. Breuer's and Freud's therapeutic tactics were also the same as Janet's—to make the unconscious conscious by reintegration, assimilation, and liquidation, as Janet put it, was identical to Breuer and Freud's abreaction and catharsis. The vocabulary differed, but the concepts were indistinguishable.

An interesting omission in Janet's critique is any reference to Breuer's penetrating recognition of "hypnoid" or "self-hypnotic" states. Janet furthermore had major objections to Freud's tendency to overgeneralize. Hidden traumatic memories are found in hysterics, but this does not allow one to extend these unconscious mechanisms to all neurotics. As Janet wrote, "I have myself drawn attention to the subconscious character of some of the fixed ideas of hysterical patients. This characteristic of subconsciousness is ascribed by psychoanalysts to all the morbid manifestations of the neuroses."

Janet objected to free association as a therapeutic and investigative tactic, stating, "I do not think much of the method." He questioned Freud's assertion that the patient's unconscious complexes reflect repressed wishes, since Janet found many cases in which there was no wish but only fear. In this connection, Freud had also concluded that these repressed traumatic memories were sexual in nature—experiences of masturbation or sexual molestation. Janet protested that this was an old theory going back to Hippocrates—the concept of a wandering uterus being the responsible agent in hysteria, and inadequate sexual gratification the culprit. As a result, some physicians had continued to advise marriage as the treatment of choice in hysteria. Janet agreed that distressing memories with a sexual content could be detected in perhaps three-quarters of his cases, but he strongly objected to Freud's hyperbole of "all" cases. There were other traumatic memories that were not sexual, such as accidents, losses of key figures, abuses, and fears. Finally, Janet considered some of Freud's hypotheses to be scientifically unsound, including the Oedipus complex, psychosexual development—the oral, anal, phallic, and genital stages—the castration complex, and the like.

At the frontier of science there are differences of opinion, contradictory observations, and alternative interpretations. Janet and Freud had observed comparable phenomena, had agreed on some things, and had drawn different conclusions about others. This controversy might have continued exposing their differences to scientific inquiry—to new observations and continuing experimentation—if Janet had not been forgotten and Freud had not become a prophet and his writings scripture.

Unfortunately, for these and other reasons, this natural scientific process was aborted.

Janet had made fundamental observations. He had identified the close relationship between hypnosis and hysteria but never clarified precisely how the two related and interacted. He discerned the presence in his hysterical patients of "subconscious fixed ideas" and devised a treatment to make them conscious, but he never clarified the "weakness of the mind" that allowed the dissociations. One is left with his observations, but no resolution of how they fit together into a simple scheme. There is no question that his observations, so similar to Breuer's and Freud's, antedated them, and he deserves priority if honors need be bestowed. But for simplicity and clarity, Breuer's synthesis, in my estimation, supersedes both Janet's and Freud's, and if Janet is dimly remembered, Breuer is virtually forgotten. Such are the injustices of history.

## *Josef Breuer and Sigmund Freud*

It is popularly believed that Sigmund Freud (1856–1939) discovered the unconscious mind, a place in which malevolent forces operated to subvert human reason. This thesis reinforced the doctrine of determinism, since there could be no free will if unconscious forces were at work. But it was also Darwinian, since these concealed processes presumably had evolved unregenerate from humanity's animal ancestors. The solution was to make the unconscious conscious, so that these forces could be mastered by the rational mind. Free association and psychoanalysis would liberate human beings, allowing them the freedom to direct their own behavior after the unconscious was revealed in therapy.

This is a simplification and a distortion of a much more complex discovery. The recognition of unconscious mechanisms has a lengthy past, but a part of the story began in Vienna between 1880 and 1882 in the encounter of two protagonists, Anna O., the patient, and Josef Breuer, her physician. Breuer (1842–1925), whose name is now known only through his early association with Sigmund Freud, was a prominent and highly esteemed internist—a doctor's doctor—in general practice. Early in his career he had worked under Eward Hering, a famous physiologist, on the mechanisms of respiration, and had discovered its automatic control by the vagus nerve. Later Breuer also contributed to an understanding of the function of the semicircular canals, a small structure in the inner ear that allows us to orient ourselves in space and maintain equilibrium (71).

In 1871, Breuer went into private practice. An estimate of his prestige can be measured by his election to the Vienna Academy of Science in 1894. From December 1880 to June 1882, Breuer treated "Fräulein Anna O.," the name applied to Bertha Pappenheim to conceal her identity. Anna O., the patient, was a grand hysteric who suffered a galaxy of conversion symptoms, including paralyses, anesthesias, disorders of vision and hearing, neuralgias, coughing, tremors, dysphagia, and amnesias.

Anna O. entered altered states of consciousness spontaneously, and under these conditions a remarkable shift would occur. In her normal alert state she would have no inkling of why a symptom was present, but when she converted to what Breuer termed a "hypnoid" state, she would recognize why and how the symptom had been generated. When the forgotten episode was revealed and the feelings attending it expressed, the symptom would disappear. Anna O. called this "the talking cure" or "chimney sweeping."

From another perspective, Anna O. was an unusually intelligent girl of twenty-one. Breuer recognized her "great poetic and imaginatve gifts which were under the control of a sharp and critical common sense. Owing to this latter quality, she was completely unsuggestible; she was only influenced by arguments, never by mere assertions" (41). Her intellectual independence and freedom from suggestion should be remembered, because they contradict the long-standing dogma that all hysterics are highly suggestible people, a belief that still persists in medical circles. Anna O.'s talents were confirmed a decade later, for at the age of thirty she became the first social worker in Germany and one of the first in the world. She founded a periodical, organized several institutions in which she trained students, espoused women's emancipation, and labored to help children whose parents had perished in pogroms in Russia, Poland, and Rumania. This negates another misconception—that all hysterics are immature, inept, and unintelligent females.

For a year and a half on almost a daily basis, Breuer continued his treatment of Anna O., inducing hypnotic trances or exploiting his patient's spontaneous self-hypnotic forays as her symptoms were gradually explained and expunged. But then a series of events occurred that led him to terminate her therapy. Breuer became so deeply engrossed in the procedure that he is said (although this may be apocryphal and is the subject of historical dispute) to have bored his wife with the details until she became jealous and then morose (71). When Breuer finally recognized the problem, he announced to Anna O., who was now much improved, that the treatment was finished. In turn, Anna O. may have developed a hysterical pregnancy, reflecting presumably her erotic unconscious fantasies about Breuer. The talking treatment did not prove to be a permanent cure, and there were further relapses. However, Anna O., despite her problems, proceeded to live a creative existence.

The next element in the tale was introduced in November 1882, when Breuer told Sigmund Freud, then a young physician, the details of this unusual case. It made a deep impression upon Freud, and the two discussed the case on many occasions.

In 1885, Freud was awarded a traveling fellowship, and in the autumn of that year he journeyed to Paris, where he became a student at the Salpêtrière under Charcot. There he told the great neurologist about this discovery (91), but Ernest Jones (151) quoted Freud as saying, "Charcot's thoughts seemed to be elsewhere," and these observations did not arouse his interest. However, this vignette does confirm Freud's own preoccupation with the case of Anna O. This period in Paris served to direct Freud's attention further to hysteria, for at that time Charcot was studying this syndrome primarily. He was trying to find those scientific principles that underlay hysterical symptoms, was documenting the occurrence of hysteria in men, and was demonstrating how hysterical paralyses and contractures could be induced by hypnotic suggestion.

Freud then returned to Vienna, entered private practice, and spent the next five years, from 1886 to 1891, earning a livelihood, but also translating two volumes by Charcot and two by Bernheim, and writing two books on clinical neurology himself. Meanwhile, he was seeing in his practice a large number of neurotic patients. It was not an idle period.

During the first year or two of his practice, Freud used the current methods of rest, massage, hydrotherapy, and electrical stimulation to treat his neurotic patients, but all these treatments proved to be ineffective. At the end of 1887, he began to use hypnosis, but in a conventional fashion as a way to facilitate suggestions. It was only in the middle of the year 1889 that he revived Breuer's "cathartic method." Why he delayed so long remains unexplained. The simplest answer may have been Freud's discomfort with hypnosis. When he first introduced it into his practice, he wrote:

there was a sense of having overcome one's helplessness; and it was highly flattering to enjoy the reputation of being a miracle worker. It was not until later that I was to discover the drawbacks of the procedure. At the moment, there were only two points to complain of: first, that I could not succeed in hypnotizing every patient; and secondly, that I was unable to put individual patients into as deep a state of hypnosis as I should have wished. (91)

But there also occurred a most embarrassing experience for the intellectual and proper Dr. Freud, which led to an end of this period. One of his hysterical patients as she woke up threw her arms around his neck. After that there was a tacit understanding between them that the hypnotic treatment should be discontinued. This experience confirmed his concept of transference, but it also put another nail in the coffin of hypnosis.

In the autumn of 1892, he dispensed with the use of hypnosis, just three years after he had initiated the use of the "cathartic method," replacing it with Bernheim's concentration method aided by repeated pressure on the patient's forehead.

There came to my help the recollection of an experiment which I had often witnessed while I was with Bernheim. When the subject awoke from the state of somnambulism, he seemed to have lost all memory of what had happened while he was in that state. But Bernheim maintained that the memory was present all the same . . . and if at the same time he laid his hand on the subject's forehead, then the forgotten memories used in fact to return.(91)

This laying on of the hand is a tactic that may induce a hypnotic trance in excellent hypnotic subjects. It can become a signal to return to the trance, and such subjects can do it with a slight twitch of the mind. Freud, however, was not fully aware of this:

I determined that I would act in the same way. My patients, I reflected, must in fact "know" all the things which had hitherto only been made accessible to them in hypnosis; and assurances and encouragement on my part, assisted perhaps by the touch of my hand, would I thought have the power of forcing the forgotten facts and connections into consciousness. So I abandoned hypnosis, only retaining my practice of requiring the patient to lie upon a sofa.(91)

Meanwhile, during the late 1880s and early 1890s, Freud had been urging Breuer to report his experiences with Anna O. Finally, the reluctant Breuer acquiesced, and in January 1893 they published a joint article with Breuer as the senior author, entitled "The Psychical Mechanisms of Hysterical Phenomena" (40). It was followed in 1895 by the volume *Studies in Hysteria*, (41), which included detailed case histories and theoretical discussions by both authors. Finally, thirteen years after Breuer's treatment of his patient, the details were available to the medical world. The volume did not prove to be a best seller, but in retrospect it should be recognized as a milestone in the history of psychiatry. Let us return to Anna O.

In July 1880, Anna O.'s father, "of whom she was passionately fond," became ill with a pleural abscess, which resulted in his death in April 1881. During the first months of his illness, Anna nursed her father, but she gradually became ill, suffering from weakness, distaste for food, and a severe cough, which made it impossible for her to continue the ministration. But another strange transformation now occurred. She would become very fatigued in the afternoon, which was followed in the early evening by a "sleep-like" state, and afterward a period of agitation.

In December, a convergent squint appeared, followed by a left-sided occipital headache, double vision, complaint that "the walls of the room seemed to be falling over," other disturbances of vision, a weakness of the muscles in the front of her neck, paralysis, contractures, and anesthesia of the right arm and right leg that later extended to the left arm and leg.

It was at this time that Breuer began his treatment. He soon identified two distinct states of consciousness: in one she was well-oriented but sad and anxious, and in the other she hallucinated and was "naughty." Anna O. complained of lost time or absences—periods of amnesia—and rapid shifts in mood ranging from temporary high spirits to severe anxiety. She also showed stubborn opposition to every therapeutic effort. She developed frightening visual hallucinations. She complained of "darkness in her head," of not being able to think, of being blind and deaf. But there were multiple personalities as well, which Breuer did not recognize. Anna O. reported having "two selves, a real one and an evil one," and "a clear-sighted and calm observer (who) sat in a corner of her brain and looked on at all the mad business."

A further devastating problem of Anna O.'s was a disorganization of speech during which she became almost aphonic, speaking in a jumble of four or five languages. Then there was a period when she spoke only English, or only French and Italian. During this later period she would have an amnesia for the times when she spoke English. This abbreviated description of her complex hysterical illness indicates the magnitude of Breuer's therapeutic task.

To Breuer's great credit he listened to her, recognized her therapeutic suggestions and insights, and together they pursued a novel course. His first discovery, and perhaps his most important one, was the recognition of self-hypnotic states. These were everywhere to be perceived in her, but hysterics had been producing antics like this for centuries without their self-hypnosis being identified, and certainly without any realization of its significance. Anna O. invented the name of "clouds" for these deep hypnotic periods. Breuer stated, "Throughout the entire illness her two states of consciousness persisted side by side: the primary one in which she was quite normal psychically, and the secondary one which may well be likened to a dream in view of its wealth of imaginative products and hallucinations, its large gaps of memory and the lack of inhibition and control in its associations."

In his discussion of theory, Breuer made the bald statement that "the basis and sine qua non of hysteria is the existence of hypnoid states." Furthermore,

the importance of these states which resemble hypnosis—hypnoid states—lies in addition, and most especially, in the amnesia that accompanies them and in their power to bring about the splitting of the mind. . . . What happens during auto-hypnotic states is subject to more or less total amnesia in waking life (whereas it is completely remembered in artificial hypnosis). The amnesia withdraws the psychical products of these states, the associations that have been formed in them, from any correction during waking thought. (41)

Breuer added, "the hysterical symptom remains restricted to the hypnotic state, and is strengthened there by repetition; moreover, the idea that gave rise to it is exempt from correction by waking thoughts and criticism, precisely because it never emerges in clear waking life." Finally, he noted, "the hypnosis-like state is repeated again and again when the circumstances arise; and the subject, instead of the normal two conditions of mind, has three: waking, sleeping and the hypnoid state."

Clearly articulated are the primary importance of self-hypnotic states in hysteria; the repetition of these states; and the amnesia of self-hypnosis, which creates an unconscious reservoir of ideas and feelings—"unconscious ideas exist and are operative." "Auto-hypnosis has, so to speak, created the space or region of unconscious psychical activity into which the ideas which are fended off are driven."

But Breuer was cautious, and rightfully so because his experience with hysteria was limited. Anna O.'s case, in fact, formed the basis for his grand hypothesis. He did qualify his conclusions with caveats, as would any respectable scientist: "I am therefore far from attributing to all hysterical patients the generating mechanism which we have been taught by Anna O." And "I speak of hypnoid states rather than hypnosis itself because it is so difficult to make a clear demarcation of these states, which play such an important part in the genesis of hysteria." And again, "I do not venture to regard the course of events with Anna O. as having general application. . . . no doubt yet other forms of this process exist, which are concealed from our young psychological science." Nevertheless, it is clear from his lengthy discussion that he had strong convictions about the existence of these self-hypnotic states. The few reservations were interpolated to add a semblance of caution—or perhaps they simply reflected Breuer's indecisive, ruminative nature, which is known to have nettled Freud.

If these self-hypnotic states exist, the question arises as to their origins. Do they appear de novo, or are there antecedent self-hypnotic experiences that precede the hysterical illness? Breuer was aware of this problem. He asked, "Are hypnoid states of this kind in existence before the patient falls ill, and how do they come about? I can say very little about this, for apart from the case of Anna O., we have no observations at our disposal that might throw light on the point. It seems certain that with her the auto-hypnosis had the way paved for it by habitual reveries." The reveries cited were her daydreams, which she described as her "private theatre." As Breuer wrote:

While everyone thought she was attending, she was living through fairy tales in her imagination. . . . While she was in a situation that favored auto-hypnosis, the affect of anxiety entered into her reverie and created a hypnoid state for which she had amnesia. . . . After four months the hypnoid state gained entire control of the patient. The separate attacks ran into one another and thus an état de mal arose, an acute hysteria of the most severe type.

He now made reference to fundamental difference between his understanding and Freud's. "Freud's observations and analysis show that the splitting of the mind can also be caused by 'defense' by the deliberate deflection of consciousness from distressing ideas." But then there was the gentle admonition:

I only venture to suggest that the assistance of the hypnoid state is necessary if defense is to result not merely in single converted ideas being made into unconscious ones, but in a genuine splitting of the mind. Auto-hypnosis has, so to speak, created the space or region of unconscious psychical activity into which the ideas which are fended off are driven. But, however this may be, the fact of the pathogenic significance of "defense" is one that we must recognize.

Breuer also stressed the power of sexual conflicts in the generation of these hypnoid states. This, however, was probably Freud's contribution, because it was he who recognized the contribution of sexuality to the neuroses. Breuer wrote: "They repress sexuality from their consciousness, and the affective ideas with a content of this kind . . . are fended off and thus become unconscious . . . the great majority of severe neuroses in women have their origin in the marriage bed." But Breuer added an important reservation. "It is self-evident and is also sufficiently proved by our observations that the non-sexual affects of fright, anxiety and anger lead to the development of hysterical phenomena. But it is perhaps worthwhile insisting again and again that the sexual factor is far the most important and the most productive of pathological results."

Breuer's fundamental observation was the salient, central role of self-hypnosis. Considering his limited number of cases—really only Anna O.—his acuity was remarkable. Furthermore, he perceived the creation of an unconscious repository by this hypnotic process and recognized the proclivity of these patients to prior and future self-hypnotic states. However, Breuer did not continue his studies long enough to solve the entire problem, and Freud, as we shall see, did not pursue it.

There next followed perhaps the most remarkable twist in the tale. Freud simply rejected the concept of self-hypnosis. It is true that he was the junior author of the 1893 paper on hysteria in which Breuer in an abbreviated form espoused this explanation, but in the monograph (41) Freud made his position quite clear:

Hysteria originates through the repression of an incompatible idea from a motive of defense. . . . A hysteria exhibiting this psychical mechanism may be given the name "defense hysteria." . . . Now, both of us, Breuer and I, have repeatedly spoken of two other kinds of hysteria, for which we have introduced the terms "hypnoid hysteria" and "retention hysteria." . . . Breuer has put forward for such cases of hypnoid hysteria a psychical mechanism which is substantially different from that of defense by conversion.

Freud then labored a point that may be a misconstruction of Breuer's position:

In his view what happens in hypnoid hysteria is that an idea becomes pathogenic because it has been received during a special psychical state and has from the first remained outside the ego. No psychical force has therefore been required in order to keep it apart from the ego, and no resistance need be aroused if we introduce it into the ego with the help of mental activity during somnambulism (hypnosis). And Anna O.'s case history in fact shows no sign of any such resistance.

Finally, there is this pronouncement: "Strangely enough, I have never in my own experience met with a genuine hypnoid hysteria. Any that I took in hand has turned into a defense hysteria."

This was to remain Freud's position, and he was henceforth to exclude from his own consideration and that of psychoanalysis the role of self-hypnosis in the creation of psychopathology. There were a few final pronouncements that sounded the demise of self-hypnosis. In "The Aetiology of Hysteria," a paper published in the following year (1896), he expressed this skepticism more openly, and in a footnote to his "Dora" case history (1905), he declared that the term "hypnoid states" was "superfluous and misleading," and that the hypothesis "sprang entirely from the initiative of Breuer."

Freud cryptically summed up the issue in his autobiography (91). "He [Breuer] thought that the processes which could not find a normal outcome were such as had originated during unusual 'hypnoid' mental states. I, on the other hand, was inclined to suspect the existence of an interplay of forces and the operation of intentions and purposes such as are to be observed in normal life. Thus it was the case of 'Hypnoid Hysteria' versus 'Defense Neurosis.'"

I have documented this divergence of opinion between Breuer and Freud because it would prove to be of immense importance to the evolution of Freud's thinking, the development of psychoanalytic theory, and the course of psychiatry throughout the world. Freud had now in effect substituted repression for Breuer's self-hypnosis—"The theory of repression became the foundation stone of our understanding of the neurosis." Furthermore, he had introduced the term "defense" to connote an active process that denied the repressed complex a return to consciousness.

I have wondered what Breuer thought privately about these constructs. Anna O. had presented a plenitude of obstacles to the recovery of her hypnotically concealed memories. In fact, Breuer in his paper referred to her "obstancies." In her "hypnoid" hysteria, defenses had not been absent. Furthermore, the term "repression" was a semantic evasion. It was simply a way of dignifying the observation that some traumatic memories were forgotten. It contained no explanatory power. In contrast, the concept of self-hypnosis reflected a body of knowledge accumulated over a century, including the recognition of the amnesia of hypnosis.

The tantalizing question is why Freud rejected the self-hypnotic explanation. Breuer had identified and described self-hypnosis and had shown how it created an unconscious nexus and served to protect the individual against a confrontation with unpleasant experiences. Here was a magical mechanism. In hypnosis one could wish that a painful reality would disappear, and—presto!—it would be gone, at least from consciousness.

The first obvious reason for Freud's rejection of self-hypnosis was his discomfort with hypnosis. On at least three occasions, he wrote about his difficulties with this technique. But Freud's rejection of the concept of self-hypnosis involved more than mere discomfort with hypnosis. He asserted that he had never seen a case of self-hypnosis; certainly he had not recognized one, although it is clear in retrospect that several of his patients experienced this state (41).

Whatever the reason may have been for Freud's repudiation of the concept of self-hypnosis, it is clear that a novel therapy was being created. Janet in France and simultaneously Breuer in Austria both stumbled upon a similar therapeutic procedure. Breuer reported a startling observation: "When as a result of an accidental and spontaneous utterance . . . a disturbance which had persisted for a considerable time vanished—I was greatly surprised." Anna O. had suddenly found it impossible to drink water. But one day in hypnosis she recounted with anger and disgust how the little dog—"horrid creature"—of her lady companion had drunk out of a glass in her presence. Anna O. had said nothing at the time out of politeness, but after she expressed the anger that she had held back, the symptom disappeared.

Breuer and Anna O. seized on this strategy. "Each individual symptom in this complicated case was taken separately in hand; all the occasions on which it had appeared were described in reverse order. . . . When this had been described the symptom was permanently removed." This led to the therapeutic concept:

Each individual hysterical symptom immediately and permanently disappeared when we had succeeded in bringing clearly to light the memory of the event by which it was provoked and in arousing its accompanying affect, and when the patient had described that event in the greatest possible detail and had put the affect into words. Recollections without affect almost invariably produces no result. The psychical process which originally took place must be repeated as vividly as possible; it must be brought back to its status nascendi and then given verbal utterance.

Or as Breuer put it more succinctly, "Hysterics suffer mainly from reminiscences." Breuer's discoveries thus led him to the "cathartic" method predicated upon "abreaction."

But the question was why these memories, concealed in unconsciousness and forgotten, remained fresh and virulent, producing symptoms. The answer was "because they had been denied the normal wearing-away processes by means of abreaction and reproduction in states of uninhibited association." A novel psychiatric treatment had been discovered—and as sometimes happens, observation of an illness had demonstrated a basic scientific principle.

Unconscious painful experiences must be consciously managed if mental health is to be maintained. If they are consciously accepted and the attendant emotions accommodated, through this gradual process of desensitization they may slowly be decontaminated and eventually become "normal" memories. But when these experiences are not consciously processed and instead are hidden by the amnesia of self-hypnosis, they continue to remain fresh and vivid—and they fester. In this case, the appropriate treatment is to reenter the unconscious by hypnosis and make the memories conscious once again so that the normal reparative process can occur.

But when Freud attempted to apply Breuer's therapeutic method, he encountered a difficulty. He found that some patients diagnosed as hysterics were refractory, while others, with obsessional ideas—clearly not hysteria—responded to the "uncovering" treatment. Besides being plagued by the problem of the classification of neuroses, he was beset by the recurrence of symptoms in hysteria even after the cathartic method had been applied. "It cannot affect the underlying causes of hysteria: thus it cannot prevent fresh symptoms from taking the place of the ones which had been got rid of."

Freud clearly had extensive experience with the treatment of these conditions. He noted that in acute hysteria when the patient's symptoms are out of control (what today we might term a hysterical psychosis), the cathartic method is ineffectual. "The illness cannot be broken off short. We must wait for it to run its course." He also indicated that the cathartic procedure is laborious and time consuming. Freud also noted the magnitude of the demands upon the patient. "A good number of the patients who would be suitable for this form of treatment abandon the doctor as soon as the suspicion begins to dawn on them of the direction in which the investigation is leading."

Freud then explained how he modified Breuer's method to suit his own needs. His first concern was over his inability to hypnotize all of his patients. The problem, then, was how to obtain the pathogenic recollections through some other method. He remembered Bernheim's demonstration that the memories of events during hypnosis are only apparently forgotten in the waking state and can be revived by a command or a pressure with the hand, so he ostensibly dropped hypnosis and only asked for "concentration" while the patient was lying down with eyes closed.

Freud had thus presumably eliminated hypnosis—but precisely what did he think about it? He seemed first to ignore hypnosis, and then gradually to forget it. He stated for example, "I then found that without any hypnosis new recollections emerged." He substituted the concepts of repression and defense and went about his business.

Freud soon discovered that patients' destructive ideas "were all of a kind that one would prefer not to have experienced, that one would rather forget. . . . They were all of a distressing nature, calculated to arouse the affects of shame, of self-reproach and of psychical pain, and the feeling of being harmed." To help the patient recall painful experiences, Freud instituted a "small technical device." "I informed the patient that . . . I shall apply pressure to his forehead, and I assured him that, all the time the pressure lasts, he will see before him a recollection in the form of a picture . . . or an idea; and I pledge him to communicate this picture or idea to me, whatever it might be." Freud made a wry comment about this procedure that highlighted his ambivalence about hypnosis. "It would be possible for me to say by way of explaining the efficacy of this device that it corresponded to a momentarily intensified hypnosis; but the mechanism of hypnosis is so puzzling to me that I would rather not make use of it as an explanation."

Parenthetically, one can see how his therapeutic tactics had evolved. He had begun with the conventional remedies of rest, massage and electrical treatment; then enlisted hypnosis as a facilitator of suggestion; next tried hypnosis in the cathartic way; then stopped the hypnotic induction and substituted pressure on the forehead with the injunction to concentrate, remember, visualize, and reveal whatever came to mind. The final step was the method of free association, in which the therapist no longer applies tactile pressure to the forehead, but nonetheless maintains the imperative to concentrate and recall without censorship. This was soon to be his final strategy.

But one must notice the common element found in all of these apparently different tactics. While in a relaxed, supine position, often with eyes closed, the patient is asked to free associate, a situation conducive to spontaneous self-hypnosis. Whether the patient does it alone or is instructed by someone else to do it is irrelevant. The paramount consideration is whether the person has the hypnotic capability for a "deep" hypnotic trance. Information about this ability was gradually being accumulated during the late nineteenth century, but it is uncertain whether Freud was aware of this information or if he paid heed to it.

Freud also wrote about his experiences with hypnotherapy. "Where I have carried out a cathartic treatment under hypnosis instead of under concentration, I did not find that this diminished the work I had to do." Elsewhere, he wrote, "I have become altogether sceptical about the value of hypnosis in facilitating cathartic treatments, since I have experienced instances in which during deep somnambulism there has been absolutely therapeutic recalcitrance, where in other respects the patient has been perfectly obedient." This statement appears to have been based on his misunderstanding of Breuer's case of Anna O.; apparently his impression was that she displayed no blocks, obstacles, and resistances. In reality these patients present varying degrees of resistance. Some secrets are deeply hidden and assiduously defended, but others are not particularly painful and so are easily recalled.

One more element must be added to the tale. At the time the volume on hysteria was published, Freud had come to the conclusion that real sexual traumas in childhood underlay hysteria. But a crisis now occurred that temporarily shook his self-confidence. He decided that these events, hidden and forgotten in the unconscious, in most cases never really occurred. They were fantasies and wishes originating in early childhood. It was a striking about-face, and one that was to have far-reaching effects on later theory.

Freud's thought evolved in the following way. In 1894, he published a remarkable paper on the defense neuropsychosis. In this publication (92), several syndromes were identified as due to a process of "forgetting . . . giving rise either to hysteria, or to an obsession or to an hallucinatory psychosis." In hysteria the unbearable idea, now forgotten, was rendered innocuous by a bodily symptom—a "conversion." Obsessions were conscious ideas that had been split off from their emotional content, while hallucinatory psychoses occurred when the ego rejected the unbearable idea together with its affect.

In 1896, after further experience and reflection, he reported (93) further observations on the neuropsychoses. He cited thirteen cases of hysteria in which he had uncovered without exception "grave sexual injuries" inflicted by nursemaids, governesses, domestic servants, teachers and tutors. But in seven of the thirteen there had been sexual relationships for years, mostly with a brother. Furthermore, he concluded that there was probably an age limit, that these sexual insults must occur before the age of eight or ten. Identical experiences were at work in obsessional neuroses, and in one case of a paranoid psychosis, which he analyzed.

Another report appeared in 1896 (94). By now the series had expanded to eighteen cases with identical findings. There were six males and twelve females with hysteria or hysteria combined with obsessions. He divided the aggressors into three groups—strangers; maids, nurses, governesses, and teachers; and brothers. Furthermore, in two of the eighteen cases he was able to get evidence from other sources confirming the patient's account. This convinced Freud that these forgotten experiences, now retrieved by therapy, must have occurred.

But he then had a rude awakening and published a recantation (95). "I overestimated the frequency of these occurrences. . . . I have since learned to unravel many a fantasy of seduction and found it to be an attempt at defense against the memory of sexual activities practiced by the child himself—the masturbation of children." This is clarified in a letter (97) to his friend Fliess in September 1897, in which he refers to "the great secret of something that in the past few months has gradually dawned on me." It was that most—but not all—of the seductions in childhood which his patients had revealed and about which he had built his theory of hysteria and the neuropsychoses had never occurred.

What was the evidence for Freud's repudiation of his own theory? First, he cited in his letter to Fliess the numerous disappointments in not being able to bring his analyses to a proper conclusion. This would seem to be an unconvincing reason, since many other circumstances might have led to his defeats, including his failure to recognize the role of self-hypnosis. Second, he asked whether perverted acts against children could be so common, but that seemed "hardly credible." This was certainly at the time a powerful objection, but it could only have been settled by a careful inquiry directed at the other persons who were involved. Freud was in no position to pursue such investigations, and logically this assumption should have remained moot. There was next his legitimate consideration that in the unconscious there is no criterion of reality, so that truth cannot be distinguished from an emotional fiction. I would revise this somewhat, but my conclusion would be identical. In the state of spontaneous deep hypnosis, within the unconscious domain that it creates, fantasies can become facts, so that when the person comes out of this state, not realizing where he or she has been, the experience can be very real and can be believed. Freud finally cited the fact that such memories never emerge in even the most severe psychotic delirium.

Freud's repudiation of *real* infantile sexual traumas as a source of psychopathology proved to be a turning point in his scientific career. Henceforth, these repressed infantile recollections would be considered to be fantasies—an assumption and a reversal of opinion destined to move psychoanalytic theory in a new direction.

The conclusion that the early sexual abuses reported by patients were fantasies and not real experiences now logically redirected his thinking and cast his theories in a novel form. Such vivid fantasies in children could only mean that children were not sexually innocent. They must have a rich early sexual life that had gone undetected. Furthermore, if girls fantasized seduction by their fathers, it indicated that they wished such experiences. Why else should such fantasies be present? As a result of this speculation, Freud had "stumbled for the first time upon the Oedipus Complex."

The Oedipus complex became a fundamental assumption of psychoanalysis. Girls presumably entertained incestuous wishes toward their fathers, whereas boys had comparable wishes for sexuality with their mothers, coupled with hostile feelings toward the father. In boys this would be responsible for castration fears—the castration complex. When the child recognized the taboo against such fantasies, repression occurred to cope with the guilt, rendering the Oedipal wishes unconscious. Freud wrote that these theories of resistance, repression, the unconscious, and the significance of an early sexual life with its fantasies became the "primary basis of psychoanalysis."

In the last years of the nineteenth century, Freud turned his attention to dreams. In his volume *The Interpretation of Dreams* (90), the dreaming process was incorporated into his theoretical structure. The model of the dream was similar to that of the neuroses (71). For Freud the dream became the royal road to the unconscious, allowing penetration to the infantile amnesia, serving as a substitute for the task previously assumed by hypnosis.

After developing his theory of dreams, Freud investigated other phenomena. He explored the numerous slips of speech of everyday life and the nature of wit. He created concepts of narcissism, put forward a theory of instincts, and attempted to apply psychoanalytic concepts to the psychoses. He postulated a repetition compulsion, and divided the structure of the mind into the id, superego, and ego.

But Freud was now into his latter speculative period, in which he indulged his remarkable capability for the building of theory. Instincts were subdivided into Eros and Thanatos—love contrasted with death, destruction, and hate. His universal law of the Oedipus complex was applied to the tragedy of Shakespeare's Hamlet; he made an attempt at describing the personality of Leonardo da Vinci. In *Totem and Taboo* he explored the incest dread. But this was late in his career, when his theories had been reified. The essential elements had been forged much earlier, and these represented metapsychological extensions.

This has been but a brief survey of Freud's clinical experiences and his theoretical creations. He lived a long life, writing brilliantly and prolifically. This discussion is limited to his central concepts and basic observations. There is no question that he, like Janet, the earlier hypnotists, and Breuer, was exploring remarkable properties of the mind, but his system contained underlying assumptions that must be recognized and scrutinized.

Freud was the greatest advocate of the unconscious, the man who convinced the world of its existence—and this may remain his most important and enduring contribution. There seems to be little doubt that he was first led to the concept through his experiences with hypnosis and hysteria. Evidence was later to be adduced from slips of the tongue, the analysis of dreams, and the probing of mental symptoms via free association. As late as 1938, a year before his death, he wrote a paper, "Some Elementary Lessons in Psycho-Analysis" (96), to demonstrate that "mental acts which are unconscious do exist." Hypnotic experiments were used as evidence, and the example was posthypnotic behavior—"experiments made by Bernheim at Nancy in 1889 at which I, myself, assisted."

But from the perspective of my studies of hypnosis and experience with patients with multiple personality, I believe that Freud's system was

flawed by two conceptual commitments. Both came early, were fundamental to his thinking, and directed his later speculations.

The first concept, and the most important one, was Breuer's recognition of "hypnoid" states, which created an unconscious by "self-
hypnosis." It was a powerful concept, but Freud disclaimed it and
instead postulated "repression." This was one of those curious approx-
imations, the near misses that have occurred frequently in science.
Breuer had observed these self-hypnotic states in Anna O., had given
the concept to Freud, but he had repudiated it. Why this happened will
forever be a mystery, since neither participant is available for questioning. Whatever the reasons, Freud was deprived of the concept that then
might have led him in many different directions. By the end of the nineteenth century, an abundance of information about the capabilities of
hypnosis was readily available, and he might well have unravelled its
implications. Instead, he posited "repression," which was a euphemism
for "forgetting." It contained little conceptual direction, whereas self-
hypnosis would have led to the well-known amnesias of hypnosis. The
identification of these amnesias, if they are spontaneous (Breuer's self-
hypnosis), then leads to the recognition that traumas and emotions may
be hidden by this hypnotic mechanism to create a special hypnotic unconscious, but one of prime importance in some mental illnesses. Instead
of recognizing a variety of unconscious processes, Freud was forced to
postulate an unconscious with a confusing conglomerate of elements
that defied scientific examination.

Freud wrote in his autobiography that the theory of repression became the foundation stone of the understanding of neuroses. If he had
replaced "repression" with "self-hypnosis," such a sweeping generalization would not have been possible, since many people are poor hypnotic
subjects. In the same volume, he also stated that the theory of resistance,
repression, the unconscious, sexual life and infantile experiences were
the principal constituents of the theoretical structure of psychoanalysis.

This leads to the second conceptual problem. Freud initially discovered sexual molestation by fathers of their daughters as the basis for
later neuroses. These memories had been "repressed" but later were
revealed in therapy. I would suggest instead that they had been self-
hypnotically concealed. But more important to Freud's theories was his
later embarrassing insight. He reversed himself and became convinced
that what his patients reported were not real experiences but fantasies.
This was startling, because logically it led to the assumption that young
children must have heterosexual fantasies. Their presumed sexual naiveté must be an illusion. Furthermore, however, such fantasies were
"repressed." One could only assume that they were obliterated because
of guilt. The child wished for a sexual relationship with her father, but
the incest taboo instilled guilt, necessitating repression.

The concept of infantile sexual fantasies ineluctably led to the Oedipus complex, castration fears, and the theory of psychosexual development with its oral, anal, phallic, latent and genital stages, and further elaborations. Unfortunately, my own data and much contemporary evidence supports Freud's original hypothesis and rejects his reversal, which logically mandated many of his seminal concepts. All evidence indicates that incest is surprisingly common. These infantile traumas, whether in the form of sexual molestation, physical abuse, or psychological injuries, really occurred. A few may be concealed by screen memories, but the amnesias are not dictated by heterosexual fantasies.

Any further critique of Freud's analytic theories would go well beyond the scope of this volume. I am convinced, however, that his dismissal of Breuer's concept of self-hypnosis and the postulation of a fantasy theory were major errors. Since these occurred early in his career, they inevitably influenced his later metapsychological concepts. But any criticism of Freud should not distract from his stature. Freud was a remarkable innovator with unparalleled influence on twentieth-century psychiatry.

## The American Hypnotists—and the Unconscious

### Morton Prince

Morton Prince (1854–1929), Professor of Psychiatry at the Tufts College Medical School in Boston, is best remembered for his account *The Dissociation of a Personality* (219), and other reports of multiple personality. However, his book on the unconscious (220), an elaboration of articles published in 1908 and 1909, was the best exposition of his theories and experiences. He stated that the subconscious is not only the most important problem of psychology, it is *the* problem. He divided the unconscious into two parts, the unconscious, or the neural processes, and the co-conscious, the actual subconscious where ideas reside that are not accessible to conscious awareness.

He cited automatic writing, hypnosis, visual and auditory hallucinations, dreams, and crystal gazing as demonstrations of the subconscious, for all reveal "forgotten" experiences. Furthermore, hysterics, although they have anesthesias or other conversion symptoms, can be shown by hypnosis to have another part of the mind that records these sensory events. He cited dissociated states in which amnesias are commonplace although the experiences are conserved, and discussed posthypnotic phenomena in which suggestions in hypnosis are followed without recall of the instruction.

Prince referred to Breuer's and Freud's cases of hysteria and commented, "Now we have known for many years from numerous observations that emotion tends to disrupt the mind and to dissociate the experiences. . . . In certain cases the amnesia (or dissociation) is a dissociation (repression) induced by the conative force of conflicting emotion."

At that time, dispute about the unconscious was commonplace, and Prince made it clear that Freud's repression was simply Janet's and his dissociation. He cited cases of fugue states and also multiple personality in which amnesia for large epochs in the subject's life was prominent. Furthermore, he observed two striking facts about these amnestic experiences—the minuteness of the details with which forgotten experiences may be conserved and the long periods of time during which the conservation may persist. However, he did not explain how such old experiences could be retained with exquisite detail of thought and feeling. Instead, he postulated that "neurograms" conserved experiences—dormant ideas were conserved by some physiological process.

Prince was convinced that the same unconscious processes identified by Janet caused many hallucinations and contributed to religious conversions. Prince also, like Janet, attributed fixed ideas—obsessions, or imperative ideas and fanaticism—to these unconscious complexes. Furthermore, anxiety neurosis is simply another example, in which the "obsessing fear" repeatedly emerges, being one component of the unconscious memory. Phobias, he believed, are of a similar nature.

Turning to therapy, Prince observed that if one simply explains to a person who has a true obsession the falsity of his or her point of view, the explanation has little or no effect in changing the person's viewpoint. Even given a desire to do so, the person cannot modify the idea. But if the original complex, which is hidden in the unconscious and which gives rise to the meaning of the idea, is discovered and so altered that it takes on a new meaning and feeling tone, the patient's conscious idea becomes modified and ceases to be insistent. One must bring into consciousness the past forgotten experience.

Prince, like Janet, Binet, Breuer, Freud, and Bernheim, knew much about hypnosis and unconscious processes. But like them (Breuer being the exception), he did not quite grasp the simple idea of self-hypnosis as a coping mechanism that creates an "unconscious" reservoir from which many symptoms, ideas, and feelings can emanate—all manifestations of the versatility of the hypnotic process.

## Boris Sidis

Sidis (1867–1923) was an American psychiatrist of erudition and superior intelligence who was profoundly influenced by Janet. For nearly three decades, he studied hypnosis both clinically and experimentally. A prolific writer and an imaginative theorist, he published over a dozen books between 1898 and 1922 that focused on hypnosis and its relationship to psychopathology. These included texts of experimental studies of hypnosis (244), normal and abnormal psychology (246, 248), the psychology of suggestion (242), multiple personality (245), and the symptoms, causation, diagnosis, and treatment of psychopathic disease (245, 247). Any brief analysis of his work does a disservice to his contributions.

Sidis, like Janet, was hostile to Freud's dogmas and his preoccupation with sexuality. Like many others, he felt that Freud was concerned with the same psychic processes as were they, but without the recognition of the close relationship of these processes to hypnosis. Sidis wrote that Freud's suppressed complex is but another term for Janet's dissociated system, which is commonly accepted in psychopathology. In an appendix to his book *Symptomatology, Psychognosis and Diagnosis of Psychopathic Diseases* (245) is an address by Mitchell summarizing Sidis's position. It contains this statement: "Freud by his method of conducting the analysis unconsciously induces the hypnoidal state, and his therapeutic success may be due in part to the virtues inherent in the hypnoidal state rather than in psychoanalysis."

Sidis presented the interesting hypothesis that the hypnoidal state is the primordial sleep-state from which is derived hypnosis, sleep, and dreams. He was well aware of the many capabilities of hypnosis as well as dissociated states and considered hysterical symptoms the result of subconscious experiences. Furthermore, he perceived that these unconscious memories and emotions could produce much more than conversion symptoms. He thought that they could be responsible for fixed ideas and for morbid impulses such as kleptomania, homicidal mania, and the like. Furthermore, all could be traced to subconscious experiences, originating in early childhood.

Sidis contended, furthermore, that many patients could be cured only when this unconscious material is reintegrated into consciousness by hypnotic tactics, since it nourishes, guides, and controls the neurotic disorder. Unless it is reached and "disintegrated," the patient cannot be regarded as cured.

The causes of these dissociations or subconscious complexes for which the subject has amnesia are severe emotional shocks. There is usually a long series of such shocks affecting the central core of the patient's life, first experienced in childhood, which are coupled with a predisposition to dissociative states. But Sidis never made clear precisely what he meant by a predisposition to dissociative states. Although Janet had considered this to be a constitutional mental weakness, it apparently was not Sidis's conviction, but he didn't clarify his perception.

Sidis considered these hypnoidal dissociations to be central to many forms of psychopathology—a basic mechanism forged in the evolutionary process, somehow gone amiss. He recognized that hypnoidal states, dreams, hallucinations, and hypnopompic and hypnagogic states were all closely related, reflecting a common origin. However, he was unwilling to identify the mechanism of hallucinations in schizophrenia as that of experimental hypnosis, preferring to view experimental hallucinations as a deception—a product of the suggestive influence of the hypnotist.

Like Janet, Prince, and other students of hypnosis, Sidis, despite his prolific production of books and papers had no school, no disciples, and little impact on twentieth-century psychiatry, and his works, unlike Freud's, have been ignored and forgotten.

## Historical Résumé

Since the time of Mesmer, hypnosis has been a curiosity. For more than a hundred years, reputable professionals described the remarkable feats of hypnotic subjects and the therapeutic triumphs of hypnotic techniques. Unfortunately, this vast literature went unnoticed by most physicians and scientists, and its impact on the practice of psychiatry and medicine was negligible.

This neglect had many causes. Hypnosis is subjective, something that occurs in the black box of the mind. How does one prove with rigor that subjects really can hear the buzzing of an imaginary mosquito; can perceive another person as the size of a house or with the proportions of an ant; can feel such heaviness in their eyelids that they cannot be opened; can return to intrauterine existence and perceive it as a real experience; or can forget information upon request? Cynics could dispatch such accounts as fraudulent, the acts of weak-minded, suggestible individuals, or compliant behaviors aimed at pleasing an authority figure. But these explanations are unsatisfactory, if for no other reason than that too many strong-minded, honest, and critical people reported these experiences in hypnosis.

Most professionals, furthermore, had neither witnessed nor personally experienced such strange happenings, and it taxed their credulity to believe them. Part of the problem was the "slipperiness" of subjective events, which made them seemingly less accessible to scientific scrutiny and verification.

But all objections to hypnosis have not been the result of prejudice, since there have been reasons to discount it. The process was compromised by the antics of stage hypnotists, whose performances may have been dishonest. Another taint was contributed by uncritical advocates, who promulgated hypnosis as a therapeutic panacea capable of curing every disease from scrofula to epilepsy. Any therapy claiming such efficacy had to be viewed with skepticism.

Hypnosis also came to be associated with mysticism and parapsychology. It was claimed that subjects in a trance could diagnose their illnesses and prescribe proper remedies. They could revert to previous incarnations or predict the future; could return to intrauterine existence or have clairvoyant experiences. Presented with this melange of the preposterous, it is little wonder that the scientific establishment threw up its hands in horror and turned its back on the entire mess.

Nevertheless, those who had extensive experience with hypnosis had observed remarkable events that demanded explanation. Hypnosis, although contaminated by many extraneous elements, did reflect a capability of the mind with medical, psychiatric, and social implication that merited unprejudiced and critical attention.

This has been an abbreviated history of hypnosis, one that has focused on a few prominent figures. Since hundreds of books and thousands of articles have been written on the subject, emanating from most countries in Europe and from the United States, many important contributors have been ignored. Scholarly histories of the movement are needed, but they will necessitate a familiarity with many languages and a profound dedication. Ellenberg's volume, *The Discovery of the Unconscious* (71), is an outstanding achievement, and it contains a wealth of information. Janet's opus, *Psychological Healing* (148), is another source, but many others may have been overlooked. Nevertheless, the basic questions surrounding the history of hypnosis are probably represented in this chapter.

By the early part of the twentieth century, the fundamental problems of hypnosis had been identified and studied. Experienced hypnotists finally agreed that hypnosis was a distinct psychological state in which unusual mental processes were possible. A wide variety of sensory, motor, and intellectual changes could be induced during trances. There had been dispute about the nature of parapsychological experiences so often reported in deep hypnosis—whether they were figments or facts. Patients continue to report them, and it remains an unresolved issue.

The fluidists had initially dominated the scene. They were convinced that some force emanated from the operator to produce hypnosis. This led to a preoccupation with the critical role of the hypnotist, but gradually some hypnotists became aware that the subject's hypnotic capability was an important variable. Since people differed in this ability, it became apparent that it was a psychological trait that was unevenly distributed throughout the population. The role of a focusing of attention was perceived and emphasized, but it was recognized that this focus need not be on an object, but could also be on a mental image.

A bewildering number of tactics were advocated for the induction of hypnosis—all successful with some people. This led a few hypnotists, such as Braid and Bramwell, to believe that the common denominator was a fixation of attention, no matter what strategy was used. Little heed was paid to the inductions occurring without benefit of a hypnotist, but these were occasionally noted.

The role of the hypnotist continued to dominate the thinking of practically all prominent hypnotists, preventing the recognition of the existence and the importance of self-hypnotic states. The only major exception was Breuer, but his postulation of self-hypnotic processes was soon buried beneath Freud's repudiation of their existence.

The data from experience with thousands of subjects had been accumulated and roughly codified. Approximately 15 to 20 percent of the entire population had proved to be "somnambulists," those capable of a deep trance with posthypnotic amnesia, whereas another 30 percent were identified as good hypnotic subjects. No precise instrument to measure hypnotic capabilities had yet been devised, and these estimates remained clinical judgments, but the high percentage of people capable of hypnosis had been documented.

Many hypnotists had been aware of the remarkable similarity between natural somnambulism (hysteria) and artificial somnambulism (hypnosis), but none, with the exception of Breuer, boldly accepted their identity. Since the importance of self-hypnosis went unrecognized, only the parallelism between the two was acknowledged.

Hypnotic treatments were mainly exhortative and suggestive. The major exceptions were Janet, Breuer, Freud, Prince, and Sidis, although there must have been others. All five recognized the existence of hidden complexes that had to be revealed in hypnosis, made conscious, and processed.

# 2 / Contemporary Hypnosis—Further Developments and Spontaneous Self-hypnosis

There have been two main approaches to the study of hypnosis. The first involved investigation by clinicians who were primarily interested in the treatment of patients. These were often superlative hypnotic subjects who demonstrated extremes of hypnotic trance behavior—the feats that hypnotic virtuosos can achieve. These demonstrations of dramatic trance states convinced experienced hypnotists that hypnosis could induce an altered and remarkable state of consciousness, one radically different from the normal alert condition.

More recently, some have recognized that hypnosis must be studied with greater scientific rigor—under controlled conditions where variables can be defined, isolated, and measured. Hypnosis was displaced from the clinic to the laboratory, and the tedious but necessary scientific process began, probably with Hull's volume in 1933 (142). In the preface he wrote, "Throughout the history of hypnotism the clinical approach with its preoccupation with remedial exigencies, has greatly predominated. In contrast to this tendency the approach of the present work is experimental rather than clinical; the persons employed as subjects in the program of research were normal rather than pathological; the ends sought were principles and relationships rather than treatment and cures." This has remained the credo and operating mode of his successors. Commendable scientific rigor has been the goal; experimental subjects have been culled from a normal population, often college students, among whom superlative hypnotic subjects are infrequent. Few laboratory investigators have had the opportunity to work therapeutically with hypnotic virtuosos—one of the clinician's prime sources of data. Modern experimental studies have been summarized, carefully examined, and criticized in many volumes and reviews (43, 88, 98, 129, 155, 238, 267), including two excellent books by Hilgard (128, 130), which contain many references.

Both approaches clearly have merit—in fact, they ultimately must be reconciled if an understanding of hypnosis is to be achieved. These divergent approaches recapitulate the history of science. In medicine, clinicians first studied patients with diseases. Examples (180) are thyroid failure and adrenal cortical insufficiency; cases of myxedema were first described by Paracelsus (1603), Plater (1656), Hoefer (1675), Curling (1850), and Gull (1873), while Addison (1855) documented the disease of the "suprarenal capsules." But these were only the beginnings of the scientific quest. In the twentieth century, the chemical structures of the hormones secreted by these glands were identified. These hormones now have been isolated, means to measure them in minute amounts have been devised, and many studies previously unattainable have become possible. But these advances have not negated the earlier astute clinical observations. Instead, they have complemented, enhanced, and explained—penetrated more deeply into the basic chemistry and physiology of the process. In like manner, the clinician's experiences with hypnosis now are being reexamined critically in the laboratory.

Although the very existence of hypnosis has been questioned, anyone who has observed excellent hypnotic subjects cannot doubt that the state they enter is unusual and different from the normal alert, awake condition. The more pertinent questions are whether hypnosis is a unique state unrelated to normal consciousness; whether it encompasses many different states; and what its essential features and neural mechanisms are. To answer these questions it is advantageous to turn to superlative hypnotic subjects and to examine the features of their experiences since they, like patients with myxedema and Addison's disease, demonstrate the extremes. If one studies cases of myxedema and hyperthyroidism, for example, one can learn much about thyroid function. More penetrating chemical and physiological studies are needed, however, to clarify further the precise actions of the hormones.

## Heterohypnosis—Hypnosis Induced by a Hypnotist

The importance of the hypnotist to the induction of hypnosis has been an implicit assumption for the last two centuries. It was Mesmer whose "passes" mesmerized patients, and later studies have mandated a hypnotist to induce a trance. The implication has been that hypnosis is a latent capability waiting to be elicited by the expert. Acknowledgments of spontaneous trances are scattered throughout the literature, but few

professionals have perceived the remarkable implication of this observation.

## Methods of Inducing Hypnosis

Many procedures have been used to induce hypnosis (32, 60, 195, 281,
292) including those identified by Bramwell in Table 1. They have included asking subjects to listen to repetitious and monotonous speech, to
focus on somnolence or relaxation, to visualize an image or an imaginary
scene, to fix their vision on an object, to imagine a sense of lightness or
heaviness in an arm—almost any strategy that ingenuity can contrive.
Since many techniques used to induce hypnosis succeed, the question
arises whether any are superior or preferable. At present, the evidence
favors no particular method, although people do vary, and some find
one form of induction more congenial than others.

Spiegel and Spiegel (258) reviewed current information about induction techniques. They emphasized that the hypnotic state is not so much
induced as it is evoked in subjects who already have the capacity to experience trances. They reviewed a study by Kranzler, who found no differences in the scores of subjects on the Stanford Hypnotic Susceptibility
Scale, Form A, when three different induction techniques were used.
They concluded that trance induction can occur in a matter of seconds;
that the formalities of various methods of induction have receded in
importance; and that the main consideration is the subject's native hypnotic capacity—although fears, wishes, trust, and resistances may facilitate or block the procedure.

By chance—certainly not by any calculated selection—I began to do
hypnosis as an untrained novice by requesting subjects to fixate visually
on a spot on the wall, with the injunction to concentrate on a heaviness in
the eyelids until they closed. Initially, to my amazement, subjects rapidly
entered trances, some within thirty seconds and most within a few
minutes.

## The Hypnotic State

Descriptions of the hypnotic state are available in the older literature
(see Chapter 1) and in more recent reports (75, 128, 268). For example,
Tart (268) described the various stages that one superlative subject experienced when he passed from consciousness to the profound depths of
hypnosis. The hypnotist's voice gradually became remote and distant;
the environment receded and then disappeared; time became meaningless; the body extinguished; peacefulness increased and then became
meaningless while self-awareness gradually disappeared. Any clinician
who works with these hypnotic virtuosos can reduplicate these observations, although idiosyncratic variations occur.

After inducing hypnosis in excellent hypnotic subjects, I have asked them what they were experiencing. Common answers are "things are strange, I'm spacy, dizzy, floating." Most subjects comment about changes in their sense of their own bodies and alterations in their perception of the world around them. Furthermore, subjects report various stages of hypnosis, usually identified as superficial or deep. I have requested them to rank the depth on a scale of 1 to 10, and some typical reports of deep hypnosis are included in Table 6.

*Table 6.  Deep Hypnosis—Induced*

At stage 7, a patient reported being relaxed, happy, and feeling peaceful. At stage 10 she said, "It feels so good—your voice is far away. My mind is here but not my body. When I go very deep—well beyond 10—there is nothing, just a void."

I asked another hypnotized subject if she could wish for a castle or a fairy godmother. "Oh yes, that can be done. It amounts to this; imagine something, wish for it and it appears." I then asked her to come out of hypnosis. "I'm very deep, about 10. I can't feel anything. I'm spinning. My body is gone, the world is gone, I'm floating. Your voice is the only thing that is there." When she emerged, her comment was, "While I'm in that world it all seems sensible and logical."

It would seem that the dimension of depth for subjects primarily involves the degree of their inner absorption, the extent to which they relinquish the external world and the body until finally they seem to disappear altogether.

After working for some time with patients, I asked them about the nature of their experiences during hypnosis (Table 7).

## *The Capabilities of Hypnosis Induced by a Hypnotist*

By the turn of the century, many of the capabilities of excellent hypnotic subjects had been documented in thousands of patients. Bramwell (32) (1903) summarized them in his textbook, but they have been described by many investigators both before and since his exposition (12, 63, 64, 83, 142, 145, 148, 155, 195). Bramwell cited subjects' ability in hypnosis to experience catalepsy, paralysis, and flaccidity of muscles; to find all sensations altered—vision, audition, smell, taste, touch, pressure, temperature, and pain—either make them more acute or diminished or arrested; to experience anesthesia, analgesia, or amnesia; or to have delusions, hallucinations, and illusions. In fact, many of these capabilities have been incorporated into standard hypnotizability tests to measure hypnotic abilities (128, 138, 283).

To confirm these observations for myself, I studied five adult females with unusual hypnotic capabilities. All were able to reach the point of

*Table 7. Recollections of Induced Hypnosis*

"My eyes may be open, and I can talk, but I'm still in hypnosis."

"When I'm in hypnosis everything is rational, fits, makes sense. While I'm in that world, it all seems sensible and logical."

"When I'm under hypnosis, I can do or see anything—but not always by my choice."

"In one kind of deep hypnosis I disappear—almost like I die."

"You are in your own little world. Sometimes it can be so peaceful. There are no troubles. Nothing else is there. It is a state of nothingness—like you are just born. It is a wonderful state. It is like going on a trip and leaving everything."

"There are degrees of hypnosis. When I go back into the past I must go deeper or I can go very deep and disappear."

"In hypnosis you are focused. Everything is more intense. The intensity and focus is unbelievable. Even normal feelings like love and hate are intensified. Your mind is totally focused on it and you feel every bit of it. Not only can you tune into something, but you can tune it out."

I asked a patient about the advantages of that state. "There can be no feelings—either emotions or physical. You can make anything, good dreams or nightmares. It isn't crowded. The emotions are real—happiness can be intense and real. You can control your emotions. If you want one you can have it, or you can stop one if it hurts." But what are the disadvantages? "There can be nightmares, ghastly experiences. You don't have vigor—like a wet noodle. The real world is a place where people can hurt you."

oblivion or nothingness in the hypnotic state. In hypnosis, I tested their abilities to manipulate vision, audition, smell, taste, and memory; to influence the sensory modalities of pain, touch, temperature, and position; and to achieve motor paralysis. Three subjects could perform every task, but the other two were unsuccessful in some. For example, subjects were requested to go into hypnosis and then to open their eyes while remaining in a trance. I then held my index finger about four feet in front of them. I requested that they make it much bigger, much smaller, wider, thinner, make it disappear, see right through it, and place it on the wall. I then brought them out of hypnosis. The three successful subjects confirmed that the events did happen and were very real in the hypnotic state. I then asked the three to do the same things, but this time without hypnosis. One was unable to repeat the feats in the alert state, but two reduplicated the experiences. However, the latter two explained that they had reverted instantaneously to hypnosis to accomplish them.

I also studied some of the failures experienced by my subjects. I had added to the list of requests, to satisfy my curiosity, the mandates to sit on the moon and to experience their births. One subject could sit on the moon with ease and realism, since that had been a part of her childhood world of fantasy, but she could not experience her birth because "that was silly." Another could sit on the moon, but when I asked her while she was ensconced there whether it was real, she said that it was real, but then added an afterthought: "It is very real, but it can't be, because people on the moon must wear space suits."

These exercises, easily verified in talented hypnotic subjects, illustrate several properties of this state. Although these subjects have in common unusual hypnotic capabilities, there are individual differences. These probably relate to each person's past experiences. Even in hypnosis, some subjects are specialists, able to perform certain gambits but not others. Hilgard (128), based on his factorial studies, concluded in the same vein that hypnosis was sufficiently a single domain to permit a strong general factor to emerge, but there were variations that reflected individual idiosyncrasies.

But hypnosis induced by a hypnotist has remained controversial. Experimentalists have recognized that the presence of a hypnotist can provide cues, covert and overt suggestions, and other contaminants that might distort or determine the experiences that hypnotic subjects report. Ingenious tactics, such as the use of unhypnotized simulators as controls, have been introduced by Orne (207, 209) to circumvent the many objections and to gain access to the essence of hypnosis. Orne concluded that it was possible for unhypnotized controls to feign much when instructed to mislead the hypnotist into thinking that they were in hypnosis, but that these controls do not demonstrate the strange twists of "trance logic." By this he means the logical contradictions that hypnotized subjects casually accept. An example would be the report of seeing a person sitting on a chair but also seeing the outline of the chair through him. These responses presumably might be learned, but the ordinary untutored simulators from the general population do not know that such reports are typical of deep hypnosis.

Unfortunately, obvious examples of trance logic are not always present, and extremes like the example are demonstrated only by superlative subjects. As a result, these cannot be relied on to distinguish the presence or absence of a hypnotic state. When present, however, they are helpful indicators.

## Spontaneous Self-hypnosis

Formal hypnosis beginning with Mesmer focused on the mesmerist or hypnotist and his importance to the hypnotic process. It became doctrine that a mesmerist induced the trance, but Mesmer's spectacle and that of his disciple, Puysegur, gave reason to discount this dogma. Poor people attached themselves by cords to a "magnetized" tree, where many fell into trances, convulsed, or were "cured" without benefit of a therapist (61, 71). Abbé Faria (217), another early hypnotist, noted subjects who went into trances upon crossing his threshold, before he could perform an induction. Historical documentation, coupled with the experiences of excellent hypnotic subjects, suggests that the primary process is a natural capability, long used but unrecognized by the individual as hypnosis. Hypnotists presumably simply tap or exploit this trait, often introducing subjects to other aspects of their ability that they have not previously discovered. For example, a subject repeatedly may have experienced vivid "daydreams," but never discovered "lid heaviness."

The concept of spontaneous trances or spontaneous self-hypnotic states is not new. De Boismont (1855) (62) was aware of these states, although Breuer (1895) (41) was the first to identify them in hysteria. More recently, West (285) has analyzed them, many experienced hypnotists have recognized them (74, 86, 106, 165, 185, 257), and they have been noted in normal individuals (62, 181, 289). Their relevance to psychopathology has not been appreciated, however, and even those who have noted the existence of spontaneous trances have not recognized their compelling implications.

In this and succeeding chapters, my discussion will center on spontaneous self-hypnosis. To avoid confusion, it should be recognized that self-hypnosis has come to be identified with autohypnosis—a trance consciously induced by a subject after he or she has been taught the technique by a hypnotist. But spontaneous self-hypnosis is quite different. It is a rapid, unpremeditated withdrawal into a trance, a dissociation, untaught and instinctive, a primitive defensive reflex that people experience usually when anxious or fearful—often in response to some psychological or physical threat. Spontaneous self-hypnosis is the conceptual focus of this volume, and I shall attempt to demonstrate that it is a powerful concept with importance to human behavior and psychopathology.

## The Induction of Spontaneous Hypnosis

The diversity and number of hypnotic inductions, all frequently successful, pose the problem of their common denominators—the elements essential to the process. A likely place to look for the essence of hypnosis is the mode of spontaneous self-hypnosis, the natural process that is not contaminated by the biases of the hypnotist.

Most excellent hypnotic subjects, in my experience, enter spontaneous trances so rapidly that it is difficult for them to decipher the mechanism. It is virtually an unpremeditated, instantaneous reflex. Something happens and they are "in that space." For many of us the only comparable experience is a daydream or reverie, when suddenly our attention is turned inward and focused on a world of fantasy. How does one do that? There is simply a snap, and you are there. The difference is the nature of the experience. For the excellent hypnotic subject, this "space" has a reality and features that go beyond the dimensions of a simple reverie.

One can, however, identify the antecedent conditions, those that provoke spontaneous hypnosis in excellent hypnotic subjects. These include boredom, relaxation, play, and reflection—but also strong emotions such as fear, anxiety, rage, and panic, often with the sense of being trapped. In some, drugs and alcohol may facilitate the process.

The natural process of spontaneous self-hypnosis may be divided into two types for clinical purposes. First, there are the calm and tranquil spontaneous inductions. One subject commented, "My best memory of when I started self-hypnosis was in kindergarten, playing in a sandbox. I could be anything, anywhere, anybody any time. It was real—I just never grew out of it." Another excellent hypnotic subject told me, "I had little places to go where I could sit, close my eyes and imagine until I felt relaxed."

But there is a second class of spontaneous inductions, those provoked by intolerable emotions. As one subject reported, "A sense of terror totally overwhelmed me. All I knew at the moment was that I could endure no more. I began to revert backwards in age to where I felt no sense of pain or terror. I literally became an infant for the next eight hours." On another occasion, "I felt anger for a second, but then went into that space to be calm. I gave the anger away at that time [to a personality]." These spontaneous inductions frequently occur in patients when they feel trapped, terrified, and unable to cope. In those situations, separate personalities, when present, are sometimes invoked. A personality told me about the patient, "She delegates only when she can't handle her emotions—when they become unbearable. Her amnesia is time out which she deserves and needs."

I have unintentionally induced hypnosis by noxious tactics while desensitizing excellent hypnotic subjects to feared objects. One patient had been slapped repeatedly on the face as a child by her mother. Initially, just touching her forehead with my hand was sufficient to provoke a trance. Another patient was assaulted by a knife while being raped. Later, in therapy, when she simply cut paper with a letter opener she entered a trance.

An unresolved problem is whether some subjects can *only* enter a deep trance under dysphoric conditions. At present, no heterohypnotic inductions and no test of hypnotizability relies on such tactics. It is possible, however, that some of those who are apparently poor hypnotic subjects might prove to be excellent subjects under these adverse circumstances. For example, one patient with tormenting spirits (possible multiple personalities) who spoke to her in auditory hallucinations had a plethora of somatic symptoms. She reported trancelike states and was skilled at automatic writing. Her symptoms had begun a decade ago when she was desperate in a crisis and had turned to automatic writing to find some solution. Despite this suggestive evidence for multiple personality and hypnotic capabilities, many attempts to induce a trance in this woman were unsuccessful. Patients like this one, and they are not rare, pose questions about hypnosis that at present cannot be answered.

## The Nature of Spontaneous Hypnotic Experiences

Another source of information about the hypnotic state available when one works with superlative hypnotic subjects is the nature of their spontaneous hypnotic experiences. These may occur while the patients are in the hospital or in therapy (Table 8), and their descriptions may offer us further clues to the essence of hypnosis.

*Table 8. Spontaneous Hypnotic Experiences*

"I'm on the edge of panic, the walls are moving, the floor isn't there, real dizzy."

"Right now I'm totally lost in time. Nothing looks right. I'm hearing voices. It is very bizarre. Sometimes I'm back in reality for a few seconds."

"The world becomes too much and I separate. I was in jungles with headhunters laughing at me."

"An hour ago, I was overwhelmed and crazy. I'm clear now. I'm not scared, and I'm not going into hypnosis."

"I was conscious but in the twilight zone like a surrealistic experience with visions and voices. The physical state is like on drugs."

"In that state, I can hear and understand people, but I'm someplace else."

"I hurt myself yet I didn't feel it. I felt it for a moment, but then I turned it off."

"I can't think. I don't know what to do. I think 'hit me.' I've done something wrong—need to be punished. I'm scared. I feel like a dumb little kid. There is distance from you."

"All my senses were wrong. Everything was very bright. It was real weird."

"I became more and more separated from myself. I remember looking down at my hands and seeing them, but not feeling that they were a part of my body. It is a frightening sensation which I've had many times before. It was a time of unimaginable terror and suffering."

I initially asserted that the fundamental hypnosis is the spontaneous, unpremeditated form—unrelated to a hypnotist—but a skill well learned and much practiced by certain people. I would amplify this by proposing that excellent hypnotic subjects are not novices by the time they encounter a hypnotist. They are people who hypnotize themselves spontaneously. The hypnotist only elicits a repeat performance of old practices—with new wrinkles added to embellish the repertoire.

If my claims are valid, it should be possible to verify them by examining the past experiences of these excellent hypnotic subjects, antedating any encounter with hypnotists or psychiatrists. To test this assumption, I have asked a number of my subjects to write descriptions for me of any bizarre or unusual occurrences in their past, with reference to their thinking, memory, hearing, time, taste, smell, physical sensations, and vision, as well as any other experiences that they might now perceive retrospectively as hypnotic. Many recall a multitude of these events. In fact, some subjects have spent an inordinate amount of their lives in this bizarre world of hypnosis. Their spontaneous hypnotic experiences are similar to those that have been induced by hypnotists over the centuries and cover the same spectrum of modalities (Table 9).

A number of my subjects have written descriptions of early spontaneous hypnotic experiences antedating any contact with a hypnotist. One recalled:

The body loses all sensations. The mind is detached in essence from the body. The words time and space lose their meaning. One falls deeper and deeper into this ether. One is conscious but not conscious. At times, I have been in the midst of a fantastic pink and yellow star-studded spiral galaxy. At other times, the mind takes over, meandering down its secret pathways. One's mind can be at the level of the physical when one's body is "frozen," not responding to commands. There are times when everything is just blank. There is no consciousness, just "nothing."

It would seem that spontaneous hypnotic experiences, innocent of a hypnotist or any recognition of their hypnotic nature, are similar to those induced by hypnotists, if not identical to them. For example, Aldous Huxley's report of his experiences in deep hypnosis, although initiated by a hypnotist (75), is an eloquent account of an imaginative author's sojourn in this domain. Apparently, excellent hypnotic subjects may have these "classical" hypnotic experiences, often beginning in childhood, unaided by any external agency.

But the careful scientist may object to general conclusions drawn from these data, since all my subjects have been patients. Fortunately, there is a recent report by Wilson and Barber (289) based on a study of twenty-seven adult females with outstanding hypnotic abilities—"normal" individuals without multiple personalities or disabling symptoms. The authors reported, "We discovered that, with one exception, the excellent hypnotic subjects had a profound fantasy life, their fantasies were often 'as real as real' (hallucinatory). . . . It has been shown that there exists a small group of individuals (possibly 4 percent of the population) who fantasize a large part of the time, who typically 'see,' 'hear,' 'smell,' 'touch' and fully experience what they fantasize."

As children, the subjects studied by Wilson and Barber lived in a make-believe world much of the time. "Dolls and stuffed animals seemed to be alive," and these objects had "their own things to say" and "their own feelings." As children, most believed in fairies, elves, and guardian angels. They played and interacted with imaginary compan-

*Table 9. Examples of Past "Spontaneous" Experiences of Patients Who Are Excellent Hypnotic Subjects*

*Thinking*

"I completely lose the ability to think at times. Nothing comes, nothing goes, and it seems as though nothing is or was."

"Sometimes my mind sees so fast that I can't pick up anything—I'm overwhelmed. Other times it is as though my mind was totally stopped. As strange as it sounds, I sometimes feel dead."

*Memory*

"I have on six occasions blacked out. I feel this was caused by an unwillingness to accept an experience out of deep pain, fear, or anxiety. The largest one being a fear that I was crazy."

"A couple of glasses of wine and I have an amnesia for 30 minutes. When I have returned, my mother would say that I acted terribly."

(Past amnesias are reported by many subjects.)

*Hearing*

"I can go so deep into concentration that I don't hear anything, like people talking to me. Other times I hear them but I literally don't understand them, it is only sound."

"Sometimes I just return my internal tape to the start because I missed a good song on it and didn't' remember hearing all of it."

"As an adolescent I would wish for music, then hear it."

"I have heard loud gunshots that scare the hell out of me. I get into a panic. I can smell the smoke when I get into that state." (At the age of 11, this subject saw his father shoot and kill his brother.)

*Time*

"Time may be speeded to where I could go into the library at 8 A.M. and stay there totally occupied until 5 P.M., while I do not know where the time went or what I did, or it drags so slowly that I can't handle it."

"I have lost a great deal of time when in deep thought or trips, but had always attributed this to being 'busy' or 'time flies when you are having fun.'"

*Taste and smell*

"With taste, I can intensify flavors or totally turn them off. My sense of smell is easy to turn off. At camp I couldn't smell the latrine while others just sat there and gagged."

"When I was a child I would play games with foods. I would drink water and imagine it was a coke, down to the taste, the sensation of carbonation, even to the point of burping the gas."

"I could always think about a taste or smell and really taste or smell it. I just assumed that everyone could do it."

### Sensations

"I never have Novocain at the dentist—I am allergic to it. So I just sit there calm and quiet and block out the drill and pain."

"When I hurt myself I don't feel it. I know that I do it, and may feel it for a split second, but I can totally block it out."

"I can turn things off such as coldness. I can go outside without a coat while others have thick coats on and are still freezing. I just don't feel anything. I can also be freezing while it is 107° F. outside and everyone is dying of heat. I call it 'mentally cold.'"

"I could pretend that I was in a dentist office, just injected with Novocain—taste the bitter aftertaste of the shot, and numb any portion of my jaw or face."

"I wanted to learn to fly and would think about this while driving a car. I could feel the increased G-force of the takeoff on my chest while pulling back on the 'steering wheel.' I could do this while almost being totally aware of my driving as though I was in both places at once."

### Vision

"I wrote a report about witchcraft, read about frightening things, then saw the 'spirit'—a hooded figure. It happened many times. Those times I was fully awake but other people with me couldn't see the 'spirit.'"

"I looked up at church. There were the faces of my mother and father on the bodies of two total strangers."

"When I have sex with my husband, up to the time of actual intercourse which I do not remember at all, I always see another face—someone who has sexually abused me. I have never told a soul about this. It sounds crazy but I can do it."

"At age 11, I found that I could make someone so small that he would be standing in a crack. Then I also discovered that I could look at someone and make him as big as a house—sometimes a mountain."

"My father smacked me one across my face. This was the first time (age 7) that I was aware I could look at someone and make him disappear. I looked at my father with hate, and somehow he wasn't there any more."

### Jamais vu and déjà vu

"When I got home it seemed like a strange place, another world, like I had never been there before. Even my own room didn't look familiar."

### La belle indifférence

"I may be crying inside, but am laughing or expressionless on the outside."

### Early self-hypnotic experiences

"I had little places to go where I could sit, close my eyes, and imagine until I felt relaxed

*Table 9. (Continued)*

like hypnosis. At times it was very deep. I can remember total darkness, no feeling, where I didn't have to cry any more. It was an escape."

"It began at age four when I sat in a cornfield for five hours in a fairyland being a princess."

"I used to sit either in my bedroom or out under a big tree in the back yard and dream of all the beautiful places in the world I wanted to be. Sometimes it was as if I really was there."

*Self-hypnotic experiences—often accepted later
as "real" events*

"That world is a place of imagination, one is relaxed, a greater awareness of what is happening to your body, a place of profound insights which later prove to be trivial, a state of intensification where a mild headache can become an agonizing disaster."

"It seems that I have heard voices all my life, as long as I can remember. As a kid I assumed that everyone had them—they were very friendly."

"Sometimes just my body is paralyzed. I cannot move anything, and usually cannot feel anything. My mind is active but I cannot move. This may happen to only parts—my legs, arms, or hands—or I'm stuck in one place or position. It occurs with little or no warning."

"At times my body has become huge or disproportionate."

"Since my mother died when I was ten, there have been many times when I have seen her and talked with her."

"I often created new words in school. Imagine getting up in high school and using a word like 'etrofanic.' Though I have never taken a foreign language, there have been times when I have heard someone speaking in another language. I seem to know what they are saying. It has frightened me because it is almost like speaking in tongues. I've never told a soul about this."

"In a silent, alone moment, from nowhere I heard voices. As I raised my head, my eyes beheld what I now would have to classify as a vision—but it frightened me very much."

"I have always had a great imagination, but there were many, many times I knew what I saw and heard were definitely not imagination."

"As a child I could produce weightlessness. A wall was a magnet pulling me towards it."

"I have often had the sensation that someone was after me and I just had to escape. This often occurred after a mind trip. I would get up and behave like a 5-year-old or a 10-year-old with fear and terror."

"I could create high fever, colds, vomiting, or pain. I could think of a situation of vomiting and begin to do it within 15 seconds. Once I focused on my foster mother writing me a letter that her friend had died of an aneurysm. I felt a balloon-like sensation on my right frontal lobe—things became unreal and dreamlike. For several weeks I went to the doctor and he did all kinds of tests to prove to me that I wasn't going to die of an aneurysm."

"I repeatedly see a horrible face [of the man who had raped her]. It frightens me terribly. Logic told me it couldn't be, but it seemed very real."

"I remember vividly a ladder in the middle of space, and at the top of the ladder was God or Jesus. I began to climb the ladder crying hysterically. God kept telling me, 'Come on, you can make it if you only try.' Jesus or God was sitting in a chair and I crawled into his lap and he hugged me as I cried and cried. He told me I was a special person with a specific mission to fulfill, so I must return to earth and live the rest of my mother's life. She had died. I had the most peaceful, serene feeling inside filled with the spirit of God, and knew I was a special person with a specific deed to fulfill. I knew I had experienced a revelation from God."

"At times I see a ghastly arm floating. I've thrown it away three times—even put it into the garbage can. When I was young, there were always guests in my room or ghosts. I could see them when they walked into the closet. Sometimes they would fly around overhead."

"There are times when I don't know what is real and what isn't. I ask my husband to verify appointments, like parties, because I'm not sure whether the invitations really occurred. I casually tell him to telephone and ask what time we should come."

ions whom they clearly saw, heard, and felt as living people or animals. Some could later read books and become one of the characters. Through fantasy, they could become someone else—an orphan, a princess, or Cinderella. One subject at age seven distinguished her fantasy from the real world by asking people whether they were also perceiving her experiences.

As adults these subjects continued to spend much time in fantasy— about 50 percent of their day. Many have vivid sexual fantasies, so realistic that three-quarters achieve orgasms in this way. When they are asked to imagine a dog, they will see it run into the room and feel it lick their faces. Furthermore, "they tend to confuse memories of their fantasies with real events." Many become ill when they see violence on television or the movies because the experience can become so personal and real. Most have had illnesses or physical symptoms directly related to their thoughts, fantasies, and memories. Practically all have had "extrasensory" occurrences, precognitive dreams, and out-of-body experiences. Most have encountered spirits or ghosts. Wilson and Barber also comment, "Apparently most hypnotists did not realize that these excellent hypnotic subjects . . . were able to experience the classical hypnotic phenomena primarily because they had had practice in experiencing similar phenomena during their daily lives."

Although I have not had the opportunity to study a group of "normal" excellent hypnotic subjects—I have encountered three with comparable experiences who fit this description—the following conclusion seems plausible. Many people are not excellent hypnotic subjects, hence their realistic worlds are restricted to the real Newtonian world and to dreams while they are asleep. But excellent hypnotic subjects have the added dimension of a third "real" world—that of hypnosis. Some can live normal lives, with only vivid realistic fantasies. Others, due to noxious circumstances, unwittingly exploit their hypnotic skills and create personalities, amnesias, and a plethora of symptoms.

## The Realism of Hypnotic Experiences

One of the most dramatic occurrences in hypnotherapy can be the abreaction by a patient of an early traumatic event, particularly one that has been lost in amnesia for decades. Only the most hard-bitten cynic would deny the genuineness of the patient's behavior. In the process of therapy I have seen this happen many times and will cite one example here.

A homosexual man was referred for the treatment of intractable vomiting, which had led to a major esophageal hemorrhage. Since his symptoms were suggestive of "self-hypnotic" problems, and as his vomiting continued to be a danger, I suggested that we get at the cause, but immediately lest there be a recurrence of the bleeding.

In hypnosis, he commenced, "The vomiting began two years ago after sex with a male. I was at the gym, then went into the sauna. A fellow was sitting on a shelf. I had a sense of anguish and attraction. We got into sex. He grabbed my head and rammed his penis down my throat. I began to vomit all over him. He loved it, climaxed, and left. Then I began to bleed from my nose and mouth. I began to sob, ran into the restroom, and began to vomit. I actually enjoyed the vomiting. When I vomit, it reminds me of that experience—I've now repeated it many times. Food in my throat is sexually exciting. When I vomit I have an orgasm, but it is getting more and more painful because of the injury to my esophagus."

I innocently commented that it probably had an earlier cause. The fireworks began as he shouted in terror, "Keith has a knife at my throat, arching my back—sticks his penis in my rectum—his hand on my throat makes me want to vomit—I vomit—he has an orgasm. Oh God, it hurts—but I have an orgasm. He takes the vomit—rubs it over me, calls me a pig." All this had occurred at age eight with an alcoholic stepfather.

"The movie is going again. Keith turns off the television—I know what is going to happen. My rectum is sore from sex. He grabs the blanket—slaps me across the face—I start to cry, 'Please, it is so sore, please.' He grabs my ears—rubs his penis over my face. He says spit on it—he shoves it in me—climaxes in my mouth—keep vomiting all over him."

Out of hypnosis, he was exhausted. "I'm sore as if it has just happened. My rectum is sore." As he walked out of the office, he made this final acknowledgment: "All of that has been forgotten for years. I understand now why I've been vomiting. If I hadn't been here and experienced this, I wouldn't believe it—that things can be hidden so long and cause so much trouble."

But excellent hypnotic subjects spontaneously have comparable experiences. On the ward, a patient begins to scream hysterically. She is seeing blood on the walls and the horrible face of a hideous man. He is coming toward her, and she runs terrified. She has to be restrained, but the terror persists for half an hour as she shouts, "He has a knife. He will kill me." It is a spontaneous reenactment of a ghastly rape experienced twenty years before.

When she discussed the assault in retrospect, she gave the following description: "He jumped me while I was walking to my car and held a knife at my throat. He took me to a room in a dirty hotel. He unlocked the door. The knife cut my throat. He tied me down. I can't think about it! When I go back to it, I get lightheaded, physically ill and feel it. When I try to do it, my nose even bleeds. My ulcers start to bleed and I vomit. The 'nightmares' [her reversions to hypnosis] come back, and I can't tell the difference between 'nightmares' and reality."

When it is reactivated in hypnosis, a memory is not a bare recollection. It seems to contain every element of the experience—the emotions, physical sensations, the auditory and visual components, the tastes and smells. When the patient returns to consciousness, all elements are still present as if the experience has just occurred. "My body hurts all the places he cut me. There isn't any blood, but it hurts the same way."

Ordinarily we consider a memory to be a simple recollection—we merely recall an event. But these subjects either record information in greater detail, or they demonstrate that memories contain imbedded within them vivid sensations and feelings, which the penetrating focus of hypnosis can reveal.

Hypnotic experiences, whether induced by a therapist or spontaneously experienced, can be as real as events in the real world—in fact, they are often indistinguishable from reality. There appears to be a continuum extending from the alert state, to daydreams and fantasies, to hypnosis, and finally to dreams in sleep. The awake state and fantasies exist in the real world. Fantasies—of fabulous accomplishments, for example—are not mistaken for facts.

At the other end of the spectrum, dreams contain weird elements that are perceived as "real" while one is asleep, but on awaking one usually recognizes that the dream was an illusion, because it has a marker of sleep to identify it. Unfortunately, there is no obvious marker such as sleep to denote a spontaneous self-hypnotic state. The subject is neither aware of slipping into this hypnotic realm nor cognizant of its strange reality. The subject unwittingly has entered the "dream world" of hypnosis, which is every bit as real as the real world or the dream world of sleep. Therefore, when the victim comes out of hypnosis after experiencing a vision, a ghost, or a paralysis and returns to reality, these experiences, if remembered, may be fully believed in. These events must have occurred, since the subject was fully conscious and they were "real." Innocent of the presence of hypnosis, how is the subject to know it was a deception. It is a confusion that can have devastating effects.

Let us examine the evidence to this point. There seems to be an extraordinary mental process that has been named hypnosis. Historically, the assumption has been that it was induced by hypnotists, but in excellent hypnotic subjects it can be demonstrated that these inductions occur spontaneously under both tranquil and dysphoric conditions. The spontaneous transition into hypnosis usually evolves very rapidly, often in a split second. Comparably, induction by a hypnotist can occur on the first trial within thirty seconds.

In the hypnotic state induced by a hypnotist, there appears to be a gradation of responses varying in degree of depth. Mild reactions evoke a subjective sense of dizziness, floating, and disorientation, with a perception of depersonalization and unreality. But as the subject is induced to go deeper, if he or she has the capacity, the real world becomes distant, the hypnotist's voice becomes faint, and the body fades, until finally all may be gone and there is nothing, a total void.

Identical experiences are reported as spontaneous occurrences by excellent hypnotic subjects. These can be observed at times in therapy and in the hospital, but many of these subjects can also recall similar experiences in the past.

Finally, substantial literature supports the fact that when hypnosis is induced by a hypnotist, some subjects are able to experience catalepsy, paralysis, and flaccidity of muscles; to experience all sensations as altered more acute, diminished, or arrested; to experience anesthesia, analgesia, or amnesia; or to have delusions, hallucinations, and illusions. But excellent hypnotic subjects also report all of these experiences as spontaneous occurrences.

My excellent hypnotic subjects have had a fantastic array of hypnotic experiences, both induced and spontaneous, but all were perceived as very real at the time. A few subjects have returned spontaneously to intrauterine existence, while one found himself in the primeval world of dinosaurs and was terrified. Upon request, several have traveled to the moon, and one reported, "I shook my skirt before leaving because it became so dusty." Some, with eyes open, could make me as large as a house or as diminutive as an ant. One subject in hypnosis reported, "There is a tree ahead of me, but it just moved. The tree just fell, but it didn't make a sound." This illogic is the "incongruity" of deep hypnosis or "trance logic" described by Orne (207).

If one examines all these subjective feats, whether spontaneous or induced, it becomes apparent that hypnosis offers a remarkable array of potential experiences. These considerations have led me to scrutinize all functions attributed to the neocortex, either focal or general, ranging from the frontal cortex to the occipital poles. It can be demonstrated that all neocortical functions can be manipulated with realism in deep hypnosis, since all can be diminished, enhanced, distorted, or obliterated. This leads to the general conclusion that all functions of the cerebral cortex, either focal or general—motor, sensory, mental, or emotional—can be manipulated in deep hypnosis and experienced as real. Deep hypnosis may thus be said to offer a "mental neurology."

The implications of this conclusion are far-reaching. In principle, any mental aberration, any mental and many physical symptoms, and any syndrome known to psychiatry might be induced by spontaneous self-hypnosis and be accepted as real. The question is whether theory and logic will fit the facts! A theory may be elegant, but it is of limited value unless proved valid.

## Transcendence of Normal Capabilities in Hypnosis

The bizarre, preposterous antics of excellent hypnotic subjects have led many observers either to discount all alleged hypnotic experiences as "humbug" and a hoax or to accept any claim as valid. It is necessary first to recognize that deep hypnosis is a subjective or mental experience, occurring in that obscure part of the brain, the mind. Any function of the neocortex can be isolated and manipulated with utter conviction by the subject, but when someone under hypnosis returns to intrauterine existence, reverts to childhood, experiences a previous incarnation or feels as strong as Superman, it does not mean that those things are valid as judged by the standards of the real world. They are happening for him, in this world of hypnosis, but his fundamental muscular apparatus has not been transformed. Nor, when he regresses to fetal life or childhood, does his neurological apparatus change, allowing Babinski reflexes to be present. The body is still the same; only the mind has been altered to allow these experiences and convictions.

But those of us who do not have such hypnotic ability should not be so startled by these phenomena. Every night during sleep, our dreams are equally preposterous. Even the scientific, critical, and skeptical enter a world of dreams in which the illogical is commonplace, yet when dreaming and asleep they perceive these events as real. It is surprising that while much study has been concerned with the symbolism and the nature of dreams, so little attention has been directed to their reality. We uncritically accept the vividness of dreams—in fact, usually ignore it, with the simple explanation that "I was asleep." The startling feature of hypnosis is that the subject is awake, as witnessed by the ability to communicate with the hypnotist. If these events can happen while one is sleeping, why not when one is awake?

A hypnotic phenomenon of theoretical interest is age regression. Orne (208) reported a study of an excellent hypnotic subject who was asked to regress to the age of six. "Accordingly he began acting like a child, talking like a child and apparently thinking like a child. He made some drawings and wrote his name at the bottom of the drawing with typical childlike printing." On a hunch, Orne asked him to write as he dictated, "I am conducting an experiment which will assess my psychological capabilities." The subject printed slowly and laboriously, but with perfect spelling. Orne concluded:

It struck me that such an obvious discrepancy may be the cause of much controversy about hypnosis. Not only does it negate the view that age regression involves a return to intellectual functioning of early childhood, but it would be wrong to believe with the skeptic that such data shows age regression to be a fraud. If it were really a fraud, if the subject were merely seeking to put one over on the hypnotist, would he be so stupid as to write such a sentence without spelling errors. The subject's behavior can, therefore, be taken as an indication that we are not dealing with mere conscious role playing and that, at the very least, the hypnotized individual's judgment is affected.

I have had many comparable experiences. When my subjects have regressed to childhood for therapeutic reasons to resurrect amnestic traumas, some have acted like children. In retrospect, they have told me that they were back there realistically reliving an early event—but our conversation while they were there had been replete with polysyllabics and adult concepts, which they managed without self-consciousness. I have considered them back in childhood in contact with old memories, some hidden for many years, but oblivious to temporal contradictions. It is a fantastic mental realm, and if one treats patients with hypnosis one must reconcile oneself to its inconsistencies.

It has also been alleged that deeply hypnotized subjects can transcend their normal muscular capabilities. Common sense would suggest that a flabby subject can hardly match the feats of strength of a burly athlete, so reason must first be applied to these claims. But stage hypnotists have frequently demonstrated the ability of some subjects to suspend themselves off the ground supported by chairs beneath their head and feet. The question is whether hypnosis has allowed them to supersede their normal strength or whether other, nonhypnotic, considerations were responsible. Orne (210) has considered the possibility that motivation is the prime variable and has demonstrated that by motivating subjects in the awake state they can be induced to exceed their previous hypnotic performance on an endurance test. He summarized the work on the transcendence of normal volitional capabilities by stating, "All of the claims concerning significant changes due to hypnosis [these transcendent capabilities] can be mimicked by highly motivated [unhypnotized] individuals in well controlled studies."

## Tests for Hypnotizability

Perhaps the most important recent development in the study of hypnosis has been the creation of standardized hypnotizability tests. Science mandates measurements, and it is now possible to quantify this hypnotic capability. These tests hardly rival hormonal measurements, where there is precision to the picogram level, but behavioral assays are inherently more difficult because of the greater complexity of behavioral processes. These tests nevertheless offer a standardized means to measure the trait of hypnotizability.

Although a number of tests have been devised (138), those by Weitzenhoffer and Hilgard (128) are probably psychometrically the best standardized and the most widely used. The examiner reads to the subject the prescribed instructions for every item so that tests are administered in an identical fashion. There are several test forms (A, B, and C, 1 and 2) and the twelve items in forms A, B, and C—the scales most often used—are graded as positive or negative. Scores, therefore, can range between 0 and 12. Hypnosis is induced in a standard way and the test then begins. One test item is hand lowering, and the subject receives a positive score if his or her hand has lowered six inches in ten seconds. Another item is age regression, and a positive score is received if there is a clear change in handwriting between the present and the return to childhood. The hypnotized subject is presumably in the suggested subjective state, but it is the behavior emanating from this state that is observed by the examiner and scored.

It must be recognized that these tests have been devised to measure hypnotizability and so are predicated on our present understanding of hypnosis. In most ways they are vastly superior to idiosyncratic clinical opinions, but in the laudable and necessary pursuit of greater objectivity they may neglect some richness that comes from prolonged clinical experience with hypnosis. The tests, although time consuming, are very helpful, but like any tests or laboratory procedures they must be evaluated in the context of the entire clinical picture.

Scores on the test are predicated on the subject's willingness to relax and to enter the proper reflective state. Subjects who are apprehensive, suspicious, or antagonistic may perform in a way that does not reflect their true capabilities. Since hypnosis is a subjective experience, the tests can also be falsified. A subject bent on deception, or perhaps motivated to please, could inflate his or her score artificially. The assumption must be that most subjects will give honest performances.

In my experience, the major problem in testing psychiatric patients has been the underestimation of hypnotizability. This is consistent with the clinical observation that some patients initially refractory to hypnosis may prove later to be excellent subjects once their concerns are minimized and some trust is engendered. A number of our patients, whom we initially suspected were excellent subjects, had low scores when first tested. After reassurance, some were retested and their scores rose dramatically. When questioned, they reported an initial distrust of the tester, an unwillingness to go deeply into hypnosis with a stranger, a fear of deep hypnosis, or a hostility to the impersonality of the procedure.

Examples of such patients are three rapists who were studied at the state hospital. Despite the mandate of the hospital program for painful honesty—and they were candid about their crimes—when they were given the hypnotizability test by a strange psychologist, the three scored 0, 3, and 5 on the first test. All reported a reluctance to cooperate with or trust the psychologist, in part because he was Oriental. After being reassured, they were retested and scored 9, 6, and 11.

This is consistent with clinical experience with hypnotic inductions, where guarded, wary, or paranoid patients may initially resist a hypnotic procedure, while later they prove to be excellent subjects. A male patient could not go into hypnosis initially because two women were present, and he was afraid that he might divulge shameful information. Later he entered hypnosis rapidly, proved to be a multiple personality, and scored 12 on the test—the highest score possible. Another patient when first admitted to the hospital failed to go into hypnosis because he was paranoid and didn't trust the staff. He was then discharged after some improvement, only to be readmitted again after he had slashed his wrists in a suicide attempt. This time he was desperate for help and went into a deep trance within thirty seconds.

Comparable observations have been recorded by many hypnotists. Bramwell (32) in 1903 referred to the number of attempts at an induction that might be necessary. He quoted Tuckey, who would make three or four attempts before desisting, whereas Moll reported forty or more attempts before finally succeeding in some instances. Vogt, in one case, only triumphed after an astronomical seven hundred sittings. Bramwell concluded that "in many of my cases which yielded the best therapeutic results, hypnosis was only obtained after repeated failures."

Furthermore, many patients with concealed traumas are intuitively fearful of passing into a trance, losing conscious control, and encountering painful emotions and noxious memories. Consequently, they may be initially resistant to a hypnotic induction. This is illustrated by one patient, a woman with multiple personality and extensive hypnotic pathology. When initially tested she scored a 6—a normal score. Later in therapy she proved to be a hypnotic virtuoso—a superlative subject who could perform any hypnotic feat with ease. When queried about the test, she admitted to a conscious resistance at the time, since she was afraid that she might lose control totally and enter a deep hypnotic state. Later, under more reassuring conditions, she scored a 12.

The frequency of these underestimations of hypnotic abilities in patients has not been rigorously examined, but they occur often enough to merit attention. This contrasts to studies of a "normal" population of college students where test-retest reliability is very high, with a correlation coefficient of .80 to .90, which has led to the conclusion that hypnotizability is a stable characteristic over time (128). Presumably these students do not have psychopathic hidden agendas and so can cooperate without the fears that some patients harbor.

Another consideration is the test items. In the commendable effort to achieve greater objectivity, most items are scored by elicited behaviors—the arm lowering six inches or handwriting changing with regression to childhood. The more pertinent experience to which these behaviors are a response is whether the arm felt heavier or whether there was a realistic experience of being a child. There is now some movement to redevise tests in this direction (284)—to incorporate the subjective experience and the involutary nature of the response. As an example, some subjects clinically will regress to childhood, experience early events with realism, and then act and speak like a child. But others who report equally realistic experiences are poor mimics, and they continue to behave like adults although presumably their subjective states are identical.

The tests are somewhat faulty in the identification of hypnotic amnesia. A positive score for amnesia is recorded if the subject recalls fewer than four test items. It has become apparent that this scoring reflects an admixture of two forms of memory—the varying normal capacity to remember, and hypnotic amnesia. This would be only a minor problem except for the key role of hypnotic amnesia in psychopathology. A more reliable determination of hypnotic amnesia by a testing procedure would have clinical importance. But despite all reservations, the tests have been a major achievement. Further improvements and refinements will also come in time. Like all tests, however, they must be understood and interpreted in the light of their assumptions and limitations.

The Stanford hypnotic tests have the disadvantage for clinicians of taking about one hour to administer. Shorter procedures are available, although they are less reliable than the full twelve-item scales of standard tests. Graham (109) reported that the induction of eye closure alone correlated 0.68 with hypnotizability on the A scale of the Stanford tests. More recently, Hilgard (131) studied arm levitation as a single indicator of hypnotic ability. For practical purposes, if the arm levitates 10 cm in 6 minutes, the probable score on the full test would be at least 6.5; whereas if the elbow were resting on a table and it rose, the probable score is 7.5 or more. Although rigorous studies have not been done, my experience with the tests suggests that the presence of multiple personalities, major conversion symptoms, or auditory hallucinations when the voice can talk to the hypnotist, indicate even higher scores—in the range of 8 to 12.

One way to view hypnosis is through the perspective of hypnotizability tests. About 90 percent of the general population when tested will exhibit hand-lowering, presumably because the suggestion is enhanced by the weight of the arm in an elevated position. It is a simple task and a subjective state easily achieved by most individuals. In contrast, only about 10 percent of the general population can create realistic auditory or negative visual hallucinations, because this requires a deeper penetration into the inner mind than most people can achieve.

## Differences in Susceptibility; Age and Sex Variables

In the nineteenth century, a measure of outstanding hypnotizability was considered to be the ability to experience posthypnotic amnesia, and it still remains an excellent criterion. Abbé Faria, based on his experience with over five thousand subjects, estimated that one out of five or six people in the general population was an excellent hypnotic subject.

The major studies published in the nineteenth century, first cited by Bramwell in his textbook, were more fully tabulated by Hilgard and his colleagues in 1965 (128). The fourteen studies included more than 19,500 people. In this large population, 26 percent of the subjects were identified as somnambulists—excellent hypnotic subjects. The percentage varied between studies, but even if one excludes the two highest and the two lowest percentages, reducing the number of studies to ten (since the extremes might be discrepant), the mean percentage of somnambulists and the standard error of the mean would be 21 ± 3 percent.

Hilgard and his colleagues (128) also cited six studies of more recent vintage (1931 to 1958). With one exception these were of college students, a sample probably not representative of the total population. The mean percentage of excellent hypnotic subjects in these studies was 13 percent. Spiegel (256) cites a figure of about 10 percent. Although these figures may be analyzed in many ways, it would seem likely that somewhere between 10 and 20 percent of the general adult population have excellent hypnotic capabilities—a very large number when one considers the size of the world's population—20 to 30 percent are good subjects; and 10 to 20 percent are refractory to hypnosis (Table 10).

Females are believed commonly to be more suggestible, emotional, and hysterical than males, and therefore more hypnotizable, but this is probably incorrect. In a study of 100 males and 100 females, half of each sex hypnotized by a male hypnotist and half by a female hypnotist, no difference between the sexes was found (282). Hilgard (128) summarized data from use of the Stanford test. There were 272 males with mean scores of 5.6 compared with 261 females with mean scores of 5.7. These findings are in agreement with observations in the nineteenth century (32), and indicate no difference between sexes.

The age distribution of hypnotizability was first compiled by Liébe-

*Table 10. Studies of Hypnotic Susceptibility*[a]

| Studies | Number of subjects | Refractory | Light | Moderate | Deep |
|---------|------------|-----------|-------|----------|------|
| Nineteenth century (14 Studies) | 19,534 | 9% | 29% | 36% | 29% |
| Twentieth century (6 Studies) | 519 | 20% | 47% | 20% | 13% |
| | | Scores low | Scores medium | Scores high | Scores very high |
| Weitzenhoffer and Hilgard | 533 | 42% | 28% | 19% | 11% |

[a] Modified from a table by Hilgard (128).

ault and reported by Beaunis (32) (1887). He found children to be more susceptible than adults, with a peak between ages seven and fourteen. Thereafter, there was a decline with age. London and Cooper (176) in a study of children and adolescents reported maximum susceptibility between ages nine and fourteen.

For the clinician, several of these observations have particular relevance. Many young children are excellent or good hypnotic subjects (58, 59, 102, 176), so early spontaneous self-hypnosis is compatible with clinical experience. Next, children when hypnotized experience hallucinations and amnesia in larger numbers and with greater ease than do adults (58, 59, 176, 196, 200)—an observation pertinent to psychopathology. Finally, this hypnotic ability is a trait that slowly fades with advancing years. These facts merit reemphasis and further consideration, since they explain why spontaneous self-hypnotic states are common.

Table 11 contains the remarkable observation that one-half of all children, both male and female, are excellent hypnotic subjects. This means, in principle, that half of the world's population, during late childhood and early adolescence, is potentially at risk for self-hypnotic experience, including amnesias and hallucinations, if other influences, such as various abuses or severe stresses (13, 18), are imposed. Furthermore, the data imply that one-fifth of the adult population could be at risk if stresses are excessive.

A perplexing question is why there should be this curious rise in hypnotizability during childhood and early adolescence, with decrements during adult years. No answer is yet available, but it may be that hypnosis is like other skills. A mathematical ability or an athletic capability may be present in latent form, but if it is neither frequently used nor practiced, it may diminish. Self-hypnosis may be comparable.

*Table 11. Comparison of Hypnotic Susceptibility Scores of Children and Adults*[a]

| General level | Raw score on test | Percentage of cases Children | Percentage of cases Adults |
|---|---|---|---|
| High | 12 | 13 ⎤ | 2 ⎤ |
|  | 11 | 19 ⎥ 54 | 5 ⎥ 18 |
|  | 10 | 10 ⎥ | 7 ⎥ |
|  | 9 | 12 ⎦ | 4 ⎦ |
| Medium | 8 | 7 ⎤ | 6 ⎤ |
|  | 7 | 7 ⎥ 31 | 9 ⎥ 37 |
|  | 6 | 10 ⎥ | 8 ⎥ |
|  | 5 | 7 ⎦ | 14 ⎦ |
| Low | 4 | 6 ⎤ | 11 ⎤ |
|  | 3 | 4 ⎥ | 10 ⎥ |
|  | 2 | 3 ⎥ 15 | 11 ⎥ 45 |
|  | 1 | 1 ⎥ | 7 ⎥ |
|  | 0 | 1 ⎦ | 6 ⎦ |
| | N = | 240 | 124 |
| | Mean of raw scores = | 8.16 | 5.25 |
| | S.E. = | 0.20 | 0.29 |

[a] Modified from table by London and Cooper (176).

## The Depth or Difficulty of Hypnotic Feats

The nineteenth-century hypnotists recognized that only 10 to 20 percent of all subjects experienced posthypnotic amnesia—the "somnambulists" who could forget the happenings in a trance. From one perspective they can be viewed as a minority of the population, but the feat can be identified also as a difficult one, since it is the privilege of few.

This epitomizes some of the problems implicit in the term "depth"—an elusive construct. At times, the term reflects the progressive loss of contact with the body and the external world. In other contexts it denotes the extent of departure from alert consciousness analogous to stages of sleep. Clinically, "depth" may refer to the ability to achieve amnesias or negative hallucinations, presumably "deep" feats. Experimentally, depth may be measured by the number of items the subject passes on a hypnotizability test; the ratings (1 to 10) he or she fixes to the depth at the moment; or the type of experience being encountered (241). Each may be implied in the concept of depth, and all are probably interrelated, which creates some semantic confusion. But a fuzzy term should not be a problem as long as it is defined by specific observations and these are available for scrutiny. The frequency and therefore the difficulty of various items on the Stanford Hypnotic Scale (Form C) was tabulated by Weitzenhoffer and Hilgard (128, 283) (Table 12).

*Table 12. The Stanford Hypnotic Scale (Form C)*

| Item | Percent passing ($n = 203$) |
|---|---|
| 1. Hand lowering | 92 |
| 2. Moving hands apart | 88 |
| 3. Mosquito hallucination | 48 |
| 4. Taste hallucination | 46 |
| 5. Arm rigidity | 45 |
| 6. Dream | 44 |
| 7. Age regression | 43 |
| 8. Arm immobilization | 36 |
| 9. Amnesia | 27 |
| 10. Anosmia to ammonia | 19 |
| 11. Hallucinated voice | 9 |
| 12. Negative visual hallucination (sees only two of three boxes) | 9 |

It is apparent that certain items, carefully defined in the protocol of the test, can be passed by many—hand lowering and moving hands apart; but other items, such as auditory and negative visual hallucinations, are passed by a few—therefore these are difficult hypnotic feats.

Many other scales have been devised (141) to identify simple and difficult feats. One published by Shor (141) has been modified to serve as a rough guide for clinicians (Table 13). It lacks psychometric precision, but it can be useful for identifying excellent hypnotic subjects.

## Genetic Versus Acquired Trait

When hypnotic responsiveness has been measured by standard tests over time it has proved to be stable. Test-retest coefficient correlations over a period of months are in the .80s and .90s, while undergraduates who were retested in their home communities ten years later showed a correlation of .60 (130).

A tactic frequently employed to detect the heritability of a trait is the comparison of identical and fraternal twins. Morgan (198, 199) studied the hypnotic capabilities of fifty-eight pairs of identical twins whose scores correlated at the .52 level; in contrast, 82 pairs of dizygotic twins

*Table 13. Scale of Easy to Difficult Hypnotic Feats[a]*

*Very easy*
　Hand lowering

*Easy*
　Hand levitation
　Eyelid closure

*Intermediate*
　Realistic age regression with eyes closed
　Visual hallucinations with eyes closed

*Difficult*
　Complete amnesia
　Negative visual hallucinations
　Elimination of severe pain
　Clinical Symptoms
　　Personalities
　　Major conversions—functional blindness,
　　　body anesthesia, limb paralysis,
　　　and seizures

[a]Modified from Shor (141).

had correlations of .17 and 132 pairs of siblings a correlation of .19. These values support a genetic factor. Adoption studies, which are a more precise means to distinguish nature from nurture, have not yet been done.

More studies are needed, but the implication of those done so far is that hypnotizability contains a genetic component. This is to be expected, since evidence from animal behavioral studies supports the general principle that many common behavioral traits are in part determined genetically. The fact that hypnotizability is widely distributed throughout the human race makes it a likely candidate.

Any trait in animals, be it exploratory, sexual, aggressive, social, or territorial, if it can be experimentally defined can be enhanced or diminished by appropriate inbreeding. Dogs are an excellent example of this process. Although all are presumed to have a common ancestry, through the centuries they have been selectively bred to enhance various abilities such as docility, ferocity, exploratory behavior, and herding. Presumably the same process with respect to hypnotizability has been at work in human beings, but it has operated in a random, rather than a planned way.

Although I have not done studies to separate genetic endowment from learning—definitive investigations are both onerous and expensive—occasional clinical information has been of some interest. One excellent hypnotic subject had a mother who held seances. In a trance she would call up spirits, hear voices, and do automatic writing. Two had fathers whose concentration was so intense that they could screen out anything said by their wives. One had a mother who lived "in another world." She could blot out feelings—even the murder of a son had left her unemotional. "She acted as if it never happened."

Two outstanding hypnotic subjects had fathers diagnosed as paranoid schizophrenics, but their psychoses had peculiar features. One was a Dr. Jekyll and Mr. Hyde. At times he was a gentle, loving parent, but at other times he was a sexual sadist. When he sexually assaulted his five-year-old daughter, he frequently called her by her mother's name. When he was finally committed to a state hospital, the doctor noted in a report that the patient claimed long periods of amnesia. The other father became psychotic after a near-death experience during World War II. He was hospitalized for eight years, but then made a miraculous recovery and was "cured" for many years without further relapses. These are anecdotes, but they may prove to be relevant, supporting a familial or genetic hypothesis. Similar observations have been reported (56, 235).

These observations, however, do not imply that hypnotizability is immutable. Most experimental studies demonstrate slight gains in this ability with either training or modeling procedures, although final scores usually correlate with initial ones (130). But these laboratory studies have not been lengthy, and more relevant although less exact information may be garnered from accounts of yogis, mystics, and transcendentalists, which suggest that long practice under expert tutelage will improve hypnotic ability.

Furthermore, many of my patients have unwittingly engaged in hypnosis, without recognition of the process, since childhood. They have had many years of spontaneous practice. Most are hypnotic virtuosos, remarkable performers of the kind that Hilgard (130) estimates occur in 1 to 4 percent of the population, and Wilson and Barber (289) in 4 percent. It may be that all were born with outstanding abilities, but it seems likely that practice has perfected their skill.

The preceding information is sparse, but more general considerations of the heritability of behavioral traits may be pertinent. In primitive organisms, genetic information controls behavior, and learning when it exists is minimal. As one ascends the phylogenetic scale and the central nervous system enlarges, genetics continues to influence behavior, but learning becomes a more and more powerful factor. Finally, in primates and human beings there is a bewildering intermingling of both. Even biological traits are subject to the same principle. An example is height, in which genes indubitably play a role, but this genetic predisposition is influenced by nutrition, which often accounts for a considerable variation in growth.

Caution must be applied, since our knowledge of the heritability of hypnosis is still limited. It seems likely, however, that hypnotizability will prove to be a complex ability genetically coded in the central nervous system with varying degrees of individual differences—and also one that is subject to learning, especially if it is cultivated over many years.

## Posthypnotic Phenomena

To this point our concern has been with events such as lid heaviness or visual hallucinations that occur while the subject is in hypnosis. But if proper instructions are given, automatic behaviors may be elicited after the subject has left hypnosis and is in the conscious state. These are the posthypnotic phenomena, or the posthypnotic suggestions, which have been recognized as part of the hypnotic repertoire for two centuries. These give an added dimension to the hypnotic process—and a crucial one—because they demonstrate that hypnosis has the potential for continuing effects long after a trance is terminated. Hypnotic feats are puzzling enough but the posthypnotic processes present a further conundrum, and one with important clinical implications.

The Marquis de Puysegar in 1784 "mesmerized" a young shepherd, Victor, who fell into a sleeping trance, in contrast to Mesmer's subjects, many of whom convulsed and contorted. Victor then displayed sleep-walking-like behaviors but afterward had no recollection of them. Thus, hypnosis came to be considered an artificial somnambulism with post-hypnotic amnesia as a cardinal feature.

In the experimental situation, posthypnotic suggestions are given by a hypnotist, usually with the injunction to forget the instructions but to perform the request. The future behavior has been defined in hypnosis, an amnesia for the instructions has been requested, and the act will later be performed without cognizance of its source. A simple example is the hypnotic suggestion to rise from the chair in two minutes and stretch. When the subject is asked why he or she rose at that time, a feeble excuse may be offered, such as "I've been sitting for awhile and needed to stretch," but the instructions are forgotten.

Another twist should be noted. Hypnotists may recommend that subjects carry out the posthypnotic suggestion even if they remember the instruction and hesitate to comply. Subjects when they do comply are seemingly demonstrating a compulsion, a behavior important to psychiatry. To the observer, these artificial acts may seem fraudulent, simply efforts to please the hypnotist, but all evidence indicates otherwise. For one thing, too many impeccably honest subjects who have demonstrated these behaviors have recaptured the memory in retrospect and then realized that the forgotten instructions compelled the act.

One question sometimes posed is how long these behaviors will persist when they are *experimentally* induced. Janet (148) studied thirty highly "suggestible" persons. In three-quarters of his hypnotic experiments, the requested behaviors lasted only briefly. In one-quarter of the instances there was a prolongation—in some cases for several days, in one individual for sixty days, and in another for ninety days. Janet stated, "As might have been foreseen, the suggestions whose effects were most obviously transient were those which conflicted with the subject's habits and tastes, those which were especially difficult to carry out, and those whose performance made the subject feel awkward or ridiculous." More recently, Edwards (70) studied the decrements in a posthypnotic finger response to a buzzer. Although there were variations from individual to individual, there was evidence of a response at 405 days, the longest interval tested.

Orne (128) gave subjects the posthypnotic suggestion to mail a postcard daily from a stack of fifty provided. The daily receipts declined gradually, long before the fifty cards were mailed. A control group, without hypnosis but with a monetary incentive, performed more faithfully than the posthypnotically instructed subjects. Orne accepts the authenticity of posthypnotic behaviors, but his study indicates that artificial dull tasks, when directed either in hypnosis or requested in consciousness, will rapidly be neglected unless a strong motivator is introduced.

An amnesia for the instructions is the usual accompaniment of a posthypnotic suggestion, and it is a phenomenon that has been investigated in many studies. A salient feature of hypnotic amnesia, a core consideration, was stated by Hull (142) fifty years ago. Logic mandated, he suggested, that if the amnesia is reversible, which it is, the underlying mechanism could not be at a level of registration or retention, but must be at the level of reproduction. Reviews of experimental studies of amnesia have all arrived at the same general conclusion that the key to hypnotic amnesia lies in the retrieval mechanism. The information has been recorded and coded, but it can't be retrieved (59, 78, 157).

In a rudimentary form an unconscious has been experimentally created by posthypnotic suggestion—a repository in memory containing directions not consciously known by the subject. But behaviors will emanate from this unconscious nexus as directed, unless they are too outrageous or repugnant. Furthermore, even if the instructions are remembered, they may be followed compulsively. There seems to be a compelling need to pursue them whether they be forgotten and unconscious or remembered and conscious. Finally, most hypnotic experiments are artificial or discordant, in contrast with what occurs with spontaneous hypnosis in patients. If a hypnotic suggestion is to persist, whether it be experimental or spontaneous, it should harmonize with the individual's needs and feelings.

A discussion of these processes that occur spontaneously in patients will be deferred, but the simple elements delineated in experiments with posthypnotic suggestion reveal the fundamentals from which complex behaviors seen in the clinic develop.

## The Personality Structure of Able Hypnotic Subjects

The term "suggestibility" has been associated with hypnotizability since the early nineteenth century. This semantic trap has led many to believe that able hypnotic subjects are highly suggestible; usually this can be translated as naive simpletons. In fact, they *are* suggestible, but only in the sense of being able to enter trances in which many suggestions can be implemented.

Breuer, Freud, and Janet rejected this claim of "suggestibility" and recognized that some subjects had critical capabilities that permitted persuasion only by information and logic. Many of my hypnotic virtuosos have been equally analytical and skeptical. They have frequently rejected my explanations with a scientific disdain for mere opinion. In fact, in trances some have been intellectually as stubborn as mules.

Experimental studies support the distinction between primary suggestibility (hypnosis) and social suggestibility (gullibility). Moore (197) used an autokinetic test, a persuasibility test, and an influencibility test in a study. Apart from postural sway, a hypnotic item, the correlations with hypnotizability were near zero.

The only trait thus far identified that correlates highly with hypnotizability has been the capacity for deep imaginative involvement (128, 133). Subjects with high hypnotic scores reported a variety of these experiences, whereas they were uncommon for those with low scores. This included involvement with reading, especially fiction; activities in the dramatic arts and religion; adventures in mountain climbing, cave exploring, or skin diving; and experiments with drugs, parapsychology, and oriental beliefs. For example, when really interested in reading fiction or looking at a movie, these people feel that they literally are there and become the characters. Shor (240) reported similar findings in a study of book reading fantasy.

These involvements are reminiscent of trance states reported by my excellent hypnotic subjects and those of Wilson and Barber (289). When reading a book or watching a movie, they are likely to move from being an observer to being a participant; to switch spontaneously into a hypnotic mode. Three patients with outstanding hypnotic abilities (tested 10 to 12 on the Stanford Scale C) described similar experiences on the stage. All engaged in amateur theatrics, and all reported that they did not play the role but instead became the character. What has been identified in highly hypnotizable subjects as imaginative involvement may be another aspect of the spontaneous slippage into a trance that will enhance the vividness of an experience.


## Animal Hypnosis

There is the need for an animal model of hypnosis, since animals offer investigative possibilities not available in humans. This option may exist; a trait so widely distributed in humans, presumably coded in the genes, should have an evolutionary ancestry.

A likely approach is to examine the modes of human spontaneous hypnosis for their analogues in animals. The first spontaneous human mode is a peaceful hypnotic repose, a calm reverie while awake. This is also the state usually produced by a hypnotist. Edmonston (69) reviewed the literature and came to the same conclusion: "that the responses to traditional hypnotic procedures (whether subjectively reported or objectively measured) equate neutral hypnosis with relaxation."

This mode can be detected when wild animals are observed in their natural state. The animal is lying down, relaxed and resting but simultaneously alert to any sign of impending danger. It appears to be in two states, internally directed while in repose but also tuned to the outside world, attentive to any threat. An unusual sound will catapult it instantly to a rigid, alert posture. This is akin to the normal heterohypnotic induction, in which the subject is requested to enter a tranquil trance while remaining alert to the operator's voice. The difference, apparently, is that the human subject usually has no reason to be attentive to an external danger.

The second spontaneous hypnotic mode in human beings is in response to a perceived threat, a fear reaction seen very frequently in patients. Similar behaviors can be observed in wild animals when they are confronted by a danger and helpless. Faced with a danger, the animal first assumes an alert, tightly focused attitude. The animal then has one of three options: to fight, to flee, or to do nothing and remain immobile. The last presumably is hypnosis.

Immobility has preservative virtues, since it is the attitude least likely to provoke an attack. Furthermore, if the animal is trapped and helpless, this posture of death, being catatonic, may avert destruction. Bramwell (32) related this to hypnosis by explaining the catalepsy as "a conscious simulation of death adopted by the animal from the instinctive knowledge that certain birds and beasts of prey, except under pressure of extreme hunger, will not attack what is dead."

This behavior may also be seen when an animal is cornered. A naturalist told me that he had observed this immobile behavior both in a badger and a bear cub in the wilderness, when they seemingly had felt endangered and unable to escape. I witnessed another example in a movie of animals on the African plains. An antelope was being pursued by a pack of wild dogs. His fate was sealed, death was imminent. Unperceived by the pack, the antelope frantically veered into a clump of trees and assumed a catatonic posture, while the dogs sped by in hot pursuit. The immobility saved the animal from destruction while depriving the dogs of a succulent meal.

Both types of hypnotic-like behaviors can be witnessed under natural conditions in the wild. The question is whether they can be artificially reproduced in the laboratory. Primates, mammals, birds, reptiles, and amphibians will all demonstrate a persistent immobility with flaccid or rigid postures when the animal is rendered helpless or when the tactic of visual fixation, similar to human induction, is applied. So a frog, when placed on its back and then lightly tapped on its stomach, will remain immobile for hours. An alligator rolled on its back becomes catatonic, whereas a bear, lion, dog, or cat made to stare at a bright object will assume an inert position but continue to keep its eyes open. A remarkable description of these processes with photographs is to be found in a volume written by Volgyesi (278).

How does one prove that animal hypnosis is akin to the human experience? One should note that this is a problem common to all animal investigation, when the results of studies in animals are extrapolated to humans. With respect to hypnosis, since animals cannot give a verbal report, one must rely on similarities in behavior. The postures—rigid, flaccid, and catatonic—seem to be identical, as are many of the induction procedures. Furthermore, surgery has been performed on pigeons, rats, guinea pigs, and hares that were in a hypnotic state without evidence of pain, analogous to the human situation (48).

A major objection (52, 100) has been the argument that animal hypnosis is a fear response, a consideration that has convinced some scientists of its unrelatedness to human hypnosis. This opinion has been based on the relaxed nature of "artificial" trances induced by a hypnotist. But spontaneous inductions in human beings are consistent with the fear hypothesis. Many people enter hypnosis spontaneously when they are frightened and trapped, a situation identical to the animal predicament.

If one tentatively accepts the universality of hypnosis in man and animals, certain inferences may be drawn. Hypnosis must be phylogenetically very old, with a special neural circuitry akin to those now being defined for aggressive, sexual, and eating and drinking behaviors. Furthermore, it must have served to enhance survival, otherwise it would not be omnipresent.

In fact, patients have repeatedly told me that as children they were trapped by the psychological, physical, or sexual brutality of parents. Unable to escape, to flee or fight, they have disappeared internally by spontaneous hypnosis. It was a tactic that many, unprompted, have said allowed them to survive. Unfortunately, unlike animals, their hypnotic sojourns became habitual and eventually destructive. Any animal who used hypnosis in this way would perish.

## Summary

My central concern in this book is the concept of spontaneous self-hypnosis. A hypnotist does not create a trance but merely facilitates its emergence. The capacity to enter trances is probably a genetic endowment, distributed almost normally over the population, although long practice may improve it. Therefore, many induction tactics may succeed, although the critical considerations are the fears, wishes, trust, and resistances of the subject, which allow or inhibit the emergence of this ability. Furthermore, to produce a trance, a hypnotist relies on a tranquil, relaxed induction. Spontaneous hypnosis, in contrast, is often induced by a fear response, akin to animal hypnosis.

Able hypnotic subjects rarely recognize this trance capability as hypnosis and under benign conditions it seems to be harmless. In childhood it may promote realistic fantasies, while in adulthood spontaneous self-hypnosis may facilitate imaginative involvement (128, 133) and perhaps creativity (28) in a few persons with other special talents. Many subjects with excellent hypnotic skills report past spontaneous experiences long before they ever encountered a hypnotist, and these seem identical to the classical hypnotic state.

If one examines the capabilities of the neocortex, it becomes apparent that deep hypnosis, either spontaneous or induced, can manipulate with realism *all* neocortical functions. It offers a vast array of possibilities. In fact, it has the potential to produce almost any symptom known to psychiatry and, in principle, can simulate or induce almost any psychiatric syndrome.

Deep hypnosis is a world of realistic fantasies, but it is also a region of realistic vivid memories, where amnesias occur. A salient feature is the phenomenon of posthypnotic suggestion, in which instructions, although forgotten, will produce some particular behavior after the subject has come out of hypnosis.

The ability to be hypnotized is common in children, peaks in adolescence, and gradually diminishes in later years. It is evenly divided between the sexes.

Finally, there is evidence to discount the alleged transcendent properties of hypnosis. Hypnotized subjects cannot exceed their normal physical capacities.

# 3 / *A Theory of Hypnosis*

Many theories have been proposed to explain hypnosis. Shor (23) sees hypnosis as a departure from the normal alert state: when this orientation to reality is temporarily reduced or eliminated, the subject enters a trance. In a deep trance, the distinction between imagination and reality is lost, and rational control of behavior is suspended. Hypnotic role playing ensues in which early feelings toward parents are transferred to the therapist. Hilgard (128) summarized the many aspects of hypnosis that have been regarded as central features of the hypnotic state:

1. Passivity or lack of initiative, evident in the quiet repose of relaxed hypnosis, when the subject responds docilely to suggestions or experiences a peaceful state of relaxation.
2. Redistribution or selectivity of attention, as when a subject focuses primarily on a memory while the environment is extinguished except for the hypnotist's voice.
3. The capacity to reexperience vividly and visually past memories or to experience a fantasy with realistic intensity.
4. A reduction in reality testing or the tolerance for reality distortions. This includes all of the suggestions present in standard tests for hypnosis including hallucinations and delusions, which subjects accept during hypnosis as real events. It is the heightened suggestibility emphasized by Bernheim and the early hypnotists, in which judgment is partially or completely suspended and illogical events are accepted as real.
5. A certain kind of role enactment. This is seen in regressions to childhood, during which the person may act and speak like a child. These role expectations or "demand characteristics" are not sham behavior, however, since the subject at the moment experiences them as real. There is a deep involvement in the role.
6. The amnesia of hypnosis, which has perplexed observers since the time of Mesmer.
7. The psychoanalytic hypothesis of a regressed state, a return to the primary process thinking of an early period of development in which impulses are dominant, rationality is suspended, and transferences reflect earlier relationships to parental figures.

More recently, Hilgard (130) has elaborated a complex "neodissociation" theory. It is based on Janet's early detection of dissociations, the splitting of consciousness, but incorporates modern cognitive theory and includes concepts from recent research on information processing, divided attention, and brain function.

Any theory of hypnosis, therefore, must encompass the many facets of the phenomenon, including realistic role enactment (230); the redistribution of attention; the loss of initiative; vivid images, realistic memories, and realistic fantasies; the reduction in reality testing—trance logic; and increased "suggestibility"—the many feats potentially possible in hypnosis, including amnesias.

I hope that the theory to be presented here will prove a useful way to conceptualize hypnosis, although it may be that no theory will succeed until there is a better understanding of underlying neural mechanisms. Nevertheless, a theory, even if imperfect, may direct research in productive ways and may clarify clinical problems.

## Normal Mechanisms—A Neural Model

A simple model of the central nervous system—one that might offend a neurophysiologist—is first presented here to lay the groundwork for our later analysis of the hypnotic state. We will arbitrarily divide the central nervous system into four components that are conceptually the most relevant to the hypnotic process. First, there are peripheral receptors, detectors of distant and proximal stimuli—those for audition, vision, and olfaction, and those sensitive to taste, touch, pain, temperature, and position. This exteroceptive input of stimuli will be classified as *sensations*. Enteroceptive receptors affiliated with the autonomic nervous system will be ignored.

Some nerve fibers conveying sensations are short-circuited low in the spinal cord or brain stem, but most are transmitted up the nervous system in segregated tracts. These tracts relate to elemental "instinctual" organizations in the limbic system, where primitive eating, drinking, sexual, agonistic, and emotional behaviors are clustered. These signals enriched by the limbic system provide the cerebral cortex with information. This is the region of the higher mental functions, and for the sake of brevity we will term these complex elaborations of the simple peripheral stimuli, now in the cortex, as *experiences*—the second component of the model. Experiences are classified, coded, and then recorded by a mysterious process into *memory*, short- and long-term, the third component. The reticular activating system, diffusely distributed in the core of the neural axis with radiations to the cortex, is the alerting mechanism that functions to focus *attention*, the fourth component.

These then are the four elements of primary concern in a consideration of hypnosis—*sensations* at the periphery, *experiences* and *memory* in the cortex, and the mechanism of *attention* with its diffuse distribution.


## Attention Mechanism and Conscious Experiences


The next consideration is the nature of conscious experience. At any moment one has only a meager breadth of awareness—that being perceived by the attention mechanism. All else at that time is out of awareness; therefore, for a fraction of time all else is unconscious.

As one reads a book, one's attention is focused on it, with rapid reference to data in memory and some awareness of the immediate environment. An infinity of other possible experiences and memories potentially available are temporarily unconscious. But attention to the contents of a book is not like a laser beam with coherent synchronous waves that create a cylinder of uniform light surrounded by darkness. Rather, attention is like a beam from a flashlight—with a concentration of luminosity in the center, which fades and grows gradually dimmer toward the fuzzy edges until finally there is darkness.

When the center of the attention beam is on a mild pain, it will hurt. Persistent central attention may then even intensify the distress. As attention is slightly redirected, the pain now on the dim periphery will diminish until a more remote distraction temporarily commands the focus, totally eliminating awareness of the pain. As long as this redirection persists, the pain, now unattended, is unconscious—although presumably the receptors for pain are still firing, but perhaps with diminished intensity since feedback to them from consciousness has been eliminated.

A further element is the mobility of attention. It flickers, darts hither and yon, and only with deep concentration will remain relatively immobile. In human beings, this concentration often depends on such elements as taste and motivation. Each person has his or her own idiosyncratic interests and preferences, and these determine where the person will concentrate attention. A professional golfer may focus most intensely on a putt, whereas a carpenter may be most fixed on a neat joint, and a scholar on a dusty tome. Animals best demonstrate a fixed focus when stalking a prey or alerting to a danger. One unanswered question is how much peripheral, dim attention is normally recorded in memory—a little or more than we recognize? One patient told me that she would voluntarily enter hypnosis when she wanted to recall a forgotten detail of an innocuous experience, revisit the event and find in this vivid recall the missing elements.

# Memory

Experiences once attended to are then coded and placed in their proper niches in memory. Memory banks are a filing system with labeled, interconnected receptacles; without them information would be chaotic and scattered, inaccessible to rapid retrieval.

This system of coding must be both determined and limited by the structure of the brain, its anatomy, chemistry, and physiology—properties all human brains have in common. This is the basic machinery, but the brain has a capability which distinguishes it from all other organs, that of learning. This flexibility should allow experiences to modify the coding system, to introduce differences between individuals and also between cultures. This is comparable to computers: the hardware may be similar, but the software—the programs—will vary.

Free association probably taps this memory coding process. A common association to man is woman; a rare association to man is danger. Presumably, men and women are coded partly in the class of people, but a few individuals, due to indoctrination or misadventure, have man and danger in the same category, or the danger category is closely affiliated to that for man.

Memory may be short- or long-term. Short-term memory is short-lived and probably electrical, unless it is translated into the long-term process, which is believed to be chemical. This is a highly simplified description, kept short for purposes of analysis. Many studies of memory are available (156).

Since memory is a component of behavior, it follows the general laws of behavior, either behavioral and operant or classical Pavlovian. Some memories apparently are vividly fixed by one experience—one trial learning—although they are probably reinforced by sporadic recall. Ordinarily, however, memories remain distinct and vigorous only when they are reinforced and used—otherwise they fade, recede, and disappear. Calculus when first learned, for example, may be understood and remembered, but when long neglected it will grow faint until finally it atrophies and virtually disappears.

A summation of specific experiences coded in memory, whether distinct and rapidly retrievable, faint and difficult to recover, or lost, forms a residuum that linked to genetics determines habits, attitudes, prejudices, and culture.


## Hypnotic Processes

If a rational explanation for hypnosis can be devised, it should be consistent with these more general considerations of the central nervous system and with what we know about both animal and human psychology.

It would be inconceivable for hypnosis to be such an odd fellow as to be totally unrelated to the normal functioning of the central nervous system, the cortex, and its masterpiece, the mind.

During the nineteenth century, ideas about hypnosis were gradually formulated, but it was primarily Braid (1843) who identified the central process (30, 31, 32). At first, Braid was convinced that a fixity of gaze was mandatory to an induction, but later, after the successful hypnosis of blind subjects, he concluded that this was not essential. A fixation of the eyes was only one aspect of the riveting of the mind on one idea, and this concentration on a single idea was the essence of the process. This narrowing or focusing of attention internally continues to be viewed by some as the essential element in the induction and the state of hypnosis; in this view, hypnosis is a function of the reticular activating system (201, 203), although the nondominant hemisphere may also contribute to the process (99, 113).

If the attention mechanism is the crucial component in what is termed hypnosis, then internal focused attention should somehow account for the features of hypnosis, although many aspects might appear to be dissimilar and unrelated to one another.


## Hypnotic Amnesia

The phenomenon of hypnotic amnesia is a promising place to start, since it has occupied such a prominent role historically in "somnambulism." It is also a crucial element in the development of multiple personalities. In addition, it is a component of dissociation and it has been extensively studied experimentally.

Therapy may resurrect traumatic experiences forgotten for as long as thirty years—a long time to hide an unpleasant occurrence. Most events that have occurred before age five and are not recalled during the intervening years are irretrievably lost, but these amnestic memories can be recalled under hypnosis in minute detail. Such amnesias are easily demonstrated in excellent hypnotic patients by a simple experiment performed during the initial interview, something I have done many times. Under hypnosis, patients are questioned about general matters, but inquiries are also made about hidden forgotten experiences. If patients acknowledge the presence of such experiences—and many patients in the conscious or hypnotic state have this intuition—they may then be asked to look into the "deeper" mind to find a mild trauma. In many cases, patients immediately retrieve forgotten material, although it had previously been unavailable to their consciousness.

Before the interview is terminated, patients are given the option of remembering or forgetting the traumatic experience. Those who forget then come out of hypnosis and return to full consciousness blank, but those who decide to remember are now fully aware of and remember the content of the interview as well as the traumatic experience. This exercise is revealing. Information known a minute ago, coded in short-term memory, has been immediately forgotten by some, but a past event, in long-term memory, has also been expunged. Whether memory is coded electrically or chemically seems to be irrelevant to the process, since both short- and long-term memory are subject to an amnesia. Comparable experiments can be performed with sensations, since all sensations induced in hypnosis can be eliminated or recognized. A pain such as a headache—but also an experimental pain—can be reduced or eliminated in hypnosis, and moments later, upon request, it can be reactivated.

A more general principle emerges from these observations. Sensations, when consciously detected, as we noted in our model of the central nervous system, become experiences when recorded by the neocortex. They then are coded as short-term, simple memories. But memories, either simple or complex, may be hypnotically manipulated–recognized or forgotten. Conscious sensations in this sense belong in the more general category of memories. A pain, therefore, when hypnotically eliminated, is forgotten; sensations, when consciously detected or hypnotically obliterated, are really remembered or forgotten.

My prize forgetter constantly recapitulated this process spontaneously. In therapy we would resurrect a traumatic experience—in her case, a rape. In hypnosis, I would say, "Now, I want you to remember that. Please repeat it," and she would. Once she was out of hypnosis, I would ask her to repeat it again, and she could. But a minute later, she would have forgotten the intolerable memory—and this in a person with a photographic memory for poetry, plays, and music.

When such information, such memories, remain unconscious, it can be shown by various techniques that they still exist and flourish, although they are unknown to the subject. A dramatic manifestation of this is automatic writing, a capability of some excellent subjects. Several delightful anecdotes illustrate this. William James (128, 144) studied an excellent hypnotic subject who could perform automatic writing. In a trance, the subject's anesthetic right hand began to write. James pricked the back of the man's hand fifteen to twenty times, but he showed no response to indicate feeling. As a control, James pricked the unanesthetic left hand, and the subject asked, "What did you do that for?" Later, as the experiment continued, the anesthetic hand wrote, "Don't you prick me any more." At the end of the session, the subject said that he had been conscious of only two pinpricks, those on the left hand.

Estabrooks (77) reported an experiment with a friend using automatic writing with an anesthetic hand. When Estabrooks pricked the hand with a needle, it wrote a stream of profanity "that would have made a top sergeant blush with shame." The subject continued to read a book quietly during the entire procedure "without the slightest idea that his good right arm was fighting a private war."

The processes involved here, whether experimental or clinical, are identical, differing only in form: one is contrived to create a scientific study, while the other is naturalistic, having evolved out of dire necessity. In each case, external events—the painful prick of a hand or a rape—have been detected by sensory receptors. The messages reach the cortex, "pain" or "horror." Hypnosis is induced in one case, and it is spontaneous in the other. The experiences are relegated to memory and forgotten, one by the hypnotist's request and the other as a spontaneous flight from reality. The pain is recorded in simple form; the rape may be elaborated in the form of a personality, a feature of the syndrome of multiple personality. Essentially, sensations have been transformed by the cortex into experiences, and these experiences in memory have been made amnestic.

Both the pain and a personality are concealed from consciousness as dissociated events, but a personality in patients may then be accosted in hypnosis and can speak. Many will then reveal much about the hidden experience. How does one get the concealed pain to speak, to gain a measure of its intensity? Hilgard (130, 132) has ingeniously done this by using automatic writing and automatic talking, experimental equivalents of clinical personalities.

Using unhypnotized controls and good hypnotic subjects, he found that the latter group, when instructed while in hypnosis not to feel pain, at the highest intensity of the stimulus could block out about 84 percent of the pain produced by ice water and 90 percent of an ischemic pain. Most but not all of the conscious pain had been eliminated.

The next question is whether the pain was recorded even if it had not been consciously detected—and if so, to what degree? Automatic writing and automatic talking revealed that about 67 percent of the ice water pain and 80 percent of the ischemic pain had been recorded by these subjects. Apparently about three-quarters of the pain registered by unhypnotized controls had been perceived, but that leaves one-quarter still unexplained. The probable answer is that hypnosis eliminated the anxiety that occurs with the conscious perception of pain, and anxiety enhances the response.

I would add that some of my patients can totally eliminate pain under natural conditions. Two experienced self-inflicted, severe third-degree burns that later necessitated skin grafts. In one case, the patient had complete amnesia, and in the other, the patient had a dim, distant awareness of the act. But in both cases, the patient experienced no pain consciously at the time. Descriptions of painless major surgery done in the nineteenth century confirm the ability of some subjects to block the sense of pain completely. I have not tried to recapture the unconscious intensity and distribution of the pain from patients, but it seems probable that the same process is operating as in the experimental situation.

There seems to be little doubt that simple sensory modalities and complex external events can be forgotten hypnotically, but the first problem is where in the memory process this occurs. Experimental studies of hypnotic amnesia have been analyzed in several review articles (59, 78, 157). These reviews have concluded that the problem is one of retrieval. The information has been experimentally introduced hypnotically, and recorded and transcribed into memory, but there is a retrieval failure. This is precisely what is seen in patients—the only difference is that the patient has long ago introduced the information self-hypnotically. That it is still hidden in memory can only be proved when it is resurrected hypnotically, which frequently occurs in therapy. But even before the precise memory is discovered, there are symptoms that suggest the presence of this hidden nexus. Only after therapy can it be shown, with less precision than in the experimental situation, that the symptoms came from these hidden repositories. Headaches vanish, voices are abolished, and depressions are lifted when therapy is successful.

## Theory

Since all evidence, both experimental and clinical, points to a retrieval failure as the cause of hypnotic amnesias, the problem is how this failure is accomplished. The probable agent is the attention mechanism, "retrieval process" being the designation given it when it calls information forth from memory. A plausible explanation is that excellent hypnotic subjects can control this attention apparatus with unusual precision. If the attention apparatus is carefully directed, it can avoid forbidden memories and keep them out of consciousness. But this is only a first approximation to a theory. The many aspects of hypnosis must be considered to refine it.

Under normal circumstances, when a person's internal focus is mobile there are thoughts, memories, and fantasies. But this inner attention is flickering and divided, with a distinct awareness of the outside world. These mental experiences under normal conditions are easily distinguished from external events and are recognized as occurring in the mind.

Hypnosis is an intensification of this inward attention. As the patient's internal focus becomes sharper, external awareness diminishes until the patient is primarily preoccupied internally, with only a faint awareness of external events. Finally, when the patient is totally absorbed internally, when his or her focus is only on these mental processes, the external world and one of its components, the body, vanish, leaving only the mind. Somewhere in this sequence, what is termed hypnosis begins. Like all traits or skills, this one also displays every gradation in the population—only a small minority can reach the extreme of nothingness. It seems likely, since this capability is so widely distributed along virtually a normal distribution curve, that hypnosis is the upper range of a general skill (128).

This internal absorption explains many hypnotic phenomena, since the primary focus in hypnosis is on memory and its derivative—fantasy. For example, the hand when directed in hypnosis to become lighter and rise does so because the patient is concentrating internally on the sensation of lightness, available in his or her memory. Similarly, an auditory hallucination, which probably takes greater concentration, also taps the memory of voices coded in memory.

Patients have repeatedly explained that frequently they are totally involved with their inner world in spontaneous deep hypnosis, so much so that the outside world is not present. However, one patient said, "When I work with you in hypnosis [and talk to you], you pull some of that concentration away and I am sometimes more aware that it is a vision. I have two awarenesses until it gets very intense and then I lose you. That event in hypnosis has such a degree of overriding importance to me, my life, and what has happened, that it concentrates almost all of my attention." Not only is there an internal focus, but its intensity is a function of its meaningfulness. Its significance for the patient plays an important role in determining the degree of his or her fixed focus. Furthermore, attention seems often to be divided in hypnosis, but whether it is only a single beam or is multiple will be left unsettled. A single beam of attention with mobility and changing diameters, if these alterations were very rapid, could create the illusion of a divided attention.

*Lack of Initiative*

One feature of heterohypnosis cited by Hilgard is the subject's passivity. This seems to be a function of the usual induction tactics, since the hypnotist requests relaxation. But in spontaneous hypnosis, we see that the subject is not necessarily passive. If the patient's spontaneous focus of attention is on relaxation or pleasant fantasies, he or she experiences a tranquil state, one that is comparable to the semisomnolence of resting animals. However, if the subject's spontaneous focus is on a terrifying experience or a horrifying fantasy, the subject will experience a state of panic which is comparable to the alerting, fearful response of animals to impending danger. The crucial consideration is where the subject's memory and fantasy attention are focused.

## The Reality of the Hypnotic Experience

In deep hypnotic states—but not the most profound, in which attention may be reduced to a single minuscule point—there are two foci of attention, a minute one on the external world, often only the hypnotist's voice, and an intense one on memory and fantasy. This intense internal focus creates for the subject a sense of realism. He or she is now in the world of hypnosis, in the world of realistic fantasies and realistic memories. As one patient told me, "Your world and my world are different." In this other world any feat that memory and imagination can contrive may be experienced, but with a sense of utter reality. Fantasy is not limited by the laws of physics, so anything, no matter how illogical it may seem to the observer, may occur in this fairy-tale domain. Scientists may term this "trance logic," "thought disorder" or "primary process," but all fail to convey the phantasmagoria permissible.

But why is neither reason nor judgment applied in this state? Apparently this intense focus on memory and fantasy makes these experiences real. Patients simply explain that these events are indistinguishable from real events. This fixed, virtually unwavering concentration of attention, now like a laser beam on the inner mind, creates a realistic illusion or delusion.

What is termed reality testing is essentially the ability to distinguish events in the outside world from events in the inner world of the mind. Both are recorded in the cortex, but ordinarily we can easily differentiate an event in the outside world from a memory or a fantasy. Excellent hypnotic subjects, when they are not under hypnosis, can do this in a normal fashion. They only experience confusion when they misidentify a spontaneous hypnotic experience as a real experience.

Under normal circumstances, all people, whether hypnotically gifted or not, have learned the distinction between reality and memory or fantasy. The ability to make this distinction may be an acquired skill, or it may be a genetic feature built into the central nervous system. In either case, when not under hypnosis, with rare exceptions that will not be considered now, everyone has this ability.

But when a subject is asked to enter a trance and find a traumatic experience, let us say one that occurred at age five, why doesn't the subject realize as he or she relives the experience that it is only a hypnotic exercise? Let us recall that at any moment only information at the focus of attention is available to consciousness. Much collateral information can ordinarily be reached with ease, but this is so because attention can flicker back and forth and rapidly retrieve information from memory. When attention is deprived of this mobility and is transfixed on a memory (a form of animal fascination), it has lost this ability. Consequently, all that a person consciously knows at that moment is what is in the forefront of the mind—in this example, the memory of an abuse—which is so realistic as to be undeniably happening now. Under these conditions of fixed attention, information about the hypnotic induction must be retrieved from memory, but the unwavering focus prevents it. Collateral information, which allows reason to operate, has been eliminated.

But even if rationality is introduced in the form of the therapist's voice or the statement "this is only hypnosis," the information doesn't significantly reverse the delusion. The overriding feature is the reality of the experience, which convinces the subject. A woman will report, for example, that a man is beating her, and the pain is terrible. She is being raped; it is happening. Her mother slaps her face, it hurts, her ears ring. There is blood all over. A gun fires, a bomb explodes. She is sitting in the lap of God.

A patient's description of this inner state may clarify its subtleties. "It is confusing when you speak [in hypnosis]. I don't quite understand what you are doing there. But when I'm in the middle of it [an old traumatic memory], you are totally blocked out. There is some divided attention when you speak, but then the experience [from the memory] is distant like watching it on a movie screen, or it may be coming in flashes or bursts. But when I'm really there, nothing else exists. Sometimes when I'm between both worlds I can't figure out which is real, you or that place. I'm not sure which way to go—where the real world is."

After hypnosis is terminated, her face still hurts where it was slapped; she feels vaginal pain from the rape. Patients see, hear, smell, and feel these experiences! Only after a return to full consciousness do they recognize that it was a memory, and even then the emotional and physical aftereffects may persist for hours. Many have told me in retrospect that these long-hidden memories just retrieved feel like the experience has just occurred.

Another feature of these lifelike experiences is their meaningfulness for patients. A confirmed atheist at peace with his or her beliefs doesn't spontaneously sit in the lap of God; patients who have this experience consciously already have faith in religion and a crying need for protection. Vivid memories in hypnosis, furthermore, are reactivations of traumatic experiences so distressing that they were long concealed. As such, they are highly important.

### Why Traumatic "Forgotten" Memories Do Not Extinguish

Memories concealed for years have been discovered, but learning theory mandates that behaviors—and memory is a facet of behavior—must be reinforced else they extinguish. In fact, these traumatic memories are repeatedly reactivated, often in nightmares, but in cryptic or disguised forms. Furthermore, chance contemporary encounters containing elements associated with the original event also frighten the person and provoke a flashback, a sudden trance, when the memory is relived only to be forgotten once again. Although there is not conscious awareness, these memories are not dormant. In a strange way, they are active and repetitive, producing symptoms. One patient led a double existence. During the day she was a competent administrator, but at night she would usually revert to her hypnotic world where childhood horrors were revisited and then forgotten. Patients with these problems have specific activators that in daily life revivify and perpetuate these occult memories, although the victim recognizes only anxiety, panic, depression, pain, or amnesia.

## Why Unconscious Memories Produce Behaviors

A further problem is how these hidden memories in the conscious, unhypnotized subject can produce behaviors, the counterpart of experimental posthypnotic suggestions. Something buried or well concealed from consciousness should be inert—or at least that is the intuitive deduction. It seems necessary to postulate some force or pressure deriving from these buried memories; otherwise, they should not produce behaviors. Freud found it imperative to postulate a dynamic "id"—which has been criticized for its hydraulic properties, reminiscent of nineteenth-century physics.

When one examines the nature of ordinary memories and normal behavior, it becomes apparent that there is a substructure of biological needs and primitive drives that profoundly influences behavior. These behavioral patterns in primitive form are organized in the limbic system of the brain, then refined in the cerebral cortex, but they do direct our eating, drinking, sexual, and agonistic behaviors in many ways unknown to consciousness. Furthermore, an amalgam of old experiences coded in memory creates habits, attitudes, prejudices, value systems, religious convictions, political certainties, and cultural beliefs that direct behavior in an infinite variety of ways, although most of these memories are unrecognized or forgotten—and therefore unconscious. In fact, many of our important behaviors are initiated and directed by these concealed engrams.

The intuitive conviction that hidden memories should be inert is contradicted by such evidence. Apparently this transformation of unconscious information into behavior is the rule of the mind rather than an exception. Information stored in the unconscious—either genetically coded or introduced by experience—will lead to behavior if internal or external events activate it. For example, an honest man doesn't steal, but he doesn't stop to consider it a prohibition or a social taboo introduced by indoctrination; nor can he recall the many early experiences that created his conviction that stealing is wrong. Similarly, a dishonest man does steal, but is usually ignorant of the early antecedent determinants of his act. Conscious behaviors have been blocked or facilitated by a repository of unconscious engrams in memory.

Hypnotically concealed memories in the conscious subject should be equally lawful, and they are. These memories do produce behaviors often classified as symptoms, since many of them are disabling, antisocial, or distressing. Furthermore, these hypnotically hidden engrams are not in some distant nook in memory where unused calculus learned thirty years ago resides. They seem to be in the forefront of memory, as evidenced by hypnotic automatic writing, hypnotic dreams, their rapid hypnotic recall by some, and the presence of their derivatives—symptoms. They appear to be "on the tip of the tongue" just out of conscious awareness, but nevertheless forgotten.

In summary, then, we can say that the "hypnotic" focus of attention can hide old information by avoiding it; can make memory and fantasy real by fixing on them; can perform many feats of hypnosis by centering on memory and fantasy; can allow subjects to forget themselves by eliminating awareness of information about themselves; and can create an unconscious whence behaviors and symptoms will emanate.

### Amnesias

At first glance when one examines the complexities of some amnesias they seem inexplicable by a simple model of focused attention. Experimentalists (59) have classified amnesias into several categories depending on the tasks presented to subjects. These include posthypnotic recall amnesia, an amnesia for the events within the hypnotic session; posthypnotic source amnesia, a retention of the material learned within the hypnotic state, but a forgetting of the fact that it was learned under hypnosis; posthypnotic amnesia for material learned with the hypnotic condition; posthypnotic partial amnesia, an amnesia for only some of the events or material; and amnesia within the trance for earlier trance experiences.

Clinical experience with spontaneous amnesias suggests that these distinctions are artificial, although they may be experimentally useful. In patients anything or everything may be excluded, depending upon the person's needs. Sometimes an entire period is expunged; at other times the amnesia is fragmented. For some, the memory is there but the emotions are hidden. And sometimes the emotions are evoked but the memory is concealed. Furthermore, the memory, either intact or fragmented, may be partially dissociated—shrouded in a dim awareness at a distance so that it is neither experienced intensely nor perceived as a personal event. Every permutation and combination may occur.

Let us analyze complicated amnesias and see whether any theoretical clarity emerges. The patient remembers the prodrome to an assault—being accosted by a man with a knife and being terrified. A few fragments of the assault itself can be recalled, but these are highly selective. The more brutal parts over a four-hour period are forgotten. The permissible parts of the memory apparently have been somehow previously identified by the victim, and only these can consciously be retrieved.

Multiple personalities are another example of complicated amnesias. The characters were created in hypnosis to be male or female, young or old, and with specific responsibilities. Some can only cry; others are specialists in suicide, larceny, anger, or happiness. Any attribute, ability, or appearance, anything imaginable can be ascribed to them, depending on the patient's needs, past experiences, and imaginative capabilities. When they are retrieved by the attention apparatus in hypnosis they contain these elements, but an infinity of other elements are excluded. A very specific but highly complicated memory, a personality, has been created that consciously cannot be retrieved, although it may be accessible in hypnosis.

But this same process occurs normally without the intrusion of an amnesia. A medical diagnosis by a physician is one example. A history of epigastric pain followed by nausea and vomiting, then right lower-quadrant pain with a low fever and moderate leucocytosis causes the doctor's attention mechanism to find in memory a differential diagnosis that includes appendicitis. This diagnostic memory is both inclusive and exclusive. It contains certain possibilities but automatically eliminates others—a brain tumor and gout, for example—because this is the way the memory was originally designed and programmed by a learning process. Certain diagnostic possibilities are remembered, others are excluded—temporarily forgotten. Memories may be complicated, but they are programmed with remarkable specificity to include designated information while excluding a plethora of other information.

Patients with functional amnesias have done the same thing. The permissible memory has been coded, but the unacceptable elements have also been registered, and these are avoided. The only difference between this process and the diagnostic process is that the physician can rapidly retrieve information about brain tumors and gout because this information in memory isn't taboo. The brain clearly has the ability to segregate information in conformity with the instructions it has received.

Retrieval, therefore, is predicated on the way information has been coded and the capabilities of the retrieval mechanism. In the case of patients, the coding has been complicated, with some information labeled as anathema. Given a finely tuned attention mechanism, the patient can now avoid forbidden information.

A further consideration is how the fully conscious subject, not under hypnosis, can avoid these unconscious memories. At these times excellent hypnotic subjects have an attention mechanism that is operating in the normal mode, that is indistinguishable from the attention mechanism of hypnotically unendowed persons. In this normal state, these virtuosos cannot perform their hypnotic feats. They have the normal flickering, unconcentrated attention with a central focus and a dim peripheral awareness. One might assume that the relaxed attention mechanism would inadvertently stumble on the concealed information and reveal it, but this doesn't happen.

The animal model is a useful point of reference. A rabbit under safe conditions may be calmly scampering. The "hypnotic" mechanism is available but is not operating. At this time it is only a potential ability. The mechanism is instantly mobilized when a danger is sensed, however. Suddenly the rabbit is tensely alert, totally fixed on the threat, prepared to run or, if trapped, to become immobile.

Excellent hypnotic patients under tranquil conditions are not usually in trances. During these quiescent periods they are out of hypnosis, unless they are requested to enter a trance or choose to do so on their own. But, like rabbits, when their peripheral attention detects a threat, they can instantaneously enter the hypnotic mode, using their potential capability, and alert to the danger can avoid it. The difference between the rabbit and the patient is that the animal alerts to an external threat while the patient alerts to an internal danger—the appearance in consciousness of the repudiated memory.

In sleep this alerting mechanism appears to be less sensitive. Now poorly responsive, it works sluggishly, and elements of concealed experiences enter dreams frequently in the form of nightmares, a common symptom in these patients. Many develop insomnia, often recognized by them as a phobia of sleep, because their dreams can be so terrifying. Furthermore, in the process of therapy, when hidden experiences are being recaptured, these nightmares often increase. During the day the patient has better control over retrieval and may avoid trouble, but in sleep the control diminishes.

## State-Dependent Learning and Resistances

There is another puzzling feature of this retrieval process. In most and perhaps all cases in which these memories have been spontaneously sequestered by hypnosis, they can only be retrieved by hypnosis. The path into the cave is the path leading out. This may be a form of state-dependent learning (266), but it has several features that are seemingly contradictory. A simple experiment illustrates one. A subject in hypnosis is given a number such as eight and is asked to forget it. She then forgets it while in hypnosis, but when she comes out of hypnosis the number is still unretrievable until she is told to remember it. At that point, in full consciousness, she does remember it. She says it was on the tip of her tongue and suddenly upon request it appeared. Apparently she was able to retrieve the number consciously; hypnosis was unnecessary. Furthermore, the assumption in state-dependent learning is that a return to the state in which the learning first occurred—a drug-induced state, for example—provides cues leading to retrieval and recall. This is like a sudden recollection of a name. The cues to the retrieval have been absent until an event with the proper associative network activates the memory. For some patients these cues in hypnosis may play a role in the hypnotic retrieval, but in many instances other factors seem to be more important.

The evidence, although imperfect, makes it unlikely that traumatic memories are so well concealed that a state of hypnosis is necessary to find cues. All evidence indicates that many are superficial despite the amnesia. But why then should hypnosis so often be mandatory to retrieve them?

In the case of the number eight, the patient consciously found it easily. I can only assume that it was innocuous, and that therefore no resistance blocked finding it once permission was given. But naturalistic amnesias involve powerful resistances; the patient unconsciously fears the buried memories. There apparently are two forces at work to promote recall when the hypnotist induces the retrieval. There is the motivation introduced by the hypnotist's demand. It is much easier to face a phobia if a powerful person is there urging and supporting the effort. In difficult cases I often discuss the problem of these confrontations with the patient to instill courage before using hypnosis. But even in hypnosis, some have to be cajoled and pushed. They may say, "There is a wall" or "There is darkness." The answer is, "Try harder, we must find it." Resistances can be formidable.

Patients indubitably show resistance and reluctance to face their phobias. Given this, the fine focus of hypnosis is a crucial element in their recall. It permits a confrontation: the patient is no longer at a long distance from the feared object, protected by a fringe detection alerting system. A line of defense has been breached. A patient explained the process: "You leave behind those conscious reservations, so you can zero in. Instead of avoiding clues, you pick up on them and know they are meaningful. When conscious you dismiss them." The fine focus of hypnosis seemingly eliminates some mental elements that facilitate avoidance. In another sense, some reservations are excluded or rendered unconscious by the hypnotic focus. The feared memory can still be avoided, to be sure, but avoidance is no longer as easy. The full intensity of the patient's attention may now reveal it.

The intense hypnotic focus facilitates the retrieval process, but it doesn't automatically force recall. If the patient is very timid or if the experience has been very traumatic, even focused attention is insufficient. Such patients must be motivated to try. Any tactic calculated to reduce their fear and to increase their will may be employed. They may perceive their buried experience only at a distance or they may cautiously nibble at it a bit at a time. In these cases progress may be discouragingly slow, because patients' resistances and fears are so intense.

### Conscious Awareness

A curious twist is the way amnesias present in multiple personality patients. From the whimsical perspective of personalities, a personality ordinarily lives in the hypnotic world but is aware of both worlds—the real and the hypnotic one, whereas the conscious patient is aware of only one world—the real world. In other words, the unconscious has full information while the conscious mind has restricted knowledge.

But both these descriptions are insufficient. It seems preferable to consider three components of the mind—consciousness, the attention mechanism, and memory. The content of consciousness is determined by what the attention mechanism focuses on. For patients with amnesias memory is intact, but it has been subdivided into the retrievable and the inaccessible. Certain memories have been concealed from the patient by a hypnotic amnesia.

When a personality assumes the body, what is essentially occurring is a shift in conscious awareness. The patient's attention is now avoiding all memories of "self" and has substituted an awareness of someone else, the personality. There is an amnesia for self-awareness; the patient becomes someone else.

The personality in consciousness may then reveal part of the hidden material, because the block to retrieval of concealed memories has been partially lifted. The patient may be consciously aware of secrets only because the "self" is absent. When the "self"—the patient—returns and assumes consciousness, this information in memory once again can be avoided, perpetuating the amnesia.

Amnesias, like the memories they hide, are often of long standing. They lie pristine as originally conceived, isolated from the patient's later experiences and so unchanged. Only when the patient focuses on them can they be retrieved, reevaluated, and altered. But the patient's preference is to let them be, unless a therapist motivates a confrontation.

### Summary of the Model of Hypnosis

The model of hypnosis in its simplest form relies on the capabilities of a finely tuned attentional focus, and the fact that only what is attended to is conscious. Intense concentration on a role, a sensation, an emotion, a personality, a fantasy, a book, or a memory makes it real. A fixed focus *partially* away from an event makes it dim, distant, and distorted (derealism, depersonalization). A total focus away from an event renders it unconscious—out of conscious awareness. In principle all hypnotic experiences, despite their apparent complexities, should be explicable by these fundamental maneuvers.

In summary, the theory of hypnosis is essentially this:

1. In the central nervous system, sensations become experiences and then memories.
2. Hypnosis is primarily a function of the reticular activating system—the attention system—directed upon the mind.
3. Excellent hypnotic subjects, when relaxed, have normal attention mechanisms. But these subjects have the potential capacity to concentrate and to mobilize this mechanism with greater precision than do most people. Therefore, hypnosis is simply the extreme of a normal capability.
4. This fixity of attention accounts for hypnotic feats.
5. Information in memory when not attended to is unconscious. When attended to, it becomes conscious.
6. An intense focus on memory or fantasy makes it real to the subject.
7. Information may be placed in memory and then may be avoided by the capabilities of this hypnotic mechanism.
8. This avoidance of traumatic memories creates an unconscious repository of memories that then produces behaviors.
9. These unconscious memories are reinforced and so persist in vivid form in the mind, but they are avoided when cues to them are peripherally detected.
10. In the conscious patient, these behaviors coming from unconscious memories will appear in a compelling form. In patients these behaviors are usually symptoms.
11. The fundamental hypnosis is spontaneous self-hypnosis, which is often induced by intolerable experiences.
12. Hypnosis, either spontaneous or induced by a hypnotist, can manipulate any function of the neocortex.
13. Therefore, any symptom or syndrome known to psychiatry may be created by this self-hypnotic mechanism. That doesn't mean that self-hypnosis is responsible for all neurotic and psychotic syndromes, but it does mean that excellent hypnotic subjects may create or simulate all.

Having summed up my theory, I must add a caveat. The brain is a neural network, a dynamic mechanism with chemical processes producing structural changes. A simple explanation of a focusing apparatus like a light beam has utility, but clearly it is a crude approximation. Unfortunately, until these more basic physical processes are deciphered, and this may be a long time hence, a simpler theory must suffice.

Theories are frequently put forward, but a worthy theory must conform to reality. It must be precise enough to be testable, and it should have predictive capabilities. One of the problems with Freud's analytic theory has been a lack of precision. It has been almost impossible to put his concepts into acceptable statements that could be tested experimentally. I have used my theory to make predictions, some of which have been tested by experimental studies. These are discussed in Chapter 5.

## Summary

A theory of hypnosis has been postulated. It is based on the ability of the reticular activating system to focus attention on the inner operations of the mind. This focus, if sharp and unwavering, can create a sense of realism. In turn, this can produce realistic fantasies and vivid memories; can deprive the mind of reality testing and produce "trance logic"; can allow "dissociations," amnesias, and the "suggested" feats of hypnosis; can produce, in its relaxed form, passivity and the loss of initiative; and may create an unconscious repository of memories.

# 4 / *The Syndrome of Multiple Personality*

In the preceding chapters the focus was on hypnosis, to give the reader an overview of its history and nature. Emphasis was placed on those features of hypnosis most important to clinical problems. An analysis of this information next led to the conclusion that the fundamental trait was spontaneous self-hypnosis, rather than a trance induced by a hypnotist. Logic seemed then to mandate that this spontaneous form, due to the versatility of hypnosis, should have the potential to create psychiatric symptoms and syndromes in hypnotically endowed people. Evidence to support this reasoning comes first from cases of multiple personality.

Multiple personality is considered first because it is probably the best example of spontaneous self-hypnosis, demonstrating the ability of hypnosis to produce a galaxy of symptoms, personalities, and irrational behaviors. It was Paracelsus in 1646 who first recorded a case of multiple personality: a woman reported that the personality pilfered her money, while she remembered nothing about it (278). Rush (229) described several possible examples in 1812, and in 1817 Mitchell (194) reported the case of Mary Reynolds under the title, "A Double Consciousness or a Duality of Person in the Same Individual." Between 1889 and 1906, cases were reported by Dana, Dessoir, Binet, Azam, Laurant, Janet, Myers, Sidis and Goodhart, and Prince. In 1944 Taylor and Martin (271) summarized these examples and several others, reviewing a total of seventy-six cases.

Sporadic cases since 1944 have been published, and more recently Greaves (111) identified fifty cases between 1970 and 1980, while Boor (22) added twenty-nine more. A complete survey of the world's literature has not been published, although a bibliography, mainly limited to articles in English, is now available (23). More cases could be found, since many earlier ones must lie undetected in the vast repository of pamphlets, articles, and books published all over Europe on hypnosis during the nineteenth century. But a rough estimate of three hundred cases may be an approximation of the number currently available in the literature.

This number suggests that cases of multiple personality are rare. This is the general belief, but it is probably incorrect. Cases are now being detected in large numbers (159, 162), and I have myself seen more than a hundred during the past five years. If my experience is reliable, these cases are relatively common, but they go unrecognized because most clinicians are not alert to the possibility. The very obvious cases, in which personalities are on parade, are uncommon, but more subtle examples are frequent. If one wishes to see bacteria, one needs a light microscope; if one wishes to see a virus, one needs an electron microscope; and if one wishes to encounter subtle cases of multiple personalities, one needs to use hypnosis.

Returning to the history of the disorder, a few of the more famous cases in the early literature deserve notation. Mary Reynolds (71, 194) had hysterical attacks. One, which occurred at age nineteen, left her blind and deaf for five or six weeks. On another occasion, she awoke without any memory for her past. She was cheerful and sociable, but did not recognize her friends and in addition had lost the ability to read and write. Five weeks later she returned to her previous condition again, dull and depressed but with no recollection for the intervening period. Both periods continued to alternate for fifteen years until she settled into the second, more pleasant, condition, where she remained for the last twenty-five years of her life. Her memories of the two states were absolutely distinct, without overlap or knowledge of the events in the other one.

In 1828, Von Feuerbach (271) described his patient Sorgel, who had two states. One person was quiet, pious, and industrious. The other person was often violent and assaultive; one time he chopped an old woodcutter to death and drank his blood. Azam (71) described a case that was often cited in the nineteenth-century literature. He first saw Felida in 1858, when she was fifteen. She was a timid, depressed adolescent with a variety of hysterical symptoms, including motor agitation, eating disturbances, pains, and insensibilities. At times, she would pass into a transitional phase of semisomnolence, and then wake up gay and active without any anxiety, pain, or other symptoms, but with a total recall for her former state. This comfortable state would last for several hours. Then she would return once again to her preceding dismal condition, but with no recollection of the preceding period. During one episode of emancipation and gaiety, Felida had sexual intercourse and became pregnant, but when she returned to her usual sickly state, she was quite unaware of her sexual transgression. As her abdomen began to swell, she consulted M. Azam about the abdominal protuberance. Some time later she returned to her physician in the other state and apologized, since she now understood her problem. During the greater part of her life these two states alternated, and it was only in her old age that the better state became dominant.

Janet (71) also had a number of cases, including Marceline, whom he first encountered in 1887, when she was twenty. She had not taken any food for several months, obstinately refusing to eat because she would vomit any food or drink that she might be forced to swallow. When Janet first saw her, so weak and emaciated that she could not stand, she had a generalized anesthesia, with diminished vision and hearing. Under hypnosis, however, Marceline would enter another state, one in which she could move, accept food, and eat without vomiting. Sensation returned to her body, and she could hear and see perfectly. During this period she had total recall for her previous state. But after she had eaten and regained weight, she would return to her former pitiful condition, with an amnesia for the asymptomatic period. Things continued much this way for fifteen years. She would come to Janet to be put to sleep, would enter her alert state, and then return home happy without symptoms, but the recovery would only last a few weeks. These cycles were repeated over the years until she died of tuberculosis.

Perhaps the most famous case in the literature was Miss Beauchamp, who was studied by Morton Prince (219) and presented in great detail in a lengthy volume. In her case, four personalities were discovered. More recently, a number of lengthy biographies of multiples have been published (23), the best known being those of Sybil (235) and Eve (273).

## Definition

It would be premature to cast the syndrome of multiple personality into a rigid form by proposing a restrictive definition, although many have been offered (13, 33, 56, 57, 111, 161). Greaves (111), for example, designated eight diagnostic signs: (1) reports of time distortion and blackouts; (2) reports of being told of behavioral episodes by others; (3) reports of notable changes by reliable observers, including the patient referring to himself by another name; (4) alter-personalities elicited through hypnosis; (5) use of the self-referent "we" as a collective in conversation; (6) discovery of writings, drawings, or other productions among his or her belongings that the patient does not recognize; (7) a history of severe headaches accompanied by blackouts, seizures, dreams, visions, or deep sleeps; and (8) hearing of voices that the patient identifies as internal and not coming from without.

The present criterion for the diagnosis of multiple personality is the DSM-III definition that it is "the existence within the individual of two or more distinct personalities, each of which is dominant at a particular time. The personality that is dominant at any particular time determines the individual's behavior. Each individual personality is complex and integrated with unique behavior patterns, and social relationships" (260).

Retracing my experiences with these cases may illustrate the variations and the complexities that any definition must encompass. The first patient, a nurse, had a personality who emerged in the presence of a supervisor. When the patient was transferred to the University Hospital under my care, I had the hunch that hypnosis might be the proper approach to her problem. Untutored but willing, I muttered a few "hypnotic" incantations, and miraculously the patient went into hypnosis. It was high drama. When I asked for the personality, at first she couldn't be found, but when I urged the patient to look harder, there was a pause with a sudden transformation. From a quiet, demure, polite and diplomatic matron, my patient changed to a gum-chewing, outspoken, no-nonsense female. The personality did apologize for causing the patient so much trouble, but her intentions were commendable. "Her back hurt her so much. Oh God, it was terrible. She refused to take any drugs for the pain, so I injected them when she wasn't there. She's stupid."

The personality had first come when the patient was six years old. "We played together when we were little. We have been best friends, played dolls, and made pies together." What about those spells of amnesia? "The worst one was for eight hours. That was after some root canal work. Oh God, how it hurt. I decided to let her rest—I would work that shift. She was so tired." On another occasion, I asked the patient to describe her husband, which she did in glowing terms. He was kind, devoted, an excellent provider, and a wonderful person. But her personality bluntly commented, "He's a bore." Personalities sometimes speak the unadorned truth.

One observation I made while treating this patient, which I did not initially appreciate, was her ability to enter a deep trance in a minute on the first trial. This is the more interesting since I was able to induce this trance as a novice with no hypnotic skills.

My next patient had a plenitude of personalities, eighteen identified and named, who would emerge spontaneously and act in different ways. When questioned, they could specify when all came into being with their functions. She had been raped by her father and brother, abused by other children, and had had a harrowing early life. In her case, the personalities were frequently on display, marching around the ward completely alert and often obnoxious. She had made many suicide attempts.She also was an excellent hypnotic subject. In desperation we called all her personalities together and mandated an integration. The necessary therapeutic work had not been done and the integration lasted only a day.

At that point, the syndrome was a tantalizing puzzle to me, one that generated many guesses but few answers. My next two cases were identified almost by accident. By that time, I had a suspicion that hypnosis was the key to the puzzle, but how it might operate was not obvious to me. The first of the two patients was a classical hysteric with a multiplicity of somatic symptoms and a long list of major surgical operations. She had never been perceived as a multiple, and no one in her family had recognized distinct characters. Nevertheless I tried hypnosis, which opened Pandora's box. Out came a host of personalities, with names and functions—at last count almost fifty.

The other patient was also a clandestine multiple. She had a past history of hysterical blindness lasting eight years, but personalities had never been recognized, perhaps because she lived alone. Nevertheless, in hypnosis eighteen personalities eventually appeared as a history of early rape, maternal brutality, and neglect emerged.

I spent many hours exploring these cases, interrogating and treating both the patients and their personalities. I was able to identify and study more cases as it became apparent that hypnosis was the key to open the door. As I worked, general principles gradually emerged. "Spontaneous self-hypnosis" appeared to be the crucial concept that penetrated the mystery and led in many unsuspected directions.


## Multiple Personality—The Controversy

Since the syndrome of multiple personality was first described, it has been a source of controversy. It has been alleged that personalities were the unsuspected creation of naive therapists or that personalities represented dramatic role playing by compliant patients bent on pleasing their physicians. As the number of reports increased, a few obvious cases were accepted as bona fide since it could be documented that the personalities antedated therapy, but the more subtle cases continued to be viewed with skepticism by critics.

There is no doubt that personalities can be readily interviewed when the patient is under hypnosis. But have these personalities really been there all along, or are they the creation of the psychiatrist? They do not seem to be an artifact of therapy (264). In some cases, there are reports that before therapy the patient had assumed another name, identity, and behavior. In most cases, personalities can identify their age, the patient's age when the personality appeared, the circumstances under which it occurred, why it was necessary, and a history of past appearances. Furthermore, auditory hallucinations in these people usually reflect the presence of personalities, because in most cases the offender can be identified easily with hypnosis. In seventy of my cases, 50 percent had auditory hallucinations before hypnosis, further evidence that the personalities predated me.

But are personalities fabricated to please the therapist because these patients are so compliant? It is a misconception that they are docile, obedient individuals. In my experience many are hardheaded, stubborn, and unsuggestible. Several respected authorities—Freud, Breuer and Janet—all came to the same conclusion about their hysterics. Furthermore, a few patients created new personalities during therapy. All were readily acknowledged as recent additions, whereas most other personalities dated their inception to much earlier periods, usually childhood or adolescence.

The cautious scientist may find such evidence unconvincing. Flamboyant acts can be used to please a therapist; patients may decide to deceive a credulous doctor. The crux of the problem is whether patients are consciously playing a role or *are* someone else. Whether these behaviors are to be judged as real or feigned ultimately depends on what is happening within the black box of the mind, and this knowledge is the privilege solely of the patient. Therefore, one must rely on the patient's honesty. I can only affirm that most of my patients have been honest about other matters, which has led me to believe their reports. I would agree, however, that if a patient's honesty is suspect, caution is necessary.

But one also observes behaviors and judges whether the actions of personalities seem genuine. Many are convincing. Should these considerations leave doubts about the authenticity of the phenomenon, one must rely on the number of similar observations made by many psychiatrists. In this regard, personalities may be compared to the auditory hallucinations that many schizophrenics report. The observer does not hear the voices, but accepts them as valid because so many schizophrenics, in many places under diverse circumstances, have claimed them. The same can be said for multiples.

However, it is also true that key figures in patients' lives—such as parents, siblings, mates, and children—can be visualized in deep hypnosis and will speak un-self-consciously. Unless it can be ascertained that they were created at an earlier date to cope with forgotten traumatic experiences or serve functions unacceptable to the patient, I have not considered them to be personalities. For example, one patient's deceased father kept speaking to her, urging that she commit suicide and join him in heaven. My verdict in that case, since I could speak with the voice, was that the father was a personality. On the fringe of the phenomenon, however, there is clearly room for dispute and differing opinion.

At times I have interviewed patients, induced hypnosis, and searched for personalities. When the patient has told me that someone was there, I have asked to speak to the individual. This often brought out someone, who then spoke. The question arises as to whether the speaker should be considered a personality. Is it necessary for the speaker to assume the body at some time to qualify for the designation of a personality? I don't think so because I have encountered such personalities but this remains a controversial question, one that hinges on one's definition of the syndrome. My conclusion, anticipating much that follows, based on my experience with diverse cases, is that the fundamental process is one of spontaneous self-hypnosis. If the individual hypnotically has concealed repugnant experiences, intolerable emotions, or unacceptable functions, and they are embodied in personalities, I consider the process one of multiple personality. But if these painful experiences and emotions, now hypnotically unconscious, are not personified, I do not classify these patients as multiple personality. The basic maneuver, however, is essentially identical—a self-hypnotic amnesia.

From one viewpoint, the controversy about the hypnotist inadvertently creating personalities is a red herring. The key consideration is whether self-hypnotic processes are partially or mainly responsible for the psychopathology exhibited by the patient. Some patients with many symptoms rapidly recover after a few sessions during which their amnestic traumas are revealed and made conscious. In these cases, if all symptoms disappear and the recovery persists, there is considerable assurance that the amnesias were the culprits. But in lengthier cases, those in which therapy may extend over many months or years, it becomes difficult to prove with scientific rigor that the return to consciousness of unconscious traumas was the essence of the therapeutic process—although both patient and therapist may have this conviction. These are some of the considerations that make these processes both fascinating and controversial.

## The Role of Self-hypnosis

There are many converging lines of evidence that support the importance of self-hypnosis as a major factor in multiple personality (13, 16, 38, 159, 264). All of the multiple personality patients with whom I have had experience are excellent hypnotic subjects. Most are capable of posthypnotic amnesia, and many can do automatic writing. Some are hypnotic virtuosos who can perform all the feats described by the nineteenth-century hypnotists. This clinical impression has been supported by formal hypnotic testing. Twenty-eight patients with multiple personality have been administered the Stanford Hypnotic Susceptibility Scale (Form C) (283). Scores on this test range from 0 to 12. The test was originally standardized on 307 Stanford University students. The mean score for this group and the standard error of the mean was $5.2 \pm 0.18$. We have studied a group of eighty-nine heavy cigarette smokers who scored $6.6 \pm 0.28$. It is difficult to know which population should be designated as a "normal" one, but in this case it has not made any statistical difference, since the patient population scored $10.1 \pm 0.36$, a remarkably high level, and one with a probability value of less than 0.001. These figures confirm the clinical impression that patients with multiple personality have unusual hypnotic abilities.

But everyone does not have this hypnotic ability, since it is a trait roughly normally distributed throughout the population (128). Presumably many people do not have sufficient hypnotic talent to create realistic personalities. In a study by London and Cooper (176), 18 percent of adults scored in the high range of 9 to 12 on the Stanford Hypnotizability Scale. In contrast, 54 percent of children attained similar scores on a comparable scale. Since multiple personality begins in childhood, these figures suggest that one-half of all children could be at risk for personalities if other predisposing factors were present.

The fact that many of my multiple personality patients entered trances rapidly when formally hypnotized, usually in a few minutes, also must be noted. This could not be attributed to the rare skills of this hypnotist nor to any unusual technique employed. Initially I was a hypnotic novice and yet I was able to perform rapid inductions regularly on the first trial. Since these hypnotic performances could not be ascribed to my abilities, and as subjects had only been asked to relax and to focus their attention—commonplace behaviors in everyday living—I was led to believe that this must be a much-practiced exercise but one that is unrecognized as hypnosis. Most of my patients claimed never to have been hypnotized, but when they were questioned about past comparable experiences, many recalled them. One patient was first hypnotized when she went to a pain clinic to be treated for severe headaches. She protested that she had never been hypnotized and doubted that she would be a good subject. A deep trance was rapidly induced and she had a strange feeling of familiarity. It later turned out in therapy that she had been spontaneously entering trances since the age of five and had undergone every variety of hypnotic experience. Many patients were questioned about past hypnosis-like episodes, and some of their typical descriptions are included in Table 9 in Chapter 2.

It is possible in many cases to obtain, without prompting, descriptions by personalities of how the patient created an alter ego, a process identifiable as akin to a hypnotic induction. Personalities, in fact, are often perceptive observers. Thus a personality said of one patient, "She creates personalities by blocking everything from her head, mentally relaxes, concentrates very hard, and wishes." Another description was, "She lies down, but can do it sitting up, concentrates very hard, clears her mind, blocks everything out and then wishes for the person, but she isn't aware of what she is doing."

On one occasion I intentionally induced a new personality, "Dr. Bliss," via hypnosis with the hope that he might be able to assist me in therapy. This was accomplished rapidly, and henceforth he could be called at will. Unfortunately, he was not helpful but instead would complain that the region was both overcrowded and unmanageable. Similar experimental inductions of personalities have been reported by Harriman (125, 126), Leavitt (169) and Kampman (152). There has been disagreement about whether these are bona fide personalities (39, 111, 159). It should be recognized that experimental personalities, like experimental amnesias, paralyses, posthypnotic suggestions, and hidden observers (130, 132), because they are artificial, do not reduplicate in every detail their clinical counterparts, but they do reduplicate the basic mechanism.

But the most persuasive evidence for spontaneous self-hypnosis comes from observing these patients in therapy. Many will drop into trances when they approach painful events. For one patient my white coat was sometimes the self-hypnotic provocateur, since it could bring back early memories of her father's sexual assaults when he played doctor and raped her. Another patient, during the process of desensitizing her to snakes—since she had been brutally assaulted with a snake—initially would disappear into hypnosis when asked to look at a picture of a snake. In her case, there was an obvious marker to identify hypnosis: her eyeballs would roll upward just before she disappeared (257).

Not only do multiple personality patients repeatedly and rapidly enter these dissociated states, but many in the process of therapy have for short periods become aphonic, blind, paralyzed, depersonalized, anesthetic, and amnestic. Most report many past hypnotic experiences of an identical nature dating back to childhood. In fact, they frequently recognize that an inordinate amount of their lives has been spent in altered states—either as personalities or in trances.

The "spontaneous" transformation of the alert patient into a personality usually occurs when the patient encounters a stress with which he or she cannot cope. The switch can be rapid, almost instantaneous, but the repetitive explanation by patient and personalities is simply that the patient "disappears" when the alter ego assumes the body.

In one case there was a more illuminating report. A patient at my behest discussed with her husband sexual problems that they had been having. Unfortunately, she became so distressed that a personality emerged who verbally flayed her husband for his clumsy sexual behavior. The patient felt that she "was being pulled into darkness." She had given her body to this personality, but a fragment of herself remained that allowed her to view the process. She explained that her state of near-oblivion was indeed hypnosis, but very deep, the next step to total darkness. Previously, under hypnosis, she had experienced this endpoint and so recognized it. Her explanation was, "In deep hypnosis you give up, are calm, totally numb, your body is relaxed and you can't move. The next and final step is you are gone—everything is black. When Lisa (a personality) takes over it is the same feeling."

Finally, there are forgotten traumatic experiences resurrected in the course of therapy. Many are identified by patients, in retrospect, as self-hypnotic concealments.

The crux of the syndrome of multiple personality seems to be the patient's unrecognized abuse of self-hypnosis. This unintentional misuse seems to be the primary mechanism of the disorder. The process begins very early in childhood, and thereafter self-hypnosis becomes the dominant mode of coping with stress. Unpleasant experiences are henceforth forgotten or delegated to a personality by the switch into a hypnotic state. It seems likely that multiples are excellent hypnotic subjects by virtue of years of unrecognized practice as well as a genetic endowment.

This syndrome is an example of Murphy's Law: "If something can go wrong, it will," or stated more scientifically, any aberration may occur in some people, from the structure of a molecule to a behavioral trait, if it is compatible with survival. In the case of multiple personality, the hypnosis system is misused to produce amnesias and alter egos. Personalities are first unwittingly created by self-hypnosis and later perpetuated by the same process. In the famous case of "Anna O," who was probably an undetected example of a multiple personality, Breuer was well aware of her self-induced "hypnoid" states (41).

## Imaginary Companions or Invisible Playmates—The Prototype of Personalities

That adults should have multiple personalities seems strange if not bizarre. When there are dozens, some benign and others malignant, one is overwhelmed by the complexity of the process. Yet there is a simple model of this process which many parents recognize—the imaginary companions of children. It may be viewed as the prototype of the adult condition, although in most cases it is benign and quite normal.

In an article by Pines (218) there is a description of children's invisible playmates or imaginary companions. A large proportion of children have them, as high as 65 percent. One three-year-old has an elf who scares away monsters. But he shares in good times too. Another child has Hubert, a mouse. Hubert hides under the table and eats food when he thinks nobody is looking. But sometimes intelligent animals, fairies, and invisible humans inhabit children's minds. Many are true companions with the virtue of being steadfast, loyal, and always available. These playmates talk a lot and they listen even more. They fill the empty space in children's lives during the times when they are alone or when playmates are not available.

But many children actually hear the voices of their friends. Jaynes reported, "At least half of the people I have talked to who have had them remember that they hallucinated the voices of their imaginary playmates" (218). In questioning my patients about early imaginary playmates, I have encountered identical reports. Patients with multiple personality often recall these early experiences as being very real, with conversations that were audible and distinct. Their imaginary playmates were every bit as real as real friends and parents.

A personality told me, "We played together when we were little. She [the patient] was five or six. She had no playmates, only a doll [Lucy was the name of the doll and was this personality's name]. She attended a Catholic school but wasn't Catholic, so the kids wouldn't play with her." But there were problems with her brother, which added a twist to the process. The personality continued, "I put ants on his crackers. Once when we crawled over a picket fence I left him caught on a spike. Her brother had a piggy bank but she [the patient] broke it and cut her thumb." The patient then interrupted, "I was so scared. My mother said, 'Wait until your father comes home, you'll get a spanking,' but someone else did it. I remember getting into my bed with my doll. I didn't want to be spanked, I wanted to disappear, just hide. When Dad came home, he didn't spank me." To which her personality retorted, "I got the spanking."

This anecdote depicts the transition from a simple realistic imaginary playmate—the realism being a characteristic of a hypnotic state—to the next step, the dissociation of self-hypnosis, which can range from a simple detachment to total amnesia. In this case there was amnesia to cope with the spanking.

Another patient created her first personality at the age of four or five. David, a male personality, told me, "I came to protect her. I'm strong. She wanted a brother—everyone else had one, but her brother, David, died. I'm the first she made. I began when she found some pictures of her brother in a casket." But the process continued, and Donnie was created when the patient was five. "She had a good friend who died, so she created me to take her place. She was happy when I was around because then she felt loved. She doesn't let me out very often but I'm here." Next came Cathie, when the patient was seven. "People hurt her, they hurt her bad. I express anger for her and if someone hits her, I hit back. She needed someone to do what she couldn't do." When the patient was ten, Denise emerged. "I want her dead. She hasn't enough guts to commit suicide for herself, but I'm going to get those pills and do it for her." At 16, Janice came. "I'm seductive and a flirt, outgoing and sexy. She tries to block out sex, but I like it. She was raped at seventeen, and Cathie and I tried to help." There was an episode of blindness. The personality, Cathie, explained. "Denise [the suicidal personality] tried to kill her. She made her heart go faster and faster and then she lost her sight." The patient added, "I was afraid that I was going to have a seizure. I'm an epileptic."

This patient, like many of these patients, frequently had auditory hallucinations. A female voice coming from a distance kept repeating "You're stupid." Such frightening voices had been present for years. Under hypnosis, Cathie blithely admitted to being the culprit, because she becomes annoyed with the patient's unwillingness to handle problems.

These excerpts illustrate the transition from benign imaginary companions of childhood to the malignant progression that these patients experience. The commonplace occurrence of having imaginary playmates would seem to be divisible into two classes. Children with limited or poor hypnotic capabilities simply play, but their companions lack realism and are easily identified as imaginary. But children with excellent hypnotic abilities have very vivid experiences with these creations. Their playmates can be seen and heard with the reality that hypnosis permits.

Many patients with multiple personality report realistic experiences with their early imaginary companions, but then noxious experiences introduce a further transformation. The personalities then are delegated to cope with rape, murder, isolation, unhappiness, and other experiences, thus depleting the individual's responsibilities. A partial or complete amnesia is introduced by another capability of hypnosis—the ability to forget. As some patients describe it, "Those memories are hidden in the back of my mind."

But all patients do not recall childhood imaginary companions. Some apparently skip this stage and immediately begin with personalities to cope with early traumas. These personalities are not playmates; they are allies who assume noxious memories and feelings and allow the child to survive.

A patient late in therapy told me about her "voices." "They began in preschool. They weren't voices, they were my friends—my family." This family lives in hypnosis, concealed from the patient by an amnesia, but endowed with any function that the imagination can contrive.

The question is how to define when imaginary companions cease to be simply that and become the syndrome of multiple personality. It is an arbitrary decision. My inclination is to separate the two at the point of partial or complete amnesia when the individual's autonomy is being compromised, but other partitions are possible.

## First Appearance of Personalities—Age of Patient

The age of the patient when the first personality appeared was determined in fourteen subjects (13). In most cases the subject was four, five, or six years old. In several other cases a personality was said to have emerged as early as three, and there have been examples as late as eight to ten, but the first appearance in early childhood has been the rule. Whether personalities can emerge for the first time in adulthood is uncertain. I have not seen a case with convincing clinical evidence for this, but in principle it should be possible.

Allison (39) reported that 45 percent of his thirty cases first had split before age five, and 85 percent before age ten. This pattern usually emerges early in childhood, setting the form for this mode of adaptation. Thus, a remarkable pattern of coping with stress is established early. The wish for someone else is magically fulfilled, but it is often accompanied by amnesia, since the experience with its unpleasant emotions may be sequestered and forgotten. For example, the patient is no longer angry at her mother, nor can she recall the terrifying experience. Henceforth, this is the alter ego's responsibility, not hers.

## The Number of Personalities

Thereafter, as the need arises, more personalities may be created, further depleting the subject's autonomy. In these patients the eventual number of personalities has ranged from two to over a hundred, corresponding to reports in the literature (162). Early investigators usually cited only a few, but larger numbers are now being detected in some patients. Kluft (163) in a series of seventy cases reported a modal range of 8 to 13.

Some patients cluster traumatic experiences around a limited number of personalities, while other patients are less parsimonious, and a few seem to cope with each new need by generating another one. Furthermore, all personalities are not ordinary people. I have been privileged to encounter a Cheshire cat who represented a patient's father leering over her bed at age seven, Jesus, Sister Mary, the Devil, ghosts, even God. Many have names, but some appear nameless. There was one personality contrived to cope with anger, suicide, and rape who remained nameless until I christened him "the voice." "The voice" would periodically emerge to affirm his mission "to kill her"—a most unpleasant character.

In fourteen cases, an analysis was made of the age of the patient when various personalities appeared. Peaks occurred at four to seven years of age and in early and late adolescence, probably corresponding to periods of enhanced conflict and stress when assistance became necessary (13).

## The Functions and Nature of Personalities

The various functions of personalities depend on the particular needs of the patient, but there is some pattern to the process. Most personalities embody painful emotions that cannot be expressed, skills that are craved, and sexuality that cannot be tolerated. Suicidal, sexual, angry, and weepy personalities are most abundant, but the possibilities are myriad (Table 14). The types have been classified in many ways (9, 13, 161). Personalities can be of different sexes or ages; have separate wardrobes; appear with diverse symptoms, handwriting, handedness, vocabularies, accents, and even language (3, 13, 56, 161).

*Table 14. Some Functions of Personalities*

| Patient's problem | Personality's task |
|---|---|
| *Memory* | |
| Wants to forget trauma | To assume memory and feelings |
| *Emotions* | |
| Fear | To be afraid or not be afraid |
| Unhappiness, depression | To be depressed or be happy |
| Fear of crying | To cry for the patient |
| Sense of shame or guilt | To assume guilt |
| Suicidal feelings | To master courage to commit suicide |
| Anger and rage | To assume rage |
| Homicidal feelings | To assume lethal impulses |
| Loneliness | To provide a playmate, a sibling |
| *Introjected parent* | |
| Brutal or rejecting parent | Is internalized to continue mistreatment or to perpetuate the same upon others |
| Unloving mother | To be a good, kind mother or a punitive mother |
| *Protector* | |
| Wants to die | To save her from suicide |
| *Skills* | |
| Feels stupid, incompetent, or untalented | To be an intellectual, singer, artist, or writer |
| Is shy and afraid of people | To be friendly, gregarious, uninhibited, and assertive |
| Feels physically weak and afraid | To be strong, pugnacious, and fight |
| Wants to escape | To run away |
| Lacks courage | To have courage and retaliate |
| *Sexuality* | |
| Is unable to cope with sex | To be sexual, promiscuous, assume sexuality |
| Needs money | To be a prostitute |
| Feels homosexual impulses | To be a homosexual |
| *Motivation* | |
| Feels incompetent or inadequate | To push subject to achieve or be an overachiever |
| *Somatic symptoms* | |
| Has multiple conversions and somatic complaints | Is asymptomatic |
| Has no symptoms | Has somatic problems |

One example is a personality who explained, "I came to help when she was raped. She needed someone to take over. I don't like sex but I can manage it—I'm a whore and a prostitute but she [the patient] is very moral and proper. I'm a tramp, just dirt and filth, but I take over the sexual part of life, which she can't tolerate." In another patient, there was a personality who announced, "I want her dead. She hasn't enough guts to commit suicide for herself, but I'm going to get those pills and do it for her."

All personalities begin as friends and allies or, if you will, invited guests. Some are amicable and pleasant, so they make the patient happy and give her confidence. But others are macabre, bent on assault, suicide, and homicide. For example, in the process of therapy, a personality named Ann, who has been carefully guarded, is released. Another personality tells me, "Ann has so much anger that she is ready to fly, hitchhike, do anything to find her mother and kill her." Fortunately, the patient is able to restrain this personality, which allows me some temporary peace of mind.

The personalities may appear only once for a single mission and thereafter remain dormant, or they may continue to function either as shadowy, unconscious influences or as a dominant force when they periodically take over the body. One personality assumed control of the body for an entire year, leaving the patient with an amnesia for that period.

There are incredible episodes. A personality (Lois) told me, "Joan [a personality] went out for a walk, Rebecca [another personality] ran into the middle of the road to commit suicide, but a policeman drove up and stopped her. So Joan took over again. When the cop tried to touch her she told him to stay away. He didn't, so she threatened to wrap his balls around his neck. Then she punched him, so he put her in handcuffs and shoved her into the patrol car. I [Lois] then took over and gave the body to [the patient], who started to cry. At the police station they telephoned Jan [a friend] who said there were eighteen different personalities. I [Lois] told the police that we were making splendid progress in therapy. When he said that I was plenty cool and composed for such a problem, I told him it was not my problem and furthermore the body didn't belong to me."

Another personality says, "I just have fun. I go out with the kids and drink beer." The patient, who has been instructed to listen, comments, "So that is the reason why I wake up drunk in the morning with terrible headaches."

The tales are endless, but there are two sides to these transformations, both preservative and destructive. A personality speaking about her mistress tells me, "She is twenty-two but she wouldn't be here now if it weren't for us." But a fellow personality estimates that the patient has been absent about two-thirds of her life. Another patient admits to losing ten hours a day. It would appear that an innocent infantile ploy has inadvertently become an adult disaster.

When they are numerous, personalities may develop a loose organization or hierarchial order. In one case, the personalities established a schedule so that all had an opportunity to assume the body and seek their recreation. Furthermore, the more aggressive or physically stronger members often intimidate the rest. But there is also some balance of power to avert disasters. One personality attempts suicide, while others abort it. The patient is nauseated and cannot eat or drink, so several personalities take command of the body to nourish it. But only good fortune saves some of these patients from disaster. When a personality drives down Main Street at eighty miles per hour while singing at the top of her lungs, she is courting death.

The personalities may be viewed from another perspective. The activation or emergence of an alter ego usually indicates that the subject experiences an intense emotion that has previously been delegated to a personality whose specialty it is—be it fear, anger, rejection, loneliness, or a sense of inadequacy. But the process of fragmentation and delegation, with an accompanying amnesia, allows these feelings to be amplified, so that even if the patient is only mildly depressed, the assignment of a suicidal personality to handle the melancholy may result in a suicide attempt. Similarly, a personality takes to the streets to solicit men, an act that the intact patient would never attempt, although she might have a passing impulse to do so. In the integrated person, many of these actions would be inhibited or counterbalanced and judgment would be applied. In these fragmented people, however, judgment and inhibition are impaired or absent.

Personalities have functions that are specific and limited. Unless further attributions are assumed, their repertoire remains static. At the time of their creation, their roles are well defined by the patient, but as time passes and with further experience, they may mature and become more complex, with new responsibilities. For example, one personality was commissioned to be bitter toward men, but later she became a leader of a women's liberation group, an automobile mechanic, and a lesbian.

When a personality assumes the body, any experiences in the real world during this period become those of the personality. The personality then has the memories and feelings generated while he or she was in control. This explains why some personalities may grow, mature, and change. A personality who never emerges into the real world will remain in nascent form precisely as first conceived, unless it is "treated" by the patient or the therapist, or more traumatic experiences are hypnotically donated to it. Furthermore, personalities are limited by their functions. They are incomplete, lacking the contrasts, contradictions, and versatility of real people. Many seem to be automatons with an unswerving dedication to a single mission. They are programmed and persistent—one thinks but does not feel, another cries but cannot laugh, a third specializes in self-mutilation.

These behaviors reflect a major rule of the hypnotic world and a general psychological maxim. Experiences and traumas if isolated cannot be processed, since they have not been integrated into the ongoing stream of consciousness. A painful experience, for example, the death of a parent, must be processed through the torment of mourning, a procedure that will eventually convert it to a memory and relegate it to a proper niche in the past. If such an experience is concealed hypnotically, it remains an irrational force, noxious and immutable.

The stubborn persistence of these hypnotic implants, in their nascent form even after the passage of decades, was an attribute that I initially found perplexing. Andrea, aged thirty-five, has a five-year-old hidden in hypnosis who has been sexually abused by her father and rejected by her mother. The little girl sits there terrified, laden with guilt and filled with rage. She personifies and encompasses all of these traumatic experiences, which were forgotten by the patient at the age of five by self-hypnosis. I am told by a personality, "There is a young, little girl, Andrea-Ellen. She is frozen . . . like in a cage . . . she can't get out and has been there for many years . . . she stands like a picture in the Bible . . . like an adulteress, and people spit on her, hit her, and call her bad names. She stands and takes it because she thinks that she deserves it."

Traumatic experiences may be relived and personalities may be reencountered if the patient spontaneously reenters hypnosis in a frame of mind that elicits this process. When Andrea overworked, she became exhausted, depressed, and felt guilty about her failure to reconcile with her mother before she died. These feelings triggered the self-hypnotic trance and transformed her into the little girl—someone whom I have seen and treated on many occasions. In this state, she strangled a cat—for the cat symbolized a ghastly experience: when she was five years old, her father threw a live cat into the furnace and promised to retrieve it alive from the flames if she would permit intercourse. For Andrea it was a choice between killing a cat or killing herself for her guilt and homicidal rage. At other times she reverted hypnotically to childhood and then severely burned herself to expiate her sins.

These early hypnotic implants are carefully guarded. Later experiences in the real world, no matter how helpful they may seem, do not alter them. Andrea has an advanced degree in psychology. She has lived for over two decades, acquiring an understanding of life, religion, and psychology. But despite all her learning, including three years of competent psychotherapy without hypnosis in another city, these implants remained hidden in her hypnotic unconscious, unmodified, as pathogenic now as they were when first conceived. Events thus relegated to the unconscious remain unaltered unless they are hypnotically recovered and reinserted into the stream of consciousness.

## The World of Personalities

To enter the domain of the personalities is simple. The key to the door is hypnosis, and these patients are excellent hypnotic subjects. During hypnosis, personalities hidden for decades can be accosted and interviewed, or forgotten memories can be encountered and relived by the subject with all the emotional intensity of a contemporary event.

But by conventional standards, the world of personalities is an illogical world. Personalities may admit to being created by the subject, but the process is unbiological and fantastic. When I ask Martha how old she is, the answer is, "I'm eleven, she [the patient] created me to be eleven." Feigning surprise, I reply, "But most children are born as babies," to which she replies without concern, "No, I wasn't. She must have had a reason. I trust her." Then I ask whether she has grown older, only to receive the answer, "No, I just stay eleven, that's a happy age."

Another patient, who is about to come to trial for conspiring to kill her husband, has a personality who is the culprit. The personality, now frightened, protests that it was only a prank. "If she goes to prison, do I have to go, too? . . . I'm not going to prison . . . she can go, but I won't. . . . I'm leaving."

Suicidal personalities are similarly stereotyped and irrational. At first I would argue with them, logically observing that if the patient died they would also perish. But the answer always came back, "That is my mission," or "Only she will die." The logic of self-preservation rarely penetrates. This illogic is the "incongruity" of deep hypnosis, or "trance logic" (207).

Magical thinking is typical of this disorder. A patient wishes for someone and—presto—a person appears as a new personality to handle the problem. Some personalities are malignant, bent on suicide or homicide, whereas others are preservative, dedicated to saving the patient. There are those without emotions, who are wonderfully insightful but devoid of feelings, and others who embody only fear, depression, or rage. Vocalization and vision are a part of the repertoire of the personalities in this domain. They are reported to converse with one another, to scream, cry, and squabble, although the observer hears nothing. They are described as babies, children, adolescents, or adults by other personalities who "see" them, but when they assume the body the appearance is that of the subject.

Amnesia is another property of this hypnotic world. A personality or an experience may be placed here and forgotten, or it may be retrieved and remembered. Under hypnosis, the patient is introduced to personalities who have been unknown to him or her for many years. If the patient elects to remember them, he or she is henceforth aware of their existence. Furthermore, this may be the prototype of "state-dependent learning" (266), for experiences forgotten with hypnosis are rediscovered in hypnosis.

The capabilities of hypnosis may be fully exploited, and every aspect of mental and emotional functioning may be perverted. All sensations can be reduced, enhanced, or distorted; movements can be inhibited or distorted; experiences can be made familiar or strange; thinking can be blocked or scrambled; memory can be inhibited; emotions can be obliterated or enhanced. Any aspect of these functions may be the focus, depending on the patient's inclinations and needs.

The barrier separating the real world from the hypnotic world is not always impervious. Ordinarily, the naive patient is not aware of the personalities, but some naive subjects experience auditory hallucinations—hear voices. One patient heard voices intermittently for years telling her, "You are no good," or shouting, "You never stand up for yourself." They later proved to be those of two personalities. Another patient kept hearing a female voice that cried, "You're stupid!" Under hypnosis, I spoke to a personality who blithely admitted that she was the culprit. Patients who hear voices may perceive them as coming from inside their head or from the surrounding environment.

This land of fairy tales is nonetheless very real. When patients enter the domain either spontaneously or in therapy, they are literally living in another world. The Devil terrifies them; suicidal personalities frighten them; homicidal personalities are hidden and imprisoned; they sit in the lap of Mother Mary for protection. A rape at age seven is relived with all the anguish, anger, and physical pain of the original event. One personality steals, another starts fires, a third solicits men as a prostitute, another slashes the patient's wrists. This is not merely a benign world of fantasy, but a vicious place where any insult is possible. A constant struggle is being waged within the patient between preservative forces and destructive powers.

## Experiences of Personalities—Fantasy or Fact?

The domain of personalities—the realm of hypnosis—is a world of fantasy. Personalities are obviously imaginative constructs. Furthermore, in this hypnotic world any conceivable feat can be realistically experienced. But when patients recall early traumatic experiences during hypnosis, are these facts, or are they fictions so easily contrived in this world of fantasy?

Freud was aware of this problem, and it was one reason for his reversal of opinion when he decided that the infantile traumas reported by his patients were fantasies rather than actual experiences. He wrote to Fliess that "there is no 'indication of reality' in the unconscious, so that it is impossible to distinguish between truth and emotionally-charged fiction" (97). Freud by that time had abandoned hypnosis, and so did not recognize that this "unconscious" was the amnesia of self-hypnosis. Nevertheless, his observation was correct, and it must be considered. But what are these hidden traumas reported by patients? Freud had encountered only sexual abuse. Janet, in contrast, found a predominance of sexual misadventures but also other kinds of unhappy experiences.

Since patients usually delegate major traumas to personalities, the records of twelve patients were examined, and fifty-three personalities were randomly selected to determine the traumas that they had assumed. Eight percent represented early "imaginary" playmates, were pleasant experiences, and had been created because the individuals were lonely. All the rest represented experiences that were intensely dysphoric. These severe traumatic experiences ranged from incest and rape (25 percent) and physical brutality (15 percent) to suicidal despair (12 percent). This evidence suggests that most personalities, at least in patients, are produced by abuse and mistreatment, usually in childhood.

Many patients have been battered children. Brutal treatment by parents, sexual molestation, and other disasters are commonly reported (13, 56, 111, 163, 288). But many of these experiences were forgotten, then resurrected in hypnotherapy and relived vividly as if they were again occurring. The question is, then, did these traumas ever happen, or are they fantasies—permissible constructs in hypnosis?

It has not been possible to establish the veracity of these experiences in all patients, but in thirteen subjects collateral evidence was available from parents, siblings, and other sources. In one case, a father was questioned, and he verified early incest. In two other cases, the patient had been told by sisters that they also had been raped by the father. In another case, the patient consciously remembered fragments of the trauma at age seven—her pain, bruises, bleeding, and vaginal infection. Unrecalled, but resurrected in therapy, was the actual rape by a vagrant. A mother confirmed her daughter's molestation in another case.

All traumas were verified as actual occurrences, with two exceptions. In one case, the hypnotic recall of amnestic early rapes represented fantasies or screen memories, since an aunt reported that the patient had a premarital vaginal examination, which the doctor stated had demonstrated an intact hymen. However, I suspect that her many alleged rapes concealed some intolerable early abuse by her father, who later was psychotic for a decade. Unfortunately, she was a therapeutic failure, and her terror precluded any hypnotic penetration to the presumed real experience. In the second case, a rape by a stranger was first revealed. But this proved to be a screen memory, a fantasy concealing the real event—a sexual assault by her father—which was even more intolerable. The evidence, at least from thirteen cases, suggests that almost all of these traumas have been actual events, hidden by a self-hypnotic amnesia.

In Freud's defense, it must be recognized that the frequency of incest

(280) was not recognized in his day, and it would have been a bold if not an unthinkable assumption to insist that so many middle-class fathers had sexually mistreated their daughters. He wrote, "There was the astonishing thing that in every case . . . blame was laid on perverse acts by fathers. . . . It was hardly credible that perverted acts against children were so general" (97). Only in the last decade have articles and books begun to appear verifying the frequency of child abuse and sexual assaults upon children.

But all of these patients have not been sexually abused, raped, or physically assaulted. One patient was never physically abused, but the psychological abuse by her mother proved to be equally devastating. "She never touched me. Never gave me a hug—just gave me the silent treatment. She threatened always to leave. No matter what you did was bad—robots could do it better. She loved the damn dog more than me—at least she would pet it. Whatever I was, wasn't good enough. Nothing ever worked. I would have preferred to have the hell beat out of me. Emotional abuse can be worse. You don't show the scars on your body, but you feel them. You want to die." Her first personality, "the kid," came early in childhood to seek love, hugging, and recognition, while the patient herself became an isolate, fearful of human closeness or affection.

There are some patients who were not mistreated; these seem to be overly "sensitive" or highly "imaginative" individuals, genetically endowed with excellent hypnotic capabilities. One was a delicate woman who felt rejected early in childhood because "my parents wanted a boy and got a girl." Later she felt disliked by playmates and classmates and so turned to imaginary companions and a fantasy world of hypnosis. A hypnotic virtuoso, she had auditory and visual hallucinations from an early age, and soon populated her imaginary realm with specters and apparitions as well as friends. Later, as she spent more time in self-hypnosis, while the real world became increasingly unrewarding and alien, her depressions intensified and a suicidal personality was introduced. The patient proved to be a partial therapeutic success; she refused to give up her hypnotic world for the real world, where she found only repeated rebuffs and displeasure.

Another patient had devoted parents, but she was lonely because younger siblings usurped her parents' attention. She was another excellent hypnotic subject, but one with a flair for the dramatic. She aspired to be an actress, but living in a drab small town thwarted this ambition. Her personalities got her into all kinds of scrapes, and headaches finally led to therapy. But meanwhile the personalities had introduced her to drugs, some seamy characters, and a disastrous marriage. Hypnotherapy cleared the headaches, abolished the personalities, and allowed her to restrict her flamboyant urges to amateur theatricals.

### Personalities Hidden and Manifest

Many patients' personalities remain undetected by clinicians and families until hypnosis uncovers teeming populations of them—in one case eighteen, in another fifty, and in a third more than a hundred. All three patients had disabling symptoms justifying a variety of diagnoses, but the existence of multiple personalities had not been suspected.

One patient had been a "closet" multiple. She had virtually a schedule for the personalities when each assumed the body. In fact, she even had separate apparel for some members of her entourage, including an adolescent and a militant feminist. One specialized in high style, another wore skirts, and a third preferred uniforms and suits. Unknown to the patient, there were boxes of clothes in the storage room. Since she was afraid of the dark, as herself she never entered that area.

After I had begun to treat this patient, I was surprised one day by her appearance as Rhoda, a personality encountered in hypnosis, but one who spent most of her time restraining several other personalities bent on homicide and suicide. Rhoda strode into my office dressed in a quasi-military outfit, smoking a cigar. In contrast to her mistress, who was a shy stutterer, Rhoda arrogantly sat down and berated me in an angry voice for being such a fool. When I replied that such an accusation might be justified, but then asked why she considered me so stupid, she loudly denounced me for considering herself and her fellow personalities to be personalities. They were all people, she said, and it was high time that I recognized it. My lame response was, "You may at least concede that there is only one body." After a few minutes, I induced her to leave, and out came the demure patient.

But some personalities may exert a subtle influence without taking over the body, like imaginary playmates during childhood. One personality, Joan, never allowed the patient to sit next to a man or stand near a man, although Joan never appeared.

The absence of confirmation by other people of manifest personalities does not eliminate the diagnosis. In some cases the switches are subtle, leading the unalert to conclude that the subject is immature, moody, or unpredictable. Moreover, the family may ignore all transformations. What happens inside a patient's mind is not always evident to casual observers.

### Personalities May Emerge and Take Over the Body While the Individual Disappears

Personalities may take over the body while the individual disappears. One patient, for example, developed a personality known as the "voice" —a nasty, malevolent individual. Initially he was created to protect the patient, as a friend and ally, but when she was brutally assaulted, he assumed the memory for almost the entire experience. After repeated panics and depressions finally demoralized her, he was assigned the additional responsibility of expressing suicidal feelings—a previous suicide had almost been successful. When "the voice" assumed the body, he assured me that the next attempt would be lethal. Meanwhile, the patient had totally disappeared. When she returned, she was puzzled and perplexed and asked what happened. She was discouraged to learn that the "voice" had returned, said that she hated those blank amnestic periods, but claimed that she has no control and simply didn't know how to prevent them.

In another patient, a punitive personality emerges in therapy to pound her head with her fists and to strike her head against the wall while the patient is "absent." I have to grab her and forcefully restrain the self-abuse. The personality—a man—keeps shouting that she is no good, a sinner. As this case suggests, therapy can be strenuous. It is often neither a feast of reason nor a tranquil tête à tête. A personality may be in command momentarily or for long periods. One personality may pursue prostitution, another may consume drugs, and a third may skillfully manage a large agency—while the patients involved are in a distant limbo or totally extinguished.

The process whereby a personality might emerge while the patient disappeared was initially puzzling. Short episodes, such as those often witnessed in therapy, seemed to be explicable by the alchemy of hypnosis, but there were histories from several patients of personalities who had control for as long as a year. That seemed too long a time for a hypnotic state to persist. Furthermore, personalities kept telling me when we discussed this question that they were not in hypnosis after they emerged and had the body. Such statements made no sense at the time, but my mistake was to underestimate the acuity of some personalities.

When the patient's normal self is replaced by a personality, the initial transformation is hypnotic, but the hypnotic transition can be very rapid. As one watches the patient, one sometimes observes a pause or a momentary blank state. The personality then appears, but now out of hypnosis. The key to the puzzle is the recognition that if hypnosis can allow such patients to forget experiences, feelings, or even their native language, why should they not be able to forget themselves? After a rapid switch, patients forget themselves—or to describe it in a slightly different way, patients go into hypnosis, disappear, and then are hidden in hypnosis like personalities, while the personalities emerge into the real world, no longer in hypnosis. If an experience can be concealed by the amnesia of hypnosis, then in principle anything in memory can be hidden, including personalities, feelings, sensations, and one's own identity. All do occur.

## The Patient's Awareness of Personalities

Every gradation of awareness of the existence of personalities can be found if enough patients are studied. A total awareness is often present with imaginary childhood companions, where there is realistic play without any need for subterfuge. The subject cavorts with his or her companion, watches, converses, and remembers. There isn't an amnesia. This is also true for some patients, since there are those who are consciously aware of their personalities. Although some investigators (57, 274) posit an amnesia for personalities as necessary for the diagnosis, this has not been my experience. Just as the therapist can introduce patients in hypnosis to personalities, so patients by themselves may stumble upon them and remember the encounter.

The next step is a detachment, a depersonalization, in which the patient is once removed, dissociated, observing a personality while dimly aware of what is happening. One patient, for example, had a personality, Sonny, whom "I knew since the age of eight. Sonny could handle anything. He could talk his way out of any situation. He helped me survive in a tough neighborhood and in the Marines. When a situation demands a 'con' all of a sudden the thought comes into my head. Okay, Sonny, what do we do now, and he goes. I have the control to activate him, but he does crazy things. Sonny once took LSD and wanted to kill people. I won't take drugs. I'm afraid to lose control." In hypnosis I spoke to Sonny, but gingerly, with respect for his assaultive tendencies. When I asked him, since he is a "con" artist, how I could be sure that the entire tale wasn't a "con" job, he smiled and said, "You can't, can you?"

Another patient, despondent and guilty on the anniversary of her mother's death, watched a personality put her arm in a fire, producing an extensive third-degree burn later requiring skin grafts. The patient had no control over the movement and felt no pain as she watched her skin char. Here two aspects of self-hypnosis were at work, dissociation and anesthesia.

Another patient has a personality, "Willow," who acts as a prostitute and makes a handsome living. When I asked the patient about surprising or unpleasant experiences in her life, she said, "People approach me and say they know me but I don't know them. Men say 'Hi, Willow, when are you going back to work?' They sometimes say shocking or insulting things which I don't want to repeat. I don't like forgetting things. There was one period of six months which I entirely lost. People tell me I'm a show-off, but that doesn't sound like me." When I asked her about sex, her reply was, "I'm scared of sex. It is sometimes painful." Have you ever read *Sybil*? "It's scary!" Do you have multiple personalities? "I think so, but I've never met them. They come out when they want."

Many similar encounters have led me to the conclusion that patients' recognition of their personalities is variable. In some cases they are known to patients, but usually they exist in a twilight zone of dim consciousness or are totally out of awareness.

## The Hidden Observer

Many personalities know information that is inaccessible to the patient, but a few personalities are remarkably omniscient. They are insightful psychiatrists without any recourse to texts. These superb allies are not always present, but those whom I have encountered have been immeasurably helpful and instructive. My first tutor was "Doneata," who had been created to be an intellectual.

Doneata described herself. "I came to live with her when she was four. Although she is only twenty-two, I believe that I'm forty years of age. I am intelligent and enjoy visiting with people of intelligence. I enjoy quiet evenings, going to places of historic interest. If I had all the time to myself, I'd live in a library. Most of all I want to help Doris [the patient]. After all, isn't that why I've stayed so long?"

When I first met Doneata my note read, "She has a beatific smile and a quiet, thoughtful manner. One would never suspect that quaking, stuttering Doris could have such a star hidden within her." But Doneata wasn't whole either, since, as she said, "all feelings belong to some of the others."

Early on, Doneata began to offer direction and advice. I would frequently ask for her suggestions in therapy. "She must be freed from the past because she has never admitted that those things really happened. One possibility is to relive those experiences. If she does, it will then not be possible for her to deny them. We certainly kept those other psychiatrists hopping."

Doneata kept supplying me with information that the patient didn't know. "What a bastard her father was. He tried to rape her for the first time when she was twelve. Before he had only masturbated her. When he was leaving the room, Rhoda [a personality] appeared for the first time, picked up a hammer and threw it at him. It just missed, but he beat the shit out of Rhoda."

When I pushed too hard for an integration, Doneata admonished me that "A one-time memory won't banish a personality because there were other experiences which have been nurtured." These included memories of the patient's father. "When she was young, she saw nothing wrong with her father when he sexually caressed her. She saw it as a gesture of love. It was only at the age of seven when her mother discovered it that she realized his behavior was wrong. Tammie Jean came then when she learned the truth, to handle the shame."

This was one of my early cases, and I was uncertain about a proper method to integrate personalities. Doneata's advice was a model of clarity. It has remained a basic principle. "The first step is to recover the memory. Next, the memory becomes more and more real. It is Oh No—No—and then me. At that point, the personalities turn up the heat. As it becomes uncomfortable for them, it becomes distressing for Doris. The next stage is acting out or losing time. If she momentarily drops her guard or turns her back, the personalities take over. Then she gets the determination and desire—admits the memory, admits and experiences the feelings and works it through, until finally there is the integration."

But there are many personalities with limited knowledge who can be informative primarily about their own histories, some personalities who initially know little or nothing about themselves, and those who know a great deal but refuse to reveal anything. The "voice" was one of those. He could have saved months of work but refused to cooperate in any way. It was necessary to wander in hypnosis searching for clues to discover what traumas the patient had experienced—then to put it together piece by piece, knowing all the time that the "voice," if he would only cooperate, could reveal all in short order.

But what does this tell us about the fundamental process? It tells us that a part of the mind in these excellent hypnotic subjects knows much if not all of these experiences, but the experiences have been split off from normal consciousness and hidden hypnotically. In another sense, it can be said that these memories are in the forefront of the mind, but not available to consciousness. Hilgard (130, 132) in his studies of hypnosis has termed this reporter the "hidden observer," and has used this capability, experimentally, to reach hypnotically concealed information.

### Personalities Represent Hidden Phobias

But why do personalities remain concealed from the patient for so long? They do because many of these fantastic constructs represent traumatic experiences, unacceptable impulses and intolerable emotions that the subject fears and would like to avoid and forget. Miraculously, patients have this ability: their hypnotic skill enables them to obliterate repugnant, frightening memories, emotions, and urges. This can be done easily, instinctively, without guilt or a sense of responsibility.

Some hidden memories are easily recalled in hypnosis because they are no longer terrifying. But many are so traumatic that they are defended and avoided indefinitely. One patient had a horrible experience with a sexual psychopath who inflicted every form of sexual torture a twisted mind could conceive. She had blocked out the sordid details but had the intuitive conviction that she could never consciously tolerate the experience. This led the patient to a firm resolution to commit suicide, and a previous attempt had almost succeeded. Since suicide seemed the only alternative, there was little choice but to tackle the problem, knowing either way courted disaster. This patient's therapy lasted several years, as we chipped away at the concealed trauma. Every detail evoked terror. Four hours of torture experienced twenty years before could only be recalled in minuscule fragments against formidable resistances.

But the complex phobias that multiples demonstrate are encumbered by an obstacle ordinarily not found in simple phobias of snakes or heights. The feared object is not easily identifiable; instead, it is internalized and hypnotically concealed, hidden by a protective amnesia. So the first task in therapy is to identify the traumatic event and to reactivate the emotions associated with it. Sometimes this requires a major task of detection, since clues may be scanty and obstacles powerful. But the task must be done if the trauma is to be returned to consciousness, where it can be processed and eventually accommodated.

## Confusion of the Real World with the Hypnotic World

Unless one works with these patients or has extensive experience with excellent hypnotic subjects, it is difficult to grasp how *real* deep hypnotic experiences can be. When a patient enters the world of hypnosis and encounters an early traumatic episode, whether it is induced by a hypnotist or it occurs spontaneously, the event can be relived with the intensity of the original event. The patient is literally there reexperiencing all.

A recurring complaint from these patients is an inability at times to distinguish between events in the real world and those in the hypnotic world. One patient exclaimed, "I feel like a Ping-Pong ball going back and forth. I know that one world is real and the other isn't, but sometimes I don't know which is which. I spoke to you last night in the hospital. But you weren't here—*or were you?* We talked for a long time about how confused and how frightened I am. You talked to the 'voice' and said that you were stronger because you were real. He said that he was stronger because he was just as real. He said, 'Watch—I'll show you'— and he put his hands on my throat and began to strangle me." In turn, I explained that I had been home with my own fantasy life.

## Personalities Are Activated by External Events in the Real World

The patient's ongoing state of mind and conscious experiences will determine whether personalities will gain control. For example, Andrea overworks, becomes exhausted, and is reprimanded by her supervisor. This causes her to panic. Unknowingly, the supervisor represents her mother, and Andrea then goes into self-hypnosis, hears her mother saying she is no good, becomes depressed, and a personality beats her, inflicting an injury.

Andrea, who is typical of these patients, has a plenitude of activators associated with past traumas, including fires, rejection, criticism, white uniforms, hospitals, physical violence, and a host of other provocateurs that can tap amnestic experiences. They are not always overwhelming, but they become so when she is enervated or depressed. At these times her abilities to cope with stress diminish, she panics, and she reverts to her primary coping tactic, self-hypnosis. Like a trapped animal, she dodges instinctively into a trance to escape.

### Special Capabilities of Personalities

Personalities, as has been noted, can assume many functions—the many that self-hypnosis permits. Their versatility is limited only by the imaginative scope of the patient and the restrictions imposed by the real world. If there is a physical injury while a personality is in control, both the patient and the personality must assume it since there is only one body, but this is a trivial restriction compared with the plenitude of options potentially available.

PHYSICAL OPTIONS   One personality is blind, or virtually so, because her field of vision is fragmented into pieces, representing an intolerable event the patient witnessed at age six when the patient's mother cut her live puppy into pieces as part of a voodoo ritual.

"Nothing," another personality, has no physical sensations, a state designed to cope with repeated sexual and physical assaults by the patient's father. But the most versatile personality is "Anna," who is a hypochondriacal disaster. Her many physical symptoms keep physicians busy and pharmacists prosperous. She has migraine, multiple pains, insomnia; complains of shortness of breath, palpitations, pain in her chest that radiates into her arms; she also suffers from dyspareunia, urinary frequency, and nocturea. It is best to stop there, because her litany of physical ailments is virtually endless. In contrast, her counterpart, "Sally," also a personality, sometimes assumes the body but is never sick and never takes pills. Sally warned me about Anna. "If she comes to your office, it is only to get pills. She thinks that she is sick, but there is nothing wrong. It is all in her head. I specialize in happiness, but Anna's thing is misery."

An unbelievable experience occurred with Doris (the patient) in therapy when she was in the throes of assuming her blind personality's experiences. Doris was now partially blind. She wobbled into my office guided by two friends, since she could barely see her way. In hypnosis, my ally, Doneata, explained. "She has hysterical blindness but it is very strange. There are images but they are shattered—broken up. Everything she sees is scrambled in some way—upside down, split or something. It amounts to Christina [the blind personality] not wanting to see." She continued, "Christina is not yet integrated but she is very close. Doris now knows her experience but she has not assumed all of the emotions so she is partly blind now."

I decided that this was a rare opportunity to record a hysterical blindness on videotape, but it would be awkward and slow to ask Doris to walk down the stairs to the audiovisual studio. I asked Doris to go into hypnosis and then suggested that Doneata walk with me instead. Out came Doneata conversing. She walked down the corridor, joyous and sprightly, with perfect vision. After we were seated in the studio, I called Doris and out she came, blind.

There have been aphonic personalities but as yet no paralyzed or deaf personality has appeared. However, in principle any sensory or motor disability could be inflicted on an alter ego.

INTELLECTUAL OPTIONS    Several personalities have been structured to be intellectual specialists—one example being Doneata. These personalities had considerable utility since they could think without experiencing emotions. When the patient was emotionally disabled—unable to think because of panic, depression, or rage—these personalities could assume control and think quietly and rationally. In effect, they were personifications of another feat of hypnosis—the ability to hide emotions.

But the converse can also occur. There was another remarkable personality, Keith, who made the patient stupid. Keith kept his master a functional illiterate. Keith told me, "When he was young, I kept him out of trouble. His Ma and Pa beat him. People teased him. The baby sitter poked him with needles, and his uncle ran over his dog." But the patient said, "Keith was afraid of people—they wanted to hurt him. Keith was very dumb, he couldn't do anything. He was uncoordinated, his brain didn't work, and he couldn't read."

Therapy in that case was brief—only two hours of hypnotherapy. I casually integrated Keith because both he and the patient were willing, not realizing that a minor miracle was in process. The next time I saw the patient, several months later, he told me, "Keith grew up and you helped make him part of me." As he was driving home after Keith had been integrated, he began to read the highway signs for the first time. "Before, I couldn't read the headline of a newspaper and could barely read a Dick and Jane book."

On his own, he had done hypnosis to treat himself and rapidly began to regain memories. He proudly said, "Anything I saw or memorized before, I would forget thirty seconds later. Now I can memorize anything. My coordination is much better. I don't feel like the same person. I am rapidly learning to read. I have just finished reading a book on geology, and I didn't have any trouble except for a few words. I was never able to do anything—now I can." Presumaby learning went on during the patient's school years, but it was hypnotically hidden and unavailable as long as Keith was present. The integration, with further hypnotic exercises on his own, cleared the block and released forgotten information, allowing him to use his native abilities.

EMOTIONAL OPTIONS     Many examples have already been given of personalities who assumed abhorrent emotions. Most often delegated to personalities are depression, suicidal despair, anger, rage, and fear. Personalities who cry for patients, are dedicated to suicide, become angry, or carry homicidal rage are common. All have been created because such feelings were forbidden, punished, immoral, or terrifying.

But there are also personalities designed to be happy. Andrea had one, a child, who gaily walked in the fields picking flowers—usually dandelions. "Julia" was a joyous child designed to compensate for despondency over neglect by her mother and abuse by her father.

IMPULSE OPTIONS     Many personalities assume sexuality for patients. For example, one personality handled all variations of sex with a patient's husband for years, without his recognition of the transformation. It was only during therapy that the personality rose up one night in wrath and announced her presence—to the husband's amazement and displeasure.

I have known at least six personalities who have worked as prostitutes. One patient in the course of therapy, during a period when we were uncovering early forgotten sexual abuse, created a new personality—a prostitute whose job it was to be sexually abused—a strategy designed to make those early sexual experiences more realistic and believable. She inserted an advertisement in the newspaper reading, "Desperate Debt! Have day job but need $500 extra cash by September. 30-year-old female, attractive, intelligent, strong, willing to consider any legitimate job." There were many male applicants!

Many personalities fight for patients. I have not examined male murderers, but it seems likely that homicidal personalities will be found in some, since indicted murder suspects with multiple personality are now being reported by the press. Homicidal personalities in females have frequently been encountered, but they usually abuse the patient and not the physician. A sense of self-preservation or cravenness has led me to avoid male patients with such characters. I examined one huge, muscular man, presumed by the staff to be schizophrenic, while he was a patient in the hospital. He rapidly entered a trance, but when a personality appeared who announced, "I want to kill," I politely said "thank you," and decided against hypnotherapy.

Larcenous personalities are not uncommon. "I take over and do the stealing. She doesn't know about me, and isn't there when the stealing happens. I tell her she is no good, and she has to prove it." Another patient, a middle-aged matron, shoplifted—but with complete amnesia. In hypnosis the reason was revealed: "They were all needs of my family, but never for myself. My husband was carrying two full-time jobs. I felt desperate because I could remember how I felt growing up—so poor, never having anything. I don't want my children to feel like that."

A few personalities have had the added function of being pyromaniacs, but fortunately none whom I have met have ignited a major con-
flagration. It does seem likely that some pyromaniacs may be multiple
personalities.

## Self-hypnotic Processes Without Personalities

Impulses, emotions, traumas, and conversion symptoms that have been
self-hypnotically concealed need not be personified. Many can be found
unaffiliated with personalities. The fundamental process is the self-
hypnotic concealment. A personality is an added fillip frequently employed presumably because animism is a human proclivity. Early human
beings attributed spirits to trees, thunder, and lightning. Their lives
were replete with mysterious spirits, deities, and powers. Frazer in *The
Golden Bough* (89) wrote much about this trait. Patients with multiple
personality follow this mode, but there are patients with comparable psychopathology devoid of personalities in whom traumas have simply been
hypnotically hidden.

In essence, the presence of personalities creates a syndrome that is
known as multiple personality, but the fundamental mechanism that
produces personalities is self-hypnosis. This mechanism of hypnosis has
remarkable versatility, and it can produce amnesias, fugue states, somnambulism, conversion symptoms, and parapsychological experiences,
to cite a few examples, but often in the absence of personalities. In turn,
many multiples have experiences that are blotted out and hypnotically
forgotten without recourse to a personality. The essential ingredient is
the use of self-hypnosis as a coping tactic in its many forms.

## Personalities and Experimental Posthypnotic Suggestions

The roles personalities fill, their missions and gyrations, at first glance
are hopelessly complicated and may seem to defy any simple explanation. To facilitate understanding, it must first be recognized that personalities operate in two spheres—one is in hypnosis, but the other is in
the real world, out of hypnosis. Ordinarily hypnosis is induced by the
therapist, and a personality is encountered while the patient is in hypnosis. The personality has been hidden, is therefore unconscious, but now
it emerges. If the patient still in hypnosis meets the personality, then at
that moment both, so to speak, are in hypnosis. But the personality spontaneously may emerge while the patient disappears. Now the patient is in
one sense unconscious while the personality has the body out of hypnosis. Personalities therefore can be present either in or out of the hypnotic
state.

Looked at from another perspective, personalities have been created
in the past by the patient during self-hypnosis. They then continue to

exist but are hidden from consciousness. Some may never appear but will periodically influence the patient's conscious behavior. Other personalities sporadically assume the body and in full consciousness perform their functions. But all personalities when they operate are partially or completely divorced from judgment, moral mandates, and other factors in memory that ordinarily would function. A small segment of the mind at these times is directing behavior, while the rest of the mind is dormant.

Two types of unconscious processes can therefore be at work, one during hypnosis and the other out of hypnosis, but in both states the patient has an amnesia or a dissociation for them. This conundrum can be best understood in terms of the simpler experimental process—the phenomenon of posthypnotic suggestion, which has been known to hypnotists since the time of Mesmer.

It may be useful to describe this paradigm once again since it is so relevant to the clinical process. The hypnotized subject is given a simple suggestion such as "You will forget my instructions, but you will go to the blackboard in five minutes and write your name." Many fine hypnotic subjects will then comply. It may look conspiratorial but it isn't. This same process works in patients, but in the guise of personalities. They have been hidden by self-hypnosis and are the counterpart of the hypnotist's simple suggestion. In both cases, the hypnotic process is terminated with an amnesia—after personalities have been programmed by the patient or the hypnotist has planted his instructions. Later, now out of hypnosis—the posthypnotic part—the experimental subject performs the act, whereas the personality assumes the body and performs its function. Neither the experimental subject nor the patient, now "replaced" by a personality, is then in a trance. Both situations operationally are identical, because in both unconscious instructions direct the behavior of the conscious mental apparatus. The experimental subject is fully conscious, but the unconscious suggestion has gained ascendency. It has acquired control and propels the subject to the requested behavior. By the same token, the unconscious programs in the patient—the personalities—have emerged, assumed control, and then acted. In both, unconscious programs direct behaviors without conscious control. The steps in this process have been tabulated to demonstrate the essential identity of the experimental paradigm and the more complex clinical process (Table 15).

A simpler process occurs when a personality does not emerge but at some point is said to direct the conscious behavior of the patient. Here there is an unconscious program at work analogous to the unconscious instructions in the experimental paradigm.

There is also a curious compulsive component to a posthypnotic suggestion. Whether the suggestion is remembered or forgotten, the subject seems compelled to perform the act, although it may be awkward or

*Table 15. The Posthypnotic Suggestion—Clinical versus Experimental Paradigm*

| Patient | Experimental subject |
|---|---|
| *In Hypnosis* | |
| 1. The patient spontaneously enters hypnosis (self-hypnosis). | 1. A hypnotist induces hypnosis in the subject (heterohypnosis). |
| 2. The patient in hypnosis creates a personality with a mission. | 2. The hypnotist gives the subject, in hypnosis, a mission—the suggestion. |
| 3. The mission of the personality is mandated by the patient's needs, emotions, and experiences. | 3. The suggestion is artificial and contrived. |
| 4. The patient wishes to forget the personality and the circumstances that made it necessary. A hypnotic amnesia ensues. | 4. The hypnotist requests a hypnotic amnesia. |
| *Hypnosis Terminated—Out of Hypnosis* | |
| 5. The patient has an amnesia for the personality and its mission. They are unconscious. | 5. The subject has an amnesia for the suggestion. It is unconscious. |
| 6. The personality persists in the unconscious for many years. The patient needs it. | 6. The suggestion persists in the unconscious for a short time. It is unnecessary. |
| 7. The personality assumes the body. The unconscious complex gains control | 7. The suggestion directs the body. The unconscious suggestion gains control. |
| 8. The patient disappears or dissociates. | 8. Conscious control is reduced or lost by the subject. |
| 9. The personality activates the body to perform a behavior. | 9. The suggestion activates the body to perform a behavior. |

embarrassing. Personalities either hidden or manifest display this same driven behavior. The frightened conscious patient suddenly bolts for the door and runs down the corridor. Only later will the culprit be discovered by hypnosis. It is a personality whose task is to protect her and make her run, although she has not been aware of the personality's presence. Conversely, a personality assumes the body and declares that she is there to commit suicide for her mistress. No argument will deter her; this is her mission and she must perform it. Later she does make a suicide attempt, after which the patient has complete amnesia for the act. Seemingly there has been a driving force, a compulsion to suicide, despite all entreaties to reason.

Such demonstrations by patients have convinced me that the experimental model of posthypnotic suggestion is neither fraudulent nor trivial. The spontaneous enactment of these behaviors in countless forms by patients is essentially identical to the performance of subjects in the laboratory. The major difference is the complexity of the clinical situation and the fact that patients introduced the hypnotic suggestions many years earlier without the guidance of a hypnotist.

The model of an experimental posthypnotic suggestion is a crucial paradigm and deserves thoughtful consideration. The hypnotist's suggestions or programs—synonymous with the patient's traumatic experiences, forbidden urges, personalities, or other mental processes—have been attended to by the experimental subject and then forgotten. Ideas have been hypnotically implanted and hypnotically forgotten. An unconscious repository has been created.

But this model demonstrates a perplexing observation. The amnestic suggestions of the hypnotist, akin to the amnestic autosuggestions of the patient, have a compelling power. They can now cause the alert, conscious individual to behave in ways that are contrary to his or her logic and judgment. Unconscious programs, hidden by hypnosis but coded in memory, will compel behavior in the now unhypnotized subject. In experimental subjects these behaviors are trivial and evanescent, but in patients they can be devastating and persistent.

It should be recognized that behaviors that are promoted by unconscious programs in the conscious patient need not only be motor acts. Replacing actions may be thoughts, emotions, or sensations. Therefore, in the conscious patient, the unconscious programs may produce "behaviors" that we designate as hallucinations, delusions, phobias, conversions, personalities, or depression. The unconscious program has created symptoms in the conscious patient.

## The Diagnosis of Multiple Personality

It has been recognized that many chronic patients refractory to conventional therapies prove to be multiples (161). Furthermore, many symptoms once thought specific for schizophrenia, for example, Schneider's primary symptoms (234, 250), are common in these patients (16, 161). At present, more females than males have been identified as multiples. Eighty-five percent of Allison's patients were female (3), and Boor (22) estimated a ratio of eight females to one male. However, it seems likely that males will be found in the antisocial criminal population (3, 5, 16, 20)—a group still untabulated.

Many patients display multiple lacerations and scars on their forearms, while unrecognized sojourns in hypnosis cause them to feel possessed or reincarnated. They have amnesias, but sometimes forget they have forgotten. They hear voices, awake in strange places, are accused of outrageous behaviors, and experience dysfunctions in movements, sensation, hearing, and vision. But these patients usually go undetected as multiples, and their disorder is misdiagnosed as schizophrenia (3, 13, 15, 111, 177, 227, 235, 272, 273), borderline state (9, 15, 53, 111, 112, 137), affective disorder (15), antisocial personality (3, 5, 20), or other personality disorders.

I have studied forty-eight females and twenty-two males who met criteria for multiple personality to determine their symptom profile and diagnostic features (16). Since the current criteria for this syndrome are those of DSM-III (260), subjects were divided into two groups. The first was composed of twenty female and twelve male adult patients who met the DSM-III requirements for multiple personality. In the second group were twenty-eight female and ten male patients who were interviewed under hypnosis but could not be studied and treated intensively to determine whether they met all the DSM-III criteria for multiples. They were tentatively identified as multiple personalities because in hypnosis "persons" could be accosted and would speak. These "persons"—possible personalities—claimed to have been there many years and identified functions and traumatic experiences that had been delegated to them, although the patient had an amnesia or partial amnesia for their presence and duties. The first group will be designated as DSM-III multiples, and the second group, temporarily, as possible multiples.

All patients completed a self-report containing 327 items, symptoms characteristic of eleven major psychiatric syndromes. Controls were twenty-four females and twenty-four males culled from a church group, nurses, technicians, and graduate students.

Excellent hypnotic subjects were defined clinically as those who entered a trance rapidly; experienced lid closure and arm with elbow elevation (131); perceived hypnotic events with realism; could regress realistically to early experiences; and usually had amnestic capabilities.

Since the estimates of hypnotizability were clinical judgments, the Stanford Hypnotic Susceptibility Scale (Form C) (283) was administered to patients to establish a more objective rating of hypnotic capabilities. Controls for the hypnotizability scale were a group of cigarette smokers, who smoked one and a half packs a day, as well as other controls (87, 283) culled from the literature.

The two groups were contrasted to determine whether the abbreviated tactic of interviewing patients in hypnosis and identifying "persons" with functions typical of "personalities" would select patients who were similar or identical in their symptom profiles to DSM-III multiples. There were *no* significant differences between the twenty females diagnosed as DSM-III multiples and twenty-eight female possible multiples on any of the syndromes, and only a single significant difference (self-reported anxiety, $p < 0.05$) among the twelve DSM-III male multiples and the ten male possible multiples. Since there were twenty-two comparisons and only one significant difference at 0.05 level, a difference that would be statistically expected by chance, it was concluded that the syndromes, the symptom complexes, reported by DSM-III multiples and the "possible" multiples were statistically indistinguishable.

The scores on the hypnotizability test were next compared for the two groups, the DSM-III multiples and the "possible" multiples. Not all patients were tested, because the psychologist who administered the test worked part-time and was often unavailable. Whenever he had the time, tests were given—a random process.

The highest score attainable on this test is 12. Controls had means of 5 or 6, whereas DSM-III multiples and possible multiples had mean scores in the superior range of about 10, which were statistically identical ($p$ = N.S.)—a further confirmation of the similarity of the two groups (14) (Table 16).

*Table 16. Hypnotizability Scores*

| Group | Number of subjects | Scores | $p$ Values[a] |
|---|---|---|---|
| DSM—III multiples | 18 | 10.0 ± 0.44 | < 0.001 |
| Possible multiples | 10 | 10.3 ± 0.65 | < 0.002 |
| Combined multiples | 28 | 10.1 ± 0.36 | < 0.001 |
| Controls—cigarette smokers | 49 | 6.6 ± 0.37 | |
| Controls (283) | 307 | 5.2 ± 0.18 | |
| Controls (87) | 17 | 5.7 ± 0.80 | |

[a] The $p$ values were determined by comparing the scores of the cigarette smokers, since they were the highest, to the scores of the multiples.

Since there were no significant differences between the two groups in either their symptom complexes or their hypnotizability, and as both demonstrated "personalities" with amnestic information and functions, they were combined for further analysis, and all were considered to be cases of multiple personality. It should be added that this only increased the size of the sample. The general conclusions that emerged from the study would be the same if only the DSM-III multiples were analyzed and the other group excluded, but a separation seemed unwarranted since the evidence supported their identity.

In Table 17 the mean percentge of symptoms acknowledged by the seventy patients is tabulated. The first observation is the large number of symptoms in all categories reported by the average patient with multiple personality. These cover the spectrum of the eleven major syndromes and indicate that the average patient is truly polysymptomatic.

The next observation comes from a comparison of female and male multiples. Females had significantly more symptoms referrable to anxiety states, hysteria, phobias, and obsessional fears, whereas males had significantly more symptoms of sociopathy and alcoholism. This is con-

Table 17. Symptoms Male Versus Female Multiples[a]

| Syndrome | Number items in category | Patients | | | Controls | | |
|---|---|---|---|---|---|---|---|
| | | Female multiples (48) | Male multiples (22) | p Values | Females (24) | Males (24) | p Values |
| Anxiety | 14 | 54 ± 4% | 43 ± 5% | < 0.05 | 6 ± 2% | 4 ± 1% | < 0.001 |
| Hysteria | 38  30 | 38 ± 2% | 28 ± 4% | < 0.02 | 3 ± 1% | 0.3 ± 0.2% | < 0.001 |
| Obsessions and compulsions | 21 | 32 ± 3% | 23 ± 4% | < 0.05 | 1 ± 1% | 2 ± 1% | < 0.001 |
| Phobias | 29 | 28 ± 2% | 18 ± 3% | < 0.01 | 5 ± 1% | 3 ± 1% | < 0.001 |
| Hypomania | 14 | 39 ± 4% | 36 ± 6% | N.S. | 2 ± 1% | 1 ± .04% | < 0.001 |
| Depression | 50 | 56 ± 3% | 49 ± 5% | N.S. | 4 ± 1% | 3 ± 1% | < 0.001 |
| Multiple personalities | 68 | 43 ± 3% | 35 ± 4% | N.S. | 2 ± 1% | 2 ± 1% | < 0.001 |
| Schizophrenia | 23 | 23 ± 2% | 28 ± 5% | N.S. | 3 ± 1% | 1 ± 0.3% | < 0.001 |
| Sociopathy | 16 | 27 ± 3% | 38 ± 5% | < 0.02 | 1 ± 0.5% | 1 ± 0.4% | < 0.001 |
| Hyperactivity | 14 | 34 ± 4% | 36 ± 6% | N.S. | 4 ± 1% | 3 ± 1% | < 0.001 |
| Alcoholism | 26 | 19% | 46% | < 0.05 | 0 | 4% | < 0.001 |

[a] The number of items in each category is listed in the second column. Under hysteria there were 38 items for females and 30 for males. The scores reflect the percentage of the total number of items in each category, with the standard error of the mean, which the average patient checked as positive.

Although there were 26 questions about alcoholism, a judgment was made in each case as to whether alcoholism was a serious or major problem—for female multiples, as an example, it was 19 percent of the cohort.

The p values in the last column were derived by comparing the female controls to the female multiples and the male controls to the male multiples. The p values for both comparisons were identical.

153

sistent with clinical observation that males when disturbed tend to act out and to abuse alcohol, whereas females are more likely to internalize and develop more somatic and anxiety-related symptoms.

Next are some of the more distinctive or prominent symptoms in the various categories (Table 18). Some that should particularly alert one to this diagnosis should be underscored. They include major conversion symptoms, particularly amnesias; depressive symptoms with multiple suicide attempts; a history of physical or sexual abuse when young; depersonalized and derealistic states; auditory hallucinations either within or outside the head; visual hallucinations; the ability spontaneously to block out pain; intractable headaches; and recurrent nightmares. There are clearly many others since the list is long, but these are some of the symptoms that should direct attention to this diagnostic possibility. The

*Table 18. Prominent Symptoms[a]*

| Symptoms | This study | | Study by Putnam et al. (222) Females (92) and males (8) |
| --- | --- | --- | --- |
| | Females (48) | Males (22) | |
| Depressions | 90% | 78% | 88% |
| Amnesias | 85 | 64 | 57 |
| Dazed states | 83 | 50 | |
| Nightmares | 83 | 59 | |
| Suicide attempts | 81 | 77 | 68 |
| Multiple phobias | 75 | 59 | |
| Anhedonia | 75 | 50 | |
| Rapid mood shifts | 71 | 68 | |
| Severe anxiety or panics | 69 | 61 | 54 |
| Sexual abuse early | 60 | 27 | 83 |
| Depersonalization | 54 | 50 | 53 |
| Derealization | 54 | 50 | |
| Auditory hallucinations | 54 | 45 | |
| Eliminate severe pain | 52 | 68 | |
| Fugue states | 52 | 50 | 55 |
| Pain problems | 50 | 48 | 46 |
| Headaches | 50 | 36 | 66 |
| Visual hallucinations | 48 | 32 | |
| Physical abuse early | 40 | 32 | 75 |
| Body anesthesia | 38 | 32 | |
| Paranoid delusions | 35 | 27 | |
| Limb paralysis | 33 | 23 | |

[a] These are some of the symptoms and their frequencies reported by multiples. Controls have not been included, but all percentages for multiples were significantly higher than those for controls. In fact, controls reported very few of these symptoms.

The values for these multiples have been compared with those for a group of 100 multiples reported by Putnam et al. (222), who collected their data via a national survey of psychiatrists.

presence of auditory hallucinations both inside and outside the head, which has been common in our experience, should be noted, since other clinicians (3, 56) have reported only internal voices and considered this a diagnostic feature.

These findings are consistent with an earlier, less complete analysis of fourteen female multiples by the author (13), and a national survey of one hundred cases (ninety-two female and eight male) by Putnam et al. (222).

Multiples vary widely in their symptomatology. Several reported as high as 70 percent of the 327 complaints and symptoms listed in the self-report, whereas two had only 14 percent. To demonstrate the wide divergence in symptomatology, fifty major symptoms were selected from the self-report—those most frequently reported and those seemingly most distinctive—to determine their frequency in this patient population. In Table 19 the distribution is enumerated, demonstrating the variations in these patients.

*Table 19. Individual Variations in 50 Major Symptoms* [a]

| Number of symptoms | Number of patients | | Controls | |
|---|---|---|---|---|
| | Female (48) | Male (22) | Female (24) | Male (24) |
| 40–50 | 2   ( 4%) | 1   ( 5%) | 0 | 0 |
| 30–39 | 11   (23%) | 3   (14%) | 0 | 0 |
| 20–29 | 24   (50%) | 10   (45%) | 0 | 0 |
| 10–19 | 9   (19%) | 7   (32%) | 0 | 0 |
| 0–9 | 2   ( 4%) | 1   ( 5%) | 24 (100%) | 24 (100%) |

[a] Fifty major symptoms were identified in the self-report, including those most frequently reported and some most significant when present. Scores for patients and controls were tabulated to demonstrate the distribution of symptoms for individual multiples and controls.

In my personal experience with more than a hundred patients whom I deemed to be multiple personalities, either those who met the DSM-III criteria or my criteria, all have been clinically excellent hypnotic subjects. A question is how reliable my clinical judgment of excellent hypnotizability has been. Before testing a variety of patients, I have made independent judgments of excellent hypnotic abilities. Of thirty-four subjects, many not multiples, who subsequently were tested, I have judged all to be excellent hypnotic subjects. Their mean score on the Stanford Scale was 9.6 ± .35, a very high score placing them in the upper 10 percent of the population—confirming the reliability of my clinical judgment.

My clinical judgment of excellent hypnotizability for the 70 multiples reported in this series is further supported by the hypnotizability scores of twenty-eight multiples who have now been tested. Their mean score of 10.1 ± 0.36 with a *p* value of < 0.001 is a confirmation of their unusual hypnotic abilities.

The *Minnesota Multiphasic Personality Inventory* was also administered to some patients. Fifteen female multiples who qualified for the DSM-III diagnosis of multiple personality have completed the MMPI test. This test was devised before there was recognition of the frequency of multiple personality. As a result, such patients were probably given many other diagnoses, and a typical profile was not defined.

*Table 20. MMPI Profile of DSM-III Female Multiples (n = 15)*[a]

| Category | Score | Score (Coons, 57) |
|---|---|---|
| L | 46 ± 1.5 | 47 |
| F | 85 ± 3.7 | 84 |
| K | 45 ± 1.6 | 50 |
| Hs | 79 ± 3.2 | 64 |
| D | 86 ± 2.9 | 76 |
| Hy | 77 ± 2.0 | 68 |
| Pd | 85 ± 2.6 | 85 |
| MF | 38 ± 4.2 | 47 |
| Pa | 83 ± 2.1 | 74 |
| Pt | 84 ± 2.7 | 79 |
| Sc | 100 ± 2.9 | 87 |
| Ma | 69 ± 3.7 | 62 |
| Si | 71 ± 2.8 | 69 |

[a] All values over 70 on the MMPI test represent scores 2 standard deviations above the mean—in the 95 percentile range or higher. In the third column, scores reported by Coons on 10 patients are listed.

A relatively consistent profile for these patients has emerged (Table 20). The average patient had marked elevations on the F (validity) scale and the Sc (schizophrenia) scale. There were also elevations on the Hs (hypochondrias), Hy (hysteria), D (depression), Pd (psychopathic deviant), Pa (paranoid), and Pt (psychasthenia) scales. These findings are consistent with observations from the self-report, which demonstrate a multiplicity of symptoms in all categories of psychopathology.

An explanation for the singularly high levels of the F and Sc scales is readily apparent if one examines the items that determine those scales. First, 13 items are common to both categories. But next, if one does a rough classification, the F scale contains a predominance of statements referable to psychotic symptoms (hallucinations, delusions, paranoid ideas), depression, family discord, sociopathy, dissociations, and other hypnotic phenomena—all commonly found in these patients. In turn, the Sc scale has many items referable to social isolation, depression, family discord, bad thoughts and urges, as well as a preponderance of items of a dissociative or hypnotic nature—again typical of these patients. Furthermore, the elevated scores on many of the other scales are consistent with the multiplicity of symptoms characteristic of these patients.

If experience with the self-report can be extrapolated to the interpretation of the MMPI scores, it seems likely that this typical MMPI profile will be suggestive but not diagnostic. There should be some multiples, those with a lesser number of symptoms, who do not show this profile, and there should be others with this profile who are not multiples. The singularly high F and Sc sores coupled with other elevations may be alerting, but they are probably not definitive. One must then use hypnosis to prove or disprove the diagnosis.

But why do these patients suffer a plethora of symptoms referable to many major psychiatric syndromes? An explanation for this may reside both in the general capabilities of deep hypnosis and in its ability to create an amnesia with an unconscious repository. Deep hypnosis permits the manipulation of any mental or emotional function with realism—to enhance, diminish, distort or eliminate these functions—and thus the symptomatic possibilities are large.

The hypnotic processes may produce devastating symptoms, but they also cause confusion and maladaptive modes of living, which contribute further to a polysymptomatic state. Furthermore, since these patients do vary widely in the number of their symptoms and where they cluster, they receive a wide variety of diagnoses, depending on which symptoms are most prominent.

## The Incidence of Multiple Personalities

To gain a more accurate estimate of the frequency of this disorder in patients—albeit a crude estimate—we did a survey of psychiatric inpatients and outpatients (21). Inpatients sequentially admitted to two acute wards of the University Hospital were asked to complete an abbreviated self-report containing 105 items. Those who reported symptoms suggestive of the syndrome were interviewed and studied. Eighty percent of the patients completed the self-report.

From the sample of fifty patients who returned the self-report, eight met the DSM-III criteria for multiples, while four others had amnesias without personalities. Six of the eight multiples were administered the Standard Hypnotic Susceptibility Scale (Form C) and their mean score with the standard error of the mean was 10.2 ± .65. If one assumes that there were no multiples in the 20 percent who failed to submit a self-report, the rate would be 13 percent. It was concluded that at least one out of every ten patients admitted to our inpatient service was a DSM-III multiple.

A colleague with extensive experience with hypnosis and multiples, who is in private practice with routine referrals from diverse sources, examined the records of his outpatients. Two series, each of fifty cases, were drawn at random from his files—a hundred cases in all. The results in the two series were statistically indistinguishable, and they were therefore consolidated. There were fifty-eight females and forty-two males. Nine were DSM-III multiples (eight females and one male). In nineteen other cases severe amnestic traumas, without personalities, were uncovered by hypnosis.

This study is limited in number and has methodological defects, but it does suggest that a significant number of psychiatric inpatients and outpatients—approximately 10 percent in these surveys—have multiple personality. Perhaps another 5 to 20 percent have hypnotic amnestic traumas, without personalities, which contribute to their disabilities.

## Coexistence of Multiple Personality with Other Pathology

Since many people are endowed with hypnotic capabilities, it would not be surprising to find some who also have a genetic predisposition to other syndromes, such as bipolar illness, schizophrenia, or anxiety neuroses. Such doubly marked individuals must exist, but their identification presents problems.

Excellent hypnotizability can be estimated clinically and measured by standardized tests, but even here there are exceptions since some people seem only to enter deep trances with drugs or during periods of intense emotional distress. But the proof of a genetic predisposition to other psychiatric disorders, especially in any single individual, is at present impossible since there are no reliable and indisputable markers for these disorders. A family history loaded with cases of severe depression or schizophrenia may be suggestive, but even here caution is necessary, because the patient may have escaped the genetic taint. Furthermore, family members would have to be examined for hypnotizability to be certain they were not multiples, since self-hypnosis can simulate so many disorders.

The fact that many multiples qualify by present criteria for such designations as borderline states, schizophrenia, or depression does not indicate that they suffer from two disorders. It simply demonstrates that our criteria are imperfect and our categories heterogeneous and arbitrary.

## Roles versus Personalities

All people have various facets to their persons. Human beings are bundles of contrasts and contradictions. At times we act like an adult, a sibling, or a child. We may be impulsive or restrained, punitive or kind, generous or penurious, dignified or vulgar, honest or devious. There is, however, an essential difference between these various aspects of our beings, which are normal roles, and personalities. In excellent hypnotic subjects these various personalities are dissociated, totally separated as autonomous components. They usually operate out of consciousness, while the person has an amnesia for their presence and activities. This contrasts with normal roles, in which there is an integration or linkage of various parts and an awareness of their presence and conduct. There is no amnesia, and the various parts are interrelated. There may be every gradation to the process, to be sure, but the extremes are easily separated by this amnestic feature, the privilege of unusual hypnotic talent. Only the hypnotically endowed can achieve these remarkable splits; by contrast, most people can have only normal conscious contrasts.

In "normal" people there are also times when emotions are partially separated from other aspects of the mental apparatus. There is "blind" rage, when anger is transcendent and thinking is virtually suspended. Judgment may be impaired during periods of depression, elation, or misery, and it is folk wisdom that no major decisions should be made during these periods. All potent emotions can monopolize attention, reducing our capacity to judge wisely or think coherently. This contrasts to the total schisms found in multiples, where extreme attentional dissociations create personalities who are entirely intellectual, depressed, happy, or angry. It is the normal process carried to the extreme of total splits.

## Precipitating Events versus the Real Traumas

These patients demonstrate another aspect of our mentality, one that is obvious to historians but is sometimes unrecognized by psychiatrists. A concentration on present events can be misleading. One cannot understand the contemporary reactions of the Russians, Arabs, Israelis, or Americans without a penetrating insight into their past. The "dead hand" of history directs present attitudes and behaviors, leading to prejudices and actions that are both unrealistic and inappropriate.

In the same way, multiples with amnestic agendas are reacting to present events in terms of their concealed traumas. Present stresses are activating concealed experiences often encountered in childhood. The primary problems are old; the present stresses are merely activators.

These multiples differ from many other patients by virtue of their amnesias, but many people incapable of amnesias have early traumas identical to those experienced by multiples. Some have been able to reconcile them, but others still harbor these grievances, albeit conscious ones like ancient vendettas still festering, and these must be attended to in therapy.

## Legal Problems

Some multiple personalities do commit crimes while they are in altered states of consciousness, and these pose legal problems. If a person commits a crime with an amnesia, or if a personality perpetrates the act while the individual is "absent," is that individual legally responsible for the crime?

The insanity defense in the American legal system is primarily based upon the M'Naughten rules (228). "To establish a defense on the ground of insanity, it must be clearly proved that, at the time of the committing of the act, the party accused was labouring under such a defect of reason, from disease of the mind, as not to know the nature and quality of the act he was doing; or if he did know it, that he did not know he was doing what was wrong."

This rule in essence places the emphasis on the defendant's lack of intellectual or cognitive understanding as the sole justification for legal insanity. Over the last hundred and fifty years, additional formulations have been adopted in certain jurisdictions. There has been the "irresistible impulse" rule and also the "product of mental illness" rule, first formulated in New Hampshire in 1869 and later by Judge David Bazelon in the District of Columbia in 1954. An alternative has been the American Law Institute test. "A person is not responsible for criminal conduct if at the time of such conduct, as a result of mental disease or defect, he lacks substantial capacity either to appreciate the criminality (wrongfulness) of his conduct or to conform his conduct to the requirements of the law."

This last code differs from M'Naughten in three respects. It introduces "appreciation" for cognitive understanding, thus adding an emotional component; there is no longer a need for total knowledge but only a "substantial" capacity; and there is the introduction of the "irresistible" impulse in the form of the defendant's ability to control his or her actions. The insanity defense in all forms rests on the fundamental premises of criminal law that punishment should be predicated on moral culpability, but also on the philosophical assumption of free will.

There is sufficient dispute about the legal rules applicable to ordinary cases in which there is a question of insanity, but the problems of multiple personality and amnesias offer complex questions that the courts have not addressed. This is due in part to the controversial nature of these problems, but also to the fact that they have been recognized only a short time.

Multiple personalities present perplexing problems that present rules don't resolve. An individual with multiple personality may commit a crime. At the time—and I have seen many examples both related and unrelated to criminality—there is compelling evidence that an amnesia existed, and therefore a lack of cognition; that it was irresistible—an irrational driven behavior forced by unconscious elements; and that it was alien—would not have been perpetrated by the conscious individual. Furthermore, the same person, when not dissociated, will have the cognitive capability to distinguish right from wrong, will not have irresistible urges, and will not commit crimes.

Present legal rules offer no simple solution to this conundrum. The courts must address this problem in the light of scientific knowledge, but doing so will involve many complex considerations. The fact that hypnosis and multiple personalities can be falsified must be recognized (211, 212). Ordinarily this is not a problem with patients, but it becomes one when a person is under indictment for a serious crime. A clever criminal bent on deception can study the literature and learn to mimic these states; this is an increasing possibility as this information becomes public and is disseminated. Orne (207) has demonstrated this by the use of simulators in experiments. When instructed to act as if hypnotized, some can mimic the state well enough to deceive experienced hypnotists.

Hypnosis is a subjective experience occurring in the privacy of the mind. A person in deep hypnosis, for example, may be visualizing a realistic person or a vivid scene. But one must rely on the person's report, since only he or she is seeing it. A criminal faking the process may claim to have these hallucinations, and if he or she has studied the literature may do this with verisimilitude. Only that person will know whether it is a valid report or a misrepresentation. Amnesias and personalities are of the same kind, and all may be simulated.

A forgotten memory retrieved by hypnosis is structurally identical to conscious memories, except that it has been unavailable to consciousness. When recovered it may be precise and accurate, distorted and unreliable, or totally falsified (211). Testimony derived from hypnosis is no better and no worse than any testimony presented in court. All recollections, be they hypnotically retrieved or otherwise recalled, must be carefully scrutinized and supported by collateral information.

These considerations create a problem for the court. The fallibility of psychiatric testimony has been well publicized. Less commonly recognized has been the subjective nature of these states and their private nature, which can make diagnoses controversial and elusive. Unfortunately, these self-hypnotic states may be common in criminals, but the setting of the legal process makes the diagnostic process incomparably more difficult.

Furthermore, there is the treacherous problem of unconscious processes. We all have behaviors directed by our genes and early experiences. In this sense we are all victims or beneficiaries of unconscious forces. The hypnotically endowed can have an additional unconscious component—the dramatic interplay of urges and personalities created by a hypnotic amnesia. If the law were to assume that faulty genes or unfortunate early experiences created behaviors beyond the control of the individual, and this may be, few criminals would be culpable; but this analysis would create legal chaos. The perplexing question is whether this special unconscious, provided by a hypnotic amnesia, is an exception—or does it fall into the more general category of unconscious processes, which the law tacitly assumes are subject to free will and conscious control.

The law is also dedicated to the protection of both society and the individual. Some criminals, irrespective of the causes of their behavior, are too dangerous to be allowed freedom. Society must be protected. To attain this goal a controversial measure may be indicated. It may be necessary first to decide on guilt or innocence; next to establish the diagnosis of a self-hypnotic state; and then to decide on the magnitude and danger of the crime. If the crime is a major affront to people and if the person is a danger to society, then incarceration in an institution with security facilities, be it penal with therapeutic capabilities or a hospital with a security section, will be necessary. Unfortunately, proper treatment will not always be available, and if it is, guarantees cannot be given that it will be successful.

This is the problem: the crime may be committed by an unconscious component of the mind, yet it may be a serious offense and pose a threat to society. The individual is not consciously culpable and his or her rights must be protected. But simultaneously such a person is dangerous, and other members of society must be protected from criminal behaviors even if they are unconsciously directed.

## Summary

The syndrome of multiple personality begins in childhood, usually as a defense against physical, sexual, or psychological abuse. The prime mechanism appears to be spontaneous self-hypnosis, which creates amnesias, an unconscious repository, personalities, and many other symptoms.

A prominent indication of the syndrome in many cases is a plethora of complaints referable to a wide variety of psychiatric syndromes. Unfortunately, most patients are not routinely queried extensively enough to identify their numerous symptoms, but a detailed self-report can serve as a useful diagnostic guide.

A superabundance of symptoms should be particularly alerting when several of the following complaints are included: periods of amnesia, severe intractable headaches and recurrent nightmares, depersonalized states, multiple suicide attempts, major conversion symptoms, hallucinations, and a history of early physical or psychological abuse and sexual assaults.

However, the simplest way to make the diagnosis is by the use of hypnosis as a diagnostic tool. Psychiatric patients with excellent hypnotic skills are suspect. In hypnosis one can search for concealed personalities, forgotten traumatic experiences, and hidden painful emotions.

If these "self-hypnotic" problems were rare, they might rank as unimportant curiosities, but this does not appear to be the case. At least 15 to 30 percent of all patients in a recent study displayed "self-hypnotic" processes that determined or influenced their symptoms (21). Furthermore, multiples receive many diagnoses, most frequently schizophrenia, borderline states, hysteria, sociopathy, or depression, and are treated accordingly.

It should also be underscored that a concentration on multiple personality is misleading. What needs to be emphasized is the central mechanism of self-hypnosis, its amnesia being the exemplar of the self-hypnotic process. It can not only hide traumas and personalities from consciousness; it can also conceal motor movements, bodily sensations, fantasies, language, vision, audition, artistic skills, odors, reading ability—any capability recorded in short- or long-term memory.

The converse is also evident. Just as a personality can assume consciousness while the individual disappears, any other process may likewise substitute for a personality and become conscious while its counterpart remains inoperative as an unconscious component. Thus, a paralysis or anesthesia may become the conscious component, while the functions of movement and sensation are unconscious.

The same reasoning may be applied to the concept of personalities. There is probably no need to ponder unduly how personalities should be classified; to be concerned because some have names or are nameless; to consider some partial and others complete; to argue about their numbers or the fact that some are identified as spirits, caretakers, or a spiritual core. The essence is a hypnotic amnesia hiding experiences, emotions, and functions. How these are subdivided and delegated is idiosyncratic, a function of the patient's tastes, imagination, and needs. But essentially an amnesia is operating in many forms—a simple process, but one capable of byzantine complexities.

Masquerading under diverse designations is this self-hypnotic population. But the problem is complicated because self-hypnosis seems to be the dominant mechanism responsible for some disorders, such as multiple personality, while it may be a subordinate process in others. In essence, hypnosis seems to be a defensive or homeostatic mechanism, one used to cope with childhood and adult stress (255). It may be used constructively for fantasy, repose, or one trial learning, but it may be subverted to produce disability or disease.

# 5 / *Psychiatric Syndromes and Symptoms*

The versatility of self-hypnosis offers a remarkable range of potential symptoms to excellent hypnotic subjects. Multiple personality disorder, with its many symptoms and its ability to simulate major psychiatric syndromes, illustrates this versatility. But do self-hypnotic processes extend beyond this domain and contribute to other psychiatric disorders? A test of this possibility, a first approximation, would be the identification of other syndromes or symptoms that necessitated excellent hypnotizability. The presumed mechanism of hypnosis should offer clues to likely candidates.

The key feature of hypnosis is the nature of the internal attention process. This attention skill allows a focus on mental processes, which isolates and makes them real. But conversely it also permits a fixed focus away from these mental elements, making them insensible or unconscious. This generalization can be studied by examining specific hypnotic feats, best documented by standardized hypnotizability tests (128, 283). For example, 92 percent of a normal population will exhibit arm lowering when the suggestion is given that the elevated arm is growing heavier and heavier. Apparently this is a simple achievement, well within the capability of most people. It involves tapping memory and focusing on heaviness, a feeling assisted by the pull of gravity. In this case, there is a minimum of suggestion operating, aided by a real physical force. But the opposite feat, imagining that the elevated arm is growing lighter so that it will rise, is a more difficult achievement. It demands a greater fixity on imagination and memory—more hypnotic ability. The subject must focus on the memory of lightness and ignore the effects of gravity to accomplish it. Evidence from hypnotizability tests indicates that more difficult feats are limited to a small segment of the adult population. Only 9 percent, for example, can hallucinate a voice or have negative visual hallucinations. (128, 283).

Based on these considerations and clinical observations spanning two centuries, I made the following assumptions. The most difficult attentional feats, possible only for excellent hypnotic subjects, should be realistic auditory hallucinations and negative visual hallucinations; extensive functional amnesias, blindness, seizures, body anesthesia, and paralyses of limbs; the ability not to feel the pain of severe traumas; and the creation of personalities who can assume command of the body. Other feats, such as depersonalization and derealization, need not be linked to such an unusual ability, since they are probably capabilities of a much larger segment of the population.

This analysis should not be misconstrued to mean that self-hypnosis must be the unique mechanism always responsible for these behaviors. Given what we now know, such an assumption would be unwarranted. Unidentified mechanisms other than excellent hypnotizability may well account for exceptions. In fact, exceptions should offer exciting possibilities for study. An example would be realistic auditory hallucinations in those chronic schizophrenics who are poor hypnotic subjects. Are they really excellent hypnotic subjects not identifiable by present procedures? Do they have biological defects in the reticular activating system? Or are there other mechanisms as yet unknown that account for the voices?

The amnestic capabilities of hypnosis suggest other potential subjects for study. Hypnotic amnesia can conceal and make traumatic experiences unconscious. In turn, these unconscious memories may produce symptoms and bizarre behaviors. Of this kind would be such behaviors as self-mutilation, some grim, senseless crimes and murders, some panic attacks, some acute psychoses, and other syndromes. If my assumptions are correct, some patients with such syndromes should be excellent hypnotic subjects. Furthermore, it should be possible to demonstrate under hypnosis that they harbor major traumas concealed from consciousness that are responsible for producing these behaviors.

Another striking characteristic of hypnosis is a fixity of attention that acts to magnify experiences. There should be patients who can focus on certain ideas, feelings, and sensations to such a degree as to make them major neurotic concerns. Some should be good hypnotic subjects, but presumably they need not be hypnotic virtuosos.

These self-hypnotic reactions, epitomized in multiples, are usually responses to severe stresses. Like their evolutionary predecessors, human beings have the options when confronted by a danger to fight, flee, or enter a trance. Since the ability to enter a trance is common, many can follow the self-hypnotic route. This option has the virtue of self-preservation, but it also may include many dysphoric experiences, such as depersonalization and derealism, which are so frightening as to intensify symptoms.

Beyond the immediate purview of psychiatric syndromes there should be excellent hypnotic subjects who have "hypnotic-like" experiences that are socially acceptable and not disabling. Examples may be normal people who have vividly hallucinated religious experiences or who report parapsychological events such as the realistic recall of previous incarnations.

A number of studies testing these assumptions have been completed, but many more are necessary to verify and extend preliminary results and refine theory. Thus far, subjects have been examined primarily for hypnotizability. The Stanford Hypnotic Susceptibility Scale (Form C) (283) has been administered to patients to establish a more objective rating of hypnotic capabilities.

## Multiple Personality

The multiple personality syndrome is probably the most extreme example of spontaneous self-hypnosis. These patients have realistic personalities, extensive amnesias, other major conversion symptoms, unconscious traumas, and a host of other self-hypnotic symptoms, including the ability of some to block severe pain. All are clinically excellent hypnotic subjects. Twenty-eight have been tested, and they scored 10.1 ± .36 on the Stanford Scale. Although self-hypnotic coping molds the form of this syndrome, the same mechanism influences other disorders; these will now be examined. In Table 21 the hypnotizability scores of patients with various syndromes which have been studied are summarized.

*Table 21. Hypnotizability Scores of Patients with a Variety of Syndromes*

| Syndrome | Number of subjects | Hypnotizability scores | $p$ Values |
|---|---|---|---|
| Vietnam syndrome (263) | 14 | 10.9 ± 0.22 | < .001 |
| Multiple personality (16) | 28 | 10.1 ± 0.36 | < .001 |
| Hysteria (Briquet's syndrome) (17) | 17 | 9.5 ± 0.49 | < .001 |
| Major conversions (17) | 18 | 9.7 ± 0.48 | < .001 |
| Anorexia nervosa (14) | 11 | 9.7 ± 0.6 | < .001 |
| Sexual offenders (20) | 33 | 8.0 ± 0.36 | < .01 |
|    Dissociations | 22 | 9.0 ± 0.27 | < .001 |
|    No dissociations | 11 | 6.2 ± 0.57 | N.S. |
| Complex phobias (87) | 17 | 8.5 + 0.5 | < .01 |
| Bulimia | 13 | 7.7 ± 0.61 | N.S. |
| Pain syndromes | 33 | 6.9 ± 0.50 | N.S. |
| Super obesity | 13 | 5.9 + .8 | N.S. |
| **Controls** | | | |
| College students (283) | 307 | 5.2 ± 0.18 | |
| Cigarette smokers (16) | 49 | 6.6 ± 0.37 | |
| Cigarette smokers (87) | 17 | 5.7 ± 0.80 | |

## Hysteria (Briquet's Syndrome)

Hysteria is one of the oldest syndromes known to medicine, dating from the ancient Egyptians and Greeks. Through the ages, the condition has been attributed to many causes and treated in many ways, in keeping with the information and preconceptions current at the time (143, 170, 277). Hippocrates and Plato identified the disorder, attributing it to a wandering uterus since it was recognized that most cases occurred in women, although occasionally men were also afflicted.

The migratory uterus theory was discarded with the advent of anatomical knowledge, but was replaced by a theory of toxic secretions originating from that organ. The conviction that hysterical women suffered from a disorder of their sexual organs caused by unsatisfied sexuality continued to be influential over the centuries. In the seventeenth century, even the great William Harvey, the discoverer of the circulation of the blood, advocated "hymeneal exercises" as a specific remedy.

As demonology gained credence during the Middle Ages and early Renaissance, authorities deemed hysterics instruments of the Devil, succubi, or victims of demonic possession. Later the disorder was attributed to vapors and humors, but with the growth of medical knowledge during the seventeenth and eighteenth centuries, some physicians came to attribute hysteria to disorders of the nerves and the brain, until it was finally perceived by a few as a condition of the mind. During this period, many theses and books were written about hysteria, and according to Diethelm (67), the term hysteria came to connote a multiplicity of physical symptoms—hypochondriasis.

A novel insight emerged with the advent of hypnosis. Although controversy was rampant, it became apparent to some that all symptoms of hysteria could be artificially induced in excellent hypnotic subjects by suggestion during trances (32). A parallelism between "artificial hysteria" (hypnosis) and hysteria was recognized, but the precise relationship between the two was not identified.

In the late nineteenth century and early twentieth centuries, a startling discovery was made. Hypnosis, when it was induced in some hysterics, could reveal forgotten early traumas that were responsible for symptoms. A new unconscious had been discovered, an unconscious which would generate psychoanalysis.

Janet in Paris first reported this process (146), but virtually simultaneously in Vienna, Breuer was treating "Anna O." and discovering the same unconscious traumas (41). In essence, Breuer claimed that Anna O. was entering "hypnoid" or "self-hypnotic" states, creating an unconscious repository that concealed her traumas, a discovery that led to his cathartic therapy. But within a few years, Freud had rejected this insight, claiming that he had never encountered a "hypnoid" hysteria (41, 94).

Freud had first published accounts of early sexual molestation in hysteria, which he claimed caused the syndrome (91, 93), but only a few years later he recanted, stating that these accounts by his patients were not real experiences, but were instead early fantasies of incest (97). Such alleged fantasies in children demanded an explanation, and this led to many theories, including the Oedipus complex. For Freud, therefore, hysteria became the result of Oedipal conflict. Janet, among others, took grave exception to this view (148). Instead, Janet attributed the dissociations—the split of consciousness from unconscious memories—to a congenital weakness of the mind (147). For him and others, a genetic defect was involved in hysteria.

More recently, a commendable effort has been made to define the syndrome of hysteria more rigorously so that it can be studied with greater precision (79, 80, 115, 117, 119, 120, 221, 291, 293, 294). To avoid unnecessary controversy, the disorder was renamed "Briquet's syndrome," a recognition of Briquet's study of hysteria, published in 1859 (42, 179). In fact, "Briquet's syndrome" appears to define and include the severe symptomatic hysterias that were described by many psychiatrists during the nineteenth century.

Despite the apparent close relationship between hysteria and hypnosis, the precise connection between the two has never been clearly defined. To clarify this problem, female patients were studied who met the criteria for Briquet's syndrome. These are not simply "hysterical" people in the lay sense, but by definition are patients with twenty-five or more specific symptoms, distributed among ten categories. Included in the sixty possible symptoms are a host of anxiety, somatic, conversion, and depressive complaints.

There were thirty-three female patients in my study who met the criteria for Briquet's syndrome. Their mean number of designated symptoms was $33 \pm 0.2$. Twenty-seven were *clinically* judged to be excellent hypnotic subjects, three were judged to be good subjects, and three were judged to be poor hypnotic subjects.

Seventeen of the thirty-three patients in this study were tested. Their mean score was $9.5 \pm 0.49$ ($P < .001$)—very high scores on the test. Fourteen subjects rated clinically as excellent hypnotic subjects scored $9.9 \pm 0.50$, whereas two judged to be good scored 8, and the one judged to be a poor hypnotic subject scored a 6. The evidence, both clinical and from tests, suggests that most female patients qualifying for the designation of Briquet's syndrome are excellent hypnotic subjects—in this study, 82 percent.

Fourteen of the thirty-three cases (42 percent) met the DSM-III criteria for multiple personality. Seven more were considered to be probable multiples (21 percent). Probable multiples were patients who were interviewed under hypnosis but could not be studied and treated intensively to determine whether they met all criteria for DSM-III multiples. They were tentatively identified as multiple personalities because in hypnosis "persons" could be accosted and would speak. These "persons" claimed to have been there many years and could identify functions and traumatic experiences that had been delegated to them, although the patient had an amnesia or partial amnesia for their presence and duties. There is evidence that the symptom complex demonstrated by patients identified in this way is statistically indistinguishable from the symptom complex of DSM-III multiples (260). It seems likely that this hypnotic procedure will identify patients with multiple personality. It was concluded that in the group of female patients with Briquet's syndrome, there was a subgroup of 42 to 63 percent who had multiple personality, depending on the criteria applied to make the diagnosis.

But all DSM-III multiples do not qualify for the designation of Briquet's syndrome. Twenty-one female DSM-III multiples have now been studied in this fashion. Of these, 76 percent qualified, but 24 percent did not have the pattern of symptoms characteristic of this diagnosis. If one limits the diagnosis of hysteria to the severe cases who are polysymptomatic—those who qualify for the designation of Briquet's syndrome—it appears that most will prove to be excellent or good hypnotic subjects, both when evaluated clinically and when given formal hypnotizability tests.

Since hysteria has defied explanation for four millennia, it may seem bold to attribute the syndrome to self-hypnotic states. The evidence for this conclusion can be briefly summarized. During the nineteenth century, the similarities between hypnosis and hysteria and the presence of early unconscious traumas were detected. Moreover, all the symptoms reported by these patients can be artificially induced by heterohypnosis (32). As a group, these patients are capable and often remarkable hypnotic subjects. Most have major conversion symptoms, personalities, and unconscious, forgotten traumatic experiences, all probably indicators of excellent hypnotizability. These observations have led me to the conclusion that the primary mechanism in many, or perhaps most cases of Briquet's syndrome (severe hysteria) is spontaneous self-hypnosis.

A tantalizing question is why there are exceptions to this rule. Patients who qualify for the diagnosis of Briquet's syndrome but are seemingly poor hypnotic subjects deserve careful scrutiny. Are they actually hypnotizable but fearful of hypnosis, or are other mechanisms operating to produce the syndrome?

## Major Conversion Symptoms

Major conversion symptoms can be found in a wide range of psychiatric, neurologic, and general medical disorders, including hysteria (79, 120). Farley, for example, studied a group of 100 postpartum females (79). Of these, 13 percent reported the conversion symptom of blindness, 12 percent of hallucinations, and 7 percent of anesthesia, all occurring at some time in the past. This was a normal population, and the findings indicate that these transient symptoms, unassociated with major psychiatric syndromes, are not rare.

Guze et al. studied incidence of conversion symptoms in 500 psychiatric clinic patients (120). A history of one or more conversions was obtained from 24 percent. Conversion symptoms were found in all diagnostic categories but were commonest in hysteria and antisocial personalities, categories that accounted for almost half the patients with multiple conversions.

Since major conversion symptoms have been a hallmark of "grand" hysteria dating back to antiquity, and as I have assumed that patients exhibiting these symptoms should have excellent hypnotic skills, I culled from my records of the past four years 60 female psychiatric patients who reported these symptoms. Fifty-five (92 percent) had amnesias, 23 (38 percent) paralyses of limbs, 23 (38 percent) body anesthesia, 14 (23 percent) functional seizures, and 10 (17 percent) a period of blindness. Thirty-seven (62 percent) had multiple conversions, which accounts for why the total of the percentages exceeds 100 percent.

In almost all of these cases—there were only a few exceptions—the conversions were short-lived and sporadic. Among the exceptions, one patient was functionally blind for eight years; another had a long-standing functional paralysis of her legs; and another had a fugue state lasting a year. All three patients were superlative hypnotic subjects.

Patients reporting these major conversions have all been *clinically* excellent hypnotic subjects, and at least twenty-five of the sixty were hypnotic virtuosos, with the hypnotic abilities possessed by only 2 to 4 percent of the general population (130, 289). Eighteen of the sixty were tested; they scored a mean of 9.7 ± 0.48 (Table 22). The limited number of tests was due to the frequent unavailability of the psychologist, but also to the fact that early cases were not tested because this procedure had not yet been initiated. It was concluded that these major conversions occur in excellent hypnotic subjects. Whether exceptions to this rule exist must be determined by future studies.

## Auditory Hallucinations and Schizophrenia

Multiple personalities not only experience hallucinations; they often report a variety of delusions. The two in combination may lead to the diagnosis of schizophrenia if the possibility of multiple personality is not considered and if there is no indication of drug or alcohol abuse, manic illness, or brain damage.

Recently, more rigorous definitions of schizophrenia have been proposed, but these have remained primarily research tools rather than clinical guides to diagnoses (7, 49, 226, 259, 260, 269). As a result, most patients with auditory hallucinations, especially when these are accompanied by delusions, are assumed to be schizophrenic and are treated with antipsychotic drugs, often for long periods of time.

Many hysterics (those patients with Briquet's syndrome) also have auditory hallucinations (42, 80, 179)—as many as 88 percent in one study (107). This is not a recent observation; Briquet (42), Janet (146, 147, 148), Breuer (41), Bernheim (11), Prince (220), and Sidis (242, 248) all cited cases of hysteria with this symptom in the late nineteenth and early twentieth centuries.

Since many multiple personalities report auditory hallucinations (50 percent in my series), and since this symptom seems to require excellent hypnotic ability when self-hypnosis causes it, a group of patients with auditory hallucinations was studied to determine how many members of the group were excellent hypnotic subjects. In my study, all patients with auditory hallucinations were sequentially identified by the personnel on the ward as they were admitted to the psychiatric inpatient service. Some patients with auditory hallucinations may have been missed, but all detected cases were then interviewed. Forty-five patients with auditory hallucinations—twenty-one males and twenty-four females—were ex amined. No attempt was made to hypnotize seven, either because they were too disturbed to cooperate or because they refused to comply. These seven were included in the cohort and defined as poor hypnotic subjects without multiple personality, to eliminate any favorable bias in the selection process.

Attempts were made to hypnotize the remaining thirty-eight subjects. Those identified as excellent hypnotic subjects with auditory hallucinations entered a trance rapidly, experienced hypnotic events with realism, and usually had amnestic capabilities. In hypnosis the "voices" could be contacted, engaged in conversation, and would readily admit to being responsible for the patient's problem. Voices included those bent on suicide and homicide, an assortment of friends and foes, and even the Devil. Since the "voices" spoke and acted like personalities, and as patients identified in this way are symptomatically indistinguishable from DSM-III multiples, it was concluded that the "voices" were personalities speaking.

It must be emphasized that the patients in this study were probably not typical of chronic populations found in state hospitals and VA hospitals, where regressed "process" schizophrenics with hallucinations are common. The psychiatric unit from which these patients were culled is an acute therapeutic facility of twenty-eight beds. Fifty-four percent of the cases admitted in 1980 were private, usually indicating some form of insurance, and 45 percent came from mental health clinics. Whether this population and the results obtained are typical of most acute psychiatric units can only be determined by further studies.

Sixty percent of the forty-five patients with auditory hallucinations were identified clinically as excellent hypnotic subjects with personalities responsible for the "voices." In 24 percent of the cases, either hypnosis could not be induced or personalities and amnestic traumas could not be found; another 16 percent for various reasons could not be examined.

It was concluded that at least 60 percent of the subjects experienced auditory hallucinations based on the presence of personalities, whereas 40 percent had hallucinations possibly based on other mechanisms. Of this 60 percent who were positive for personalities, twenty-seven patients in all, twelve were males and fifteen were females.

Charts and past records were examined to determine the diagnoses that had been applied to the forty-five patients by staff psychiatrists, residents, or referring psychiatrists who had previously treated them. Many patients had received several diagnoses in the course of their illnesses, but most had been considered to have some form of schizophrenia or an affective disorder. Patients with multiple personality had been given eleven different diagnoses in the past or during the present hospitalization (Table 22).

*Table 22. Clinical Diagnoses Applied to 45 Patients with Auditory Hallucinations*[a]

| Diagnoses | Number of diagnoses in each category | Number positive for "personalities" | Number negative for "personalities" or not examined |
|---|---|---|---|
| Schizophrenia | 31 | 20 | 11 |
| Schizoaffective disorder | 10 | 7 | 3 |
| Borderline state | 4 | 4 | 0 |
| Manic-depressive illness | 5 | 4 | 1 |
| Drug addiction | 8 | 3 | 5 |
| Alcoholism | 3 | 2 | 1 |
| Depression | 3 | 2 | 1 |
| Hysteria | 2 | 2 | 0 |
| Sociopathy | 5 | 5 | 0 |
| Pain syndrome | 1 | 1 | 0 |
| Paranoia, cerebral atrophy | 1 | 0 | 1 |
| Anxiety neurosis | 1 | 1 | 0 |

[a] The number of diagnoses exceeded the number of subjects because some patients received more than one diagnosis over the course of their illness.

Thirty-five of the forty-five patients with auditory hallucinations, 78 percent of the sample, had received the diagnosis of a schizophrenic disorder at some time. In this subgroup of thirty-five patients, fifteen were males and twenty were females. Twenty of the thirty-five were identified as multiple personality. Included in the twenty were thirteen previously judged by their psychiatrists to be delusional, eleven who were considered to be paranoid, and six who were deemed thought-disordered. Many of these twenty were chronic patients, and practically all had been or were being treated with phenothiazines, some for extended periods.

Patients considered to be multiples with auditory hallucinations were all judged clinically to be excellent hypnotic subjects. Six were tested. Their mean score was 9.17 ± 0.98—a significant elevation—and a further confirmation of the hypnotic capabilities of this subgroup.

The mental mechanisms responsible for auditory hallucinations remain uncertain (139, 155). Only one explanation at present can be both experimentally and clinically verified, and that is hypnosis (32, 130, 155). Many excellent hypnotic subjects in a trance, either induced by a hypnotist or spontaneously engendered, can hear with realism various sounds or voices, just as they can visualize with realism people or places, feel or not feel various sensations, or experience various smells or tastes. These voices and delusions may then operate even when the person is in an alert state (13). Furthermore, the voices may be experienced as either inside or outside the head.

Ten of the patients in this study were treated with hypnotherapy. Multiple personality was reconfirmed in the ten cases, and none had a thought disorder except during acute phases when there were reversions to spontaneous hypnotic states. Although the majority of this treated group had received a diagnosis of schizophrenia in some form, in no case did this seem to be justified retrospectively. All patients identified as "self-hypnotic" with multiple personalities were rational and intellectually intact during calm periods. None displayed the gross intellectual fragmentation and disorganization commonly observed in deteriorated, chronic schizophrenics. From analysis of their records, at least seven of the "self-hypnotic schizophrenics" would probably have qualified for the DSM-III diagnosis of schizophrenia.

Whatever the percentage of such cases may be, the inference seems warranted that many patients with auditory hallucinations have self-hypnotic psychopathology. Furthermore, many multiples with hallucinations and delusions continue to be misdiagnosed as schizophrenic. Rosenbaum (227) has reached the same conclusion. Some of these cases may correspond to the earlier classification of hysterical psychoses (135, 252). A relevant comment appears in a text on psychiatric diagnosis by Woodruff, Goodwin, and Guze (294). They state that a number of patients with schizophrenia met the diagnostic criteria for hysteria, but those patients were considered to be schizophrenic because of prominent delusions. Presumably these were unidentified multiples.

This poses the question of the hypnotizability of schizophrenics and the relationship of hypnosis to this syndrome. Although it is generally assumed that schizophrenics are poor hypnotic subjects, a survey of the literature does not support this sweeping generalization. Conclusions drawn from many studies have ranged from the assertion that psychotics are not hypnotizable to the observation that schizophrenics are as hypnotizable as normal subjects. A critical and scholarly review of this literature, both old and recent, has been done by Lavoie and Sabourin (167). The evidence indicates that acute or partially compensated schizophrenics who are living in the community except for temporary periods spent in hospitals tend to be better hypnotic subjects than chronic schizophrenics residing in state hospitals. Hypnotic susceptibility scores of schizophrenics who volunteer to be tested have consistently been higher than those of "coerced" schizophrenics, and highly susceptible schizophrenics have generally been found among female patients from acute treatment units. Lavoie and Sabourin concluded that recent data favored the hypothesis of normal hypnotizability in some samples of schizophrenics when the relevant variables of age, chronicity, type of volunteering, and sex are properly controlled. The relationship between hypnosis and schizophrenia still remains an unresolved but important problem.

In this connection, it should be recognized that the patients in this study—those given the diagnosis of schizophrenia by clinicians—were in an acute unit, were ordinarily living in the community, and were diagnosed as schizophrenics primarily because they acknowledged hallucinations and delusions.

We concluded that auditory hallucinations and delusions, when they occur in intellectually intact patients who are not flagrantly thought disordered, should suggest the possibility of self-hypnosis with personalities. But the findings also indicate that poor hypnotic subjects can have auditory hallucinations, since many chronic schizophrenics who hear voices seemingly cannot be hypnotized and score low on tests. This implies that either other mechanisms are producing these hallucinations or self-hypnosis is operating but is undetectable by present techniques.

This study does not explain schizophrenia, but it may add another piece to the puzzle. It has become increasingly apparent that what we call schizophrenia is actually a number of different disorders. There is powerful evidence for a genetic contribution in many, verified by family, twin, and adoption studies, although the nature of this genetic vulnerability is unknown. There is also a subgroup of patients with dilated ventricles and cerebral atrophy. Some schizophrenics respond favorably to antipsychotic drugs, which presumably act on dopamine receptors, but many others do not respond. There is also this group with self-hypnotic mechanisms, patients who often fit the diagnostic criteria but are not schizophrenic.

There are other observations that are puzzling but possibly important. Chapman (51) studied a group of early schizophrenics who later became chronic patients. They had many symptoms referable to all areas of the cerebral cortex. These included déjà vu experiences and feelings of unreality; visual disturbances, such as macropsia and micropsia, blurring, fragmentation, no depth, alterations in color and brightness; motor disturbances, including a loss of control of movements, immobility, "legs walk by themselves"; speech distortions, such as inserting the wrong word and a failure to comprehend the speech of others; thinking impairment, including stoppage of thought, blank spells, dazed periods, trances, confusion; and various delusions. Similar findings have been published (25, 26, 27, 276). It is interesting that these symptoms are identical to those reported by patients with multiple personality and are characteristic of hypnotic states.

Attentional deficits have also been attributed to schizophrenics. But a bewildering number of aberrations have been claimed for these patients in the past. Thus far, these have added confusion rather than clarity to the problem. If there is an attentional defect, its existence has not yet been proved. Schizophrenia is a conundrum, and how self-hypnosis fits in is part of the mystery.


## Sociopathy and Criminality

Although antisocial acts plague society, the causes of these transgressions remain controversial and uncertain, despite many studies. It is unlikely that a single cause for these abuses will be found, since these offenders are heterogeneous. However, a subgroup may demonstrate self-hypnosis that facilitates misconduct.

A series of studies by Guze, Clininger, and their colleagues will be cited first, relating to female felons. These studies are particularly useful from a psychiatric viewpoint because of the precision of the diagnostic procedures. Sixty-six female criminals were studied by Cloninger and Guze (55). It is a small sample, one that may not be typical of the universe of female felons, but it does reflect the complexity of the problem and the many factors that may contribute to criminality. In this group, there was a high incidence of an absent parent, while 9 percent of the females were illegitimate. Fathers of 55 percent were probably sociopaths or alcoholics, as were 27 percent of the mothers. Seventy-three percent of the women did not complete high school. At least one-third were major disciplinary problems in school and one-half had academic problems, although few were mentally impaired. One-half were unemployed; one third were on welfare; and most had poor, erratic job histories. One-third were married before the age of eighteen, and 83 percent of those married had been divorced or separated. Forty percent of their children were conceived out of wedlock. One-half of the women were problem drinkers, and almost one-half were intoxicated on alcohol or drugs when they committed the index crime.

Forty-one percent of these women qualified for the diagnosis of Briquet's syndrome. A related observation was that one-quarter were known to be prostitutes. Briquet, in his book published in 1859, mentioned that he examined 197 prostitutes, 53 percent of whom were hysterics (42, 179). Although these investigators had no theoretical concern with multiples and therefore would not have pressed for such information, five of the sixty-six women spontaneously described themselves as a "split personality" or a "multiple personality." Since only a minority of multiples will do this, it can be assumed that the probable number should be much larger.

In this welter of variables, no single factor accounted for the final result of criminality and imprisonment. Intertwined were the forces of a disorganized subculture, unstable families, poor parental models, alcoholic parents, early abuse, antisocial peer pressures, a lack of motivation and direction, academic failures, few skills, early marriage, alcohol and drug abuse, and other factors. It was a sequence of disasters.

A compelling statistic is the high incidence of hysteria (Briquet's syndrome) in this group. If one can extrapolate from my data on hysteria, most of these 41 percent should have been good or excellent hypnotic subjects prone to multiple personality, with concealed traumas and hidden antisocial agendas. Presumably many must have been mistreated when young and resorted to self-hypnotic tactics to protect themselves. Although a hypnotic mechanism cannot account for all female criminality—since the majority were not hysterics—the hysterical group nevertheless made up a substantial part of this heterogeneous population.

There is thus a relationship between hysteria and sociopathy in women, but there is also an association between hysteria in women and sociopathy in men. Guze summarized his group's findings, spanning fifteen years, of studies of these syndromes (121). Briquet's syndrome runs a prolonged course over many decades, although there are fluctuations in its intensity (115, 216). It runs in families. About 20 percent of first-degree female relatives may suffer from the disorder, while first-degree male relatives have an increased prevalence of sociopathy and alcoholism (6, 117, 118). Sociopathy and hysteria coexist in women more often than would be expected by chance, and an early delinquent and antisocial history frequently antedates the manifestations of Briquet's syndrome (54). Sociopathy in fathers appears to be particularly associated with the syndrome of hysteria in delinquent and sociopathic daughters (55). Furthermore, hyperactive children carry an increased risk for delinquency and sociopathy (186), with an increased prevalence of sociopathy in fathers and Briquet's syndrome in mothers (46, 202).

Guze (121) concluded that hysteria (Briquet's syndrome) and sociopathy have a common family origin. The earliest manifestation of the adult hysteria may take the form of the hyperactive child syndrome, and the sex of the individual will direct the course of the illness. Thus, Briquet's syndrome will predominate in females and sociopathy will predominate in males.

Turning to males, the evidence for dissociative states in male criminals is scattered and less conclusive (5, 47, 204, 275). But a pertinent observation is the preponderance of female multiples over male multiples in psychiatric practice (3, 22, 161). Since all multiples are excellent hypnotic subjects, yet this skill is evenly divided between the sexes (128), this has led to the suspicion that many male multiples not present in a psychiatric population might be present but undetected in the criminal population, a group that ordinarily does not frequent psychiatrists. This inference is supported by reports in the press of murderers with multiple personality (204, 275).

Satten et al. studied four convicted males who committed bizarre murders (233). Two claimed amnesias for the crime and one reported a dreamlike dissociated state during it. All four experienced periods of altered states of consciousness and depersonalization long antedating the murders.

Another example quoted by Bower (24) is Sirhan Sirhan, who assassinated Robert Kennedy but had no conscious recollection of the murder. He carried out his crime in an agitated state with an amnesia. Under hypnosis he was able to recall the events, sometimes with automatic writing, but this information never became consciously available in his waking state, and he continued to deny the murder. Diamond, a forensic psychiatrist, is also quoted as saying that in his experience an amnesia is frequently present following violent crimes of great passion, such as assaults or murders, in about one-third of the cases (24).

Taylor and Kopelman (270) reported that 10 percent of a sample of 203 men charged with criminal offenses claimed amnesia for their crimes. Amnesias occurred only with violence, most frequently with homicide, and none of the amnesias had legal implications. Furthermore, 26 percent of the 34 men convicted of murder or manslaughter were amnestic for the offense. Other studies of amnesia for homicide include 31 percent of fifty-one convicts (171); 33 percent of thirty-six convicts (114); 40 percent of fifty convicts (206); and 47 percent of thirty convicts (29).

It also should be noted that conversion symptoms occur most frequently in hysteria, but next most often in sociopathy (116, 120). Major conversion symptoms probably entail excellent hypnotizability (17).

Based on my experience with female multiples, I think it likely that some grim senseless multiple murders might be the product of these self-hypnotic conditions. I have frequently encountered homicidal personalities in females—none lethal—but often enough to believe that such characters in males could kill. Furthermore, in female multiples I have found an array of other antisocial behaviors perpetrated by personalities while the patient had an amnesia or was in a dissociated state. These have included theft, assault, prostitution, arson, and plotting to murder. The likelihood that dissociated hypnotic states contribute to some female criminality seems probable, but the relationship of these states to male criminality, excluding some grisly murders, is still uncertain.

It was postulated based on the finding of excellent hypnotizability and multiple personality in female hysterics (17) that the self-hypnotic processes producing hysteria might also be operating in some of their male counterparts producing sociopathy and criminality. The familial common denominator in this group might be the early physical, sexual, and psychological abuse (13, 18) experienced by both the males and females, which could lead to hypnotic defense and facilitate criminal behavior. This clearly would not explain all criminality, but it might be one factor among many promoting antisocial behavior in some male felons.

To test this self-hypnosis hypothesis, a group of convicted male sexual offenders were studied (20), a subgroup of the criminal population. Subjects included thirty-three sexual offenders—eighteen convicted of rape, nine of pedophilia, and six of incest—who were incarcerated on a forensic ward of the Utah State Hospital. This was a selected population, since all sexual offenders were not admitted to the program. Those who qualified had a normal I.Q., expressed a desire to change, were between seventeen and thirty-five years old, had been tried and sentenced, and accepted the fact that they had committed the crime. This eliminated some offenders, including those who might have an amnesia and therefore would not acknowledge the offense.

All subjects were questioned about dissociations at the time of the crime, about past dissociative experiences, and about sexual fantasies before the crime—whether they were vivid and realistic. Hypnosis was tried with most to assess their hypnotic abilities clinically and to search for personalities.

Subjects completed a self-report containing 305 items, symptoms characteristic of eleven major psychiatric syndromes, and a questionnaire containing a list of fifteen factors that might have contributed to the crime. These factors were rated by them on a scale of 1 to 5 in order of their importance. A psychologist, without knowledge of the clinical information, administered the Stanford Hypnotic Susceptibility Scale (Form C).

Possible dissociations reported to have occurred at the time of the crime included experiences such as, "like a dream; a haze over everything, can't remember all—felt compelled"; "like a fantasy—a weird feeling of unreality"; "floating feeling, not real, a third party watching"; "couldn't believe I was doing it"; "sitting back watching, saying it wasn't happening."

Past possible dissociative experiences reported by subjects included amnesias, déjà vu phenomena, no pain when beaten as a child, no pain with dental procedures, extrasensory experiences, visions, voices, micropsia, macropia, and out-of-body experiences.

Fantasies prior to the crime were common, but only those that were vivid, "as real as the real experience," were considered as possibly dissociative.

All subjects were examined for multiple personality. Seven qualified as DSM-III multiples, and six others were considered to be probable multiples since they described other parts that could assume control, sometimes with names and specific functions.

Subjects who revealed possible dissociative experiences in two or more of these four categories were tentatively considered to be self-hypnotic. In this group were three of the six guilty of incest, seven of the nine pedophiles and twelve of the eighteen rapists. In all, twenty-two of the thirty-three sexual offenders qualified clinically for possible self-hypnotic processes (67 percent), whereas one-third did not qualify.

In Table 23 the hypnotizability scores are tabulated. Twenty-nine of the thirty-three subjects were tested. As a total group they scored significantly higher than controls, but when they were subdivided into those with two or more kinds of possible dissociated states (67 percent) and those without them (33 percent), the dissociated group had very high scores, whereas the other group had normal scores. Furthermore, thirteen of the twenty-two with possible dissociations were probably multiples. Their scores of 9.2 were only slightly lower than the scores of 10.1 previously found for twenty-eight multiples (16, 18, 19).

*Table 23. Hypnotizability Scores of Sexual Offenders—with and without Self-Hypnotic Symptoms*

| Group | N | N Tested | Score | p Value |
|---|---|---|---|---|
| Total group | 33 | 29 | 8.0 ± 0.36 | < .01 |
| Qualify | 22 | 19 | 9.0 ± 0.27 | < .001 |
| Not qualify | 11 | 10 | 6.2 + 0.57 | N.S. |
| Multiples | 13 | 13 | 9.2 ± 0.34 | < .005 |
| DSM-III | 7 | 7 | 9.1 ± 0.26 | < .01 |
| Possible DSM-III | 6 | 6 | 9.2 ± 0.70 | < .05 |
| Multiples (from other studies) (16, 18) | | 28 | 10.1 ± 0.36 | < .001 |
| Controls | | | | |
| Cigarette smokers | | 49 | 6.6 ± 0.37 | |
| Controls (128, 283) | | 307 | 5.2 ± 0.18 | |
| Controls (87) | | 17 | 5.7 ± 0.80 | |

The hypnotizability scores confirmed the reliability of the clinical di-chotomy, but the high scores in two-thirds of the criminal offenders also suggested the presence of two populations—one with hypnotic pro-cesses possibly contributing to criminality and the other with identical offenses lacking this unusual hypnotic capability.

The two groups also differed significantly in their symptom profiles (Table 24). The dissociative group had many more symptoms, except for alcoholism, in all categories. They reported a mean of 31 percent of all symptoms, whereas the undissociated group had 13 percent and the controls reported only 1 percent.

Furthermore, the dissociative group had a symptom profile com-parable to that of male multiples, the two exceptions being in the schizo-phrenic and sociopathic categories. This suggests that the self-hypnotic process may have been responsible in part for their polysymptomatic syndrome.

Since all excellent hypnotic subjects and all multiples do not commit sexual crimes, other factors must contribute to the commission of these offenses. In an effort to ascertain what these factors might be, a self-report containing fifteen likely possibilities was completed by the offend-ers, who rated them in order of their importance from 1 to 5.

There were many individual differences, but a number were spec-ified as important, with high ratings. These included a lack of confidence with women (66 percent); anger at women (59 percent); intense realistic fantasies (59 percent); antisocial attitudes (53 percent); unsatisfied sex-ual feelings (44 percent); sexually abused when young (31 percent); and alcoholism (28 percent). Some cited pornography as stimulating, and a few had responded to violence and rape on television. Furthermore, as children and adolescents they had exhibited antisocial behavior and poor adaptation. They stole (61 percent), lied (55 percent), set fires (30 percent), and were major disciplinary problems in school (79 percent). Most were shy (79 percent), lonely (70 percent), and had few friends (67 percent). Later criminal problems preceding their sexual offenses were multiple thefts (58 percent), but only 9 percent were ever in a reform school. Twenty-five percent reported physical abuse as children.

These observations suggest a relationship between some criminality and hypnotic mechanisms. In females the data appear to be more con-clusive, since a high percentage of female felons qualify for the designa-tion of Briquet's syndrome (54, 55). But the evidence for the importance of hypnotic mechanisms to male criminality, except for sporadic case reports, has not been examined. This study, to our knowledge, is the first investigation in this way of a series of male offenders. They were sexual offenders and not criminals with lengthy records, but neverthe-less two were murderers and the majority were multiple rapists.

Studies of criminal populations in penitentiaries are needed, but these would present problems. Hypnosis is a subjective phenomenon,

Table 24. *Symptom Profile of Sexual Offenders—with and without Self-Hypnotic Symptoms*

| Symptom categories | Sexual offenders (N = 33) | | | Qualifying sexual offenders vs. series of male multiples | | | |
|---|---|---|---|---|---|---|---|
| | Qualify N = 22 | Not qualify N = 11 | p Value | Qualify N = 22 | Male multiples N = 22 | p Value | Male controls N = 24 |
| | % Symptoms present | | | % Symptoms present | | | % Symptoms present |
| Anxiety (14) | 33 ± 5 | 10 ± 2 | < .005 | 33 ± 5 | 43 ± 5 | N.S. | 4 ± 1 |
| Hysteria (30) | 25 ± 5 | 5 ± 1 | < .005 | 25 ± 5 | 28 ± 4 | N.S. | 0.3 ± 0.2 |
| Obsessions (21) | 25 ± 5 | 5 ± 2 | < .005 | 25 ± 5 | 23 ± 4 | N.S. | 2 ± 1 |
| Phobias (29) | 21 ± 4 | 11 ± 1 | < .001 | 21 ± 4 | 18 ± 3 | N.S. | 3 ± 1 |
| Mania (14) | 32 ± 5 | 25 ± 5 | N.S. | 32 ± 5 | 36 ± 6 | N.S. | 1 ± 0.4 |
| Depression (50) | 42 ± 4 | 16 ± 4 | < .001 | 42 ± 4 | 49 ± 5 | N.S. | 3 ± 1 |
| Multiple personality (68) | 30 ± 4 | 12 ± 2 | < .001 | 30 ± 4 | 35 ± 4 | N.S. | 2 ± 1 |
| Schizophrenia (23) | 15 ± 4 | 2 ± 1 | < .05 | 15 ± 4 | 28 ± 5 | < .05 | 1 ± 0.3 |
| Sociopathy (16) | 56 ± 6 | 35 ± 8 | < .02 | 56 ± 6 | 38 ± 5 | < .01 | 1 ± 0.4 |
| Hyperactivity (14) | 46 ± 5 | 29 ± 6 | < .05 | 46 ± 5 | 36 ± 6 | N.S. | 3 ± 1 |
| Alcoholism (26) | 36 | 45 | N.S. | 36 | 46 | N.S. | 4 |

occurring in the black box of the mind. Honesty and cooperation are necessary if valid information is to be attained, and these might not be forthcoming from an incarcerated population.

Although sexual offenders represent only a small and perhaps an atypical segment of the criminal population, this group was chosen first because it was available for study. But it was also selected because it promised more reliable data than might be expected from inmates of the state penitentiary. These patients were involved in a hospital program that required painful frankness—deception was not tolerated by the group or staff. For example, several men, when questioned about the rape, reported that they had been convicted on one count but had also committed several other rapes unknown to the court. This offered some assurance that their reports and the hypnotizability scores were valid.

Self-hypnotic dissociative experiences will produce a sense of distance, impersonality, and unreality, extending to an amnesia that will allow the individual in this altered state to perform acts that ordinarily would be anathema or taboo. This dissociation may be mandatory for some individuals, but others do not need a spontaneous subterfuge; they can commit crimes consciously with little or no remorse. Comparably, some sexual offenders seem to have hypnotic capabilities that facilitate their crimes, whereas others who commit these offenses do not have or apparently do not need this mechanism.

The fact that so many of these males—whether rapists, pedophiles, or perpetrators of incest—had these excellent hypnotic mechanisms was surprising, but there was also evidence that many other factors directed the sexual criminality. These included early antisocial practices, social isolation, problems with sexuality, alcoholism, fear of and animosity toward women, early sexual and physical abuse, and other problems. A pertinent question unanswered by the study is the relative importance of the dissociative processes to the commission of the crime, given the many variables operating. It seems likely that they played an important role in some cases, especially in those with personalities—where a switch would allow a personality to assume control—but it wasn't possible to treat these subjects using hypnosis over an extended period to determine how often this occurred. It was concluded that hypnotic mechanisms probably contributed to the sexual crimes in a majority of these cases but that other factors were also important.

Whether the findings in this study can be generalized to other forms of sociopathy and criminality cannot at present be answered, but the observations of Guze and Cloninger deserve further consideration. Their studies indicate that some but not all cases of sociopathy in males and hysteria in females have common familial origins. If one adds that hysteria is often associated with hypnotizability and multiple personalities, some tentative inferences may be drawn.

Modern western society offers many advantages to the fortunate, but it has created amid its blessings a host of social and economic problems. One is a fragmentation of many subcultures and a dissolution of the extended family, so important historically to early indoctrination and the creation of internalized codes of socially desired conduct. The result for some has been the series of disasters experienced by female felons. Such familial and social influences experienced early in life are likely to promote unsuitable models and defective consciences, conducive to anti-social behaviors for both males and females. The contribution of genetic factors to the process remains uncertain (44, 45).

But the physical, sexual, and psychological abuses common in these families will promote hypnotic defenses. In the female, hysteria may result. The question as yet unanswered is what segment of their male siblings who became sociopaths and criminals were subject to the same mistreatment and have the same hypnotic process operating. The high incidence of conversion symptoms in male sociopaths—secondary only to hysterics—has been cited. This suggests that hypnotic tactics are being used by a segment of this male population, but further studies are needed to define the extent and significance of this factor. Other subgroups of criminals—those involved in crimes of passion or grim repetitive murders—may approximate the figures found in sexual offenders, but it seems unlikely that such large numbers of self-hypnotics will be found in the population of hardened felons, among whom criminality is a profession or a way of life.

## Post-traumatic Stress Disorders (The Vietnam Syndrome)

The psychological reaction of soldiers to the stress of combat is the prototype of severe reactions to catastrophic disasters, such as natural disasters, bereavements, fires, acts of terrorism, plane crashes, confinement in concentration camps, torture, and other events that strain the adaptive capabilities of human beings. The syndrome of multiple personality should be included in this category as the prime example of reaction in childhood to the stress of psychological, physical, or sexual abuse (13, 255).

Reactions to the dangers, losses, and brutality of combat have been given many names, including combat fatigue, shell shock, war neurosis, and more recently Vietnam syndrome or post-traumatic stress disorder (PTSD) (260). For many who served in Vietnam, the war experience was extremely traumatic, and some veterans' problems have persisted for many years (279). It is estimated that 40 to 50 percent of these combat veterans have suffered emotional aftereffects, and some investigators believe that as many as 1.5 million Vietnam veterans may eventually need psychiatric help (279). These casualties exhibit a constellation of symptoms, including intense anxiety and panic attacks; recurrent battle dreams and nightmares; severe startle reactions and depression; explosive, aggressive behavior; interpersonal problems and constricted social relationships; flashbacks (hallucinations); and somatic symptoms.

Various explanations have been proposed to explain both the intensity of the reactions and the large number of veterans disabled by Vietnam combat experiences (81, 108). Many of these have pointed out that there were factors virtually unique to that war. Soldiers were rotated home every twelve months (Marines every thirteen months); therefore all rotated on their own, creating an individualized experience that was destructive to unit morale. The ideological basis for the war was bitterly disputed at home, producing unprecedented disharmony and doubt. The enemy were rarely uniformed; there was no front line, only grim guerrilla warfare and jungle combat. Women and children could be combatants; there were no safe havens. It was an endless war with no ground gained, only impotent rage, brutality, and a private quest for survival. It also was a teenage war; the average soldier was about twenty years old. In addition, the abuse of hashish and narcotics was excessive. Finally, when soldiers were rotated home, they returned not to be rewarded as heroes but to face antiwar marches, protests, and obscurity. For most, the entire experience was terrifying, dehumanizing, and later demoralizing.

Veterans' delayed stress reactions were due to many of these factors, but no specific hypothesis has been accepted to explain why some individuals and not others experienced severe disability. Premorbid emotional vulnerability has been suggested (295, 296), but there is reason to doubt this hypothesis in many cases (84, 122).

Based both on experience with several severe cases of the Vietnam syndrome in which "personalities" were discovered and on the symptomatic similarities of this syndrome to that of multiple personality, we hypothesized that veterans with severe post-traumatic stress disorder would have high hypnotic susceptibility scores and exhibit above-average imagery ability. This imagery capability is a trait frequently present in excellent hypnotic subjects (133, 237).

Fifty Vietnam veterans living in a rural community were contacted by mail, and twenty-six agreed to participate in a study (263) designed to test the hypothesis. Only four of the twenty-six had ever sought therapy, and all but one had been in combat. The dependent variable for the study was post-traumatic stress disorder (PTSD) as measured by self-report on a 15-point scale. The scale was a summation of the criteria for the diagnosis of PTSD provided by DSM-III and a scale used by a Salt Lake City veteran counselor based on reported effects of PTSD. Subjects reported a yes or no answer to fifteen symptoms, resulting in a PTSD score of from zero to 15.

The independent variables for the study were (1) hypnotic susceptibility, as measured by the Stanford Hypnotic Susceptibility Scale, Form

C (283); (2) imagery, as measured by Sheehan's Vividness of Imagery Scale (236), on which subjects received a mean score of 0–7, indicating the ability for imagery (those receiving a score of 2.0 or less were considered high imagers); (3) A symptom self-report based on the symptoms found in eleven major psychiatric syndromes, which was an augmented version of a protocol used in previous studies (16, 18). The MMPI profiles of twenty-two other veterans with severe PTSD who had been treated at the Veterans Center also were analyzed.

The veterans dichotomized sharply into two groups on the 15-point post-traumatic stress disorder self-report (Table 25). Fourteen of the twenty-six reported scores of 8 to 15, the mean and standard error being 11.8 ± 0.64. This group had hypnotizability scores of 10.9 ± 0.22, extraordinarily high scores equivalent to levels found in patients with multiple personalities (15, 16, 18). In contrast, the other twelve veterans had PTSD scores of 2 to 0 with a mean and standard error of .67 ± 0.19. Their hypnotizability scores were 7.1 ± 0.54, slightly high scores but statistically indistinguishable from normal controls.

*Table 25. Scores of Vietnam Veterans on Tests*[a]

| Item | N | Vietnam syndrome High | N | Low | p Value |
|------|---|------|---|-----|---------|
| PTSD score | 14 | 11.8 ± 0.64 | 12 | .67 ± 0.19 | < .001 |
| Hypnotizability score | 14 | 10.9 ± 0.22 | 12 | 7.1 ± 0.54 | < .001 |
| Total number of symptoms ( %) | 14 | 19 ± 3 | 8 | 7 ± 1 | < .02 |
| Imagery scores | 14 | 2.0 ± 0.27 | 12 | 3.1 ± 0.31 | < .01 |

[a]The PTSD scores had a range of 0 to 15; the hypnotizability scores from 0 to 12 (9 to 12 being very high); and the imagery scores 0 to 7 (below 2 being high). The hypnotizability scores of the high PTSD subjects compared with controls had a *p* value of <.001, whereas the difference between the low PTSD subjects and controls was not significant.

It was concluded that high hypnotizability correlated with the Vietnam syndrome—in this study invariably since all with the syndrome scored 10 to 12 on the hypnotizability test, whereas those without the syndrome had normal mean scores. Furthermore, a stepwise multiple regression analysis indicated that the relationship between the PTSD and hypnotic susceptibility explained .62 of the variance of the syndrome.

Those veterans with high Vietnam syndrome had 19 ± 3 percent of the symptoms on the self-report, whereas those with low syndrome reported 7 ± 1 percent. However, seven of fourteen highs had relatively few symptoms, suggesting that this subgroup did not have syndromes as severe as those we have found in incapacitated veterans who have been inpatients at the local VA hospital.

Since the high PTSD group had markedly elevated hypnotizability scores, symptoms on the self-report commonly found in patients with multiple personality (16) were examined and the high PTSD group and low PTSD group were contrasted. In Table 26 the symptoms distinguishing the two groups are listed, some of the symptoms often reported by multiples with excellent hypnotizability (13, 16, 222). Only four of these symptoms were reported by veterans with low PTSD scores, and two of the four symptoms came from one person who had a high hypnotizability score of 10. These findings were a further confirmation of the association of excellent hypnotic skills with these symptoms.

*Table 26. Critical Symptoms of Vietnam Veterans with High and Low Scores for the Vietnam Syndrome*[a]

| Symptoms | High Vietnam syndrome (N = 14) Percent | Low Vietnam syndrome (N = 8) Percent |
|---|---|---|
| Rapid mood changes | 50 | 13 |
| Amnesias | 43 | 0 |
| No feeling for severe pain | 36 | 0 |
| Paranoia | 36 | 13 |
| Feeling strange, unreal | 29 | 0 |
| Body anesthesia | 29 | 0 |
| Loss of consciousness | 21 | 13* |
| Ataxia | 21 | 0 |
| Suicidal feelings | 21 | 0 |
| Extrasensory experiences | 21 | 0 |
| Repeating nightmares | 21 | 0 |
| Trances—like hypnosis | 21 | 0 |
| Macropsia, micropsia | 14 | 13* |
| Visual hallucinations | 14 | 0 |
| Auditory hallucinations | 7 | 0 |

[a] The number of veterans in the "Low Vietnam syndrome" column was 8 because 4 others in this category refused to complete the self-report. The asterisks refer to the one subject with "low Vietnam syndrome" who had a hypnotizability score of 10.

The fourteen subjects with high PTSD scores had imagery scores of $2.0 \pm 0.27$, whereas the twelve low PTSD subjects had scores of $3.1 \pm 0.31$ (Table 26). From another perspective, there were nine high PTSD veterans with scores below 2, whereas only one low PTSD veteran had a score below 2, and he was the individual with a hypnotizability score of 10. Therefore, only individuals with excellent hypnotic skills showed unusual visualizing capabilities, although all excellent hypnotic subjects did not demonstrate this trait.

*Table 27. MMPI Profile of Twelve Veterans
with Severe Vietnam Syndrome*[a]

| Category | Score with S.E. |
|---|---|
| L | 46 ± 1.4 |
| F | 92 ± 3.8 |
| K | 44 ± 1.8 |
| Hs | 84 ± 5.0 |
| D | 91 ± 5.0 |
| Hy | 76 ± 3.2 |
| Pd | 91 ± 2.7 |
| MF | 73 ± 1.5 |
| Pa | 88 ± 3.0 |
| Pt | 94 ± 4.1 |
| Sc | 111 ± 3.7 |
| Ma | 73 ± 2.7 |
| Si | 68 ± 2.7 |

[a]These are the mean scores and standard error of the mean for 12 of the 22 veterans with severe PTSD syndromes who had MMPI profiles comparable to those previously found in female multiples. All values over 70 on the MMPI represent scores 2 standard deviations above the mean—in the 95 percentile range or higher.

In a previous study (16) a typical MMPI profile for females with multiple personality was reported. This same profile has been found in some male multiples, although a series of MMPIs for male multiples has not been accumulated. The profile contains high F scores and high Hs, D, Hy, Pd, Pa, Pt, and Sc scores. The very high F and Sc scores, with other elevated scores, characterize the group. This is a profile reported by Snyder et al. (251) for twenty-six male patients diagnosed as borderline personality disorders (174), although many may have been undetected multiples.

Twenty-two patients treated at the Vietnam Veterans Center identified as severe cases of the PTSD previously had been given the MMPI. Twelve of the twenty-two (55 percent) had the profile previously found in female multiples (Table 27). Given previous experience with this profile, it seems likely that it reflects a severe polysymptomatic disorder often based on excellent hypnotic capabilities (16).

This study supports the hypothesis that the PTSD of Vietnam veterans correlates with increased hypnotic susceptibility. If this study can be replicated and confirmed, it has significant implications. It implies an important, perhaps central, role of excellent hypnotizability in the genesis of severe post-traumatic stress syndromes of many varieties. All correlations will probably not be this neat, but in principle this association fits theory and experience with the childhood stress syndrome of multiple personality (13, 15, 16, 17, 18).

A perplexing problem posed by this study is the nature of this hypnotic capability. Past research indicates that hypnotic susceptibility is a stable trait, probably genetic in origin, that does not usually change over time, although there is evidence that long practice may enhance it (128). The question is whether only people with excellent or good hypnotic capabilities are susceptible to severe post-traumatic syndromes or whether severe chronic stress may convert normal hypnotic abilities into superior ones.

## Complex Phobias (Agoraphobia)

Phobias have been classified in many ways, but at present a subdivision into four categories is useful (183). The major clinical form is the agoraphobic syndrome. The total prevalence of all phobias in a Vermont study (1) was 76.9 per 1,000 population; agoraphobia had a prevalence of 6 per 1,000. In contrast, agoraphobics made up 50 percent of the phobics in a hospital population, indicating that psychiatrists treat a skewed sample, those phobics who are most disabled (1).

Agoraphobia is a chronic disorder that usually begins in late adolescence or early adulthood. Two-thirds of those affected are females. The clinical picture consists of fears of public places, walking alone, using public transportation, or being alone at home. It is further distinguished by panic attacks and episodes of depersonalization, features usually not found in other phobias. A relationship to depression (181), anxiety neurosis (124), and obsessional neurosis (183) has been suggested, but all these connections remain uncertain.

The other three types of phobias are the simple forms—phobias of animals or specific situations; phobias of blood and injury; and phobias of social situations. These include such isolated fears as those of heights, darkness, or flying; or of eating in public places or urinating in the presence of others.

The agoraphobic syndrome is our principal concern because of its possible relationship to self-hypnosis. It has the distinctive features of panic attacks and depersonalized experiences, symptoms frequently reported by patients with multiple personality, who also experience multiple fears. This poses the possibility that patients with complex phobias may have unusual hypnotic capabilities. In principle this skill could generate irrational fears by a hypnotic fixation, might create a hypnotic amnesia with an unconscious agenda, or might produce a hypnotic internal focus leading to depersonalized and derealistic experiences.

Frankel and Orne (87) reported hypnotizability scores of 8.5 ± 0.5 ($P < 0.01$) in subjects with complex phobias, elevations confirmed in other studies (82,154). In contrast, Spiegel et al. (253) found normal or low scores in subjects with fear of flying. These seemingly contradictory findings may not be inconsistent. The first study was of agoraphobics, whereas the second was of a common simple phobia. These two syndromes are probably dissimilar. It seems likely that many people can develop a simple phobia of heights, darkness, bodily injury, snakes, or flying because of a genetic predisposition to these fears. These may not necessitate any special hypnotic ability, whereas many people with complex phobias may require the additional variable of good hypnotizability. Further studies are needed.

## Anorexia Nervosa and Superobesity

The syndrome of anorexia nervosa, once rare but now common, seems to be related to the social mandate that females be thin if they are to be popular and attractive. In affluent Western societies where this cultural injunction is potent, most females are weight conscious and periodically diet. From this huge dieting population presumably at risk, only a small percentage develop anorexia nervosa, and even fewer reach cachectic levels. Those who do develop the syndrome manifest a weight phobia. They become fixed on the fear that they will lose control and become obese. They therefore cultivate leanness as a protective tactic to cope with the fear. In the process, the focus on thinness becomes all consuming, and every pound gained causes panic.

The question is why only a small percentage of the dieting population at risk develops this malignant weight phobia. One factor is the nature of these patients. Ninety percent or more are females, because the cultural injunction against overweight applies much less stringently to males. Almost all are compliant individuals. Many have been unhappy and lacking self-confidence, and some have been depressed. Seemingly they are very susceptible to the thinness mandate and to the inference that a weight loss will solve their personal problems. There is also recent evidence (141, 153, 290) that they may have a genetic predisposition to depression, since many have a family history of depression.

But these may not be sufficient explanations to account for the phenomenon. It is possible that hypnotizability may contribute to this phobia, just as it may to other complex phobias. We studied eleven females whose weight fell to a mean level of 83 pounds. This weight is close to the mean weight of 79 pounds reported for large series of these females (14). Our patients' hypnotizability scores were $9.7 \pm 0.6$ ($p < .001$). Furthermore, I have seen two cases of anorexia nervosa with multiple personality, and dissociative phenomena are commonly reported by anorexia patients. Self-hypnosis may account in part for this irrational driven behavior, the intensity of the phobia of obesity, and the distortion of body image found in this syndrome.

In contrast, thirteen bulimics, those who binge and vomit but do not lose excessive weight (mean weight of 105 ± 2 pounds) scored 7.7 ± 0.61 ($p$ = N.S.)—an elevated score but considerably lower than the score of patients with anorexia nervosa.

The presence of superobesity has been a striking observation in some of our patients—fourteen with multiple personality and three with hysterical amnesias. Fourteen were females with an average maximal weight of 279 pounds, and three were males averaging 327 pounds.

A random group of thirteen other superobese individuals was tested for hypnotizability, culled from a group of patients who underwent gastric stapling for their obesity. Their scores were 5.9 ± 0.8—a normal result. The tentative conclusion was that a subgroup of the superobese may have hypnotic psychopathology that contributes to their overweight, but the majority of the superobese are probably grossly overweight for other reasons.

## Pain Problems

I have seen a number of patients admitted to the Pain Clinic who were excellent hypnotic subjects, some who qualified for the diagnosis of Briquet's syndrome or multiple personality. These have been sporadic encounters, and no study of sequential admissions has been done. However, S. Ross Nakashima at the University of Utah Medical Center did hypnotizability tests on a random group of thirty-three pain patients. Their mean score was 6.9 ± 0.50, a slightly high but normal score. But the interesting finding was the bimodality of the graph of the scores. Thirty-nine percent had peaks at 3, 4, and 5, whereas a second peak occurred at 8 and 9, accounting for 33 percent. Nine percent scored 10, 11, or 12. The data are suggestive of two groups of pain patients, those in whom hypnotic mechanisms may contribute to pain and those with pain problems unrelated to this ability.

## Self-harm Syndrome—Self-mutilation

Self-injurious behaviors are often found in psychiatric patients (187), but self-mutilation is uncommon. Self-mutilation spans a spectrum from multiple cuts with a grid of scars covering the wrists and forearm; to self-inflicted infections, deep burns, and repetitive injections of insulin or other drugs; to self-castration and Munchausen's syndrome.

Pattison and Kahan (215) analyzed fifty-six published case reports of self-harm. They identified an onset in late adolescence with repetitive episodes; a compulsion to harm oneself in stressful situations; increasing anxiety and anger; a narrowed perspective excluding alternative solutions; a depressed mood; and a sense of relief after the self-injury. Drug and alcohol abuse, a lack of social support, homosexuality in males, suicidal thoughts in females, and psychosis were frequent.

Bach-Y-Rita (8) studied eight felons in prison who were not only habitually violent but also self-mutilators. They repeatedly inflicted wounds on themselves and averaged ninety-three scars per person. Depression preceded the acts, followed by a relief after the cutting. But they also reported a sense of depersonalization without pain during the self-mutilation.

These observations are akin to behaviors seen in multiples. Many make frequent suicide attempts. I tabulated the number for twenty cases, and they ranged from 0 to 23 with a mean of 4.5 ± 1.1 attempts. Furthermore, there have been at least eleven examples in my series of severe self-mutilation. All have injured themselves without pain, the assaults having been inflicted by personalities during amnesias or occurred during dissociated, depersonalized states. Two patients induced third-degree burns; three gave themselves severe infections; three repeatedly slashed their arms, body, or neck; one swallowed a corrosive agent, producing a large gastric ulcer; and two experienced multiple fractures.

Although it seems unlikely that all self-mutilators are of this kind, the similarities are apparent. Severe self-mutilators should be studied for hypnotizability and amnestic traumatic experiences, since these can be factors contributing to such behaviors.

## Borderline Personality

Many definitions have been proposed to identify borderline patients, but the category probably encompasses a heterogeneous population of different entities. There is evidence that a subgroup are multiples (15, 53, 137). Horevitz and Braun (137) studied thirty-three multiples, and 70 percent met the criteria for borderline personality; Kluft (159) analyzed seventy multiples and found 23 percent. Studies reversing this procedure are needed to define what proportion of borderline patients are multiples.

## Summary

These are a few syndromes which have been studied with reference to hypnosis. However, we have identified and treated a variety of other patients with self-hypnotic pathology who would be given the diagnosis of alcoholism, narcotics addiction, pseudoretardation, juvenile delinquency, obsessional neurosis, anxiety neurosis, affective disorder, and psychosexual disorders (57, 262).

A recent study (254) indicates that a random group of chronic psychiatric patients will have a low normal level of hypnotizability. This suggests that self-hypnotic syndromes are scattered throughout various categories and may not be detected by a simple survey. For example, criminality may have many determinants, but there appears to be a subgroup of criminals with hypnotic mechanisms facilitating antisocial behaviors.

Our findings to this point indicate that many psychiatric syndromes may be induced, simulated, or influenced by self-hypnotic mechanisms, but their diversity dictates that other factors or variables must also make a contribution. An obvious example is sex, since there is a predominance of females with complex phobias, anorexia nervosa, and hysteria. The major contribution of self-hypnotic processes to various symptoms and syndromes merits further research.

# 6 / *Therapy*

The number of psychological therapies that have been employed to treat mental miseries is large. Many purport to cure and are endorsed by enthusiastic advocates, but with few exceptions these are supported only by anecdotal information. At present, the count of these different therapies is at least 250 (127)—a disconcerting indication of contemporary gullibility and confusion.

Parloff and his colleagues (214) have summarized the available scientific data on the effectiveness of psychotherapy. They concluded that patients given therapy show significantly more improvement in thought, mood, personality, and behavior than do untreated patients, but they also noted—and it is an important reservation—that psychotherapy can produce adverse effects in a small percentage of cases.

The existence of so many psychotherapies designated by different names suggests that many must share common elements (85). It has been assumed that these would include the enthusiasm, assurance, genuineness, empathy, and concern of the therapist—perhaps even his or her wisdom and experience; the patient's high expectations, motivation, and resourcefulness; catharsis, or the expression and sharing of fears, guilts, and pent-up feelings; desensitization to fears; a high spontaneous recovery rate; and other undetected elements.

One would hope for more precise knowledge. We now know that lithium is a remarkable prophylactic agent for certain manic-depressive illnesses, and that tricyclic drugs resolve some depressions. The challenge is to identify comparable psychotherapeutic tactics that are specific for the treatment of particular psychiatric illnesses. It now seems possible that hypnotherapy has this potential in the treatment of spontaneous self-hypnotic disorders, but many more studies will be necessary for any consensus about the usefulness of this therapy.

The schema that follows can only be considered a preliminary approach to these self-hypnotic disorders. It is based on experience with many cases, considerable trial and error, and the logical inferences that proceed from some understanding of the nature of these disorders. In no sense is it offered as any more than a first approximation. It has yielded some remarkable results, but it has also yielded failures. Treatment is often painfully slow, and sometimes it is outrageously demanding of both patient and doctor. For many, and the number of candidates is large, it is so uneconomical as to be impractical. But it is to be hoped that this crude process can be refined and shortened—and the pyrotechnics reduced—as more investigators study these illnesses. Descriptions of methods to treat these patients are available (2, 5, 38, 162, 163). These include therapies that are eclectic (287), analytic (159, 162, 163, 166, 182, 225), behavioral (164), family (10, 172), group (50), and hypnotic (2, 4, 5, 34, 35, 73, 136, 140, 159, 162, 163). In this early stage, controversy remains the rule.

## General Principles

The therapist should keep in mind a few general principles when he or she treats patients with this form of psychopathology. Although they are helpful guides, they are insufficient; perplexing problems are frequent and one must be mentally nimble. The unexpected is commonplace, crises occur, patients can be puzzling, and one must be imaginative if not ingenious. But despite this unpredictability, these general principles can be a guide to the therapeutic process.

First is the recognition of the self-hypnotic mechanism. These patients have unknowingly used self-hypnosis to conceal from conscious awareness a variety of noxious experiences, intolerable emotions, and repugnant impulses. Many of these are early childhood traumas, and all have created an unconscious repository from which symptoms emanate. In some patients, these memories are not totally unconscious but are dissociated, distant, or impersonal—but equally pathogenic.

The next principle comes from folk wisdom and experience with the treatment of phobias. The therapist should try to avoid allowing the patient to panic or become terrified. Anxiety should be kept at a level the patient can tolerate. If the individual is overwhelmed by fear, the result may be a temporary defeat, which should be avoided if possible. Even a minor victory is reassuring to the patient, and a failure is discouraging.

Another principle relates to precipitating events. The basic problems, now hidden, occurred many years ago. Although they will be reactivated by contemporary experiences, these immediate precipitants are instigators—not the primary problem. The past traumas now buried in the unconscious must be revealed if therapy is to be successful.

There is next the need to discover these hidden experiences. The most direct method is via hypnosis, although many other techniques, including analytic, Gestalt, and primal—in fact, any highly charged experience—may produce trance states in susceptible subjects that go unrecognized by either the therapist or patient. What has been hidden by self-hypnosis must be revealed by hypnosis. The unconscious must be made conscious. But these patients harbor a special kind of unconscious information—memories that have been concealed by a hypnotic amnesia or a hypnotic dissociation.

It must then be recognized that many of these experiences, emotions, and functions have not only been hidden but also may be delegated to personalities, another product of self-hypnosis. These personalities now have responsibilities abrogated by the patient. These responsibilities must be identified and reassumed by the patient; otherwise, therapy will fail.

There are also formidable resistances to the therapeutic processes. The concealed experiences initially were forgotten because the patient could not consciously cope with them. As a result, these memories or functions have remained unacceptable and are feared. Some traumas can be rapidly identified and made conscious, but others are guarded or avoided relentlessly. The resistances must be penetrated, often slowly and painfully. A therapeutic impasse usually indicates a resistance that must be identified and resolved.

One must realize that the traumas, although they may have occurred decades earlier, are still virulent because they are unresolved and unprocessed by the conscious mind. In these patients, guilt, rage, neglect, or a rape is still frozen in its early form. Therefore, when reactivated and returned to consciousness, these old memories are experienced as events that have just occurred. When such experiences are personified, relegated to a personality, the custodian demonstrates these same features. Personalities are fragments of an individual that are still anchored in the past. Adult learning residing in the conscious mind has not penetrated into this unconscious, so personalities also remain frozen as remnants of early experiences.

Although therapy can be complex, a central concept overrides all details. Patients must accept the fact that these experiences, so artfully hidden, did occur. The hidden experiences, the concealed emotions, guilts, and urges are theirs. All must be recognized, accepted, and processed, usually by discovering and reexperiencing them in hypnosis. Although reality may be unfair, the truth must be faced; the past is unalterable and must be accepted. Coping with problems by the use of self-hypnosis is self-defeating and eventually must be abandoned. Reality must be confronted and problems resolved by more effective tactics.

Finally, after the traumas have been discovered and made conscious and the personalities integrated, there is a period of reaccommodation and learning. The patient has used self-hypnosis for many years to cope with stresses, but now he or she must learn other tactics. Relapses do occur when the patient regresses back to self-hypnosis so therapy does not end with integration.

## Identification of Cases

The first step in therapy is the identification of patients with self-hypnotic problems. Do they have amnesias, depersonalized states, hallucinations, headaches, and nightmares? Do they have a sense of other parts of them that control behavior? Are there anxiety symptoms and panics, conversion symptoms or depressions? Multiple suicide attempts or injuries without pain are alerting. But an easier and more rapid approach than searching out these symptoms in an interview is the use of a detailed self-report that the patient can complete before being interviewed. A multiplicity of complaints referable to many syndromes is suggestive, particularly when voices, amnesias, and many "hypnotic" symptoms are acknowledged. All may be suggestive, but one must identify the patient's hypnotic capabilities: this is a crucial factor in the diagnosis. A patient without hypnotic talents presumably cannot produce an amnesia or personalities.

The next step is the actual identification of self-hypnotic complexes. I now routinely test all patients rapidly for hypnotic capabilitiy. Since one is eliciting a skill that the patient either has or lacks, the prime prerequisite is to have a subject who is not afraid, or is even eager, to try hypnosis. I usually state after a brief history has been taken that it would be useful to learn how able a hypnotic subject the patient is, since the information could be very helpful both for diagnosis and treatment. I furthermore ask whether the patient feels any fear or aversion to hypnosis. If any is expressed or indicated, we discuss the matter to allay any anxieties and misapprehensions. Most patients are then quite willing to try, although a few refuse. Occasionally a patient does poorly at first but after further discussion relaxes and proves to be an excellent subject. I must admit to being a bit of a coward, or perhaps just cautious, and burly males whom I suspect have this pathology are handled gingerly. I ask about past assaultive behaviors and if they are acknowledged only proceed in the presence of a muscular aide.

I have found that hypnosis can usually be induced briefly and simply. I usually request relaxation with visual fixation on a spot. The patient is then asked to concentrate on a heaviness in the eyelids. There is a minute or two of verbal patter—"Your eyelids are growing heavier and heavier until they close and stick together." When they close, I then ask the subject to take a deep breath and to relax further with expiration. I test how well the eyelids stick together. Are they so heavy and glued so tightly together that they can't be opened? Another procedure is to test arm levitation. When the arm is made very light and a helium balloon is attached to it, will the arm and elbow rise from the side of the chair? If all goes well, I then suggest that the patient look into the back of his or her mind to see if there is anyone or anything there. If anything or a person is identified, I want to know what or who it might be. Should a person be found, I often ask to talk to him or her. When the patient has auditory hallucinations, I ask to talk to the voice. It is surprising how often a personality can be rapidly identified in this way.

If these tactics are unrewarding, I often ask the patient where he or she enjoys being, perhaps at a beach or in the mountains. I then suggest that the patient go there and relax. At that point it is helpful to know how realistic the experience is, so I ask how well the patient can see the beach and the ocean, smell the salt water, feel the bright sun. If this can be done with realism, I ask whether these experiences are as sharp, real, and clear as seeing me and the room when the patient came into the office. An affirmative answer often identifies excellent hypnotic subjects.

Several formal hypnotizability scales are available, and scores on these can be helpful. However, with experience one can become proficient at identifying excellent subjects without the tests. My clinical estimate usually approximates scores on the tests, but it is always reassuring to have this confirmation.

The induction of hypnosis, given an excellent hypnotic subject, is simple. Anyone can induce hypnosis. The real challenge is what to do with this state—how to use it therapeutically. Let us assume that I have identified the patient as an excellent hypnotic candidate. I have searched for personalities and found one who is willing to talk to me. I then make a rapid survey by asking the personality—a girl, for example—if she has a name; how long she has been there; the patient's age when she came; whether the patient knows her; whether she ever takes over the body; whether she ever directs or influences the patient when the patient has the body; her mission or function; and whether there are other people back there. After further discussion, depending on the circumstances, I may then speak to the patient and present the option to remember or forget what has happened in hypnosis. If the choice is to forget I accept the request, but often with the admonition that eventually these things will have to be remembered if treatment is to be successful. Termination of hypnosis is then preceded by the request to relax and to feel calm, peaceful, and rested. If I find no personalities, I ask the patient in hypnosis to look into the back of his or her mind for any hidden nasty experiences or painful feelings. Should any be reported, I ask whether they have really been forgotten. If the answer is yes, I may request that a mild one be remembered. In many cases this can be done. The patient is given the option to remember or forget, and the trance is terminated with reassuring statements. If the patient elects to remember after the return to a conscious state, the episode is discussed to determine whether it was a forgotten experience or feeling and whether the patient has the impression that others are still back there concealed from consciousness.

The decision now must be made with the patient whether to enter a therapeutic alliance and proceed with hypnotherapy. I explain that these hypnotically concealed complexes, usually hidden much earlier in life, will remain sources of symptoms. They must be extracted and faced consciously, but it may not be easy. It will be necessary to be stubborn and persevere. I am willing to stick at it, but it may take time, patience, and courage. I explain that some cases go rapidly, but others are more difficult. We cannot know for sure until we try.

To illustrate my procedure in an initial interview, I offer the following example. The patient had a severe pain syndrome. I was asked to see her in consultation by a colleague. After a few casual questions, I asked whether she had ever tried hypnosis. "Yes, I did it with the pain doctor." Are you a good hypnotic subject? "I think so, but I'm not sure. The pain doctor said I am." (She later scored 11 out of 12 on the formal hypnotizability scale.) Would you be willing to go into hypnosis, because I would like to determine how well you can do and it would be helpful? She closed her eyes, and I asked that she tell me when she was there. In thirty seconds she said, "I'm there now." Would you look in the back of your mind and tell me whether there are any hidden nasty experiences? "Yes, there are some, but I try to keep them there." Is there any person there? "Yes, a sailor." Can you see him? "Yes." If you prefer you need not listen, but may I talk to him? "Yes." Sailor, are you there? "Yes, what do you want?" Her voice had now dropped an octave. Sailor, why are you in her mind? "I raped her." Is there anyone else there? "There are four of us who raped her." I thanked him and called her back.

I told her that she need not remember what happened in hypnosis if she preferred. This was done because I did not expect to be her therapist and was only doing a diagnostic interview. If I had planned to continue therapy, I would have given her the option to remember or forget, but with the comment that these hidden memories must be eventually remembered if she wished to get well. She elected to forget.

I then asked her to relax, to feel calm and peaceful, and to come out of hypnosis slowly. In the alert, conscious state I asked whether she had any nasty experiences when she was younger. "No." How do you and your husband get along? "There is trouble." Do they have sexual difficulties? "Yes, I get little satisfaction from sex." Did you ever have nasty sexual experiences with other men? "No, I was a virgin when I married him."

It seemed likely that the rape and perhaps other abhorrent experiences were hypnotically hidden. These might be responsible for the pain syndrome, but that was left to future treatment with her therapist. Would these traumas have emerged by spontaneous hypnosis in the course of conventional therapy? They might have surfaced, but certainly many do not. Those most carefully guarded probably can be reached only with hypnotherapy, but I have seen a few cases where these memories returned spontaneously.

## Initial Period

The early stage of therapy can be a period of indoctrination. I describe the treatment and tell patients that they have been doing self-hypnosis for years but never realized it. When they doubt their capability to produce hallucinations or amnesias by hypnosis and view these as evidence of craziness, I sometimes ask them to enter hypnosis and visualize their mother, children, or husband and suggest that they converse together—a demonstration of auditory and visual hallucinations. Similarly, I may suggest that our hypnotic session be forgotten until I give the signal to remember—evidence of the amnestic capabilities of hypnosis. This doesn't expunge symptoms, but it reassures some patients that there is a rational explanation for their experiences—that the label of schizophrenia, which sometimes has been applied is incorrect.

Patients may insist that they do not want to know the sordid facts. These have been concealed for good reasons; why is that objectionable? My reply is that no one can cope sensibly with problems that are unknown. In this form they will continue to create symptoms. Furthermore, people can usually handle real adversities, but fantasies, specters, and vague suspicions are devastating. Most of these hidden events occurred long ago, but until they are returned to consciousness they cannot be put to rest as old memories.

The early part of therapy, furthermore, is a trial period used to assess the patient's willingness to work and establish a trusting relationship. I never know until we begin hypnosis how rapidly progress can be made and how courageous the patient will be. Sometimes the resistances are surprisingly minimal, and past traumatic events can be recovered rapidly and easily. A few patients, once they realize how therapy is done, will do hypnosis on their own and within a few sessions complete the necessary work, but they are the exceptions.

There are other patients who less rapidly can retrieve personalities, identify their functions, recapture the events and emotions delegated to them, and integrate one personality after another. In these cases before the patient enters hypnosis we discuss where we should go that day, and I ask the patient to decide which personality should be accosted. The patient will usually identify the target, and I then ask that he or she go into hypnosis and do the work. Under these circumstances, I speak to the personality while the patient is listening and ask the personality to tell me what tasks have been given to him or her. These experiences are then recounted. I then ask if there is anything else that we have missed. If there isn't, I ask the patient if he or she is willing to assume these responsibilities and, in turn, ask the personality whether it is willing to relinquish them. If both agree, I suggest that they integrate. Should the patient agree and the personality refuse, I then tell the patient this and ask why this may be. A personality's reluctance usually indicates either more as yet undiscovered traumas that are its property, or the patient's unwillingness to cope with the task. Depending on the answer, I may say that more work must be done, or if I believe this reflects merely hesitation, I may advise a temporary integration to see whether the patient can manage the new responsibilities.

I must add one admonition. My tendency is to push rapidly, but this sometimes proves to be a mistake. My impression is that most therapists who do this work go too slowly. One must try to move at an optimal pace, not overload the patient but at the same time not delay. This becomes a matter of judgment, and one must continue to ask the patient whether the pace is too fast and whether enough work has been done that day. No matter what precautions are taken, however, mistakes will sometimes occur.

As yet, I have not discovered any reliable way to detect these easier cases before the hypnotic exploration. The presence of only a few personalities is not necessarily a clue, since one of my most difficult patients had only four, but horrendous experiences had been heaped upon one that took several years to penetrate. Other patients have not had terrible experiences, but are timid, or unwilling or unable to work. Some will persist at the task and gradually can be coaxed to try, but others fail and discontinue therapy. Whether they could have succeeded with different tactics is uncertain.

Most patients, at least those identified in the hospital or referred for therapy, do not recover rapidly. They usually need months or years of treatment, sometimes as inpatients in the hospital where they can be observed, protected, and treated intensively. They represent the majority, although in the world outside the purview of psychiatry there may be many people with milder problems of a self-hypnotic nature who never come to the attention of psychiatrists. But even those who do seek help are usually not identified, since most psychiatrists are not alert to these conditions and few use hypnosis routinely to search for amnestic traumas.

## Hypnosis

Hypnosis is primarily used to gain access to hidden traumatic experiences. At times, however, it also serves as a means to quell panic, block pain, instill motivation, or focus attention on a new idea. Hypnosis has remarkable properties, but this doesn't mean that patients are obedient automatons. They often reject my logic—sometimes quite correctly—question the facts, remain critical or sceptical, and fail to reveal concealed information.

There has been considerable controversy about the use of hypnosis in the treatment of multiple personality. In part, this is based on the failure to recognize the spontaneous hypnotic states that these patients repeatedly enter, but it is also based on some of the problems encountered when hypnosis is employed.

It must be remembered that patients' concealed complexes are akin to phobias. Frightening experiences and unacceptable repugnant feelings have been put out of consciousness. These have been avoided and hidden, remaining guarded and defended. When the patient enters hypnosis and is directed toward hidden problems, fireworks may explode and crises occur (160). Tensions mount and symptoms increase. As these hidden complexes are threatened, patients often develop severe headaches, insomnia, and nightmares; flash into personalities; make suicidal attempts; have hysterical seizures; develop amnesias; run from the hospital; and do any number of disagreeable things, depending on what secrets are being threatened.

This kind of behavior is not characteristic of all patients. Occasionally the patient's hidden secrets are retrieved easily and rapidly, and one can only be grateful when this occurs. Approaching these complexes generates anxiety if not panic, and it often resurrects fragments of the forgotten experience (spontaneous abreactions). It is painful for the patient, unpleasant for the therapist, and disrupting on the ward if the patient is in the hospital. Inexperienced nurses resent it, and novice therapists can be intimidated. Critics are correct when they cite the problems of such hypnotherapy. I have come to accept the fact that symptoms are activated by the process—that patients must often get worse before they can get better. There is usually a struggle.

These unconscious niduses were concealed initially because the patient could not cope with them. Until the therapist entered the scene, these complexes remained hidden, periodically emanating symptoms. In mild cases they can be rapidly recovered, but in most instances there is very powerful resistance to retrieval. "Let sleeping dogs lie" has been the principle unconsciously directing these patients. How then does one go about bridging these resistances and gaining access to these concealed memories?

## The Relationship

Since the penetration of stalwart resistances is frightening even to a highly motivated patient, therapy requires a trusting relationship. The therapeutic effort compares to a major mountain climb in which the novice ascends with a guide and at times must rope up. The novice must be confident that the guide is experienced and able. The novice's life is in the guide's care, and there must be trust that he or she will provide safety in precarious, exposed situations. The novice must trust, but the guide must demonstrate that the trust is justified. The novice must feel that the guide is cautious and sturdy, and can cope with emergencies.

It may seem melodramatic, but something like this is involved in difficult cases. Therapy can be a long, tough, precarious climb. Misadventures do occur and trust wavers. It is an elemental relationship with the omnipresent threat of crises, if not disasters. Suicidal gestures and serious attempts at suicide may occur, for example. Gradually, however, one becomes fatalistic, weighing risks against benefits, taking chances when the odds are favorable. I have escaped fatalities among my patients, but this can only be attributed to my good fortune and their instincts of self-preservation.

Many of these patients have no reason to trust others. Those who have been abused are often wary of people. Others are timid and easily frightened: they withdraw into their hypnotic shells whenever any presumed danger is detected. This often involves a switch into personalities that are self-destructive or angry.

At times patients will enter their hypnotic world spontaneously and lose contact with reality. One patient, when she became distraught, would revert into the "angry one" who would strike her head against the wall and beat her. I would have to sit on her lap and restrain her until she became calm. At other times while in the hypnotic state, this patient perceived me as her father, about to assault her sexually. Fortunately, she was a small woman whom I could physically restrain. It seems obvious that a powerful man in a comparable confused state could be a dangerous adversary should he be back in the past, trapped in hypnotic delusions. Females tend to be self-punitive, but many men under these conditions could be assaultive.

When upset, other patients revert to childish states—become five-year-olds, for example, and demand every form of attention and care. One even drew up adoption papers, but my wife wisely demurred. In the patient's fantasy world we had become loving foster parents who would right all wrongs. These are extremes; most cases are less demanding.

In most cases, the therapeutic relationship is less intense. I try to be consistent, open, and honest. When patients ask questions, I give answers if I know them. The agreement is that I will be direct and honest, but patients must be equally honest with me. We must discuss our relationship and not ignore interpersonal problems. If we become mired in misunderstandings, there will be no progress.

I describe the usual course of therapy; we discuss theory, and I try to clarify our immediate objectives. Some patients in retrospect have told me that these clarifications were helpful, but others have acknowledged little benefit.

The therapist must be alert to interpersonal problems—they are often a source of trouble. Patients do become discouraged and depressed. They lose faith and confidence in the therapist and the therapeutic process. Reassurance is necessary, and successes must be reviewed and emphasized. If possible, the therapist should finish every session with a sense of accomplishment or optimism. "You were very brave," or "It will be easier to face memories next time," or "You succeeded again—you are showing more courage all the time."

Patients regress and project old behavioral patterns onto the therapist. Every form of transference may occur, particularly when patients spontaneously enter trance states. At these times, the therapist may be perceived literally as a threatening, abusive parent or assaultant. Given this relationship, the therapist may need to be flexible in his or her approach. I have made home visits when crises occurred; telephoned and insisted on further therapy when patients refused to return; and embraced patients when they were distressed—I think in a fatherly fashion. I am a doctor and they are patients, but we are also friends and allies, working together to find some solution to well-concealed problems.

## Gaining Access to Hidden Memories

It should be remembered that hidden memories are unconscious, but in a strange way they are known to the patient. A part of the mind has the memories, although the conscious part has no access to them. Apprehensions, abreactions, voices, fears, dreams, compulsions, forebodings, sensations, and other symptoms escape from this hideaway. The patient often has an intuitive sense of its nature and is an invaluable guide—although a reluctant one—in directing the therapist to the secrets. But hypnosis is the key to open the door, the prime tactic to discover the information.

In the usual case, one reconnoiters in hypnosis and meets some personalities, but many remain hidden. I try to learn what the concealed problems are and take histories from the personalities that are accessible. Personalities can be clustered and conceptualized in many ways. Allison (4) has grouped them into persecutors, rescuers, and internal self-helpers. Beahrs (9) uses the term "avengers" for personalities that assume rage for experiences of sadistic brutality. My inclination is to recognize that some personalities are there to help the patient and others are malevolent—violent, homicidal, or suicidal. Every manner of personality may be found, depending on the needs and imaginative capabilities of the patient. Helpful personalities should be questioned for any information they can provide. They should be urged to reveal the problems that made their assistance necessary.

The detective work then begins. I have often thought that training in Scotland Yard would have been more valuable in this pursuit than courses in anatomy. One follows the patient's leads and searches for clues. The process in complex cases is one of slow unraveling. The more accessible problems are usually the least traumatic, whereas those deeply concealed are the most disturbing—and consequently the most difficult to uncover and the last to be revealed.

When the patient is out of hypnosis, much time is spent planning strategies together. It is a process of exploration, a search for clues. The therapist may offer guesses, but the patient will often retort that they don't seem correct or they don't feel right. My own hunches are often wrong, and I am frequently surprised.

One tactic is to pose casual questions to the patient, such as, "Not recognizing a person whom your husband said you once knew seems a bit strange, although it might be trivial." In this case, the patient acknowledged that her memory was blank but said she felt a sense of fear—a feeling of not wanting to know anything more about him. It might have been inconsequential, but one pursues any lead when the clues are few. In this instance, in hypnosis the question led to an important experience, an essential element in her major trauma.

If the patient has no suggestions and I have no clues, I may ask for hunches or guesses, intuitions and feelings. These are not merely helpless queries, since the patient has a hidden part that knows the answers. Casual suggestions by the patient can be valuable, and they are usually correct.

Given some point of departure, it is then necessary to penetrate to the trauma, but usually this cannot be done blindly. Time must be spent first searching for the likely place to look in memory. The patient may say, "I don't know where to go." It is then necessary to examine and reexamine the patient's recent symptoms and feelings to detect what unconscious experience may have been activated. For example, she recalls recent thoughts of suicide, flashes of her mother, a sense of choking, and anger at me. We both agree that it must be something that happened at age five, something involving her mother. We now know where to look. In hypnosis she remembers coming to her mother for help, but instead her mother hysterically grabs her by the throat and chokes her.

A long list of tactics may be employed after the patient enters hypnosis and reports seeing only a wall, darkness, or nothing. These denote resistances, a reluctance to find the problem. The various tactics are all directed at the same goal—to circumvent the resistances and to learn the hidden experiences. Some tactics work, others don't, and some initially are successful only to fail later.

One can ask the patient in hypnosis to visualize a movie or a play, tell a story about someone else, have a hypnotic dream, or free associate. The patient can be urged to see pictures, detect odors, hear sounds, discover feelings, or report physical sensations. I ask for any words, even the first letter in a word when it is clear that the word is crucial. If I already have strong hunches, I may ask the patient in hypnosis to use the automatic lifting of a finger, which is directed to rise when what I say is correct. Automatic writing is also occasionally useful, although time consuming.

But there are moments when indirect tactics don't succeed. I am often reduced to elemental force, commanding the patient to try harder, look more, don't stop, screw up your courage and find it. The patient whimpers and the therapist becomes exasperated. It can be exhausting for both.

At times, patients have brought me writings by personalities, poetry or drawings that were revealing. It is startling to have patients with superior intelligence offer such transparent messages with puzzled expressions. They are befuddled by the content, although anyone else can decipher it. A patient called me to her room one morning to see a drawing that she had found lying on her bedside table. She disclaimed it, since she had no artistic talents and could not remember either awakening or drawing. It was a splendid rendition of a coiled fat snake done in great detail—an important element in her trauma. There was no doubt that she had done it during the night in an amnestic state, and it was a further step in the therapeutic process.

Personalities often are helpful, and I turn to them for assistance. Those that are knowledgeable can be valuable allies. Some offer much information, but most know only parts of the story. When the help is available I often brainstorm with the helpful personality to discover what is being hidden or why progress is impeded.

It should be realized that all these tactics are reflections of the central process. The patient is guarding his or her secrets, although the therapist may be using automatic writing, hypnotic dreams, or personalities to uncover them. These indirect tactics will gradually reveal them, but they are unveiled only at a rate acceptable to the patient. The secrets come, but they may remain still partially dissociated and at a distance—and therefore impersonal and unreal.

This brings us to another important principle. One must distinguish between gathering information helpful in therapy and the recognition by the patient of the reality of his or her experiences. The therapist may seek the information to understand the particulars of the problem, but this is not by itself therapeutic. When there is a block, the patient may be asked to rest in a pleasant place, perhaps by a lake, the ocean or in the mountains—wherever seems comfortable. The patient may relax there in hypnosis and *not* listen while you converse with a personality. It is then helpful to learn from this ally that the patient was molested by a stranger, beaten by a parent, or mistreated by a brother. Under these circumstances, the therapist then knows the problem—although the patient continues to have an amnesia. One must then seek ways to induce the patient to face the unpleasant facts and accept them.

An important rule is that the patient must listen while the therapist engages a personality; otherwise, there is no therapy. Whenever possible, I insist that the patient remain. He or she, too, must be privy to the information. Furthermore, one must be alert to possible tune-outs, and I repeatedly ask whether the patient is still there or has disappeared.

In my first case, I spent an entire month treating a personality while the patient tuned out. The personality had stolen drugs and injected them into my patient, a nurse, while she had an amnesia for these acts. Mistakenly I assumed that this therapy given the personality, in the absence of the patient, would somehow assuage my patient's guilt and allow her to accommodate better to the transgression. I was treating her "unconscious," but slowly and subtly, or so I believed. Finally, after a month of soul-searching discussion with the personality, I concluded that adequate preparations had been made and I then invited the patient to listen. The result was disastrous. All of our conversations were known to the personality but not to the patient. For the first time she learned about her transgression and became deeply depressed. My initial work had in no way penetrated her conscious mind, and she was not prepared for the shocking revelation.

No matter how one approaches the patient's secrets, the prime objective is to make them conscious. One way is to treat personalities in sequence. One begins with the most accessible and progresses through the array. As their secrets are discovered and accepted by the patient, each in turn is integrated.

In treating personalities, I often introduce them to the patient and ask that they work together. The personalities have skills that the patient might be willing to learn, and they have information that would be helpful. They must come to know and understand one another. Eventually they must find some compromise or an arrangement that is mutually acceptable. Differences must be resolved. The patient may ask, "Must I like her?" The answer can be, "No, but you must resolve your differences." Homework may be recommended so that arbitration can proceed outside of the therapeutic sessions.

I make friends with the personalities, although some are antagonistic. They often assert that I intend to destroy them. My answer is that such is not my intention. I cannot force an integration. My hope is to make the personality a conscious part of the individual along with other parts, but no longer hidden.

In turn, the patient may object to some of the personality's behaviors. For example, a personality wears too much lipstick, likes "sexy" dresses, or is explosive and obnoxious when angry. I reply that these responsibilities can be the patient's if she is willing. She has the privilege of deciding what compromises are desirable or sensible, but only after she accepts these obligations.

I sometimes suggest to personalities after preliminary discussion that they have carried intolerable responsibilities for many years. It is time for them to relinquish the burden so that the patient can assume it. The patient, in turn, is encouraged to assume the task—to cry, be assertive, get angry. It isn't a powerful tactic, but it can assist recovery.

As the patient reexperiences and recaptures hidden events, the personality involved often becomes weaker, more tractable and amiable. "Rhoda," for example, was a vulgar shrew created to protect her mistress, but as the patient became stronger, Rhoda began to whine and complain that she was losing her power.

At times, personalities are secretive or hostile. In one patient, personalities refused to divulge any information. It was clear that the patient did not want to know the details of her traumas. She sensed that it would be too much and that she would not be able to live with the knowledge. In fact, she openly admitted this. I kept reiterating that there was no choice. She must recover them; otherwise, she would inevitably commit suicide. An adult woman, I kept repeating, could adjust better to those hidden events than a frightened adolescent who had incurred the brutality. Furthermore, she now had help, in my assistance, whereas none had been available when that grim assault occurred. My arguments and entreaties didn't budge her, and it was necessary to chip away at the details for many months until the sordid tortures were finally revealed.

When there are threats to the patient's safety, agreements can sometimes be made such as not to commit suicide during therapy, to abstain from self-mutilations, or to notify the therapist when crises occur. This is reassuring for some patients, since they fear the loss of control, feel safer, therefore calmer, and are less likely to dissociate with this protection. Such agreements work with some patients, at least for limited periods, but in other patients they fail.

Angry and suicidal personalities are the most troublesome. One can try various gambits with angry ones. They are justifiably angry, but they should also be fair; or one may suggest that they take on mollifying traits of other personalities to temper the anger. But in my experience the only solid solution is to find the early causes of the anger and to have the patient learn the reasons and accept this as his or her responsibility. The patient must learn that anger is a good and often justified emotion, one that can be managed.

Suicidal personalities are also difficult. They continue to assert their right, and intention to kill the patient. At first I would argue with them, employing sweet reason. If the patient died, they too would die. But that proved to be futile. I now reason with such patients, since it is they who are suicidal. When they become depressed and feel life is hopeless, there may be a switch into the suicidal personality. Patients must be encouraged, reassured, and given hope so that this doesn't occur.

Despite all precautions, some patients do overdose or cut themselves, and several have made serious suicidal attempts that necessitated emergency measures and treatment in an intensive care unit. When a patient says that she is sure razor blades are hidden on the ward but that she has an amnesia for their whereabouts; or is certain that there is a hoard of drugs secreted at home, although only an uncooperative personality knows the hiding place, the therapist doesn't rest easy.

At first one is inclined to spend much time with personalities, questioning them, arguing with them, and treating them. This concentration on personalities can lead one to lose sight of the real therapeutic process. When one interacts with these alter egos, the patient must be listening. In fact, one is not doing therapy with personalities; one is indirectly treating patients. It is they who are recovering hidden memories, and it is they who must cope with the amnestic experiences. But in the whimsical world of hypnosis, this kind of indirection is possible.

As I have acquired more experience with these cases, my tendency has been to spend less time with the personalities and to concentrate on patients. They must uncover the unconscious material and learn to cope with it. Personalities may be helpful aides when the patient blocks the process, if they are willing to assist.

Instead of turning to an intellectual personality for information, I now sometimes ask patients to block out their emotions so that their minds can work with me on the problem. If a patient can do this, and it is one capability of hypnosis, I then have the equivalent of an intellectual alter ego. In the same way, if no personalities can be found but the patient has fugue states or periods of amnesia, I ask to speak to that other part of the patient's mind which is present and active during those amnestic states. I simply call it "that other part" and then proceed to question it. This allows me to acquire information that the patient may be reluctant to reveal. In a sense I am creating a personality with this technique, but in actuality I am tapping the unconscious mind, where the secrets are hidden. One patient who shoplifted with an amnesia could not penetrate to the events until I tried this tactic. It was then possible to gain access to the amnesia while the patient listened.

As one gradually bridges defenses, patients may remember first only fragments of the trauma or see flashes of pictures that are garbled and unintelligible. They next may perceive the event, but as an observer from a distance. They may then see the event, but without the feelings, until finally the feelings are added and the entire memory is regained.

Throughout therapy one assesses the patient's willingness to work. Most are understandably disinclined to approach their early disasters in hypnosis because it means reliving them. The initial experiences were painful, sometimes horrifying, and patients do not want a repeat performance. Unfortunately, this is usually mandatory. If the experiences remain hidden, no amount of "chitchat" will suffice.

Unfavorable therapeutic signs are an inability to enter heterohypnosis despite all evidence that spontaneous hypnosis occurs; an unwillingness to listen to personalities during hypnosis; and the persistent forgetting of memories found in hypnosis. An occasional patient slowly gains access to traumas but refuses to confront personalities—an indication that therapy will be a formidable struggle. When personalities continue to lie, or to mislead or deceive the therapist, however, it may be time to quit. I explain to the patient that if the deception doesn't change we are blocked. Either it is my fault or they are unwilling, but in either case we had best consider terminating therapy unless those behaviors stop. After all, personalities do reflect the patient's inclinations.

But patients are different, and tactics must be tailored to fit the individual. I sometimes think of them as children who are afraid of water. To teach them how to swim demands patience, humor, distraction, coercion, indirection—any ploy to give them courage and reduce panic. One patient regularly needed two- or three-hour sessions because the first hour so often was a period when she was in a frightened daze as a terrified child. She would insist that there was too much fighting inside. Only after tears and despair would she grow calmer and begin to work constructively. Another patient had to be handled gently. When the work panicked her it would be necessary to switch her attention from the search to neutral topics. We would talk about politics, sports, any distraction until she grew calmer, and then we could resume work.

## Magical Tactics and Suggestion

I have tried a variety of magical procedures in hypnosis, but with limited success. At times I have sought to inspire courage or tranquility, even love and human warmth. At other times I have suggested body armor to make patients less sensitive, or blotted out pain when headaches were excruciating. I have left patients in the care of the Virgin Mary during crises, or hypnotically paralyzed their bodies when they felt assaultive so that their minds could work with me. On several occasions I have asked that a troublesome discovery be put in a deep freeze or the anger placed on a shelf until we had more time to work on it. All these imaginative and amnestic feats are capabilities of hypnosis. Any imaginable tactic can be tried, but in my experience these impromptu methods often fail. When they succeed, they are only temporary expedients. For example, patients' headaches can sometimes be relieved in a half minute by hypnosis, even when it is done over the telephone. But the headaches will return until the hidden traumas are revealed. In several cases chronic intractable headaches have miraculously ceased after a crucial personality was integrated, but this occurred because the underlying reasons for the pain had been discovered.

The nineteenth-century hypnotists reported remarkable successes with suggestive therapy. Their reports cannot be dismissed, but my luck using suggestion alone has been minimal. This may be due to the nature of the patient population that I have treated. All my patients have had serious psychiatric disabilities with complicated hidden traumas. It may be that simpler cases can be treated rapidly with hypnotic suggestions, whereas these patients need extensive hypnotic exploration.

## Emotional Components

A central problem in therapy with these patients is the management of emotions. Patients are deeply afraid of their hidden memories and strenuously avoid confronting them. My repeated explanation to them is that self-hypnosis with amnesia was needed by the child who could not cope, but it is not needed by the adult, who need no longer fear abuse. As adults, patients are stronger, mature, and no longer need be victims. They can handle the memories and manage their emotions. Furthermore, an amnesia that is a long-standing avoidance of a problem follows the rule of all phobias. The longer the feared object is avoided, the greater its magnification. A fear of water, mountains, or height grows with avoidance. Fears must be faced and mastered.

I tell patients that their greatest fear is of fear itself. Their anticipation is the biggest obstacle; their fantasies are more devastating than reality. I emphasize the positive, reminding them that they have shown courage in many other ways and that they also can in therapy. I invite them to enter hypnosis and confront the nemesis.

Patients also experience guilt. They are evil because of what happened to them. A father would not have approached them sexually if they hadn't deserved or solicited it. My rejoinder is often, did you really ask for it? Did it hurt? Given the choice would you have done it? The answer is usually in the negative. A few patients experienced some sexual excitement from these episodes. I explain that they were victims of normal physiology. One patient, raped by a stranger during adolescence, was horrified because she had had an orgasm. To have such a response under these circumstances was intolerable to her, and she had forgotten it. She had to realize that prolonged clitoral stimulation, even under these conditions, was responsible. Her experience should not condemn her forever.

When I am convinced that there is no reason for guilt, I say that the guilt is misplaced. In hypnosis I ask that this faulty idea be replaced. I tell the patient that he or she has been a victim. It is someone else's guilt, and his or her problem. I urge the patient to take the guilt and give it back to the person who should be feeling it. Another strategy is to urge that patients dispose of the guilt, and if they are willing, I ask how this should be done. Would it be best to bury it, or fire it into outer space? I ask the patient to choose. It should be remembered that hypnosis is a magical realm where fantastic events can take place. Guilts can be wrapped up and shot into outer space. In turn, the void left by the extracted guilt can be filled with understanding and self-respect. Sometimes, at least, such techniques are successful.

Crying is taboo for many patients. Parents punished them for tears early in childhood, and a personality often assumed this task. Patients are urged to cry when they feel like it; it is an excellent outlet and not a disgrace. To induce them to cry when it is appropriate becomes a tedious but necessary process. It involves persistent cajoling and reassurance, but can often be accomplished if the therapist is patient and tenacious.

Anger is a major disaster for most patients. They fear that if the emotion erupts they may brutalize themselves or hurt or kill someone else. Many have personalities with homicidal rage who are kept in dungeons, in cages, or contained by other personalities. These malevolent characters do emerge; in women, they usually assault or mutilate the patient.

I tell patients that when they feel anger against themselves, it is misdirected. They should really be angry with someone who has mistreated them. They are urged to reexamine their thinking. Children are brainwashed; they do not have the knowledge or experience to make mature judgments. Adults do have this privilege, however. They must correct their early erroneous beliefs and replace those ideas with correct ideas. They have every right to be angry at an abusive parent. This kind of anger is not a sin.

Eventually the explanation must be given and accepted that anger is a normal, good emotion, but if one pursues the maxim of "an eye for an eye and a tooth for a tooth," it makes one no better than one's oppressor. If that is accepted and retribution is no longer demanded, then one may suggest that the excess anger be eliminated.

When I have asked patients to explore the extent of their anger in hypnosis, they return with the frightened assertion that there are oceans of it—too much to handle. To teach them that it can be tolerated, I have asked some to make contact with a little of it in hypnosis and then to come out of hypnosis with it. I have asked others to express some anger when it was appropriate. Patients will experiment with it gradually and gingerly. One patient, after we had worked on anger for some time, was grabbed by a stranger at a public auditorium and propositioned. She instinctively reared back and "decked" him. He incurred a bloody nose and a nasty cut, but she, despite a bruised hand, acquired some confidence in her ability to protect herself. Pounding pillows, and even "primal" procedures (149) may be tried.

Several patients have hallucinated their assaultant, actually perceived him in a pillow or against the wall and pounded away at him, screaming imprecations. This behavior isn't pleasant, but sometimes it seems necessary. One patient, when I suggested that she pound a pillow, replied "That is only a pillow. I want to find him and kill him." I don't sanction homicide, however! The prime objective in therapy is to learn why there is anger and at whom it was really directed, and then to relegate that part of the anger to the past where it belongs. The injustice occurred many years ago. The anger, still contemporary, must become a component of that early experience. It must recede into the past to its proper places as an old memory, now conscious but no longer virulent.

## Abreactions

When the patient enters hypnosis and discovers a traumatic early experience, it is relived in all its detail. There is terror, there are physical pains, there are other obnoxious elements. To be sure, these events have repeatedly been encountered in spontaneous hypnosis in the past, only to be forgotten again, but abreactions are most unpleasant. A therapist dedicated to relieving suffering is naturally reluctant to induce further misery.

Unfortunately, abreactions are usually necessary. Unless patients relive the experiences, many will not accept or believe that they really happened. Even after abreactions occur, some patients will refuse to accept their validity. "My father couldn't have been so cruel. He would never have done that to me." In one case, every abreaction was followed by denial. "I must be lying. I have a vivid imagination. It isn't real." Despite all evidence—a known vaginal infection at the age of four, the fact that two other sisters had confessed that the father had raped them, and other documentation—she refused to accept what had happened. Only after many other pieces in the puzzle had been uncovered was I finally able to turn in hypnosis to "Mother Mary" for help, since the patient was Catholic. When my patient blurted out that Mother Mary had never lied to her, I took my chances and said, Mother Mary will make the final decision. If she says those things never happened I will accept her verdict, but if she says they did, I will believe her. A minute later the patient came out of hypnosis and reported, "Mother Mary said that it is all true."

The sceptic might assert that this is an excellent example of "brainwashing." I would reply that the evidence for the paternal abuse was circumstantial but conclusive. The only missing information was a confession by the father, and he was dead. These memories were in the patient's mind, but until that moment they had remained partially concealed.

At present, abreactions are necessary—and in most cases seemingly unavoidable. A challenge for the future is to find means to lessen their intensity or to avoid them while still achieving therapeutic results. I have tried various antianxiety drugs, but none thus far has been very helpful.

Some patients have less intense encounters with these traumatic memories. They simply enter hypnosis, perceive the memories, and then remember the events. They know what happened, and can piece together other facts to prove the validity of their memories and accept them. A few patients at first have "screen" memories. One relived a rape by a friend but later recognized that this had never happened. It was a hypnotic fantasy hiding the more repugnant memory of sexual abuse by her father.

## Other Tactics and Drugs

Some therapists record sessions and then have the patients listen to the tapes. When notes are taken, one may read them back to patients or give them copies to study. Information may be requested from members of the family to document the validity of the patient's hypnotic recollections. All these are ways to make the hidden memories real, to convince the patient that these events occurred. The purpose is not to perpetuate fantasies but to uncover the truth. In the world of hypnosis, fantasies can be perceived as real and believed, but memories can also be concealed and then revealed. One must distinguish between the two. Sometimes this is a simple task, but at times it is difficult or impossible.

My experience with these hypnotic revelations suggests that most traumas patients describe are real, but there are exceptions. However, where symptoms are excessive and fantasies are rampant, I assume that real events must have occurred to produce extensive psychopathology. In some cases the real events may seem trivial, such as an early surgical procedure or the feeling of rejection, social isolation, or timidity, but when these are conjoined to unusual hypnotic capabilities, self-hypnotic coping may ensue and become the major mode of adaptation.

My patients were usually given large amounts of drugs—antianxiety agents, antidepressants, antipsychotics, even anticonvulsants—before they reached me. None has seemed to be beneficial; certainly their long-term effects have been negligible. I have also tried a variety of agents in therapy but have had little success with them. Most psychiatrists who treat these patients have had comparable unfavorable experiences with drugs, although occasionally minor tranquilizers, antidepressants, or lithium may be helpful (163). Despite this clinical impression, rigorous drug studies are needed. Monoamine oxidase inhibitors are said to have efficacy in "hysteroid" patients, and it may be that they will prove to be helpful in some of these cases.

At present, difficult cases are time consuming and distressing. I often feel like an eighteenth-century surgeon, operating on patients before the discovery of anesthesia. In fact, several patients have ruefully termed me a psychosurgeon. A powerful antianxiety drug that could suppress terror and allow tranquil hypnosis would be a boon.

At times I have resorted to the use of intravenous sodium amytal to help patients delve into frightening secrets. It is a superior antianxiety agent, but it also facilitates amnesias. Patients usually forget the sessions, which nullifies any therapeutic effect. However, in cases in which resistances block all progress, an amytal interview may help. A colleague regularly uses this tactic and records the interviews on tape. Patients then can listen to their tapes in the presence of a nurse or aide and gradually accommodate to the facts.

## Conscious Nonhypnotic Tactics

One must recognize the purpose of various tactics. Hypnosis is used primarily to gain access to hidden memories. It is the means to penetrate the amnesia; once these feelings and memories are conscious they must be reconciled. This must occur in full consciousness, because it is the conscious mind that must accept the facts. The painful past events, now contemporary, must be consciously assimilated, reconciled, rationalized, and desensitized. It is true that this may occur while the patient is retrieving memories in hypnosis, but the principle is still valid, since it is the patient who is now experiencing these events.

Furthermore, the patient out of hypnosis must accommodate to present stresses and find solutions that are not self-hypnotic. This involves the skills of conventional psychotherapy and poses all the problems that psychiatrists encounter daily. New coping tactics must be identified and used to replace the old self-hypnotic subterfuges. How to block self-hypnosis has eluded me, however. Patients repeatedly report that it is instantaneous, instinctive, and uncontrollable.

Not only must patients desensitize themselves to their early traumas; at times they must desensitize themselves to knives, snakes, animals, or other things that have been components of hidden events. This is done in full consciousness. One patient first drew a straight line and then an undulating line. Later she drew tubes with humorous captions such as "I am Herbie, you don't have to be afraid. I'm your friend." Gradually she was able to draw more realistic pictures of snakes, until finally snakes disappeared from her nightmares and hallucinations. An assaultant had sexually abused her with a snake, but she had forgotten everything hypnotically. Even when she regained the memory, her terror persisted until the desensitization was successful.

Viewed more broadly, an essential feature of this form of therapy can be perceived as a desensitization process. The therapy is returning to consciousness a previously hidden memory. These painful memories, now conscious, are not necessarily mastered. They can persist as disabling preoccupations until processed by the patient.

These patients' excellent hypnotic abilities pose an additional problem. If patients go spontaneously into hypnosis, they may again relive their traumatic experiences. The question is how this self-hypnotic process can be circumvented. To study this I have asked patients to identify an early frightening experience that they have never forgotten. For example, one subject who was just learning to swim at age nine was thrown into a swimming pool. It had been a terrifying experience, one she had not forgotten. Later she became an expert swimmer, and in fact taught swimming. She is now confident in the water—swimming is safe and pleasurable. The question posed was whether this early memory was still intense—had the later desensitization process caused the terror to diminish or disappear? In hypnosis she returned to the experience and relived the terror, smelled the chlorine, and felt again as if she were drowning. The frightening memory was still there unaltered.

This suggests that even when hidden experiences are made conscious and desensitized, those memories, like all conscious recollections of severe traumas, are retained. If they are revisited by spontaneous hypnosis, they can still be relived. So the therapeutic goal cannot be to expunge them; rather it is to diminish the emotion that activates them. When the fear of swimming, or of snakes, knives, or sex is dampened, they will no longer provoke terror, so a reversion to self-hypnosis becomes unnecessary.

It may be that some traumatic memories will wither and gradually extinguish when they are not reinforced. But the alternative hypothesis must be considered. The memories persist, but potential contemporary activators—events with associative links—have been desensitized. Water is now linked to pleasure and mastery rather than to terror, and therefore the terrifying early experience is not revisited by spontaneous hypnosis although it is still present intact in memory.

I have assumed that these patients will never forget the early traumas that necessitated self-hypnosis. They can only accept them and adjust to them in a normal fashion. Life provides tragedies; people must and do accommodate to defeats, disappointments, failures, and deaths. A mother whose son is killed in an automobile accident grieves. She may curse the fates, refuse to believe it happened, and suffer great anguish, but eventually there is a mental switch. Somehow the mind accommodates, attention is refocused, and life continues. One tries to get these patients to cope in a like fashion to these hidden memories of old events, now remembered. However, I suspect that there will be those patients who will recapture hidden memories of traumas but will not be able to accept or accommodate to their tragedies.

## Trying Moments

In dissociated states or as personalities, these patients can be taxing if not impossible. They leave messages in blood, run away from the hospital, drive recklessly, and get in trouble with the police. They cut, burn, and mutilate themselves. One regularly cut her wrists with concealed razor blades; another inflicted third-degree burns on herself; and a third swallowed a corrosive agent in a capsule, creating a large gastric ulcer. Patients have also been known to swallow pins and insert metal objects in their vaginas—one repeatedly burned her vagina with a caustic chemical.

Some personalities act as prostitutes; others steal. One patient had a particularly dangerous personality that solicited men to abuse and torture her sexually. Two had personalities who married while the patient was absent. One patient became pregnant when a promiscuous personality was careless. As she said, "It isn't fair. I wasn't there and I didn't do it," but it was the patient who suffered a therapeutic abortion.

I have known several personalities that were heavy drug users and others that abused alcohol. Three patients had "hysterical" seizures. In one patient these were harmless, but the other two toppled like logs, and only luck saved them from severe injury. In the past, several had incurred broken bones or deep lacerations when personalities punished them. In one case, self-inflicted infections sustained in altered states necessitated multiple surgeries and an amputation. One patient bought a gun in preparation for suicide, and another appeared at a colleague's house with a pistol. These are only some of the experiences that I can recall. It isn't tame psychiatry, but there is drama enough—and reward when therapy succeeds.

## Premature Victories

The time arrives when the traumas have been revealed. The therapist and patient may assume a success, only to discover that all the details are known but only intellectually. The virulent emotions associated with the traumas still remain concealed. It is back to work to get at the associated anger; then the episode can be put to rest as a past memory.

In one case, the patient and I celebrated a final victory. After a two-year struggle, we had won. She prepared a sumptuous meal and we toasted our success, but unfortunately our celebration was premature. The emotions generated by her many mistreatments had not been accepted and resolved. She had partially concealed the feelings, and further symptoms began to erupt. The job was incomplete. I must ruefully acknowledge that the distinction between an intellectual insight and an emotional one is not always obvious, nor is it always clear when mastery occurs.

When the patient has experienced years of abuse as a child, the question is how much must be resurrected. One can't recapitulate every trauma over the years, because the process would be interminable. There seems to be no simple answer to that conundrum. One follows the patient's leads and stops when a sufficient number of traumas have been discovered to expunge symptoms. But even then there are surprises. Symptoms may recur, and one may discover another unsuspected personality or a further trauma that must be managed.

My experience with difficult patients underscores the importance of these undetected traumas. In two taxing cases, the final, grimmest memories only appeared after several years of therapy. Both were discovered almost by chance when symptoms persisted. By that time, both the patient and I were convinced that the unconscious had been revealed, yet therapy was failing. In retrospect, it can be seen that these memories were crucial; if undetected, they would have blocked any recovery. The lesson seems to be, not therapy interminable, but vigilance for work unfinished (162).

I am now alert to unfinished business and cautious about triumphs. Only time can justify a cure: long-term follow-ups are necessary. An unanswered question is how much early trauma human beings can tolerate and still fully recover. What is reversible and what irreversible?

## Integrations

There are many ways to integrate personalities (38). In fact, patients follow their idiosyncratic inclinations. Some cry together and then become one, others fuse with bodily sensations. The list, I suspect, is endless. One local therapist asks the patient and personality in hypnosis to enter a room through a door. He asks them to integrate, then locks the door so that they cannot leave and separate.

My procedure is to ask both patient and personality whether they are ready. I then say that the patient now has the memory, the feelings, and the responsibilities. They may now come together and become one. It is a simple, magical ceremony in hypnosis, but I am sure that other tactics would be equally successful. The crux of the process is the acceptance of the experience, with its emotional components and responsibilities. Once this is done, any procedure should work.

Patients sometimes say that they hate a personality and would like to dispose of the nuisance by destroying it. This is not acceptable. I explain that this would be a variation on their old practice of coping with an experience or function by running from it. Unfortunately, in this case the patient has no place to run; the specter is inside the mind. It must be confronted and acknowledged.

But when the necessary therapeutic work has been done, other sensible integrating variations may be proposed to the patient. If the personality is a father or mother, now dead in reality, one may request that they be forgiven or understood and be sent to heaven. Depending on particular circumstances, many tactics may be appropriate.

Some therapists do not seek integration. Instead, they recommend as a goal that all parts of the personality be guided to function cooperatively, and each part be assured of its right to exist (9). I am uncertain whether this is a fundamental difference in method or is a variation of integration.

My premise is that traumas and functions have been hidden by self-hypnosis, creating a fragmentation that deprives the person of conscious self-control. An example would be a suicidal personality. When the patient becomes depressed, there is then a hypnotic switch into this suicidal part, and it operates independently while the patient disappears. It is hardly an ideal tactic—an automaton is now in control, allowing destructive behavior to ensue. In most instances, but not all, a suicidal gesture is made, such as a superficial cut or the ingestion of pills. But a protective part of the psyche has also been operating, taking care that the cut is not lethal, or calling for help after the pills have been swallowed. Alternatively, the patient may return to consciousness and does this.

This complex indirection creates a melodramatic scenario—hardly a script for sane living. In my view the therapeutic goal is to make the suicidal despair a conscious process, thus eliminating the hypnotic subterfuge. But this seems to necessitate the recovery of amnestic traumas usually experienced at an earlier age, which led to the creation of a suicidal alter ego. When this occurs and these traumas are converted into past memories, the suicidal gestures are often abandoned.

If the therapists who reject integration as a goal do this essential work, I would not be surprised at their success. Integration may simply be the patient's graduation ceremony. It confirms the process with a symbolic diploma, which seems to be helpful. Whether formal integration is useful or perhaps essential can only be decided by further research.

One of my patients objected to the term "integration." She proposed instead the term "reconciliation," which I accepted. No term encompasses the process, but reconciliation does aptly describe the therapeutic goal. A psychiatrist doesn't have the power to change the facts, so the patient must have the courage to accept and reconcile to them.

## Final Stages

Even after all the personalities have been integrated, the therapeutic work is not finished. Patients do regress and return to previous modes of functioning if stresses become intolerable. They have spent decades using self-hypnotic tactics to cope, and they do not repudiate this tactic without a struggle. Personalities can always be reactivated with one hypnotic snap of the mind. Patients must abandon self-hypnosis, and they must come to recognize the stresses to which they are particularly sensitive.

One patient, after our hypnotic work had been completed, experienced a recrudescence of symptoms. She was again in a twilight zone, the victim of her personalities and self-destructive urges. We discovered that the past two weeks had been particularly stressful for her; she had had several experiences reminiscent of her early traumas. She was still vulnerable to criticism and heterosexual challenges. These had panicked her and driven her back into self-hypnosis. We identified the stresses, and she recognized why the panic had ensued. Then we returned to the real world once again. As she said, "That other world has been my home for thirty years, and I instinctively go there." It takes such a patient time to learn how to avoid self-hypnosis. At least in this instance it was reassuring to find that no new traumas or personalities were responsible.

After therapy, memories of traumas are conscious and relegated to the past, but they are still present. A return to hypnosis can reactivate them with intense realism. A drug that blocked hypnosis might be useful at this stage. However, it will probably be difficult to find and, if discovered, it may prove to have adverse side effects, since the hypnotic mechanism is probably neuroanatomically affiliated with other vital systems governing sleep, arousal, and normal attention.

Other problems posed by these patients are not restricted to multiples, since they are commonly encountered in many persons being treated by psychotherapy. How does one more rapidly change erroneous convictions, faulty attitudes, and inappropriate emotional responses engendered during childhood? How does one more rapidly alter maladaptive behaviors that were learned early in life? Both these problems are major obstacles to change in multiples, and both at present are unanswered questions.

## Results of Therapy

There have been many favorable reports of therapy with multiple personality patients, but only Kluft (162), who has seen 171 cases, has treated a large number of patients with follow-up information. From his group of 123 treated cases, 83 had achieved fusion, while 40 had not. The 40 unfused patients included 20 still in therapy, 10 who interrupted therapy, and 10 failures.

In the group of 83 fused patients, 50 did not fit the criterion of a stable fusion for 27 months, either because of inadequate reassessment [7]; a fusion that was stable but of insufficient duration [16]; omission of follow-up [20]; or miscellaneous reasons [7]. That left 33 patients who met the criterion for his study. Of that group, 24 percent had some form of temporary relapse, and 76 percent remained stable.

Kluft concluded that patients with few personalities required shorter periods of treatment; that male patients had fewer personalities than females and briefer treatments; and that relapses were more common in patients with a greater number of personalities. Furthermore, treatment that terminated at the point of apparent fusion was rarely complete or stable. However, most patients, if treated for a long period—often five or six years—achieved stability and symptomatic relief, but treatment was intensive, painful, and protracted. Finally, fusion was a way station; prolonged follow-up and reassessment were shown to be essential.

## Summary

This therapy is really an elaboration of the ideas and methods described by Janet and Breuer at the end of the nineteenth century. Its purpose is to breach the self-hypnotic amnesia and to make the unconscious traumas conscious. Although the principle is simple, the details of the therapeutic process are complex.

These patients have employed self-hypnosis as a coping mechanism since childhood. It is a deeply entrenched habit, a longstanding addiction, and like all long-established habits difficult to break. There is also material hidden from consciousness. Some traumas are so devastating that there is an enormous aversion to remembering them, so the process of retrieval can be virtually interminable. Therapy must be further studied, simplified, shortened, and rendered less painful. It remains primitive surgery still lacking anesthetic agents.

# 7 / *Implications*

Thus far, the principal subject of this book has been the dysfunctional aspects of self-hypnosis—the many symptoms that it can contrive. But the number of excellent or good hypnotic subjects in the general population is huge. Presumably many must experience hypnotic processes that are considered to be normal although they may contribute to behavior. In the following section these possibilities are considered.

## Hypnotic Processes under Many Names

West's excellent analysis of dissociative states (285) contains descriptions of various self-hypnotic phenomena that occur under many designations. He included such hypnotic by-products as highway trances, ecstasies and trances in mystical and religious rites, the fascination or fixation of aviators, hallucinations and delusions during sleep deprivation and sensory isolation, psychotomimetic episodes under drugs such as lysergic acid diethylamide (LSD), out-of-body experiences with anesthetic agents, the frenzy or delirium of combat soldiers—"3-day schizophrenias"—the trances of mystics and fakirs, Ganser syndrome, pathological intoxication, and states of altered consciousness seen in primitive cultures—amok, berserk, latah, and arctic hysteria.

I would concur with West's list and add near death out-of-body experiences, many parapsychological phenomena, and others either neglected by oversight or as yet unidentified. All seem to be self-hypnotic, although few, if any, have been rigorously studied. A perplexing question is whether most people are capable of these reactions or whether they all demand unusual hypnotic capabilities. There are a few suggestive reports in the literature. For example, Gibbons and DeJarnette administered the Harvard Group scale of hypnotic susceptibility to 185 undergraduates (105). Those who reported a profound religious experience in the past had high scores, while no one with a low score had had one. Many more such studies are needed.

## Group or Social Hypnosis

If one accepts a conservative estimate, that 10 percent of all people are excellent hypnotic subjects and 20 percent are good ones, this would imply that one-third of the human race could be at risk for hypnotic experiences, particularly when strong emotions are generated. A feature of hypnosis is a focused attention, and this may eliminate other mental functions, including critical faculties, when the message being received is concordant with the individual's beliefs and values.

The suggestibility of a mob is well known. Although the reasons for this must be many, an unanswered question is how many people swayed to act irrationally in a group situation may be able hypnotic subjects who have entered spontaneous trances. Under such circumstances powerful ideas could be implanted rapidly, which might lead to uncharacteristic behaviors if the messages were basically congenial.

Sidis in *The Psychology of Suggestion* (242) gave many examples of this process. "When the preacher, the politician, the stump orator, the ringleader, the hero, gains the ear of the crowd, an ominous silence sets in, a silence frequently characterized as 'awful.' . . . Disturbing impressions are excluded, put down, driven away by main force. . . . All interfering impressions and ideas are inhibited. The crowd is entranced and rapidly merges into the mob-state."

Consider the description of the "modern Messiah," Francis Schlatter, who appeared in the United States in 1895 and worked miracles. People believed in his divine powers and flocked to him. He cured many by the laying on of hands, as had so many of his predecessors throughout the ages. A reporter described the scene. "A sudden movement went through the assemblage, and even the faintest whisper was hushed. . . . Schlatter had come. . . . As I approached him I became possessed of a certain supernatural fear. . . . My faith in the man grew in spite of my reason. . . . As he released my hands my soul acknowledged some power in this man that my mind and my brain seemed to fight against. When he unclasped my hands I felt as though I could kneel at his feet and call him master." Was the reporter an excellent hypnotic subject? Had he entered a trance unknowingly?

Sargent in his book *Battle For the Mind* (232) has explored the same process. In reviewing the activities of John Wesley, the preacher and revivalist of eighteenth-century England, he analyzed the conversion of disciples. It was a sudden process generally brought about by the induction of states of great anxiety, fear, or mental conflict, often about the existence of a hell hereafter and the impossibility of salvation from hellfire except by faith. The acquisition of a "saving" faith took place only under tremendous pressures, with a sense of personal helplessness and impending disaster. It might occur during the heightened emotional frenzy of a religious meeting itself or later as a result of a spiritual struggle when people were home alone, their minds still dominated by the urgent need for a solution.

The group "insanities" of human beings are innumerable, and many are discussed by Sidis (242). There were the Crusades, which disrupted European nations for two centuries with the loss of about 7 million lives. People were moved by an irresistible urge to regain the Holy Sepulcher. The Western world of Christendom fell into a transformed state; many people had religious visions and perceived miracles. Swarms of men with their wives and children, with infants and the elderly, many sick and dying, came to conquer the Holy Land—only to be decimated before they reached Palestine.

During this demented period there were also crusades against the Arabs in Spain and the Albigenses in southern France. It is said that in the latter movement, a peculiar religious mania erupted among the women. Thousands of them, stark naked and silent, ran frantically about the streets, while many fell into ecstatic convulsions.

But one of the most bizarre crusades was the Children's Crusade, which took place about 1212. Stephen, a shepherd boy at Cloyes, imitating his elders preached to children, exhorting a holy war. Stephen became the prophet of the day, even working miracles. This epidemic rapidly spread, claiming children as young as eight and ten.

This form of madness took other forms. In 1260 there appeared the holy insanity of the flagellants, first in Italy, but soon spreading throughout Europe. "An unexampled spirit of remorse," wrote a chronicler, "suddenly seized upon the minds of people. The fear of Christ fell on all, noble and ignoble, old and young, and even children of five marched on the streets with no covering but a scarf round their waists. They each had a scourge of leather thongs, which they applied to their limbs with sighs and tears with such violence that blood flowed from their wounds."

As the flagellant epidemic subsided, a new disaster spread over Europe—the bubonic plague, or Black Death. People were seized by another mania, one endemic throughout the Western world but now in a more virulent form. A frenzy of anti-Semitism swept over Europe. Thousands of Jews were brutally burned, tortured, and killed in retribution for their alleged sins against Christ.

Then began the dancing mania; by about 1370, thousands of dancers filled the streets of Europe. In Italy, this craze assumed a slightly different form. The belief became rampant that anyone bitten by a tarantula would become dangerously ill and could only be cured by dancing to the tune of the tarantella. Many, convinced of their affliction, became blind, aphonic, and anesthetic. At the sound of music they would awaken from their lethargy and begin a frenzied dance. Tarantism became the plague of Italy. Crowds of people thronged the streets, dancing madly to the tune of the tarantella.

At the end of the fifteenth century, another fearsome idea began to occupy the mind of Western humanity. Demonophobia, the fear of demons and witchcraft, became widespread. For more than two centuries, the fear of the Devil was rampant. In Europe the insane idea prevailed that impious people, especially old women, could effect supernatural mischief—fly through space; convert themselves into dogs, cats, wolves, and goats; kill and terrify others; feed on the flesh of the innocent at horrible banquets presided over by the Devil; and sexually subvert the innocent. The old and helpless, hysterics and the insane, Jews and the unfaithful were victimized. All were accused of intimate relationships with imps, incubi and succubi, and even intercourse with the Devil himself. Witchcraft, long believed to be a reality, now seemed a perilous menace.

In his Bull of 1484, Pope Innocent VIII appealed to all Catholics to rescue the Church from the power of Satan and to expunge sorcery from Christendom. Everywhere disciples appeared to identify and burn sorcerers and witches. The doctrine was carefully and cruelly enunciated in the *Malleus Maleficarum* (261) by two monks, Sprenger and Kramer, who were delegated by the pope to investigate these depravities. The Bull was printed as a preface to the *Malleus Maleficarum,* and the volume became a part of European jurisprudence for nearly three centuries, mandating holy combat against witches. The volume lay on the bench of every judge and on the desk of every magistrate.

The witch hunt was a grim affair. Inquisitors examined suspects concerning meetings with the Devil, and whether they had attended the witches' sabbath, could raise whirlwinds, or had submitted to sexual intercourse with Satan. Torture was the usual tactic employed to elicit evidence.

Sprenger now embarked on his holy mission and burned as many as nine hundred victims a year. The German commission condemned thousands of victims to the stake. Each successive pope appointed new commissions as the epidemic of witch hunting grew. In Geneva, five hundred persons were burned in the years 1515 and 1516. One inquisitor, Remigius, was proud of his nine hundred victims in fifteen years.

This epidemic spread from the continent to England, where in 1562 Queen Elizabeth I declared witchcraft to be a crime of the highest magnitude. In Scotland, finding witches became virtually a profession. It was believed that the Devil put his mark on his victims in the shape of a spot free from pain—something we now know is common in hysterics. The witch finders, armed with long pins, roamed the country testing for the Devil's disciples. To be accused of witchcraft almost always resulted in death.

The treatise on demonology published by King James I in 1597 inflamed this orgy, for he wrote, "Witches ought to be put to death, according to the law of God, the civil and imperial law, and the municipal law of all Christian nations." He specified "two good helps" to identify the culprits: "the one is the finding of their mark, and the trying of the insensibleness thereof; the other is their floating on the water."

During the reign of James I and Charles II, the fury of demon-ophobia raged, with victims swiftly accused, hanged, and burned alive. Three thousand witches were executed during the time of the Long Parliament, and during the first eighty years of the seventeenth century, it has been estimated that a total of 40,000 were executed in England.

A notable witch hunter was one Matthew Hopkins, distinguished for his dedication and methods of detection. His favorite test was swimming. The hands and feet of the suspected witch were tied together. The victims were then wrapped in a blanket and laid on their backs in a pond or river. If they sank and drowned they were innocent, but if they floated they were guilty of witchcraft and were burned alive. Another test was the repetition of the Lord's Prayer. No witch could do it correctly. If she missed a word or even if she pronounced one indistinctly, she was guilty. Tearlessness was also a good test.

The final chapter (277) in this infamy occurred in Wurzburg, Germany, when some nuns suddenly thought themselves bewitched. They all felt themselves suffocating and had paroxysms. A nun, Maria Sanger, was suspected of witchcraft and charged with sorcery. At her trial, witnesses testified that she could change herself into a cat, a pig, or a hare and terrify the other nuns by appearing before them in their rooms in animal form. She was condemned and burned alive in the marketplace.

The purpose of this dismal recital is not to reaffirm human cruelty or humanity's long history of brutality and ignorance, for it is only too well documented in the incessant wars, persecutions, and torture of the innocent down to the present day. It is rather to identify the possible role of self-hypnosis in these behaviors. Prejudice, fanaticism, demonology, and cruelty need not be brought about by hypnosis, but the self-hypnotic process can introduce powerful ideas into the recesses of people's minds, which then can motivate and direct their behavior. Just as one's rage or a past sexual assault can be concealed in the unconscious and then act to produce illness and disability, so other potent ideas can also be imbedded within and direct malignant behaviors.

How many inquisitors were so driven can never be determined, but the contagion of these beliefs must have entered many minds by this route. Certainly many of the "victims" of witchcraft must have entered hypnotic states and developed the conviction of infestation by the Devil or anesthesias by this unwitting tactic. In an age dominated by such universal beliefs, it would only be necessary for an experience of fear, mass hysteria, or panic to induce spontaneous trances in the susceptible.

## Normal Hallucinations

DeBoismont in 1855 published a remarkable analysis of hallucinations (62). He recognized that reveries, states that I have termed spontaneous hypnotic experiences, are "eminently favorable to the production of hallucinations." He commented on celebrated subjects inflamed with ecstasy who are enamored of religion, morality, poetry, the fine arts, science, and philosophy, and devoted to the contemplation of divinity. "Such a state of mind is eminently favorable for the production of hallucinations, which are very common among such people."

Included were prophets, saints, philosophers, and many illustrious persons who had "fallen into a state of ecstasy from profound meditation." But these experiences were also reported by nuns, Shakers, convulsants, and the sick; and by the Illuminati and Quietists, many of whom boasted of seeing God face to face.

DeBoismont noted that many persons after experiencing ecstasies described "the ineffable joy they felt, the dreadful phantoms they saw, the divine visions and angelic assemblages which they witnessed. Many undertake to predict the future."

A long list of eminent persons who had reported these experiences was given by DeBoismont, and later by Parish (213). Socrates had auditory hallucinations and was said to have stood all night in a rigid attitude communicating with the voices. He was often restrained and admonished by an inner voice. Savonarola saw visions even in his early youth. Luther was subject to numerous auditory and visual hallucinations. Cardan had a guardian spirit, and the philosopher Hobbes was haunted in the dark by faces of the dead. During one part of his adulthood, Descartes was followed by an invisible being who urged him not to abandon his search for truth. A vision of the Madonna was granted to the painter Raphael; Byron was often haunted by specters; and Schumann had auditory hallucinations. Swedenborg believed that he had seen God.

Ben Jonson confided to a friend that he had passed a whole night sitting in his armchair watching Tartars, Turks, and Roman Catholics rise up and fight. Goethe asserted that on one occasion he saw the counterpart of himself coming toward him. Oliver Cromwell was stretched sleepless on his bed when suddenly the curtains opened and a woman of gigantic size appeared and told him that he would be the greatest man in England.

General Rapp, on his return from the siege of Danzig in 1806, desiring to speak with the emperor, entered the cabinet unannounced. He found Napoleon in such a deep reverie that he did not perceive the general's entrance. Finding him immobile, the general intentionally made a noise. Napoleon then recovered, and seizing Rapp by the arm, pointed to the ceiling, saying "Look up there." The general made no reply; but the question being repeated, he answered that he saw nothing. "What," said the emperor, "You do not see it? It is my star; it is before you beaming." Growing more animated, he continued, "It has never deserted me; I see it on every great occurrence; it urges me onward, and it is an unfailing omen of success."

Francis Galton, a cousin of Darwin and himself a creative genius with rare imaginative talents, in 1883 reported a study of mental imagery (101). One hundred men, nineteen of them Fellows of the Royal Society, and most of very high repute, were questioned. Twelve acknowledged very vivid visual pictures that were distinct, clear, and as bright as an actual scene indistinguishable in all particulars from reality. A member of the Royal Institute often wished that his visual perceptions would go away, because they were so brilliant and persistent. Other subjects had mastery over their mental images; they could call up the figure of a friend at will and make it sit on a chair or stand up. One reported that he had difficulty defining the difference between a normal visual perception and his mental images.

One of Galton's relatives saw these phantasmagoria frequently. "It gave her amusement during an idle moment to watch these faces, for their expression was always pleasing, though never strikingly beautiful."

But some of these people had auditory experiences. The daughter of an eminent musician often heard her father playing the piano; another lady was plagued by voices. The words were at first simple nonsense; then the word "pray" was frequently repeated; this was followed by coherent, trivial sentences; and finally the voices departed. Galton concluded that this trait is more common in females than in males; is frequent in young children; and is a natural gift with a tendency to be inherited.

Parish (213) in 1897 referred to a questionnaire devised by James, Marllier, and Von Schrenck-Notzing to which there were 27,329 respondents. Twelve percent reported hallucinations; of these, 10 percent were males and 15 percent females. There was some evidence that this trait was familial. Most of these people experienced the hallucinations while fully awake; a minority had them while lying in bed awake. Visual hallucinations were the most common, followed by auditory, then tactile. Parish attributed these experiences to a "dissociation."

This impressive array of anecdotes and studies does not meet modern scientific standards. We will never know what the hypnotizability scores of these hallucinators might have been, but it is nevertheless pertinent to recognize that "normal" persons, and many eminent figures, experienced vivid realistic hallucinations. The commonest were visual, but there were many examples of auditory and tactile hallucinations. It seems clear that hallucinations are not solely the privilege of the insane and the mentally ill.

In recent years there has been a renewed interest in imagery (238). Many musicians and artists report perceiving auditory and visual images with hallucinatory intensity (175). But evidence indicates that this capability is not limited to excellent hypnotic subjects. In a study by Sutcliffe et al. (265), twenty out of twenty-two subjects with high imagery had high scores on the Stanford Hypnotizability Scale (A), but fifty-three out of seventy-three subjects with low scores also had high imagery. Similar results were found in a study by J. R. Hilgard (128, 133). The inference seems to be that high hypnotizability is almost always associated with excellent imagery, which is also the clinical experience, but a report of imagery is no guarantee of high hypnotizability.

Imagery is analogous to many other traits that are promoted by high hypnotizability. These include concentration, excellent memory, creativity, and fantasy; and syndromes such as phobias, depression, criminality, and pain disorders. All may be facilitated by excellent hypnotizability but may also exist in its absence.

In conclusion, two considerations deserve reemphasis. The first is the large number of psychiatric patients with hypnotic hidden memories. How many others harbor these amnestic traumas and never come to the attention of therapists can only be guessed, since no studies have been done to identify their number. I myself have been shocked to discover that I spent thirty years in psychiatry totally oblivious to their presence, never realizing what lay festering in many patients' self-hypnotic unconscious. Nor did I ever realize how many patients were switching into various personalities. I always attributed these changes to emotional lability, infantile behavior, or just irascibility. Colleagues often perceived these behaviors as caused by a lack of ego control or fragmented egos, or as histrionic and borderline manifestations. I found this vocabulary unhelpful but never had a suspicion that hypnosis might clarify the problem.

Finally, I would like to offer an admonition about future research. If spontaneous self-hypnosis is a central process in many psychiatric patients, we would do well not to repeat past errors, which have misdirected and confused research in hypnosis. Preposterous capabilities have been attributed to hypnosis. These have misled thinking and taken many decades to dispel. Even if one acknowledges that our knowledge of the brain is modest and much is yet to be learned, it is apparent that the brain and its derivative, the mind, have limitations. We would do well to remain attentive to Sarbin and Slagle's admonition about hypnosis (231). After reviewing the alleged somatic powers of hypnosis they concluded, "It would be more rewarding to count and catalog the rocks of New Hampshire than to reread the literature on the somatic effects of hypnosis." They drew two conclusions from their review. "Conclusion one concerns the question, Are observed alterations in physiological processes specific to the hypnotic trance? The answer is an unqualified No. Conclusion two concerns the question, Can symbolic processes produce changes in biological processes? The answer is an unqualified Yes." A summary of their findings is that any physiological change induced in hypnosis can be reproduced out of hypnosis. Physiological, electrical, or chemical changes uniquely associated with hypnosis have not been demonstrated convincingly.

This has been a hard-learned lesson, and it should not be neglected. Future investigators should be cognizant when they study these clinical self-hypnotic processes that information about hypnosis must be applied to clinical observations if we are to protect ourselves from past errors. The many physiological changes attributed to "personalities" may not withstand critical scrutiny; they may have simpler explanations (36, 37, 223).

## Summary

Many more people than has been suspected spontaneously enter self-hypnotic states. These are a special domain, where remarkable experiences are permissible. Those unable to enter a deep trance can only infer its nature from experiences with fantasies and dreams. Deep hypnosis, in a sense, blends the two. It has the freedom of fantasies but usually without the extremes of bizarreness possible in dreams. Simultaneously, it has the realism of dreams, which is not present in ordinary fantasies. This amalgam of mental freedom and realism creates an inner world where "magical" events may be encountered.

For many, this spontaneous hypnotic transformation will provide innocuous experiences that are restful and relaxing. It may be a sojourn in realistic fantasies, where wishes can become temporary realities; a vivid reliving of a memory; a deep imaginative involvement; a mesmeric indoctrination; a bizarre experience; or, for a few, a creative process. But some people, out of dire necessity, spontaneously resort to self-hypnosis as an escape from intolerable realities.

Since an excellent hypnotic capability is the privilege of many adults and a larger percentage of children and adolescents, the population potentially at risk is huge. Furthermore, self-hypnosis must contribute to many other forms of behavior, both individual and group, directing people's activities and beliefs. It is a powerful mental mechanism important to psychiatry, medicine, psychology, and human affairs.

Hypnosis need not be an odd fellow, excluded from respectability, since in the form of spontaneous self-hypnosis it is a basic property of the mind—a powerful force directing behavior. Assigning it its rightful place in science is a step long overdue.

# 8 / *The Patient Speaks*

The writings of some patients have been included to document the nature of their experiences. The psychiatrist is prone to generalize and sterilize with professional jargon, but patients have first-hand experience, and their accounts must be respected. They may not have been schooled in science, but they have somehow survived that extraordinary world and can describe it as participants rather than observers. Some have literary ability; others are less gifted but nevertheless manage to convey the stark details of their lives, which science misses.

Patients describe the multitude of hypnotic phenomena that excellent hypnotic subjects can and do experience spontaneously. It can be a list of disasters, befuddling and terrifying to the victim and confusing to the psychiatrist who doesn't recognize their self-hypnotic origins.

## 1. An Early Personality

"I remember being on the playground. It was a warm day. My classmates wouldn't let me play jump-the-rope with them and told me to go away. So I went off to the far end in the corner where no one else was. I looked into the weeds, closed my eyes, and wished with all my might. I asked Jesus for someone who would be my friend—one person my own age who'd like me too. I didn't understand. I didn't look or talk that different. I never meant harm to anyone. I would help them. I'd be their friend. Why wouldn't they be mine? So I remember looking into the weeds and hearing Joy. Joy said, 'Hi, I'll be your friend. You don't need them anyhow. I'll be your friend and I won't hurt you either. I am here to help you.' Then the bell rang, and I went back to class feeling better.

"Thereafter, I went back to the corner to 'play' with Joy. We caught ladybugs and put them in the old milk containers. Then we'd give them to Dad—he liked them for his aphids. I remember Joy always being around. Like we'd pick the cockleburs and give them away. We'd run to the bus and she'd 'help' me when I missed the bus, if I had to go back and face Mother. Joy was always around to be my friend. Everyone else was mean to me. Besides, I got away with it—she was my guardian angel.

"I remember Mother screaming at me for not cleaning up. I couldn't hear. I could just see the anger and feel the hurt. I remember I froze. Joy 'took over.' Neither of us said anything. Joy put a smile on my face, but I was angry and hurt. She kissed my mother and agreed with her pleasantly. She made my mother happy, which was what I wanted, and she fixed it. Then I was praised for being good. I was always praised for being such a good daughter and not sassing back like the other children. So Joy helped me and she seemed to grow along with me. She was there when I needed her. Sometimes I'd ask her questions on tests. And when I couldn't move she'd take over and be happy. That was the best part. Joy is very happy and playful, so sometimes when I'm down and the situation is called for, she becomes me. Sometimes it cheers me up, but sometimes it is only Joy who is happy and I'm still upset.

## 2. The Inner World of a Grand Hysteric

These are the experiences of a patient whom psychiatrists would classify as a typical grand hysteric (Briquet's syndrome). She had more surgical operations than I could count and kept psychiatrists and physicians busy for years. Personalities were not suspected until hypnosis revealed more than forty. She scored 12 on the hypnotizability test.

"Many different and unexplainable things have been happening most of my life. I never understood or could explain the reasons for them, and because I was afraid others would think me lying or just plain crazy, I said nothing to anyone.

"From the time I was about five years old, maybe a little younger, I have been a great daydreamer. I must have had a great imagination. I used to sit either in my bedroom or out under a big tree in the back yard and dream of all the beautiful places in the world where I wanted to be. Sometimes it was as if I really was there. I remember one particular time a couple of hours had gone by and my folks had been looking for me. When they found me out under the tree, they asked where I had been all of that time. I was very excited and told them I had been to Canada with a friend of mine and we had had such a good time! My mother asked me a little about my 'trip.' I described in my childish way that Jill had gone with me and we had seen some beautiful country, how peaceful it had been, how much fun Jill and I had running through fields of flowers, and how nice the people at the farmhouse had been to us. My mother asked me a little about the people. I must have described them pretty well, for my mother looked very shocked, and my father told me to quit lying, that I was upsetting my mother. This was the first time I was told my mother's home was Canada, and what I had described to them was the farmhouse my mother had grown up in and the people were her parents who had died when she was a teen-ager. My father insisted I was lying and smacked me one across the face.

"This was the first time I was aware that I could look at someone and make him disappear. I looked at my father with hate, and somehow he wasn't there any more. This is the first of hundreds of times I've made people go away or 'disappear.' Usually it is someone I am angry with, someone I don't like, or sometimes when I just want to be 'alone.' I not only can make one person 'disappear,' but I found out when I was around ten years old I could be in a room of people and make them all 'go away.' These things happen quite often, even now. Though I didn't know how, it has always been so nice to be able to be all by myself in a crowded room.

"When I was in grade school, I can remember some of my teachers saying to me, 'You are the top little girl in this school in every subject. You are in all of our little plays and musicals, and yet so much of the time you seem to be somewhere else—not in class with the others, but in places far away.' We used to laugh about it, but there were times I don't remember even being in class, and somehow I passed all the tests with an A grade.

"I remember one particular time when I was a senior in high school. I was in a class which was taught by one of my favorite teachers of all time. This one day he was going over the test material for our final exam of the year. As he spoke, he stopped and said, 'Where are you?' I didn't respond. He again said, 'Where are you? You must be with us or you will fail tomorrow's exam.' He told me that for the whole hour it seemed as if I was just 'not there.' He told me later that he knew I would fail the exam and he was sad. But much to his surprise, I got an A on the test and received the highest score in all of his classes. I recently had the privilege of attending his eightieth birthday party. I asked him if he remembered that day, and he told me it was one he would never forget, as he had never understood what had happened. But he also said that this kind of thing happened many other times, and that other teachers of mine had also mentioned similar experiences with me to him. During these times, I never remembered being in class.

"After I found out at the age of eleven that I could make others 'disappear,' I found that I could make people so small that they would be standing in a crack or a small corner. Then I also found I could look at someone and make him as big as a house—sometimes a mountain. I began to realize I could do these things not only with people, but with other things. It used to be great fun when I was a child, but I never dared tell anyone about this. I was too afraid! I can still do these things now, and it seems great to be able to tell you about these experiences without fear of being called crazy and being locked up.

"Since my mother died when I was ten, there have been many times I have seen and even talked with her. Do you think I'm crazy now? I can go to the cemetary and by concentrating, my mother is there with me. So many times I have wanted to go with her. Once or twice, I've almost made it with pills and once with a knife. There is one more burial plot beside her saved for my father. That is *my* spot!

"Because of my hate for my father, there have been times I have looked at someone I really liked, who was nice to me, and as I concentrated on his face, I could see my father's face.

"Most of these things I have related have frightened me very much— even as an adult! I just couldn't understand why these things were happening to me—I wondered if I had a form of extrasensory perception."

## 3. A Life in Self-hypnosis

After working with this patient for some time and observing her many hypnotic forays in therapy, I asked her to write about the role of hypnosis in her life. She was another multiple personality and a hypnotic virtuoso (scored 12), with devastating depressions and several suicide attempts.

"I feel as though I have *always* been able to get 'inside' myself, and I always thought everyone could and did. I was always alone so I just went inside and then I wasn't. Later when I made friends in the neighborhood, I found I was often alienated from them so I just went inside. I also found my head to be much more reliable. The friends in my head were easily attainable and always there, so I didn't have to depend upon anyone. There also wasn't any pain, as there was with people. Sometimes I almost preferred being there. At least I was 'safe' from everything and everyone, and no one could or would bother me.

"In about second grade, I found an imaginary friend who seemed a little more than imaginary. I don't think I could have made it through recess without my friend. I thought that everyone had one. I thought it was a part of growing up.

"When I was home, it was really easy to go inside when I read or watched television. Mom used to get really upset because I wouldn't hear her calling for me. She would get so angry! That was about the only negative aspect of being inside. One time she got so angry that Dad stood up for me and said it was good concentration, and it was.

"When I was a freshman at college, I took a class in parapsychology where we were taught self-hypnosis. We were taught to enter our mind by walking down a stairway. To go further, we'd get on a boat and travel. After class, the teacher said that I was a fantastic hypnotic subject. I didn't really think about it other than I was very 'flattered,' but it was no big thing.

"At the end of my freshman year, I began to go inside myself a lot more. We always called it spacing out. I began to space out in classes, which was totally out of character—I'm one who is not only there every day but usually ten minutes early. I'd take long walks and find myself somewhere wondering where I was. I'd go to the store for something important and right in the middle not know what I was doing there. I'd also have bad nightmares. I went to the school counselor because I knew something was wrong. We had a few visits, but it was the end of the year and he was busy.

"The day I was raped, I went to class anyhow. I remember thinking that I just couldn't go, so Elsie [a personality] took over. At the time, I didn't know it was she, all I knew was that I was someone else and that I did not feel anything. I think Elsie was there through most of the class, because I don't remember the class except for bits and pieces, and then I don't remember really being there, just sort of watching myself partici- pate, and being surprised at 'myself.' But then it wasn't me. I did very well at whatever it was, and got an A in the course.

"School resumed and I did okay the first couple of weeks. I remem- ber telling Mom that something was wrong. That I felt as if I were going insane. She said that was an indication of just how sane I was. I tried to explain that it wasn't so. No success. So I put up a stronger wall, hid behind a better mask, and acted normal. I can put up the best front! It's like there are two of me. There is the outside who is happy and pleasant, who not only responds normally but participates as well—the one who does everything right, whom everyone sees. But the me inside some- times is opposite. The me is crying inside, instead of smiling and saying everything's great. The one inside is afraid and hurt, doesn't understand why things have to be that way. Oftentimes there is such a split that I can't handle it. Then I either totally black out or am just not there. I don't know where my mind goes, but it's gone. It's as though I were in a white box: no sensations or thoughts, nothing, just blank. Sometimes, but very rarely, I can't move at all, not only my mind stops but my mus- cles won't move either—I can't do anything. Most of the time my body still functions. I think someone takes over and lives for me, so I am not caught. Evidently there are times when I am caught. I am told I did this or that, which doesn't fit—and I don't remember any of it. A lot of little things like that happen when I totally 'space out.'

"Someone makes a date or appointment with me and then I don't remember. It's embarrassing when someone comes to get you and you don't know what's going on. Sometimes two of me make two different dates for the same time. One must forget to tell the other, or something. Times like that can be pretty hairy! If I do make an appointment, I have them write out a card and then I write it down. This oftentimes does little good because I'm usually too 'spaced out' to remember anyway. I have problems with time! It does get embarrassing when I think it's sum- mer and I dress in shorts and a top and go bee-bopping to find it's winter. Then everyone around just stares. Soon you begin not trusting yourself or anything around.

"Anyway, in school I began 'spacing out' for days. I'd find myself here or there wondering what the heck was going on or what I was doing.

"They were very frightening times, and they'd leave me totally out of it for days. I don't really remember what happened during them or how I coped, because I'd totally black out. Sometimes I'd find myself walking miles away from the campus or sitting somewhere on the grass or somewhere strange. I don't know what I did or what happened during those times. I guess nothing bad ever happened because I never got into trouble.

"Summer came and I didn't feel well. I didn't feel bad. I did not feel at all. I just survived. I became completely dumb! My mind quit. I could not think. I could not feel. It was exactly as if I were dead.

"My 'tune-outs' became blatantly obvious! I could not say a word, and a lot of the time I couldn't move either. I'd sit there totally numb, mentally and physically. Sometimes I'd tune out so well I couldn't even hear. I don't know where I went. I just went. Most of the time my voices would really jump at the chance. They would really get down on me. I think that I just could not fight them so I went totally blank. It got so that I didn't feel anything: sad, happy, good, bad. I couldn't think anything so I didn't talk much. My voices began calling me dumb. On the one hand, the voices would say, 'You see, you must die—you cannot even think— you'll never survive—you must die.' And on the other hand, they said, 'You have already died—you *are* dead—now all you must do is to stop your body.'

"Sometimes I get so suicidal! Sometimes I look at it all as useless! I never know who I am. When I think I'm in reality, I find I'm not, so I don't know if I'm here or there. And I don't know if I can be or have been. I think perhaps half my life has been lived in another realm or time."


## 4. The Many Facets of Hypnosis

I asked the same patient to write about the nature and the reality of her self-hypnotic experiences.

"When something happens that you, yourself, experience, how much do you question its reality? If you go outside and the sun is shining, do you question if it is night or day? If it is snowing outside, do you question if it is cold?

"Now suppose you heard voices in your head? No one told you that it was not 'normal' to hear voices in your head. Now suppose these voices are favorable and in a way help you, how much would you honestly question their reality? My reality is not that far different from yours. Like you, I did not question until I had reason to question, and by then it was too late.

"Subtlety is one of the major keys. If you saw a big purple monster walking toward you, you would know it was unreal. But nothing that far out of reality or without explanation happens. There is first a buildup. Something 'small' happens that may be a little strange, and when it is accepted inside as good or okay, then it can get a little more off. But it doesn't happen or continue without an acceptance, or without a rationale. At first, you don't 'see' keys or a book, later you can make a person disappear. Again, the person would not be able to disappear or change without an 'acceptance' or explanation. Mine is that it is done in another dimension, which I may add is becoming a socially accepted idea.

"Once you find you can do one thing, you soon learn that you can do more, until you can do anything inside your head. First inside your head you go somewhere very pleasant, say swimming in a warm pond, which is very real. I can even be perfectly 'normal,' no one would ever even suspect I wasn't 'there.' I can walk, talk, anything, so my being is in the real world, my 'soul' or other self isn't. And where do you decide one reality stops? And if you can be one place like the pond, you can go to the moon just as easily.

"When these 'happenings' occur, I am completely conscious. Everything that happens to me is real, just as it is to you. I am living, just as you are. There is no clear-cut unreality-reality line. There is an odd, partial exception—when you 'come to' and wonder where you are and what you are doing or are losing time, sometimes days. But there again, it takes years before you begin to question.

"Next time you see or feel something, ask yourself if it is real. How do you tell, how do you know? Touch something next to you and ask yourself if it is real or not. If you can feel it, see it, smell it, or taste it, and I can do that for 'unreal' things, then it is real.

"When I am in that state, I can make everything fit—one way or the other. Everything is rational and makes sense. But I completely lose the ability to think at times. My mind goes totally 'white.' Everything is gone! At these times, I am almost totally out of reality.

"Other times, I see and hear what's going on around me, but cannot understand or comprehend any of it. This happens when I'm under great stress and am upset. My thinking becomes very unclear and very disconnected. I begin a sentence, and right in the middle I don't know what the heck I was saying or what was going on. It sometimes gets to where I cannot function. I literally cannot think.

"One of the hard parts is that it is mostly done in a totally conscious and wide-awake time. This brings about a mistrust in what is or isn't and a fear of what will happen. You never know quite what to expect or what is going on. It can happen at any time, but I think mainly when I am tired, have no energy, under stress, when I am upset, or when I am down.

"I can become someone totally different, which helps because I have some very diversified friends [inside]. This can bring about a total identity crisis. Sometimes two people clash, which creates problems. One says yes, the other says no. Whoever gets there first or is the strongest, wins.

"I can turn things off, or tune things out, such as coldness. I can go outside without a coat while others have heavy coats on and are still freezing. I just don't feel anything. I can also be freezing while it is 107° outside and everyone is dying of heat. I call it 'mentally cold.' Oftentimes my hands will also feel cold to others.

"I can go so deep into concentration that I don't hear anything, like people talking to me. Other times I hear them, but literally don't understand them—it is just sound. Sometimes I can pick up a book but can't read it. It is only ink on paper. I realize it has meaning, but I don't know what it is.

"Sometimes my mind works so fast that I can't pick up anything. Other times it is as though my mind has totally stopped. As strange as it sounds, I sometimes feel dead. Other times my body does things without my really being there, and sometimes I am even surprised at what my body is doing. Other times just my body is paralyzed. I cannot move anything and usually can't feel anything. My mind is active but I can't move. Sometimes this happens only to parts—my legs or arms or hands, or I'm stuck in one place or position. This happens often with little or no warning.

"It also may go to the other extreme where I can feel too much, like the blood pumping or the air current. I become very sensitive. I can honestly feel electricity go through someone if they are touching something electrical like an electric blanket.

"I can see things or not see them, look at a book, turn around, go back to it and it won't be there, or find something there that wasn't before. Things sometimes become distorted, especially people. Sometimes they look totally strange, as if they came from somewhere else. At times they just change, get small. But sometimes they fill the entire screen. Often everything around the person becomes distorted or blurry, and I see only the person or object against a black background. I can experience a feeling of weightlessness or spinning or flipping.

"When I am in that state, my thoughts become very intense. I become literally obsessed with an idea or thought, and always they are not what I want to think about! These thoughts and feelings are normally always negative—this has been especially true for the past few years and more so recently. It was a major factor in my suicide. Some of the ideas and feelings are how life is utterly useless—a complete hopelessness!

"My memory can be very good, as if I were reliving the entire experience again. I can recall exact things from years back and just amaze people. Several people have mentioned how my mind is more like a tape recorder. Usually along with the memory comes the feelings. You remember and feel everything so intensely.

"I also lose days, sometimes weeks. I'll just 'wake up' and it will be another day. I'd be doing what I'd normally be doing, and I knew or rationalized that I must have lived.

"My mind often races! It goes almost too fast for me, and way too fast for others. At other times my mind would go so slow that it would just stop, or get stuck on one thought—normally a negative one.

"Feeling is something else. You can either feel something very intensely, or not at all. Just the lightest touch can be felt as a blow. You can feel air or water currents. Often you can actually feel what people are saying or feel what they are thinking. Sometimes I think I can feel another person's pain better and more intensely than I can my own. It's as if I am that person and I can't turn it off like I can my own feelings.

"I turn feelings off sometimes without wanting to do it. I am a hopeless case with a dentist! At the orthodontist, he'd tighten up the bands on my teeth and ask me if it felt tighter? 'No, no change,' or 'feel better?' 'I don't know.' The poor guy broke a lot of wires asking me that. All these 'I don't knows' meant return trips to try again and fix it right. I suppose I'm in hypnosis, perhaps out of sheer fear, while I'm there, then when I'm out and home I come back to reality.

"I know I go into hypnosis at the dentist. I never have Novocain. I just sit there calm and quiet and block out the drill and pain. No big deal! The problem is that I stay in that sensationless state, so I can't tell if it's better or not. I just have to guess along with the dentist.

"When I hurt myself I don't feel it at all. I know I do it, and may feel it for a split second, but I can totally block it out. When I cut off the end of my finger at camp, the director almost had a nervous breakdown, while I sat there calmly—no big thing. I was told that I was 'so brave.' What brave? I wasn't really there.

"With taste, I can intensify the flavor or totally turn it off. My sense of smell is easy to turn off. At camp I couldn't smell the latrine while others just sat there and gagged. It was convenient because it was about the only place to be alone, and the only place with a mirror and a toilet. So I didn't mind. Rarely, I'll smell really bad odors, and then it's just myself—self-hatred might tie in with it. I can stay in a tub all day long and still stink. This also makes me stay as far away from people as possible!

"When I'm stoned on grass, it's no big thing because I can normally feel that way. I can attain the exact same state and feeling without a drug—maybe even better, and definitely easier. When you're stoned, everything is intensified! You can hear things better, see things in a different perspective, notice things a lot more, feel things more. There is timelessness and you can't really grasp or keep track of time. Eating is totally out of control. Food tastes 'better,' and you can eat and eat and eat. All those things are very common to me—without getting stoned! All I have to do is will them. No one would know I wasn't stoned. I can enter their conversations and feelings, and do anything they're doing, and not be stoned. It's easy. It's as though they are finally getting on my level for a change. Even the total paranoia people sometimes get, I have without the drug.

"A lot of times people have mentioned that I acted naturally stoned. One time I blew a friend's mind. She was taking a bath, and I was sitting on the toilet waiting and talking to her. She asked me what I was thinking and feeling, and she said, 'My God, you're stoned.' I wasn't. I just told her what was happening. I was feeling the warmth from the hot tub, and really getting 'into' the color of the bathroom—as if I could feel and sense the color. This was long before I knew much about being stoned. My friend had been stoned, but no one had ever told me what it was like, and I didn't get stoned until years later. The main thing I'd stress is the intensity or lack of intensity of emotions, feelings, and senses and reality.

"In that state, reality just *is*. Everything is and can be justified and explained. Everything fits, like a puzzle. Things just are, and you appear to be normal 99 percent of the time. I've lived there for years and years without any concern or wonder or suspicion that anything was wrong. Everything was okay until my voices and idea turned on me, and I was totally engulfed and totally into death. And even then, it was years before it got so bad that I couldn't fight and reason, and I began to show on the outside that something was wrong. It wasn't until I was at the end that I began to question.

"You are in a world where anything can happen and at the same time you are totally conscious. Very, very few people can pick it up. If it's done well enough, no one can know—not until there is a conflict. For me it was my voices. They turned against me and told me I must die. Then I became suspicious that maybe I wasn't okay inside. I had always thought everyone felt and thought the same as I did. It never really dawned on me that others didn't have the abilities I had, or didn't have their own 'friends' or voices to help them out.

"I can also be outside of my body watching myself and the situation. A kind of total detachment. I can also travel and be anywhere within seconds with no problem. One thing that I feel to be important is that my world of 'hypnosis' is just as real as your world of 'reality.' It takes a lot to recognize a difference. And then when you do say something's not right, people don't understand and tell you nothing's wrong, so you keep on believing that the world of hypnosis is the way it is."

## 5. A Religious Revelation

This is an account of a religious experience that occurred while the patient, who had bulimia, was in the hospital. It happened while she was under extreme duress, but it also raises interesting questions about self-hypnosis. This subject scored only a 6 on the standard hypnotizability scale—a normal rating. Yet she was a good hypnotic subject clinically, and in hypnosis could visualize an experience at the ocean clearly. She could see herself on the beach, hear the waves, and feel the breeze with the verisimilitude of a real experience. Scores on tests may be deceptive. It may be that mediocre scores do not always reflect true capabilities. Some patients may only go into deep trances under the most stressful circumstances or perhaps they are hypnotic specialists or simply capable of vivid imagery.

"I couldn't sleep at all that night because I was thinking of many things. I was very upset with myself because I had been doing so terribly in everything. I was getting more depressed each day and had almost given up. I had lost faith in my doctor, me, and my heavenly father, and I was ready to give up everything.

"In the morning, I was awake, *very much awake.* There was a little light in the room, *light enough to see everything in it!* Suddenly a very dark and dreary feeling came into the room, and I could hear footsteps coming toward my bed but the door had not opened. I turned around and held my pillow tight because I was very frightened. I felt something brushing against the side of my bed. Then suddenly there was something heavy on me. I knew that it was evil. I have always been taught what to say if I ever had an experience with an evil spirit. So I tried to say, 'In the name of Jesus Christ, Satan leave,' but I couldn't say anything. My lips would move but nothing came out. I tried and tried again, but I could not even move my body because it was bound to my bed, but I could move my head. So I moved it to the side and I saw a man—an evil-looking man with dark hair snickering at me. I quickly turned my head and tried and tried to talk but my lips wouldn't move. I heard a movement outside and I kept trying to talk. Finally I got out, 'In the name of Jesus Christ, Satan leave,' and suddenly there wasn't any heavy thing on me and I heard light footsteps walk away. Then within a second, the dreary, dark feeling was gone, and everything brightened up. I stood up, opened my shades, opened my door, and walked out.

"I finally found a Mormon doctor who would understand what had happened, and told him my experience that morning. He would understand and not think I was going crazy or having hallucinations, *because I wasn't.* He understood perfectly and talked with me about spiritual things and maybe why this happened. Well, that was the biggest help anyone could have given me—to realize that I wanted to live with my heavenly father and good people and not Satan's evil, bad people. It proved to me that there was really a Devil and his followers.

"I know this experience was an answer to many prayers, and I know that my heavenly father knows me, my actions and reactions. He let me see the other side because he knew my heart and what kind of a person I am. I know God lives and that he truly loves us, and answers my prayers. I know there is a Devil who is deceiving and evil, and wants to tear us apart. I have been doing very well since this happened. I am out of the deep depression that I was in, and I'm going to fight to win because I have my father in heaven and people who love me on my side."


## 6. Neocortical Manipulations by Self-hypnosis

This patient, like a number of other excellent hypnotic subjects (she scored an 11 on the test), wrote about her "self-hypnotic" experience before she ever saw a psychiatrist. This report and the one that follows are typical: they document the many faculties that can be affected.

"*Smell:* Many times I would not be aware of an odor others smelled; but other times an odor would stand out very sharply for me, but not for others. This does not include an odor I am very phobic about—the smell of smoke.

"*Hearing:* There is nothing pathological about my hearing (I've been tested), yet at times when someone is talking to me, their speech is garbled and totally un-understandable, although at other times I have no problem. Sometimes sounds around me just fade away, or else they just 'jump' right out at me.

"*Time:* Time, for me, is like an accordion: often it stretches out, or it may bunch up. At times it's been 'forever'; at times it's as though it's never been. Once, time stopped completely—I call that experience 'the eternal now' for lack of a better description.

"*Fantasies:* Very strong. I've gotten completely caught up in them to the exclusion of everything else around me. The line between fantasy and reality can be very thin—I've 'gotten lost' very easily. As a child, I spent a lot of time fantasizing; I've also done this as an adult. They 'spin themselves' so to speak.

"To use the word 'fantasy' is a rather uncomfortable term for me—it implies a distinction, but for me, there is none or very little. What I have been referring to is my life, not an illusion or a delusion. This is an attempt to be understood by others whose definitions of fantasy versus reality differ from mine.

"*Motor Movements:* There have been times my body has been 'frozen' when I wanted it to move. Once, in late adolescence, my right hand was paralyzed for several weeks—neurological tests were negative.

"*Sensations:*

"*Pain*—I can block out most pain at will. As a child, I had extensive oral surgery and clearly remember the experience, but have no memory of any accompanying pain whatsoever. My attitude toward most pain is that I just can't be bothered by it.

"*Touch*—I can turn off the sense of others touching me at will, most times. However, there have been times when I have been unable to 'feel' another's touch, even when I've wanted to.

"There have been times when my touching others has been a very 'distant' experience. I once described this to someone as 'it was as if I'd been encased in an invisible balloon.' Touch, for me, can be as alive as lightning, or as dead as dead can be.

"*Vision:* Apply the words 'fade in' and 'fade out' here. Things around me blur at times, especially when I 'leave the world of the body,' so to speak. My vision has been distorted (semiblind) at least once, like someone on a bad LSD trip, which I was most definitely not on as this took place in the late fifties when I was about eleven. I've also 'seen' things that no one else could at the time. I was not under the influence of alcohol, as I had not been drinking either before or after.

"*Memory:* At times, I'm very clear for both recent and not-so-recent experiences; at other times, clear for not-so-recent experiences, but perfectly lousy for recent experiences; at times, rather vague for both types of experiences; at times, completely lost or not there at all.

"*Thinking:* I usually think quite well, but there have been times when I become stuck; the mechanisms become jammed completely; or my thoughts tear off into an entirely different direction, contrary to what I desire. One day I can comprehend a certain subject, and the very next day be completely lost. This happened in school, as an older child, a lot. I can remember times when I was thinking one thing, then sort of silently sliding into another thought, then wondering how I got there. Sometimes I've compared thinking to having Ping-Pong balls bouncing around in my head, not being sure which one is mine.

"*Emotions:*

"*Anger*—A definite no-no. That was always filed away immediately. I remember being told as a child by my mother 'Don't show your anger!' It's an emotion I've never liked. I always shied away from angry people. Anger leads to abuse. I never learned what to do with it or how to handle it.

"*Tears*—'I' cried . . . but who did it? I've thought, 'I've forgotten how to cry.' Crying is not my bag [a personality cries for her].

"*Fear*—I am still deathly afraid of thunderstorms, have been for as long as I can remember; I am afraid of the dark, of heights, of enclosed places, of being restricted from moving, of anger—my own and others'; of people in groups or alone, of getting into trouble, of not doing or saying the 'right' thing, of my mother, of unfamiliar situations. All of the aforementioned, I've always feared for as long as I can remember. Fear is the one emotion that I am very well acquainted with.

"*Irresistible Urges:* To cut myself with something sharp, even though I didn't want to; to overdose against my will; to get in a car or on a boat or go for a walk and just keep going. To deliberately endanger my life by getting drunk, knowing I had to drive. . . . I didn't care at the time;

driving like a damn fool, even though that wasn't my style; to space out and stay spaced out by whatever means possible. To stop eating; to eat even though I didn't want to; to set a fire—it was a small one—even though fires scare me; to be seriously physically ill. To deliberately irritate my boss at work, even though I knew it cost me promotions, and continued to cost me promotions that I sincerely wanted.

"Everything that I have related is what I remember—'conscious' self-hypnosis. There are times when everything is just blank, there is no discernible level of psychical consciousness, 'nothing.' This, I assume, is 'unconscious' self-hypnosis."

## 7. Neocortical Manipulations by Self-hypnosis

The patient, a male, had severe depressions and had made several suicide attempts. He was considered by the ward psychiatrist to be suffering from some form of schizophrenia. Hypnotherapy produced a rapid improvement, and two years later he is still in remission, virtually asymptomatic. He described the many facets of his self-hypnotic experiences.

"*Thinking:* Posed with the task of creating an organizational "flow chart" for a bureaucratic system, the picture would be scattered and without sense. By fixing my eyes upon a plant on my dining room table, I could enter a world that was dark with small squares—all I had to do was put the rolls or departments in the boxes, shuffle them on the 'blackboard' until it was correct, focus even further on the visual picture, and then bring the final product into awareness and put it on paper.

"At work I would receive a great deal of praise and acknowledgment for my organizational ability. People would tell me at work, 'This must have taken you forever to think out,' while in reality it may have taken two to three minutes in a state of focus, while the procedure of drafting the chart and typing my 'vision' took thirty times longer to do. The praise and acknowledgment would go over my head because I had done very little work and had not thought it out for any length of time.

"*Writing:* There were two major problems I had in writing. My first problem was my writing would 'fuzz out,' and I would feel out of control. The other problem was the tense. My writing of a past event would tend to go from past to present to past. While writing of a present or future event, my tenses would become a major problem. For example, I would move from I would like to be there to I am there.

"*Memory:* People have always said I had excellent recall—even of the most insignificant things. Emotionally charged memories come to me with almost total accuracy, even to the fine insignificant details.

"*Vision:* My vision has been tested at above 20/20. However, I have often wished my vision was poor. One way I would make my vision imperfect or jumpy would be to consume large amounts of coffee. It would make me nervous so that it was difficult to sit still or look at an object for any length of time. This could be due to my tendency when calm to stare. Sometimes what I would see would produce feelings of anxiety and fear, or feelings of pleasure, joy or laughter, depending upon my state of mind and the situation.

. "Vision, however, is my major source of self-hypnosis. My style of hypnosis developed 'eyes open' because I was always supposed to be watching something or at least appearing to be attentive. It would appear strange to people if I closed my eyes in tense situations, because they would know I was tuning them out. This way I could be pondering or just deep in thought rather than, in fact, not there at all. It is a habit I am attempting to overcome.

"*Hearing:* Some sounds create anxiety in me. I have heard loud gunshots that scare the hell out of me, and then I panic. I can smell the smoke when I get into that state. The major times I heard voices was when I was depressed. I would go into a focus of being very young; almost as though I was a little kid who needed help. Since I've learned what I've been doing, the strange voices have ceased, and it's now my voice I hear that brings me back to the present. Then I put myself back into this world to a state of calm—back to reality.

"*Smells and Tastes:* When I was a child I could pretend, in my mind, that I was in a dentist's office, just injected with Novocain, tasting the bitter aftertaste of the shot, and numb any portion of my jaw and face, depending on the target. I could also smell or taste anything I wished.

"*Sensations and Movement:* I have often had the sensation that someone was after me and I just had to escape. This often occurred after a focus or a mind trip. Unaware that I was under hypnosis (at the time, I considered it a 'thought'), I would get from the 'thought' and would behave like a five-year-old or a ten-year-old, with the emotions of fear, anxiety, pleasure, or elation, without knowing why.

"As a child, I could produce weightlessness or the feeling that a wall was a magnet pulling me toward it. I could produce any sensation or movement as long as I had experienced it and knew intellectually that it was logical and possible. I would not, for example, jump out of a window thinking I could fly, because that is logically impossible and would result in my death.

"*Time:* I have lost a great deal of time in deep thought (or trips), but I had always attributed this to just being busy, or 'time flies when you're having fun.' I have on six occasions blacked out. I feel that the amnesias were caused by not being willing to accept the experience out of deep pain, fear, or anxiety. The largest one was a fear that I was crazy because of my actions. Since realizing what is wrong—the ability to hypnotize myself—the pressure of thinking of myself as psychotic has left, and I have now gone back and remembered all situations with the emotions behind them.

"There was the time I stabbed myself with an ice pick at age four or five so my Dad would give me attention. Another time, I burned my hand with a cigarette because my foster parents told me if they caught me smoking again, that's what they'd do. I assaulted my wife twice. There was a severe depression when I attempted to take my life, but the suicide was unsuccessful because I vomited. All were blacked out and forgotten, but I got them back by myself once the fear of being crazy was eliminated.

"*Fear—Rage—Depression:* Most of my fear, rage, and depression came from experiences [hypnotic] that I had believed were simple thoughts. Not knowing that I had in fact left reality, I would go on a trip and not come down, and would have what could be described as an emotional hangover—fear, anger, depression, pleasure, elation, child-like emotions, or pain, and would respond to my real environment through this hangover. After becoming aware that my 'thoughts' are hypnotic states, I now come down and deal with the real world as opposed to a world through an emotional hangover. These previous 'unanswered' emotional states have all but disappeared, and those emotional states in the real world have become easier to handle without that emotional haze.

"*Physical Problems:* I could create high fever, colds, vomiting, pain, ulcers, etc., to the point that these symptoms existed in my mind. I would think about vomiting and begin to do it within fifteen to thirty seconds of the thought. I have vomited and could vomit on command.

"Another example occurred while driving with two girls. They put me into an anxiety-provoking situation. I focused on my foster mother writing me a letter that a friend of hers had died of an aneurysm. I wondered if I would die like that, I felt a balloon-like sensation in my right frontal lobe. I was so disturbed that I almost pulled the car to the side of the highway—things became unreal and dreamlike. My physician termed it 'separation anxiety' and put me on 5 mg Valium, which increased the symptoms. For several weeks, I went to the doctor's office almost on a day-to-day basis. It took tests and X-rays to prove to me that I was not going to die from an aneurysm.

"Another experience was a death experience. I was lying down attempting to go to sleep when I started to wonder about death. I remembered my mother telling me about how she had at one time experienced what it was like to die. She described it as something sweeping over you, a strong pulling sensation, ears ringing, and a desire to leave and stay, darkness, and general conflict, and pulling between this world and the next. My experience was precisely that.

"*What It Was Like to Hit My Wife:* I guess it could be best described by the word 'robot'—I felt like I was a robot. I could not feel or talk, I was just a machine. In fact, I guess I had hit her open-handed in the mouth or some other bony part of her face and I had bruised my hand. When I 'came down,' I just noticed it by accident while washing my hands in the bathroom. Although my hand was black and blue near the base of my fingers, there was no pain, as though it was not a part of me and didn't happen to me."

## 8. A Retrospective Account of Therapy

This patient and I have struggled together for four years. When I first saw her it was obvious that she was a multiple. She was a hypnotic virtuoso and when tested scored a 12—the highest possible score. She had symptoms in abundance referable to every syndrome on the self-report—in fact, she had as many symptoms as any multiple I have encountered.

Fortunately, I was initially naive and had no idea how taxing and lengthy therapy might be. Our sessions often lasted three hours, and what saved us both were the great moments when we made progress. Beyond that, she was a fascinating patient and a splendid person. As she said during a lucid period, 90 percent of her waking life had been spent in altered states during the past thirty years. At work she dissociated into "Super A"—an overworker and overachiever. Then she would return to her room and become a terrified child of five, without anyone else being aware of the transformations. There were twenty-three personalities, or voices and states as she preferred to identify them. In our sessions they often emerged to rant, punish, or cower, while she frequently retreated into trances when frightened.

"During the last decade I have tried many different types of therapy and drugs—all failures. Psychiatrists attempted to have me accommodate to my problems and think that I was, as one of the 'best' told me, 'a quarter of a normal person who would be dependent on "psych" drugs and hospitals for the rest of my life.' I fought that so hard—at one point even created a residential program based on the philosophy that we all needed help at different times in our life, but that *none* of us should lose her dignity, soul, or sense of identity. Other times, when I believed them, I ended up in locked psychiatric wards, often in restraints. I would 'get better' just to escape that world. Somewhere, someone inside knew that I was *not* a quarter of a normal person—that I was worth one hell of a lot more.

"I then worked with a marvelous woman therapist for three years. She was compassionate, unafraid of my deviancy, and listened to hour after hour, week after week, month after month, and even year after year of my depressions, fears, occasional times of joy, and the all too often times of total terror. She kept me out of the hospital 'psych' wards, tried various drugs, including a year trial of lithium, to no avail. She needed to take another job in another city, and we both knew we had gone as far as we could with just supportive therapy. It was helpful, but still didn't touch the core of the nightmare that had been driving me to despair and terror.

"Three months and seven other therapists followed after she departed. They kept referring to me as a poor-risk patient. One even told me I'd have to lose fifty pounds before he'd begin to see me, since my obesity showed I was not 'disciplined' enough for therapy. Another tried to commit me to a 'psych' ward after a one-hour session. So it was with little hope, after my mother died and my states of fear dominated the nights and were creeping into my days, that I called Dr. B. I hated the fact that his office was in the medical center, as I had come to view hospitals as my enemy, during the times when I needed help the most.

"My first appointment with this new therapist was just two weeks after my mother's death. He had a scholarly but ruffled look to him, but he also had a white doctor's coat, which I had come to dislike. It was not with any ease that I first sat in his large, black, overstuffed chair. I was weary though, weary of all the problems and of being shipped from one person to another for help. Almost all the other therapists had told me at the end of the first session that I had to see someone else. They would give me a list with strange names and numbers. But this time, a therapist not only didn't give me a list, but unlike any other therapist I had seen before, he said that he *knew* what was wrong with me and he was confident that he could help me. I left that day uncertain whether I had finally found the help I was desperately seeking for many years, or had stumbled upon a strange doctor who didn't grasp the terrifying reality of my mind.

"The reality of my life, however, was now my mother's death. I had tried to keep it together and handle the event with some sense of not being crazy to the outside world. I knew deep inside I was just pushing off the tidal wave of emotions resurrected with her death. Three weeks after my mother's death, and just a week after seeing this new therapist, I came to my apartment after a business meeting, well after midnight on a Friday night, closed the door, and silently died. My next memory was being in a psychiatric ward, restrained, with my left arm in a straitjacket of bandages for the third-degree burn I had inflicted on myself during that period. I had felt nothing. I remembered only sitting for days in the closet wrapped in my mother's shawl feeling so cold, so cold.

"It was in this state of total crisis that the new therapy started. Dr. B. used hypnosis, which I had come to fear as a theatrical gimmick that made people 'do' strange things which they didn't want to do. My memory of those first six months of therapy is superficial. I rarely remembered anything we discussed after I left his office. I just knew, in some strange way, that it was helping. But between those therapy sessions there was a hell of a lot of reality to handle. I was executive director of an agency fraught with problems and infighting. I had gotten along well with the male board director who first hired me. By some twist of fate, however, they elected an insecure, very religious (Catholic) woman to take his place, a few weeks before my mother's death. I found it almost impossible to cope with her demands and eccentricities, and she soon became the worst aspects of my mother. I worked long, hard hours in that agency and even attained national attention for my work. But for my 'mother/boss' nothing I did was right. Finally, in a meeting where she was berating me, I stood up and told her some of the things I wished at times I had told my mother, then quit the job.

"Both my job and therapy had come to a point of crisis. It was at that time that I remembered in hypnosis the attic of our garage at home. It was the beginning of remembering so many things. That was the place where my father kept his bedroom, his chamber of horrors, a memory which I had avoided for nearly thirty years. It was one of the critical points in our entire therapy. When I remembered the attic in hypnosis I realized I had found the key to what had been torturing my mind and spirit these many years. I came out of hypnosis remembering—conscious that it did indeed exist and was the key. To that point, the use of hypnosis and the content of therapy had been far removed from my reality. Now they were to come closer together.

"My illusion was that the events of that attic could be discovered in a rapid, conscious, and controlled manner. That illusion was rapidly dispelled. Remembering the attic meant consciously recalling all the things I had spent the past thirty years trying to erase. The horrors of sexual and physical violence that I underwent so many times for many years in that room were wrenched from their protected mental fortress, but slowly, with a level of emotional pain which at times became unbearable. I again found myself going in and out of the 'psych' unit during this period, as more memories surfaced. The problem with this therapy is that I had to remember what my mind had so carefully tried to hide; feel it, and then try to go out into 'reality' and work. Medications were tried to ease the stress, but they did little good.

"Even though I was putting the pieces of the puzzle together that had torn my mind apart, I continued to undergo the old severe states of depression and rage. I continued to mutilate myself in various ways just to have some sense of ease. As strange as that may sound, it did work. I was frustrated and feeling close to hopeless when the second major awareness came in therapy. I had always remembered my mother desperately pushing me away from her, which I had interpreted as further rejection of her 'bad' girl. I remembered in hypnosis (by being back there, so to speak) that I was caught in a crossfire fight between my father and mother. I had never before remembered my father's presence in the room. She was actually trying to protect me by telling me to go away. She was not rejecting me as I had previously remembered. I felt happy and freer than I had in a long time. I had thought that this was the last piece in the puzzle, and now I could rest. I was feeling happy and thought that this was the end to my mind's fighting itself. Not so . . . not so, but yes, it was to prove a further step to freedom.

"Through this time, Dr. B. had called my ways of being 'crazy' that of multiple personalities. I found this almost impossible to believe, as I had seen the Hollywood movies of *The Three Faces of Eve* and *Sybil* and I considered myself unlike them. I did not call myself by different names, nor did I have different wardrobes or lose memory of what I had done for a day or a week. I fought with Dr. B. so very many times over this. Yet I had long ago felt my changes in emotions to be akin to the Dr. Jekyll and Mr. Hyde classic. When pushed to put names to what I was experiencing, I could, but I had never known the people as anything but voices inside of me which I thought everyone had, a second family. I had always known these voices to have distinct tones, some male, others female, some kind and even joyful, and others full of hate and anger, wanting a human sacrifice. But that was my secret world—no one else had ever come near it. I stuck with Dr. B., fighting his theory on what was wrong with me most of the time but knowing instinctively that he was uncovering the layers of terror that would eventually end with the 'core.' I instinctively feared that core, for I had always been certain it was one of evil, or of insanity. There was a fragile sense of trusting Dr. B. and an instinctive sense that this was finally the right direction because it was no longer one of 'accommodating to my illness,' but an active investigation of why I was having these problems. But the terrors of therapy brought me back to my greatest enemy, the feelings that made me create a world apart from reality—and here was a therapist insisting that I could not run away any longer. I had to remember, had to feel, and had to fight the demons of my past.

"So began the third stage of our therapy. I thought I had uncovered most of the memories, the pieces in the puzzle. But why did I still feel like a frightened child underneath it all? What became apparent was that I had dealt with the 'facts' but had done relatively little with the feelings. We spent close to a year trying to join the memory of the traumas to the feelings. To me, it was by far the worst part of our journey. It was the most painful and frustrating. How could I possibly reexperience those feelings without some sense of revenge? I was able to maintain my job during this period but only at a minimal level. I had wished that money wasn't an object so that I could work at this to the exclusion of everything else and get through it faster. That year seemed to last a decade. As I reflect now, however, I may not have been able to cope with a faster pace. The process of remembering both the events and the feelings was full of intense pain as I actually reexperienced both the events and the feelings in Dr. B.'s office.

"The pain and frustrations of that stage of therapy finally brought a sense of completion and peace when I found the third key. I reached the core and found it a good one, not rotten or disfigured as I had convinced myself. The part of me that always told the truth was my 'Mother Mary,' and she said the memories were true. That came with the recall in hypnosis of my mother extolling, when I was a child, the virtues of Saint Maria Goretti. Maria was a virgin who was raped and brutally murdered, stabbed to death repeatedly. Religion provided my mother with the philosophy of you must accept all things as 'God's will.' That and the picture of that young girl stabbed were my early messages. It was better to die than allow a man to rape you, and I had allowed it.

"Certainly this was the final link to sanity, I thought, with almost three months of peaceful, even joyful times that followed. I even began to seriously think of terminating therapy—I was cured. Then with either divine providence or rotten luck to guide me, I was hurled into a series of crises at work that led to my request for a transfer—but worst of all, total alienation from my supervisor, who had become a friend and surrogate mother. Dr. B. went on a one-month vacation as well, and my new-found sense of sanity quickly changed to the ways, feelings, and terror of the past. I was able to figure out why this was happening on my own. I realized that I had made Dr. B. a strong parent substitute during therapy—mostly the mother I felt I never had. When he left on vacation, coupled with the problems at work with my supervisor, I was left once again alone and rejected—as I had been with my mother so many years earlier.

"Even though I knew the problem, I wasn't able to conquer it, and I quickly fell into the old behaviors and feelings. This was all further complicated with summer school at the university, where I could barely concentrate during the many times of panic. I began to fail tests, and the red marks on the test papers brought me right back to childhood again. It was true, I thought, I was also stupid and would never get better. Dr. B. had taken several other long vacations, but none of them affected me quite like this one. By the time he returned, I felt hopelessly caught in the feelings I had been so desperately working to end for over three years. I felt estranged from him, from myself, and from the entire world as I found myself immersed in self-destructive acts and constant thoughts of suicide.

"I've described that period because it holds the elements of my problems over these many years, and I believe now I can see how to intervene. The cycle is simple, but a most difficult one to break. An event in the present (such as Dr. B.'s going on vacation) will renew feelings from the past. Since those feelings are unresolved, they surface and blend with the situation in the present to make a relatively simple problem in the present an impossible one. The joint feelings become overwhelming, but the panic prevents any understanding. I am convinced now that it is almost a stimulus-response reaction. For example, if you are afraid of fire, the minute you see fire or even sense it is close to you, you panic and want to get away from it. [Note: In her—reverting to hypnosis.]

"To date, there have only been two successful ways of ending my cycles. Either I remember in therapy and deal with the original feeling that has made the problem overwhelming and thereby come to an 'understanding' of it, or during times when I cannot reach that point because my brain is too closed off to work, I must simply trust Dr. B. and get some sense of a bond with him. This would be like someone drowning, unable to swim any longer, when someone throws a lifeline into the water.

"I have also come up with some clearer ideas on how to break this cycle. The fracturing of my person into many different personalities was simply isolating and forgetting the many emotions I had at the time of my traumas. At first, we tried to identify these feelings/personalities and integrate them—the concept of 'cure' for the multiple. It became apparent that it was not working—and only made me feel worse, as I thought it was my fault for refusing to integrate. I am now convinced that integration for a multiple personality is a misleading concept. As an example, I cannot separate the emotion of murderous rage [the personality of Joe] and say that personality, that feeling, could be united with my core self. As such, at least for me, integration was a disastrous attempt to stop my cycle. Therefore, instead of integration, I prefer the concept of reconciliation.

"Reconciliation is a more active process. In reconciliation I must *remember* and *understand* what happened to me, why it happened, and how I felt about it. I must experience the feelings from my memories and *accept* that they were legitimate feelings for the circumstances. In my case, for example, that means knowing that there was a time when I wanted both my parents dead for what they had done to me. For a woman brought up in the Catholic religion, that was almost impossible to face. My religious training states that both my anger toward my parents and my desire to kill them were two of the worst sins a person could commit. So this seemingly simple process can take months and years to reach acceptance.

"The final step is *change*. Despite what I know now about my childhood, when a crisis begins I want to run to the old space in my head to run away from that pain. Since my conscious sense of self ended at the age of five when I began using personalities to cope, I have not had any realistic sense of my own person. For the past thirty years, I have thought of myself as ugly, stupid, and evil, which were the messages from that time in childhood. It has, without a doubt, affected every aspect of my being. I now have to work at changing those self-concepts and allow myself to 'grow up.' This stage demands that I tolerate my feelings in the present and have the courage not to run but face them straight on—a difficult task even for a 'normal/healthy' individual.

"It has now been four years that I have been seeing Dr. B. and trying to work all these problems out. It has been by far the most difficult therapy I have attempted, but it has given me the keys to survive as a whole person. The scars from those years of brutal torture will always be there. The changing process I am presently undergoing may be a long one and has already been fraught with setbacks. That world of personalities became my interior family and without them there is now intense loneliness. Therapy has been equivalent to surgery without anesthesia, as Dr. B. so precisely states it. I have often thought the price was too high and have been sorely tempted to give up. Fortunately, the deepest part of me knows that I am worth something and that this is my road to freedom."

# References

1. Agras, W. S., Sylvester, D., and Oliveaun, D. the Epidemiology of common fear and phobia. *Comprehensive Psychiatry*, 10:151–156, 1969.
2. Allison, R. B. A new treatment approach for multiple personalities. *American Journal of Clinical Hypnosis*, 17:15–32, 1974.
3. Allison, R. B. On discovering multiplicity. *Svensk Tidskrift for Hypnosis*, 2:4–8, 1978.
4. Allison, R. B. A rational psychotherapy plan for multiplicity. *Svensk Tidskrift for Hypnosis*, 3:9–16, 1978.
5. Allison, R., and Schwartz, T. *Minds in Many Pieces.* New York: Rawson, Wade, 1980.
6. Arkonac, O., and Guze, S. B. A family study of hysteria. *New England Journal of Medicine*, 268:239–242, 1963.
7. Astrachan, B. M.., Harrow, M., Adler, D., Brauer, L., Schwartz, A., Schwartz, C., and Tucker, G. A checklist for the diagnosis of schizophrenia. *British Journal of Psychiatry*, 121:529–539, 1972.
8. Bach-Y-Rita, G. Habitual violence and self-mutilation. *American Journal of Psychiatry*, 131:1018–1020, 1974.
9. Beahrs, J. O. *Unity and Multiplicity.* New York: Brunner/Mazel, 1982.
10. Beal, E. W. Use of the extended family in the treatment of multiple personality. *American Journal of Psychiatry*, 135:539–542, 1978.
11. Bernheim, H. *Suggestive Therapeutics.* New York: G.P. Putnam's Sons, 1902.
12. Bertrand, A. *Du Magnétisme Animal.* Paris: J.B. Bailliere, 1826.
13. Bliss, E. L. Multiple personalities: A report of 14 cases with implications for schizophrenia and hysteria. *Archives of General Psychiatry*, 37:1388–1397, 1980.
14. Bliss, E. L. The psychology of anorexia nervosa. (In) M. Gross (ed.) *Anorexia Nervosa*, pp. 163–176. Lexington, Mass.: Collamore Press, 1982.
15. Bliss, E. L., Larson, E. M., and Nakashima, S. R. Auditory hallucinations and schizophrenia. *Journal of Nervous and Mental Disease*, 171:30–33, 1983.
16. Bliss, E. L. A symptom profile of patients with multiple personalities—with MMPI results. *Journal of Nervous and Mental Disease*, 172:197–202, 1984.
17. Bliss, E. L. Hysteria and hypnosis. *Journal of Nervous and Mental Disease*, 172:203–206, 1984.
18. Bliss, E. L. Spontaneous self-hypnosis in multiple personality disorder. *Psychiatric Clinics of North America*, 7:135–148, 1984.
19. Bliss, E. L. Multiple personalities, related disorders and hypnosis. *American Journal of Clinical Hypnosis*, 26: 114–123, 1984.
20. Bliss, E. L., and Larson, E. M. Sexual criminality and hypnotizability. (In press)
21. Bliss, E. L., and Jeppsen, E. A. Prevalence of multiple personality among inpatients and outpatients. *American Journal of Psychiatry*, 142:250–251, 1985.
22. Boor, M. The multiple personality epidemic. Additional cases and inferences regarding diagnosis, etiology, dynamics and treatment. *Journal of Nervous and Mental Disease*, 170:302–304, 1982.
23. Boor, M., and Coons, P. M. A comprehensive bibliography of literature pertaining to multiple personality. *Psychological Reports*, 53:295–310, 1983.
24. Bower, G. H. Mood and memory. *American Psychologist*, 36:129–148, 1981.

25. Bowers, M. B., and Freedman, D. X. "Psychedelic" experiences in acute psychoses. *Archives of General Psychiatry*, 15:240–248, 1966.

26. Bowers, M. B. Pathogenesis of acute schizophrenic psychosis. *Archives of General Psychiatry*, 19:348–355, 1968.

27. Bowers, M. B. *Retreat From Sanity*. New York: Human Sciences Press, 1974.

28. Bowers, P. G., and Bowers, K. S. Hypnosis and creativity; a theoretical and empirical rapprochement. (In) Fromm, E., and Shor, R. E. (eds.) *Hypnosis: Developments in Research and New Perspectives*, pp. 351–380. New York: Aldine, 1979.

29. Bradford, J., and Smith, S. M. Amnesia and homicide; the Padola case and a study of thirty cases. *Bulletin of the American Academy of Psychiatry and the Law*, 7:219–231, 1979.

30. Braid, J. *Neurypnology; or The Rationale of Nervous Sleep*. London: John Churchill, 1843.

31. Braid, J. *Neurypnology*. London: George Redway, 1899.

32. Bramwell, J. M. *Hypnosis. Its History, Practice and Theory*. London: Grant Richards, 1903.

33. Brandsma, J., and Ludwig, A. A. A case of multiple personality: Diagnosis and therapy. *International Journal of Clinical & Experimental Hypnosis*, 22:216–233, 1974.

34. Brassfield, P. A. Unfolding patterns of multiple personality through hypnosis. *American Journal of Clinical Hypnosis*, 26:146–152, 1983.

35. Braun, B. G. Hypnosis for multiple personalities. (In) Wain, H. J. (ed.) *Hypnosis in Clinical Medicine*, pp. 209–217. Chicago: Year Book Medical Publication, 1980.

36. Braun, B. G. Neurophysiologic changes in multiple personality due to integration: A preliminary report. *American Journal of Clinical Hypnosis*, 26:84–92, 1983.

37. Braun, B. G. Psychophysiologic phenomena in multiple personality and hypnosis. *American Journal of Clinical Hypnosis*, 26:124–137, 1983.

38. Braun, B. G. Uses of hypnosis with multiple personality. *Psychiatric Annals*, 14:34–40, 1984.

39. Braun, B. G. Hypnosis creates multiple personality: Myth or reality. *International Journal of Clinical & Experimental Hypnosis*, 32:191–197, 1984.

40. Breuer, J., and Freud, S. On the psychical mechanism of hysterical phenomena (1893). (In) *Studies on Hysteria*, pp. 24–41. New York: Basic Books, 1957.

41. Breuer, J., and Freud, S. *Studies on Hysteria*. New York: Basic Books, 1957. (First edition, 1895)

42. Briquet, P. *Traite de l' Hystérie*. Paris: J.B. Bailliere, 1859.

43. Burrows, G. D., and Dennerstein, L. (eds.) *Handbook of Hypnosis and Psychosomatic Medicine*. New York: Elsevier North-Holland Biomedical Press, 1980.

44. Cadoret, R. J., and Cain, C. Sex differences in predictors of antisocial behavior in adoptees. *Archives of General Psychiatry*, 37:1171–1175, 1980.

45. Cadoret, R. J. Editorial. Genotype-environment interaction in antisocial behavior. *Psychological Medicine*, 12:235–239, 1982.

46. Cantwell, D. P. Psychiatric illness in the families of hyperactive children. *Archives of General Psychiatry*, 27:414–418, 1972.

47. Capote, T. (In) *In Cold Blood*, pp. 296–302. New York: Random House, 1965.

48. Carli, G. Animal hypnosis and pain. (In) Frankel, F. H., and Zamansky, H. S. (eds.) *Hypnosis At Its Bicentennial*, pp. 69–78. New York: Plenum Press, 1976.

49. Carpenter, W. T., Strauss, J. S., and Bartko, J. J. Flexible system for the diagnosis of schizophrenia: Report from the WHO international pilot study of schizophrenia. *Science*, 182:1275–1277, 1973.

50. Caul, D. Group and videotape techniques for multiple personality disorder. *Psychiatric Annals*, 14:43–50, 1984.

51. Chapman, J. The early symptoms of schizophrenia. *British Journal of Psychiatry*, 112:225–251, 1966.

52. Chertok, L. *Psychophysiological Mechanisms of Hypnosis*. New York: Springer-Verlag, 1967.

53. Clary, W. F., Burstin, K. J., and Carpenter, J. S. Multiple personality and borderline personality disorder. *Psychiatric Clinics of North America*, 7:89–99, 1984.

54. Cloninger, C. R., and Guze, S. B. Psychiatric illness and female criminality: The role of sociopathy and hysteria in the antisocial woman. *American Journal of Psychiatry*, 127:303–311, 1970.

55. Cloninger, C. R., and Guze, S. B. Female criminals: Their personal, familial, and social backgrounds. The relation of these to the diagnoses of sociopathy and hysteria. *Archives of General Psychiatry*, 23:554–558, 1970.

56. Coons, P. M. Multiple personality: Diagnostic considerations. *Journal of Clinical Psychiatry*, 41:330–337, 1980.

57. Coons, P. M. The differential diagnosis of multiple personality. A comprehensive review. *Psychiatric Clinics of North America*, 7:51–67, 1984.

58. Cooper, L. M. Children's hypnotic susceptibility, personality, and EEG patterns. *International Journal of Clinical & Experimental Hypnosis*, 24:140–148, 1976.

59. Cooper, L. M. Hypnotic amnesia. (In) Fromm, E. and Shor, R. E. (eds.) *Hypnosis Research Developments and Perspectives*, pp. 217–252. New York: Aldine, 1979.

60. Craselneck, H. B., and Hall, J. A. *Clinical Hypnosis: Principles and Applications.* Grune and Stratton, 1975.

61. Darnton, R. *Mesmerism and the End of the Enlightenment in France.* Cambridge, Mass.: Harvard University Press, 1968.

62. DeBoismont, B. A. *A History of Dreams, Visions, Apparitions, Ecstasy, Magnetism, and Somnambulism.* Philadelphia: Lindsay & Blakiston, 1855.

63. Deleuze, J. P. F. *Histoire Critique du Magnétisme Animal.* Paris: Mame, Imprimeur-Libraire, 1813.

64. Deleuze, J. P. F. *Instruction Pratique sur Le Magnétisme Animal.* Paris: J. G. Dentu, 1825.

65. Deleuze, J. P. F. *Practical Instruction in Animal Magnetism.* London; Bailliere, 1850.

66. Dibner, B. *Heralds of Science.* Cambridge, Mass.: Massachusetts Institute of Technology, 1969.

67. Diethelm, O. *Medical Dissertations of Psychiatric Interest.* New York: S. Karger, 1971.

68. Dupotet de Sennevoy, J. *An Introduction to the Study of Animal Magnetism.* New York: Arno Press, 1976. (First English edition, 1838)

69. Edmonston, W. E. The effects of neutral hypnosis on conditioned responses: Implications for hypnosis as relaxation. (In) Fromm, E., and Shor, R. E. (eds.) *Hypnosis Developments in Research and New Perspectives*, pp. 415–456. New York: Aldine, 1979.

70. Edwards, G. Duration of post-hypnotic effect. *British Journal of Psychiatry*, 109:259–266, 1963.

71. Ellenberger, H. F. *The Discovery of the Unconscious.* New York: Basic Books, 1970.

72. Elliotson, J. *Numerous Cases of Surgical Operations Without Pain in the Mesmeric State.* London: Bailliere, 1843.

73. Erickson, M. H., and Kubie, L. S. The permanent relief of an obsessional phobia by means of communications with an unsuspected dual personality. *Psychoanalytic Quarterly*, 8:471–509, 1939.

74. Erickson, M. H., Hershman, S., and Sector, I. I. *The Practical Application of Medical and Dental Hypnosis.* New York: Julian Press, 1961.

75. Erickson, M. H. A special inquiry with Aldous Huxley into the nature and character of various states of consciousness. *American Journal of Clinical Hypnosis*, 8:17–33, 1965.

76. Esdaile, J. *Mesmerism in India and Its Practical Application in Surgery and Medicine.* London: Longman, 1846.

77. Estabrooks, G. H. *Hypnotism.* New York: Dutton, 1957.

78. Evans, F. J. Phenomena of hypnosis: (2) Posthypnotic amnesia. (In) Burrows, G. D., and Dennerstein, L. (eds.) *Handbook of Hypnosis and Psychosomatic Medicine.* New York: Elsevier North-Holland Biomedical Press, 1980.

79. Farley, J., Woodruff, R. A., and Guze, S. B. The prevalence of hysteria and conversion symptoms. *British Journal of Psychiatry*, 114:1121–1125, 1968.

80. Feighner, J. P., Robins, E., Guze, S. B., Woodruff, R. A., Winokur, G., and Munoz, R. Diagnostic criteria for use in psychiatric research. *Archives of General Psychiatry*, 26;57–63, 1972.

81. Figley, C. R. (ed.) *Stress Disorders among Vietnam Veterans.* New York: Brunner/Mazel, 1978.

82. Foenander, G., Burrows, G. D., Gerschman, J., and Horne, D. J. Phobic behavior and hypnotic susceptibility. *Australian Journal of Clinical & Experimental Hypnosis*, 8:41–46, 1980.

83. Forel, A. *Hypnotism or Suggestion and Psychotherapy.* New York: Rebman, 1907.

84. Foy, D. W., Sipprelle, R. C., Rueger, D. B., and Carroll, E. M. Etiology of posttraumatic stress disorder in Vietnam veterans: Analysis of premilitary, military and combat exposure influences. *Journal of Consulting and Clinical Psychology*, 52:79–87, 1984.

85. Frank, J. D. *Persuasion and Healing.* Baltimore: Johns Hopkins University Press, 1973.

86. Frankel, F. H. *Hypnosis: Trance as a Coping Mechanism.* New York: Plenum Press, 1976.

87. Frankel, F. H., and Orne, M. T. Hypnotizability and phobic behavior. *Archives of General Psychiatry*, 33:1259–1261, 1976.

88. Frankel, F. H., and Zamansky, H. S. *Hypnosis At Its Bicentennial.* New York: Plenum Press, 1978.

89. Frazer, J. G. *The Golden Bough.* New York: Macmillan, 1935.

90. Freud, S. *Die Traumdeutung.* Leipzig and Vienna: Franz Denticke, 1900.

91. Freud, S. *An Autobiographical Study.* London: Hogarth Press, 1948.

92. Freud, S. The defence neuro-psychoses (1894). (In) Freud, S. *Collected Papers*, Vol. 1, pp. 59–75. London: Hogarth Press, 1949.

93. Freud, S. Further remarks on the defence neuro-psychoses (1896). (In) Freud, S. *Collected Papers*, Vol. 1, pp. 155–182. London: Hogarth Press, 1949.

94. Freud, S. The aetiology of hysteria (1896). (In) Freud, S. *Collected Papers*, Vol. 1, pp. 183–219. London: Hogarth Press, 1949.

95. Freud, S. My views on the part played by sexuality in the aetiology of the neuroses (1905). (In) Freud, S. *Collected Papers*, Vol. 1, pp. 272–283. London: Hogarth Press, 1949.

96. Freud, S. Some elementary lessons in psychoanalysis (1938). (In) *Collected Papers*, Vol. 5, pp. 376–382. London: Hogarth Press, 1950.

97. Freud, S. *The Origins of Psychoanalysis. Letters to Wilhelm Fliess.* New York: Basic Books, 1954.

98. Fromm, E., and Shor, R. E. (eds.) *Hypnosis: Developments in Research and New Perspectives.* (Second edition) New York: Aldine, 1979.

99. Frumkin, L. R., Ripley, H. S., and Cox, G. B. Changes in cerebral hemispheric lateralization with hypnosis. *Biological Psychiatry*, 13:741–748, 1978.

100. Gallup, G. G. Animal hypnosis: factual status of a fictional concept. *Psychology Bulletin*, 81:836–853, 1974.

101. Galton, F. *Inquiries Into Human Faculty and Its Development.* London: Macmillan, 1883.

102. Gardner, G. G., and Olness, K. *Hypnosis and Hypnotherapy with Children.* New York: Grune and Stratton, 1981.

103. Garrison, F. H. *An Introduction to the History of Medicine.* Philadelphia: W.B. Saunders, 1929.

104. Gelman, D. Finding the hidden Freud. *Newsweek*, Nov. 3, 1981, pp. 64–70.

105. Gibbons, D., and DeJarnette, J. Hypnotic susceptibility and religious experience. *Journal of Scientific Study of Religion*, 11:152–156, 1972.

106. Gill, M. M., and Brenman, M. *Hypnosis and Related States.* New York: International Universities Press, 1961.

107. Goodwin, D. W., Alderson, P., and Rosenthal, R. Clinical significance of hallucinations in psychiatric disorders. *Archives of General Psychiatry*, 24:76–80, 1971.

108. Goodwin, J. The etiology of combat-related post-traumatic stress disorders. (In) Wil-

liams, T. (ed.) *Post-Traumatic Stress Disorders of the Vietnam Veteran*, pp. 1–23. Cincinnati, Ohio: Disabled American Veterans, 1980.

109. Graham, K. R. Rate of eye closure and hypnotic susceptibility. Paper presented at the meeting of the Eastern Psychological Association, New York, April, 1971.

110. Greatraks, V. *A Brief Account of Mr. Valentine Greatrak's and Divers of the Strange Cures by him lately Performed.* London: J. Starkey, 1666.

111. Greaves, G. Multiple personality: 165 years after Mary Reynolds. *Journal of Nervous and Mental Diseases*, 168:577–596, 1980.

112. Gruenwald, D. Multiple personality and splitting phenomena: A reconceptualization. *Journal of Nervous and Mental Disease*, 164:385–393, 1977.

113. Gur, R. C., and Gur, R. E. Handedness, sex, and eyedness as moderating variables in the relationship between hypnotic susceptibility and functional brain asymmetry. *Journal of Abnormal Psychology*, 83:635–643, 1974.

114. Guttmacher, M. S. *Psychiatry and The Law.* New York: Grune and Stratton, 1955.

115. Guze, S. B., and Perley, M. J. Observations on the natural history of hysteria. *American Journal of Psychiatry*, 119:960–965, 1963.

116. Guze, S. B. Conversion symptoms in criminals. *American Journal of Psychiatry*, 121:580–583, 1964.

117. Guze, S. B. The diagnosis of hysteria: what are we trying to do? *American Journal of Psychiatry*, 124:491–498, 1967.

118. Guze, S. B., Wolfgram, E. D., McKinney, J. K., and Cantwell, D. P. Psychiatric illness in the families of convicted criminals: a study of 519 first-degree relatives. *Diseases of the Nervous System*, 28:651–659, 1967.

119. Guze, S. B., Woodruff, R. A., and Clayton, P. J. Hysteria and antisocial behavior: further evidence of association. *American Journal of Psychiatry*, 127:957–960, 1971.

120. Guze, S. B., Woodruff, R. A., and Clayton, P. J. A study of conversion symptoms in psychiatric outpatients. *American Journal of Psychiatry*, 128:135–138, 1971.

121. Guze, S. B. The validity and significance of the clinical diagnosis of hysteria (Briquet's Syndrome). *American Journal of Psychiatry*, 132:138–141, 1975.

122. Haley, S. When the patient reports atrocities: Specific treatment considerations for the Vietnam veteran. *Archives of General Psychiatry*, 30:191–196, 1974.

123. Halifax, J. *Shamanic Voices.* New York: Dutton, 1979.

124. Hallan, R. S. Agoraphobia: A critical review of the concept. *British Journal of Psychiatry*, 133:314–319, 1978.

125. Harriman, P. L. The experimental induction of a multiple personality. *Psychiatry*, 5:179–186, 1942.

126. Harriman, P. L. The experimental production of some phenomena related to multiple personality. *Journal of Abnormal Social Psychology*, 37:244–256, 1942.

127. Henink, R. (ed.) *The Psychotherapy Handbook: The A to Z Guide to More Than 250 Different Therapies in Use Today.* New York: New American Library (Meridian), 1980.

128. Hilgard, E. R. *Hypnotic Susceptibility.* New York: Harcourt, Brace & World, 1965.

129. Hilgard, E. R. Hypnotic phenomena: the struggle for scientific acceptance. *American Scientist*, 59:567–577, 1971.

130. Hilgard, E. R. *Divided Consciousness: Multiple Controls in Human Thought and Action.* New York: Wiley, 1977.

131. Hilgard, E. R., Crawford, H. J., and Wert, A. The Stanford hypnotic arm levitation induction and test (SHALIT): a six-minute hypnotic induction and measurement scale. *International Journal of Clinical & Experimental Hypnosis*, 27:111–124, 1979.

132. Hilgard, E. R. Divided consciousness in hypnosis: The implications of the hidden observer. (In) Fromm, E. and Shor, R. E. (Eds.) *Hypnosis: Developments in Research and New Perspectives*, pp. 45–80. New York: Aldine, 1979.

133. Hilgard, J. R. Imaginative and sensory-affective involvements in everyday life and in hypnosis. (In) Fromm, E. and Shor, R. E. (eds.) *Hypnosis: Developments in Research and New Perspectives*, pp. 483–518. New York: Aldine, 1979.

134. Hocking, S. Unpublished letter, 1872.

135. Hollander, M. H., and Hirsch, S. J. Hysterical psychosis. *American Journal of Psychiatry,* 120:1066–1074, 1964.

136. Horevitz, R. P. Hypnosis for multiple personality disorder: A framework for beginning. *American Journal of Clinical Hypnosis,* 26:138–152, 1983.

137. Horevitz, R. P., and Braun, B. G. Are multiple personalities borderline? An analysis of 33 cases. *Psychiatric Clinics of North America,* 7:69–87, 1984.

138. Horne, D. J., and Powett, V. Hypnotizability and rating scales. (In) Burrows, G. D. and Dennerstein, L. (eds.) *Handbook of Hypnosis and Psychosomatic Medicine,* pp. 119–132. New York: Elsevier, 1980.

139. Horowitz, M. A cognitive model of hallucinations. *American Journal of Psychiatry,* 132:789–795, 1975.

140. Howland, J. The use of hypnosis in the treatment of a case of multiple personality. *Journal of Nervous and Mental Disease,* 161:138–142, 1975.

141. Hudson, J. I., Pope, H. G., and Jonas, J. M. Treatment of bulimia with antidepressants: Theoretical considerations and clinical findings. *Psychiatric Annals,* 13:965–969, 1983.

142. Hull, C. L. *Hypnotism and Suggestibility.* New York: Appleton-Century, 1933.

143. Hunter, R., and Macalpine, I. *Three Hundred Years of Psychiatry, 1535–1860.* London: Oxford University Press, 1963.

144. James, W. *Automatic writing.* Proceedings of the American Society for Psychical Research, 1:548–564, 1889.

145. James, W. *The Principles of Psychology.* New York: Henry Holt, 1890.

146. . Janet, P. *L'Automatisme Psychologique.* Paris: Alcan, 1889.

147. Janet, P. *The Major Symptoms of Hysteria.* New York: Macmillan, 1907.

148. Janet, P. *Psychological Healing.* New York: Macmillan Co., 1925.

149. Janov, A. *The Primal Scream—Primal Therapy: The Cure of Neuroses.* New York: Putnam, 1970.

150. Jenness, D. Report of the Canadian Arctic Expedition, 1913–18. Ottawa, Canada, 1922.

151. Jones, E. *The Life and Work of Sigmund Freud.* New York: Basic Books, 1953.

152. Kampman, R. Hypnotically induced multiple personality: An experimental study. *International Journal of Clinical & Experimental Hypnosis,* 24:215–227, 1976.

153. Katz, J. L., Kuperberg, A., Pollack, C. P., Walsh, B. T., Zumoff, B., and Weiner, H. Is there a relationship between eating disorder and affective disorder? New evidence from sleep recordings. *American Journal of Psychiatry,* 141:753–758, 1984.

154. Kelly, S. F. Measured hypnotic response and phobic behavior: A brief communication. *International Journal of Clinical & Experimental Hypnosis,* 32:1–5, 1984.

155. Kihlstrom, J. F. (ed.) Hypnosis and psychopathology. *Journal of Abnormal Psychology,* 88:459–603, 1979.

156. Kihlstrom, J. F., and Evans, F. J. (eds.) *Functional Disorders of Memory.* Hillsdale, N.J.: Lawrence Erlbaum, 1979.

157. Kihlstrom, J. F., and Evans, F. J. Memory retrieval processes during posthypnotic amnesia. (In) Kihlstrom, J. F. and Evans, F. J. (eds.) *Functional Disorders of Memory,* pp. 179–218. Hillsdale, N.J.: Lawrence Erlbaum, 1979.

158. Klein, M. I., and Trebich, D. Blame the child. *Sciences,* 22:14–20, 1982.

159. Kluft, R. P. Varieties of hypnotic interventions in the treatment of multiple personality. *American Journal of Clinical Hypnosis,* 24:230–240, 1982.

160. Kluft, R. P. Hypnotherapeutic crisis intervention in multiple personality. *American Journal of Clinical Hypnosis,* 26:73–83, 1983.

161. Kluft, R. P. An introduction to multiple personality disorder. *Psychiatric Annals,* 14:19–24, 1984.

162. Kluft, R. P. Treatment of multiple personality disorder. A study of 33 cases. *Psychiatric Clinics of North America,* 7:9–29, 1984.

163. Kluft, R. P. Aspects of the treatment of multiple personality disorder. *Psychiatric Annals*, 14:51–55, 1984.

164. Kohlenberg, R. J. Behavioristic approach to multiple personality. A case study. *Behavior Therapy*, 4:137–140, 1973.

165. Kroger, W. S. *Clinical and Experimental Hypnosis in Medicine, Dentistry and Psychology.* Philadelphia: J.B. Lippincott, 1977.

166. Lasky, R. The psychoanalytic treatment of a case of multiple personality. *Psychoanalytic Review*, 65:355–380, 1978.

167. Lavoie, G., and Sabourin, M. Hypnosis and schizophrenia: A review of experimental and clinical studies. (In) Burrows, G. D., and Dennerstein, L. (eds.) *Handbook of Hypnosis and Psychosomatic Medicine*, pp. 377–419. New York: Elsevier North-Holland Biomedical Press, 1980.

168. Lawrence, R. M. *Primitive Psycho-Therapy and Quackery.* London: Constable & Co., 1910.

169. Leavitt, H. C. The case of hypnotically produced secondary and tertiary personalities. *Psychoanalytic Review*, 34:274–295, 1947.

170. Leigh, D. *The Historical Development of British Psychiatry.* London: Pergamon Press, 1961.

171. Leitch, A. Notes on amnesia in crime for the general practitioner. *Medical Press*, 219:459–463, 1948.

172. Levenson, J. and Berry, S. Family intervention in a case of multiple personality. *Journal of Marriage and Family Therapy*, 9:73–80, 1983.

173. Liébault, A. A. *Le Sommeil et Des Etats Analogues, Considérés surtout au Point de Vue de L'Action de la Morale sur le Physical.* Paris: Masson, Nancy, Nicolas Grosjean, 1866.

174. Liebowitz, M. R. Is borderline a distinct entity? *Schizophrenia Bulletin*, 5:23–28, 1979.

175. Lindauer, M. S. Imagery and the arts. (In) Sheikh, A. A. (ed.) *Imagery, Current Theory, Research, and Application*, pp. 468–506. New York: Wiley, 1983.

176. London, P., and Cooper, L. M. Norms of hypnotic susceptibility in children. *Developmental Psychology*, 1:113–124, 1969.

177. Ludwig, A. M., Brandsma, J. M., Wilbur, C. B. The objective study of a multiple personality: Or are four heads better than one. *Archives of General Psychiatry*, 26:298–310, 1972.

178. MacHovec, F. J. Hypnosis before Mesmer. *American Journal of Clinical Hypnosis*, 17:215:220, 1975.

179. Mai, F. M. Briquet's treatise on hysteria. *Archives of General Psychiatry*, 37:1401–1405, 1980.

180. Major, R. H. *Classic Descriptions of Disease.* London: Bailliere, Tindall and Cox, 1932.

181. Marks, I. M. New developments in psychological treatments of phobias. (In) Mavissakalian, M. and Barlow, D. H. (eds.) *Phobia, Psychological and Pharmacological Treatment*, pp. 175–198. New York: Guilford, 1981.

182. Marmer, S. S. Psychoanalysis of multiple personality. *International Journal of Psycho-Analysis*, 61:439–459, 1980.

183. Mavissakalian, M., and Barlow, D. H. Phobia: An overview. (In) Mavissakalian, M., and Barlow, D. H. (eds.) *Phobia, Psychological and Pharmacological Treatment*, pp. 1–34. New York: Guilford, 1981.

184. Mead, R. *A Treatise concerning the Influence of the Sun and Moon upon Human Bodies and the Diseases thereby produced.* London: J. Brindley, 1748.

185. Meares, A. *A System of Medical Hypnosis.* Philadelphia: W.B. Saunders, 1960.

186. Mendelson, W., Johnson, N., and Stewart, M. A. Hyperactive children as teenagers: A followup study. *Journal of Nervous and Mental Diseases*, 153:273–279, 1971.

187. Menninger, K. *Man Against Himself.* New York: Harcourt, Brace, 1938.

188. Mesmer, F. A. *Dissertatio Physico-medica de Planetarum Influxu.* Vienna: Ghelen, 1766.

189. Mesmer, F. A. *Memoire Sur La Découverte Du Magnétisme Animal.* Geneva and Paris: Didot le jeune, 1779.

190. Mesmer, F. A. *Rapport Des Commissaires Chargés, Par Le Roi, De L'Examen du Magnétisme Animal.* Paris: Imprimerie Royale, 1784.

191. Mesmer, F. A. *Rapport Des Commissaires De La Societé Royale De Médecine Nommés Par Le Roi, Pour Faire L'Examen Du Magnétisme Animal.* Paris: Imprimié par ordre du Roi, 1784.

192. Mesmer, F. A. *Report of Dr. Benjamin Franklin and Other Commissions Charged by the King of France with the Examination of Animal Magnetism, as Now Practised at Paris.* London: J. Johnson, 1785.

193. Mesmer, F. A. *Maxims on Animal Magnetism* (trans. by J. Eden). Mount Vernon, N.Y.: Eden Press, 1958.

194. Mitchell, S. L. A double consciousness or a duality of person in the same individual. *Medical Repository*, 3:185–186, 1817.

195. Moll, A. *Hypnotism.* New York: Scribners, 1902.

196. Moore, R. K., and Lauer, L. W. Hypnotic susceptibility in middle childhood. *International Journal of Clinical & Experimental Hypnosis*, 11:167–174, 1963.

197. Moore, R. K. Susceptibility to hypnosis and susceptibility to social influence. *Journal of Abnormal Social Psychology*, 68:282–294, 1964.

198. Morgan, A. H., Hilgard, E. R., and Davert, E. C. The heritability of hypnotic susceptibility of twins: A preliminary report. *Behavior Genetics*, 1:213–224, 1970.

199. Morgan, A. H. The heritability of hypnotic susceptibility in twins. *Journal of Abnormal Psychology*, 82:55–61, 1973.

200. Morgan, A. H., and Hilgard, E. R. Age differences in susceptibility to hypnosis. *The International Journal of Clinical & Experimental Hypnosis*, 21:78–85, 173.

201. Morison, R. S., and Dempsey, E. W. A study of thalamo-cortical relations. *American Journal of Physiology*, 138:281–292, 1942.

202. Morrison, J. R., and Stewart, M. A. The psychiatric status of the legal families of adopted hyperactive children. *Archives of General Psychiatry*, 28:888–891, 1973.

203. Moruzzi, S., and Magoun, H. W. Brain stem reticular formation and activation. *Electroencephalography Clinical Neurophysiology*, 1:455–473, 1949.

204. *Newsweek*, Jan. 8, 1979, pp. 24–26. "Double life of a clown."

205. Noll, R. Shamanism and schizophrenia: A state-specific approach to the "schizophrenia metaphor" of shamanic states. *American Ethnology*, 10:443–459, 1983.

206. O'Connell, B. A. Amnesia and homicide. *British Journal of Delinquency*, 10:262–276, 1960.

207. Orne, M. T. The nature of hypnosis: Artifact and essence. *Journal of Abnormal and Social Psychology*, 58:277–299, 1959.

208. Orne, M. T. The nature of the hypnotic phenomena: Recent empirical studies. (In) Hilgard, E. R. (ed.) *Hypnotic Susceptibility*, p. 190. New York: Harcourt Brace Jovanovich, 1965.

209. Orne, M. T. On the simulating subject as a quasi-control group in hypnosis research. What, why and how. (In) Fromm, E. and Shore, R. E. (eds.) *Hypnosis, Research Developments and Perspectives*, pp. 519–566. Chicago: Aldine, 1979.

210. Orne, M. T. On the construct of hypnosis: How its definition affects research and its clinical application. (In) Burrows, G. D., and Dennerstein, L. (eds.) *Handbook of Hypnosis and Psychosomatic Medicine*, pp. 29–51. New York: Elsevier North-Holland Biomedical Press, 1980.

211. Orne, M. T. Forensic hypnosis. Part I. The use and misuse of hypnosis in court. (In) Wester, W. C., and Smith, A. H. (eds.) *Clinical Hypnosis. A Multidisciplinary Approach.* New York: J.B. Lippincott, 1984.

212. Orne, M. T., Dinges, D. F., and Orne, E. C. On the differential diagnosis of multiple personality in the forensic context. *International Journal of Clinical & Experimental Hypnosis*, 32:118–169, 1984.

213. Parish, E. *Hallucinations and Illusions.* London: W. Scott, 1897.

214. Parloff, M. B., Wolfe, B., Hadley, S., and Waskow, I. E. Assessment of Psychosocial

Treatment of Mental Disorders: Current Status and Prospects. Washington, D.C.: Institute of Medicine, National Academy of Sciences, 1978.

215. Pattison, E. M., and Kahan, J. The deliberate self harm syndrome. *American Journal of Psychiatry*, 140:867–872, 1983.

216. Perley, M. J., and Guze, S. B. Hysteria—the stability and usefulness of clinical criteria: A quantitative study based upon a follow-up period of 6–8 years in 39 patients. *New England Journal of Medicine*, 266:421–426, 1962.

217. Perry, C. The Abbé Faria: A neglected figure in the history of hypnosis. (In) Frankel, F. H., and Zamansky, H. S. (eds.) *Hypnosis at its Bicentennial—Selected Papers*, pp. 37–46. New York: Plenum Press, 1978.

218. Pines, M. Invisible playmates. *Psychology Today*, 28–38, 1978.

219. Prince, M. *The Dissociation of a Personality*. New York: Longmans, Green, 1905.

220. Prince, M. *The Unconscious*. New York: Macmillan, 1914.

221. Purtell, J. J., Robins, E., and Cohen, M. E. Observations on clinical aspects of hysteria. *JAMA*, 146:902–909, 1951.

222. Putnam, F. W., Post, R., Guroff, J., Silberman, E., and Barban, L. 100 cases of multiple personality disorder. American Psychiatric Association Annual Meeting, May, 1983.

223. Putnam, F. W. The psychophysiologic investigation of multiple personality disorder. A review. *Psychiatric Clinics of North America*, 7:31–50, 1984.

224. Puysegur, A. M. J. Chastenet de. Memoires pour servir à l'histoire et à l'etablissement du magnétisme animal. (First edition, 1784) Paris: Cellot, 1809.

225. Ries, H. Analysis of a patient with a split personality. *International Journal of Psychoanalysis*, 39:397–407, 1958.

226. Robins, L. N., Helzer, J. E., Croughan, J., and Ratcliff, K. S. National Institute of Mental Health diagnostic interview schedule. *Archives of General Psychiatry*, 38:381–389, 1981.

227. Rosenbaum, M. The role of the term schizophrenia in the decline of diagnoses of multiple personalities. *Archives of General Psychiatry*, 37:1383–1385, 1980.

228. Roth, L., Frazier, S. H., Beigel, A., Spitzer, R. L., Stone, A. A., and Klein, J. American Psychiatric Association statement on the insanity defense. *American Journal of Psychiatry*, 140:681–688, 1983.

229. Rush, B. *Medical Inquiries and Observations Upon the Diseases of the Mind*. Philadelphia: Kimber & Richardson, 1812.

230. Sarbin, T. R. Contributions to role theory: I. Hypnotic behavior. *Psychology Review*, 57:255–270, 1950.

231. Sarbin, T. R., and Slagle, R. W. Hypnosis and psychophysiological outcomes. (In) Fromm, E., and Shor, R. E. (eds.) *Hypnosis: Developments in Research and New Perspectives*, pp. 273–304. New York: Aldine, 1979.

232. Sargant, W. *Battle For the Mind*. Garden City, N.Y.: Doubleday, 1957.

233. Satten, J., Menninger, K., Rosen, I., and Mayman, M. Murder without apparent motive—a study in personality disorganization. *American Journal of Psychiatry*, 117:48–53, 1960.

234. Schneider, K. Primare und sekundare symptome bei schizophrenie. *Fortschritte der Neurologie Psychiatrie*, 25:487–491, 1957.

235. Schreiber, F. R. *Sybil*. Chicago: Regnery, 1973.

236. Sheehan, P. W. A shortened form of Bett's questionnaire upon mental imagery. *Journal of Clinical Psychology*, 23:386–389, 1967.

237. Sheehan, P. W. Imagery and hypnosis—forging a link, at least in part. *Research Communications in Psychology, Psychiatry and Behavior*, 7:257–272, 1982.

238. Sheikh, A. A. *Imagery. Current Theory, Research, and Application*. New York: Wiley, 1983.

239. Shor, R. E. Hypnosis and the concept of the generalized reality-orientation. (In) Tart, C. T. (ed.) *Altered States of Consciousness*, pp. 233–250. New York: Wiley, 1969.

240. Shor, R. E. The three-factor theory of hypnosis as applied to the book-reading fantasy and to the concept of suggestion. *International Journal of Clinical & Experimental Hypnosis,* 18:89–98, 1970.

241. Shor, R. E. A phenomenological method for the measurements of variables important to an understanding of the nature of hypnosis. (In) Fromm, E., and Shor, R. E. *Hypnosis: Developments in Research and New Perspectives,* pp. 105–138. New York: Aldine, 1979.

242. Sidis, B. *The Psychology of Suggestion.* New York: Appleton, 1898.

243. Sidis, B., and Goodhart, S. P. *Multiple Personality.* New York: Appleton-Century-Crofts, 1905.

244. Sidis, B. *Psychopathological Researches. Studies in Mental Dissociation.* Boston: Richard G. Badger, 1908.

245. Sidis, B. *Symptomatology, Psychognosis and Diagnosis of Psychopathic Diseases.* Boston: Richard G. Badger, 1914.

246. Sidis, B. *The Foundations of Normal and Abnormal Psychology.* Boston: Richard G. Badger, 1914.

247. Sidis, B. *The Causation and Treatment of Psychopathic Diseases.* Boston: Richard G. Badger, 1916.

248. Sidis, B. *Nervous Ills. Their Cause and Cure.* Boston: Gorham Press, 1922.

249. Sigerist, H. E. *A History of Medicine.* New York: Oxford University Press, 1951.

250. Silverstein, M. L., and Harrow, M. Schneiderian first-rank symptoms in schizophrenia. *Archives of General Psychiatry,* 38:288–293, 1981.

251. Snyder, S., Pitts, W. M., Goodpaster, W. A., Sajadi, C., and Gustin, Q. MMPI profile of DSM-III borderline personality disorder. *American Journal of Psychiatry,* 139:1046–1048, 1982.

252. Spiegel, D., and Fink, R. Hysterical psychosis and hypnotizability. *American Journal of Psychiatry,* 136:777–781, 1979.

253. Spiegel, D., Maruffi, B., Frischholz, E. J., and Spiegel, H. Hypnotic responsivity and the treatment of flying phobia. *American Journal of Clinical Hypnosis,* 23:239–247, 1981.

254. Spiegel, D., Detrick, D., and Frischholz, E. Hypnotizability and psychopathology. *American Journal of Psychiatry,* 139:431–437, 1982.

255. Spiegel, D. Multiple personality as a post-traumatic stress disorder. *Psychiatric Clinics of North America,* 7:101–110, 1984.

256. Spiegel, H. The grade 5 syndrome: The highly hypnotizable person. *International Journal of Clinical & Experimental Hypnosis,* 22:303–319, 1974.

257. Spiegel, H., and Spiegel, D. *Trance and Treatment.* New York: Basic Books, 1978.

258. Spiegel, H., and Spiegel, D. Induction techniques. (In) Burrows, G. D. and Dennerstein, L. (eds.) *Handbook of Hypnosis and Psychosomatic Medicine.* New York: Elsevier/North-Holland, 1980.

259. Spitzer, R. L., Endicott, J., and Robins, E. Research diagnostic criteria: Rationale and reliability. *Archives of General Psychiatry,* 35:773–782, 1978.

260. Spitzer, R. L. *Diagnostic Criteria from DSM-III.* American Psychiatric Association, 1980.

261. Sprenger, J., and Kramer, H. *Malleus Maleficarum* (trans. M. Summers). London: Pushkin Press, 1928. (First edition, 1487)

262. Stoller, R. *Splitting: A Case of Female Masculinity.* New York: Pentangle, 1973.

263. Stutman, R., and Bliss, E. L. The post-traumatic stress disorder (the Vietnam syndrome), hypnotizability and imagery. *American Journal of Psychiatry,* 142:741–743, 1985

264. Sutcliffe, J. P., and Jones, J. Personal identity, multiple personality and hypnosis. *International Journal of Clinical and Experimental Hypnosis,* 10:231–269, 1962.

265. Sutcliffe, J. P., Perry, C. W., and Sheehan, P. W. The relationship of some aspects of imagery and fantasy to hypnotizability. *Journal of Abnormal Psychology,* 76:279–287, 1970.

266. Swanson, J. M., and Kinsbourne, M. State-dependent learning and retrieval: Methodological cautions and theoretical considerations. (In) Kihlstrom, J. F., and Evans, F. J. (eds.) *Functional Disorders of Memory,* pp. 275–299. Hillsdale, N.J.: Lawrence Erlbaum, 1979.

267. Tart, C. T. (ed.) *Altered States of Consciousness.* New York: Wiley, 1969.

268. Tart, C. T. Measuring the depth of an altered state of consciousness with particular reference to self report scales of hypnotic depth. (In) Fromm, E., and Shor, R. E. (eds.) *Hypnosis, Research Developments and Perspectives,* pp. 567–604. Chicago: Aldine, 1979.

269. Taylor, M. A., and Abrams, R. A critique of the St. Louis psychiatric research criteria for schizophrenia. *American Journal of Psychiatry,* 132:1276–1280, 1975.

270. Taylor, P. J., and Kopelman, M. D. Amnesia for criminal offenses. *Psychological Medicine,* 14:581–588, 1984.

271. Taylor, W. S., and Martin, M. F. Multiple personality. *Journal of Abnormal Social Psychology,* 39:281–300, 1944.

272. Thigpen, C. H., and Cleckly, H. A case of multiple personality. *Journal of Abnormal Social Psychology,* 49:135–151, 1954.

273. Thigpen, C. H., and Cleckley, H. M. *The Three Faces of Eve.* New York: McGraw Hill, 1957.

274. Thigpen, C. H., and Cleckley, H. M. On the incidence of multiple personality disorder: A brief communication. *International Journal of Clinical & Experimental Hypnosis,* 32:63–66, 1984.

275. *Time,* Oct. 23, 1978, p. 102. "The man with ten personalities."

276. Tucker, G. J., Harrow, M., and Quinlan, D. Depersonalization, dysphoria and thought disturbance. *American Journal of Psychiatry,* 130:702–706, 1973.

277. Veith, I. *Hysteria, The History of a Disease.* Chicago: University of Chicago Press, 1965.

278. Volgyesi, F. A. *Hypnosis of Man and Animals.* Baltimore: Williams & Wilkins, 1963.

279. Walker, J. I., and Cavenar, J. O. Vietnam veterans. Their problems continue. *Journal of Nervous and Mental Disease,* 170:174–180, 1982.

280. Warner, C. G. (ed.) *Rape and Sexual Assault.* Germantown, Md.: Aspen Publications, 1980.

281. Weitzenhoffer, A. M. *General Techniques of Hypnosis.* New York: Grune & Stratton, 1957.

282. Weitzenhoffer, A. M., and Weitzenhoffer, G. B. Sex, transference and susceptibility to hypnosis. *American Journal of Clinical Hypnosis,* 1:15–24, 1958.

283. Weitzenhoffer, A. M., and Hilgard, E. R. Stanford Hypnotic Susceptibility Scale, Form C. Palo Alto: Consulting Psychologists Press, 1962.

284. Weitzenhoffer, A. M. Hypnotic susceptibility revisited. *American Journal of Clinical Hypnosis,* 22:130–146, 1980.

285. West, J. Dissociative reactions. (In) Freedman, A. M., and Kaplan, H. I. (eds.) *Comprehensive Textbook of Psychiatry,* pp. 885–899. Baltimore: Williams & Wilkins Co., 1967.

286. Whyte, L. L. *The Unconscious Before Freud.* New York: Basic Books, 1960.

287. Wilbur, C. B. Treatment of multiple personality. *Psychiatric Annals,* 14:27–31, 1984.

288. Wilbur, C. B. Multiple personality and child abuse—an overview. *Psychiatric Clinics of North America,* 7:3–7, 1984.

289. Wilson, S. C., and Barber, T. X. The fantasy-prone personality; implications for understanding imagery, hypnosis, and parapsychological phenomena. (In) Sheikh, A. A. (ed.) *Imagery: Current Theory, Research and Application,* pp. 340–390. New York: Wiley, 1982.

290. Winokur, A., March, V., and Mendels, J. Primary affective disorder in relatives of patients with anorexia nervosa. *American Journal of Psychiatry,* 137:695–698, 1980.

291. Woerner, P. I., and Guze, S. B. A family and marital study of hysteria. *British Journal of Psychiatry,* 114:161–168, 1968.

292. Wolberg, L. R. *Medical Hypnosis.* New York: Grune & Stratton, 1948.

293. Woodruff, R. A., Clayton, P. J., and Guze, S. B. Hysteria—studies of diagnosis, outcome, and prevalence. *JAMA*, 215:425–428, 1971.
294. Woodruff, R. A., Goodwin, D. W., and Guze, S. B. *Psychiatric Diagnosis.* New York: Oxford University Press, 1974.
295. Worthington, E. R. Demographic and preservice variables as predictors of postmilitary service adjustment in stress disorders among Vietnam veterans. (In) Figley, C. R. (ed.) *Stress Disorders Among Vietnam Veterans.* New York: Brunner/Mazel, 1978.
296. Zarcone, V. P., Scott, N. R., and Kauvar, K. B. Psychiatric problems of Vietnam veterans: Clinical study of hospital patients. *Comprehensive Psychiatry*, 18:41–53, 1977.
297. *Zoist.* Vols. 1–13. London: Bailliere, 1844–56.

# Index

Page numbers followed by *t* indicate tables.